Practicing The Wisdom of Children
Our Book One

For Sharing Unconditional Love & Nurturing True Friendship

By Learning to Understand My True Self

By

William (Bill) Coulson

Practicing The Wisdom of Children
Our Book One

© 2018 by William Charles Coulson

Library and Archives Canada Cataloguing
IBSN: 978-0-9813558-2-5

Published by Coulson Press
Toronto Canada

Email: support@coulsonpress.com

Printing and Sales
by Amazon & Kindle

Introduction to Our Book One

I asked "The Child Who Lives Inside My Heart" to help me find my lost childhood ability, for loving everyone in my life with powerful passion.

During my childhood, the unresolved pain & suffering that was accumulating inside my memories from the unfair experiences in my life, started to hide my ability to live my life with powerful passion. I don't know when I lost this ability completely. By the time I became an adult, it was gone from my life. I assumed that it was hiding somewhere inside my childhood memories.

Unfortunately, after many attempts to locate it, I gave up when I could not find it.

It was not until My Son was born that I finally solved the mystery of where my ability to love life passionately was hiding, when I observed the joy, excitement and enthusiasm for new fun & adventures that fueled My Son's powerful passion for living his life to the full and I felt inspired to ask a question, that I had not asked myself for many years.

"Can I find the source of my childhood love that generated powerful passion for living my life, when I was a child?"

Once again, I searched my childhood memories for the answer to this question, so I could start to relive the powerful passion of my childhood, when I shared in the love being generated by all the life around me, especially the love from my friends & family.

And then, with the help of the wisdom of how our minds work that I was learning from our ancestors, especially the wisdom of Buddha, I found the answer to this question, so I asked myself another question to help me understand how to protect my childhood ability to love life passionately, from ever becoming lost again.

"Why was I born with this powerful ability to enjoy my childhood by sharing love & friendship and fun & adventures with everyone in my life?"

As I tried to answer this new question, I realized that I did not know the answer, when I was a child. As a child, I just accepted the precious gift of being born with the ability to share love & joy, even though I did not understand where it came from.

By the time I was a year old, I still did not know where my enthusiasm for new fun & adventures was coming from and I did not understand the concept of a God or a creator who provides us with the ability to love & forgive our friends & family. I could not ask my parents because I had not learned how to talk, even though I was beginning to understand many of the words that my parents were trying to teach me. So, I just accepted my daily struggle to live my young life with a continuous passion to learn new things, to have fun, to seek new adventures and to continue loving everyone. Instead of using words to try to understand my desires, I just accepted them as real because I was feeling them. This is why I did not need to understand where my ability to enjoy life came from. I just accepted it as real and used my ability to love every moment of every day of my childhood.

My appreciation of the value of words that describe love would have to wait until I was two years old, when I was able to talk and ask my parents, "Why do you love me?"

While I was waiting for an answer to this question, I continued to nurture the feelings of love for everyone in my life, feelings which were real & crucially important to me, as were the feelings of love that I received from my friends & family, who showered me with their love each day. I depended on these real concrete feelings of love to motivate me to seek new adventures when I woke up each morning, as I looked forward to learning new skills that were fun and a joy to learn.

Sharing love was the driving force behind my motivation to continue growing up, to learn to walk, talk & play, as I tried to satisfy my human desire to love all the life around me, and to feel loved, safe & secure, as my mind continued to develop an understanding of the ongoing love that I was receiving from my friends & family and an understanding of the compassion & forgiveness that I received from others, whenever I made mistakes, got into trouble or was treated unfairly by a friend or sibling.

Then, by the time I was three years old, I was using my feelings of love for everything in my life to help me believe that life would be fair to me in the future, because life had been more than fair to me over the last three years, as I succeeded in learning many new skills from my friends & family, as the fairness in my life continued to present me with new ways to learn and with new adventures to undertake. Life was being fair to me by offering me challenges that I could accept and master. And whenever life was unfair to me, which was not very often, my friends & family helped me to stop this unfairness, quickly.

As my belief in the ongoing fairness in my future life continued to grow inside my mind, it helped me to overcome sickness & emotional hurt whenever they entered my young life.

When I became sick or my feelings were hurt, I became a diminished child as negative feelings started flowing inside me, as I tried to hold onto my connection to my internal source of continuous love, as I struggled to get better. Even though I was hurting, I felt that life would continue to be fair to me as I learned to overcome the challenge of being sick or hurt. I felt the desire to rise above the pain that I was feeling as I tried to understand why I was suffering, as I waited for the fairness to return to my life, as the love of my friends & family continued to flow through me and as their concern for my well-being comforted me. Then, when I became well again, I automatically started to feel powerful continuous love, once more, to become a fully functioning child who loves everyone in my life, as I started once again, to satisfy my never ending desire to share the love that I was born possessing with all the life around me.

Unfortunately, I gradually lost my desire to share new fun & adventures in my daily life as I grew from childhood into adulthood, as unfair pain & suffering continued to increase in my life and started to diminish the love & joy that was motivating me to learn new skills and to accept new challenges, each day. Then, when my ability to feel continuous love was gone and I felt that the fairness in my future life was disappearing, I realized that I wanted to become a child of pure love, once again, without the burden of feeling the unresolved pain & suffering from my memories that I was reliving each day and I wanted to forgive those who had hurt me unfairly in life, so I could kill the pain of this unfairness that was preventing me from feeling pure unconditional love for friends & family, as I once did when I was a young child.

I desired to feel the continuous love, peace, joy & compassion of my childhood that I rarely felt as an adult and I wanted to rediscover my lost childhood ability to love life passionately, so I could feel my childhood sense of wonder & excitement when sharing new adventures & learning new skills.

Unfortunately, I was not able to rediscover this childhood ability and slowly over the years I forgot about my unfulfilled desire to find this lost ability, until my son was born and I started to observe his powerful passion for enjoying new fun & adventures in his life.

As I felt My Son's passion, it inspired me to search my memories, once again, for my lost childhood ability to love life passionately and when I was able to rediscover the source of this love, I decided to write a book with the help of My Son, to be able to share the wisdom that I learned as I searched for directions to the source of the unconditional love of my childhood, directions that were hidden inside my memories.

We will help you to learn this wisdom, such as the childhood wisdom for nurturing & protecting the source of the unconditional love of your childhood, a source of love that all human beings are born possessing.

This wisdom enabled My Son & me to increase the passion in our lives, as we started to share increasing love, peace, joy & compassion with those we love, powerful feelings from our childhood source of love that now live continuously inside our hearts.

Table of Contents

An Unanswered Question

Even though we decided to publish Our Book One of The Wisdom of Children series, an unanswered question remains in my mind.

Will the readers of Our Book One become motivated enough to kill the unresolved pain & suffering in their memories that is diminishing or blocking the power of their internal source of unconditional love, a source of love the readers are encouraged to find & then fully embrace, to become able to feel the continuous love, peace, joy & compassion of their childhood in their adult lives?

I hope the answer to this question is "Yes"

As Buddha's wisdom teaches us, all human beings are travelling on the same path of learning & Practicing The Wisdom of Children that is leading us to continuous feelings of joy & happiness either in this lifetime or in a future reincarnated life.

How far we progress along the path of wisdom depends on how hard we practice in this lifetime. Some of us are close to the end of the path of learning & practicing, as we continue to struggle to reach the spiritual state of Nirvana, which embodies continuous love, peace, joy & compassion.

And some of us may require hundreds of additional reincarnated lifetimes to be spent on Earth in the future, to fully learn & practice this wisdom, as we continue to kill the unresolved pain & suffering in our spiritual memories (i.e. Our Karma) that is diminishing or blocking the full power of our ability to love, as each lifetime increases our ability to feel continuous love during each day that we spend on Earth, as we practice the wisdom of enlightenment and as we learn to forgive others who do not deserve our forgiveness.

Even though I have no memory of experiencing reincarnation, I hope that Buddha's vision of all human beings experiencing continuous joy & happiness becomes true, as it is true for me in this lifetime.

Dedication to Bradley James Slauenwhite

My elementary school teacher who inspired me to share fun & adventures, as we searched for answers to our questions about the meaning of life.

(Please refer to the My Teacher & Role Model Bradley James Slauenwhite section in Chapter 6 of Our Book One)

Disclaimer

Our Book One of The Wisdom of Children Series of Books contains our understanding of the wisdom of the authors who we have referred to in the contents of our book, referenced in the bibliography and recommended in the readings list, and does not necessarily reflect the views of these authors, since our understanding is only our interpretation of the wisdom contained in the authors' books, videos & other teachings.

Our Book One describes how my mind & my son's mind works. We have made the assumption that all human minds work using the same principles that we describe in our book. Only you, the reader, will be able to determine if this assumption is true or not true by looking inside your mind and comparing what you find there to our description of how our human minds work, as we describe how our minds process the pain & joy in our lives, from the time we are born until we reach adulthood, and then into future, as we describe the challenges that we face as we endeavor to share continuous love, peace, joy & compassion with our friends & family in our adult lives.

The publication of Our Books Two through Four of the Practicing The Wisdom of Children series depends on my continuing good health as I complete the final drafts of these books and may also depend on other unknown circumstances. There is no guarantee these books will be published but My Son & I will do our best to publish them, so our readers may enjoy them and then share the wisdom in these books with their friends & family.

The US spelling of "practicing" is used in Our Book instead of the British spelling of "practising" which has the same meaning as the US version when used as a verb.

Chapter 1

My Childhood Ability to Love

I was born with the ability to feel powerful continuous love
And I used this ability to love everyone, as a child
As I do today, when I become a child of love, once again,

And I start to feel increasing childhood love
As my child looks through my eyes at friends & family
And paints my relationships with pure continuous love

Even though this love is diminished by the suffering in my life
I am helping to liberate my childhood love from pain
By Practicing The Wisdom of Children

To help me play like a child in the adult world
As I share my childhood source of love
With all the life around me

And I offer continuous love without restrictions or conditions
As I reconnect to the full power of my childhood ability to love
So I can kill any new suffering that may enter my adult life

By cleansing my mind with love, forgiveness & the truth
To become a purified child
Who increases the fun & joy in life

And transforms me into a loving adult
As I offer pure continuous love to friends & family
And they share their love with me

As our childhood sense of wonder, curiosity & delight
And our passion for living, loving & nurturing happiness
Empowers new exciting adventures in our adult lives

Chapter 2

Sharing Love & Adventures with Friends & Family

Our Book was written to help adults, like you & me, who desire to feel the continuous love, peace, joy & compassion of our childhood, feelings that fueled our powerful desire for new fun & adventures, a desire we felt each moment of everyday of our lives when we were young children.

When My Son & I wrote Our Book to share how to regain these wonderful feelings of our childhood, we came to the conclusion that our future destiny should not be about pursuing fame & fortune or any other endeavor, until we decide to become the unconditional loving human beings that we were born to be.

The Wisdom of Children is the wisdom of using my childhood ability to share unconditional love & nurture true friendship. It is also the wisdom of accepting the love from all the life around me, especially the love from other human beings and the wisdom of embracing my love for all this life. This unconditional love of my childhood is a deep affection for the well-being of all the life on Our Precious Mother Earth. It is a love that lives continuously in my heart as it encourages me to take actions to help create, nurture, serve & protect the life that I observe & interact with each new day of my adult life, as I share this love with friends & family and they share their love with me. It is a powerful love that I was born possessing, a love that has been living inside me all my life, as it fuels my motivation to live my life with great passion.[1]

As I practice this wisdom, I am freeing my mind from any unresolved pain & suffering that may try to diminish my motivation to love my friends & family.

"Freedom exists first and foremost in the mind of the rational, thinking individual. I was born to live a life using reason to enable me to rise up from any pain & suffering that may enter my life, as I struggle to fully reconnect to the continuous never ending love & joy of my childhood that lives inside me." (Modified quote from Faith of the Fallen by Terry Goodkind)

As I become free, I am learning how my mind works so I can control my mind with my reasoning ability, as I choose what is the right action to take to love everyone in my life, as I choose the feelings that I want to experience, and as I learn how to kill the feelings that are hurting me.

Unfortunately, many of us lost our childhood ability to live our lives with the immense passion of our childhood by the time we became adults, as the pain living inside our memories of the suffering that we experienced, as we grew up, began to hide our childhood ability to feel the love from all the life that surrounds us, whenever we started to relive one or more of these painful memories and this remembered pain started to reduce the intensity of the childhood love that we felt for our friends & family. These painful memories, which many of us are still reliving today, diminish our adult ability to unconditionally love our families & friends and diminish our adult ability to feel the continuous love, peace, joy & compassion of our childhood.

Fortunately, The Wisdom of Children helps us to kill the unresolved pain & suffering in our memories so they can no longer hurt us again, when we relive our memories in the future, as we learn how to reclaim our childhood ability to feel the love from all the life that is surrounding us and as we learn to reclaim our childhood ability to feel continuous love, peace, joy & compassion for all life, which includes re-energizing our adult ability to share ever increasing unconditional love and to nurture true friendship, with our friends & family.

So, if you would like to share feelings of ever increasing love with your friends & family, please ask yourself this question.

Can I remember when I felt immense love for all the life around me, when I was a young child, as I shared new fun & adventures with my family & friends? Q-1 (Please refer to the Questions to Answer in My Own Words section in Chapter 31 of Our Book One)

Fortunately, The Wisdom of Children helps us to rediscover & renew our childhood ability, to feel the love **from** all the life around us and to feel our love **for** all this life, as we become excited about accepting new challenges for fun & adventures in our adult lives.

And if you are one of the many adults, like me, who has impaired or lost your childhood ability to love all life passionately, then please join us as we begin to explore the wisdom in our book, as we begin to increase the love, peace, joy & compassion that we feel, as we rediscover our childhood ability to become the unconditionally loving human beings that we were born to be.

Hopefully, you will begin to agree with us that the primary purpose of our lives is not about doing anything that will bring us more money or other material rewards. It is about being the unconditional loving human beings that we were born to be, as we start to reap the spiritual rewards of our renewed unconditional love for our friends & family, rewards that our childhood abilities help to bring back into our adult lives.

Then, as we accomplish the secondary purpose of our lives, to live a wonderful fun filled life with our friends & family, we begin to experience an increasing richness in the quality of our adult lives, as we feel interconnected with all the life surrounding us, as we work on the goals for our life, as we enjoy the spiritual rewards of being fully connected to our childhood ability to love all life with great passion, as we use this renewed excitement & anticipation about our future adventures to put more joy into the work that we do each day, as our work helps us to provide the food, clothing & shelter that our friends & family need for their future well-being, as we begin to laugh & play like children once again while we are working, and as we begin to share empowered unconditional love & we begin to nurture renewed true friendship, with our friends, family and co-workers.

The price we pay for this wisdom is the hard work, courage & self-discipline that enables us to kill the unfair fear, anger, worry & stress in our memories that is hiding our ability to feel continuous love, peace, joy & compassion in our adult lives, a continuous life enhancing energy that we felt when we were young children, which unfortunately, has been diminished in power or has become lost to many of us, in our adult lives. To help you remember the powerful passion of your childhood, please ask yourself these questions which will help you to relive the childhood memories that will confirm the truth of your childhood ability to love all life passionately:

Will I endure the pain & suffering that my childhood memories may reveal to me, as I search my memories for the source of my childhood ability to love life passionately? Q-2

Will I forgive those who hurt me unfairly during my childhood, to enable me to kill the unresolved pain & suffering that is hiding my childhood memories of the unconditional love that I felt for other human beings, before they hurt me? Q-3

Will I use the unconditional love for the fun & adventures of my childhood, that I find living inside my childhood memories, to help motivate me to try a new adventure in my adult life? And what is my description of the fun & joy that I want to share with others on this new adventure? Q-4

Will I pay any price that is required to fully reconnect to the passion of my childhood, to enable me to feel continuous love, peace, joy & compassion in my adult life? Why? Q-5

And if your answer to these questions is "Yes, I will", then we recommend that you start to dream about sharing new adventures in your adult life by answering these questions:

How do I begin to share this powerful childhood life enhancing energy of love? Q-6

Such as, Hug & Kiss someone more often? Q-7

Forgive someone who doesn't deserve it? Q-8

Tell someone "I love you", maybe a friend I haven't told before? Q-9

Share a new exciting adventure with someone I love? Q-10

Hopefully, your answers to these questions will help you to remember sharing unconditional love when you were a child, as you dream about sharing childhood inspired fun & adventures in your adult life.

Please write down a description of a childhood inspired adventure you would like to share with someone you love. And if no new adventures come to mind, please dream one up. This will help you to find ways to make your childhood dreams become real in your adult life.

Remembering my childhood adventures has helped me to embrace the child who is living inside me, as I hope your memories will help you to embrace your child. When I found my lost child, I invited him to come out of hiding and play with me in my adult life. Now, my life is filled with childhood feelings of wonder as I observe the beauty of all the life that surrounds me, the excitement of mastering new skills, and the desire to share new fun & adventures with my friends & family, feelings that have become a powerful source of childhood motivation in my adult life, as my childhood feelings increase my adult passion for living, as I feel a renewed love for everyone in my life.

Chapter 3

Forgiving Others Who Do Not Deserve Forgiveness

In addition to the wisdom of sharing unconditional love, Our Book One contains the wisdom of forgiving others who do not deserve forgiveness.

Forgiveness enables me to kill the unresolved pain & suffering that is living inside my unfair memories.

Unfortunately, my old friends & family members created many of these painful memories when they treated me unfairly, as I grew from childhood into adulthood.

This old pain & suffering automatically starts to come out of hiding from inside my unfair memories when it re-enters my daily adult life, as new pain & suffering, whenever someone treats me unfairly again in the future. The power & intensity of this new pain & suffering is determined by the number of unfair memories that are awakened inside me when I experience a new unfairness in my future life that is similar to the experiences contained in some of my old unfair memories.

Then, when the new pain & suffering, that is generated by my old memories, builds inside my conscious mind until it becomes intense, I may lash out with new angry words or deeds that hurt the loved ones in my life, when I start looking for an excuse to release the new pain & suffering from inside me, to allow it to escape from me into the external world of people & events that surround me. This lashing out at another person, as I become abusive, allows me to reduce the stress of living with the new pain & suffering from my old memories.

Unfortunately, after this pain & suffering of the moment leaves my mind & body to go live inside the new memories that I have just created inside a friend or family member who I have hurt with my angry words or deeds, I may utter an excuse for hurting this person by saying "My pain & suffering is justified because you have treated me unfairly", without realizing that I have also treated this person unfairly by adding extra pain & suffering from my old memories to the amount of hurt that I poured upon the person who I blamed for creating the new unfairness in my life.

At this time, I may not realize that the intensity of my new pain & suffering has been increased unfairly by the power of my old unfair memories when they generated extra pain & suffering into my conscious mind, when they were awakened from sleep inside my subconscious mind because these memories contain experiences similar to the experience of the new unfair event that just occurred. It may be later when I use meditation to understand this new unfair experience that I realize I treated another person unfairly.

Relieving our daily stress by abusing friends & family members, in this way, can become an addictive bad habit in our adult lives, which we discuss in more detail in the Abusing Friends & Family section in Chapter 13 of Our Book One.

All of us endure stress in our daily lives when we work at our jobs, take care of our children, or help loved ones who need us.

Unfortunately, many of us carry around a bag of unresolved pain & suffering in our lives that adds to the amount of stress that we feel during the day.

To help you to understand this, please imagine a couple who have been living together for ten years, when one partner asks the other, "Why do I **not** feel the same intensity of love & excitement in our relationship today that I felt 10 years ago?"

In reply, the other partner says, "It is partially my fault because I have disappointed you so many times over the last 10 years that these unfair experiences have built up unresolved pain & suffering inside your memories, which diminish the love that you feel for me, whenever you relive one or more of these unfair memories of the many times that I have disappointed you.

So now, when I come home from work and you look at me as I enter the front door, some of this unresolved pain & suffering may enter your conscious mind and reduce the power of your feelings of love for me.

Unfortunately, I do not know how to help you kill this unresolved pain & suffering that is living inside your memories, so it can no longer diminish the power of your love.

I have asked you to forgive me many times in our relationship, but I do not know how our minds create forgiveness and I do not know how our minds can help us to kill the unresolved pain & suffering in our memories that we carry around with us each day.

So, please try to forgive me once again and add this new failure of my not knowing how to help, to the bottom of the long list of disappointments that I have created in your life.

During each new day of sharing my life with you, I am blessed by your continuous love and I treasure your ongoing ability to live with my many imperfections. You are the love of my life who I do not want to disappoint, so I will keep trying to be more caring, more understanding and more attentive to your needs."

This imaginary relationship illustrates why I need to learn how to forgive my friends & family members whenever they do not deserve my forgiveness, so I can kill the old pain & suffering that still lives inside me, so I do not allow this old pain & suffering to reduce the power of the love that I feel for my friends & family.

When I try to kill this unresolved pain & suffering, I do not need to use forgiveness to benefit the friends & family members who created the painful unfair events of my childhood and who may be creating more unfairness in my adult life. And I do not have to tell them that I have forgiven them, though that would help me to forgive. What I need to do is forgive them whenever I think of them, which will prevent the old pain & suffering from awakening inside my old painful memories of unfairness that is still living inside my subconscious mind and which will prevent my old memories from generating new pain & suffering inside my conscious mind, whenever I am treated unfairly again in the future.

Unfortunately, as I grew up, my memories of unfair pain & suffering began to grow in number & intensity as they started to live together inside my subconscious mind to become the thousands of memories of unfairness that are still living inside me today. Memories that will still hurt me and hurt my friends & family today, when they contain remnants of the old unresolved pain & suffering from the unfair painful experiences that I endured during my lifetime, whenever a new unfair event in my future life opens the door to My Room of Memories in my subconscious mind, when I give my old memories an excuse to enter my adult life, as I start to blame my friends & family for this old unresolved pain & suffering whenever one of my friends or a family member starts to treat me unfairly again in my future life.

To help me to visualize the amount of new unresolved pain & suffering that is being generated into my life each day by these old unfair memories, I use my mind to imagine me carrying around A Bag of Unresolved Pain & Suffering that is being refilled each day of adult life, whenever I start to relive one of these old unfair painful memories.

For many years I carried around this bag of unresolved pain & suffering, which contained feelings of resentment, feelings of unfairness, and unresolved fear, anger, worry & stress, as it diminished my ability to feel the full power of the unconditional love that has been living inside me since I was born.

As a child, I continually looked inside my mind as I tried to understand how it worked, so I could use this understanding to find answers to my questions about the behavior of friends & family that puzzled me, when I could not understand why they were acting this way.

I was also puzzled as a child when I did not understand why every human being that I knew was carrying around A Bag of Unresolved

Pain & Suffering that they did not know how to empty, which if emptied, would allow them to bring more joy into their lives.

Unfortunately, some of them carried around large bags of unresolved pain & suffering that prevented them from loving anyone because they were in continuous pain & suffering which they tried to hide from their friends & family, as they sought to relieve their pain & suffering for short periods of time through excessive use of alcohol, drugs, or promiscuous sexual encounters, etc. or by being abusive to a friend or family member to help relieve the stress of this unresolved pain & suffering whenever it was generated inside their conscious mind by an old unfair painful memory that they started reliving.

Fortunately, others carried around small bags of unresolved pain & suffering that barely diminished their ability to love everyone in their life.

Unfortunately, I could not help my friends & family because I did not know how to kill the pain & suffering that I was carrying around with me, until I studied the wisdom of our ancestors who provided me with answers that I could use to kill my unresolved pain & suffering. This wisdom taught me how to use forgiveness to kill the pain & suffering that was being generated by the old unfair memories that I was reliving each day of my life. I wanted to kill the ability of these old memories to generate new pain & suffering into my daily life, so they could not hurt me again in the future and so they could not hurt those I love.

Then, after I practiced this wisdom and the killing was done, my bag of unresolved pain & suffering became empty and it remained empty, until someone hurt me unfairly again in the future. Then, I used forgiveness to kill this new pain & suffering that had just entered my life.

And I killed my new desire for justice & revenge that encouraged me to force the person who had just hurt me to pay me compensation in remorseful words, deeds or money for this new unfairness. This killing process, which included knowing how to use my mind to forgive, enabled me to empty my bag of unresolved pain & suffering, once again

When I was a young child, I was taught to use forgiveness when I attended a Christian Sunday School, however this Christian teaching did not enable me to understand how my mind worked, so I was not able to implement The How to Forgive Process into my mind so I could become able to use forgiveness as often as I wanted to, during my childhood.

It was not until I studied Buddha's wisdom, many years later, that I learned how my mind worked, which enabled me to use forgiveness to kill all the unresolved pain & suffering that was living inside my mind in my bag of unresolved pain & suffering.

And Buddha taught me to replace this unresolved pain & suffering with unconditional love that automatically entered into my conscious mind, when I used Buddhist wisdom to choose the feelings that I wanted to experience, after I had cleansed my mind of my old unresolved pain & suffering by tapping into the full power of my Internal Source of Unconditional Love, a continuous love that allows me to forgive others who have treated me unfairly in the past, a continuous love that automatically kills the unresolved pain & suffering in my memories when I forgive others, and a continuous love that has been living inside me since I was born, but which unfortunately, may be partially hidden from me or blocked by new pain & suffering when it enters my conscious mind, whenever I relive an old unfair memory that I have not cleansed with my forgiveness.

Buddha's wisdom is also helping me to become A Compassionate Watcher each morning, as I use Buddhist meditation techniques to observe all the feelings, thoughts & images that live in my conscious mind, as they continuously compete for control of my mind & actions during the day, as My Compassionate Watcher enables me to mentally detach from all my feelings, until I decide to choose the feelings that I want to experience and until I decide to kill the feelings that I no longer want to experience, by maintaining control of my mind with my reasoning ability, which allows My

Compassionate Watcher to use forgiveness to stop an old memory from generating new pain & suffering into my future life and which allows My Compassionate Watcher to extend the life expectancy of the feelings that I want to experience.

Unfortunately, you may have to reread this section of our book several times, to completely understand this wisdom, to enable you to bring increasing love & joy into your life.

To help you understand the wisdom for forgiving the unresolved pain & suffering in our lives, I asked My Son Wil to explain his understanding of this wisdom to help you to rewrite this wisdom in your own words, to make it easier for you to explain this wisdom to your friends & family, so they can begin to benefit from your increased wisdom for sharing unconditional love & nurturing friendship by killing any unresolved pain & suffering in your life that may be diminishing your ability to love them.

My Son Wil's Wisdom for Forgiving the Unresolved Pain & Suffering in His Life

"The pain and suffering that I've accumulated throughout my life forms a barrier that prevents me from being my true self. This pain and suffering is stored in my unfair memories. These unfair memories have been created throughout my life whenever I've felt I've been treated unfairly. In order to be able to be my true self, more often, I need to learn to kill the pain and suffering in my unfair memories and remove their power over me.

My pain and suffering is triggered whenever I feel I've been treated unfairly in my adult life. When I'm treated unfairly, my negative feelings are magnified because I'm not just feeling the pain and suffering caused by the present situation but I'm also reliving the pain and suffering from all the associated unfair memories from my past.

Experiencing this avalanche of unfairness may cause me to become a different person. The anger I've accumulated in my past can come out in the present and cause me to overreact. The person I become when my emotions overwhelm me, can be angry and can treat those around me unfairly. This anger can be hard to control because it has the power of the past behind it. By learning to kill the pain and suffering in my unfair memories, I can make sure that I don't hurt the ones I love unnecessarily.

It's important that I learn to kill my feelings of unfairness so that I can limit the amount when I treat my loved ones unfairly. Whenever I'm unfair to those I love, I add to their unfair memories. By doing this, I'm inflicting my feelings of unfairness on them and passing on my anger. By controlling my own feelings I can avoid perpetuating the cycle of unfairness in others.

At times, I am unaware of how powerful my feelings of unfairness are. Since they dwell in my subconscious mind, and only surface into my conscious mind when triggered, my feelings of unfairness can hide, affect me subtly, and explode when triggered. I may also be unaware when they take control of me and cause me to treat someone unfairly. Only through reflection can I know the full impact I have on others.

If I remain unaware of the ability of my unfair memories to control me, I can live through a cycle of abuse, where I take out my anger on others without realizing the impact of my actions, and feeling my actions are justified. I need to be aware of how I act and why I act the way I do to prevent myself from hurting the ones I love.
Life can be stressful and this stress can be tiring. When I'm tired I have less control over my feelings and am more prone to acting out. I have to be careful when I'm stressed and tired that I don't take it out on those that are closest to me. I also have to understand that when someone I love takes their stress out on me, it's just because they're allowing their unfair memories to control them.

Loss of love in relationships can be caused by the failure to understand the cycle of unfairness. When I take my stress out on someone, treat them unfairly, and create an unfair memory for them, I'm building the feeling of unfairness between us. When they respond by treating me unfairly in return, the cycle is perpetuated. If we aren't mindful of what we're doing, we'll strengthen the unfairness between us to the point where it pushes away the love in our relationship. This is why couples lose love for each other over time. They don't realize that they're building a wall of unfairness between them that blocks the love.

I don't have to be angry to cause someone to feel unfairly treated. I can also trigger a feeling of unfairness when I disappoint them. If I disappoint someone I love over many years, then the feelings of disappointment I create in them will build up to the point where the disappointment can block them from loving me. I have to be aware of how not only my actions, but also my inaction, can cause pain in my loved ones and limit their ability to love me.

I can help my loved ones love me with greater passion by helping them to understand the wisdom of how feelings of unfairness can control us. I can help my loved ones understand how unfair memories can cause them to not only be angry but disappointed or indifferent as well. By helping them to understand how to kill their pain and suffering, I can help them let go of their resentment, and increase their desire to share love with me and reduce their desire to share their unresolved pain and suffering with me.

The key to killing the pain and suffering in my unfair memories is to use forgiveness. Whenever I feel unfairly treated I need to forgive the person who is treating me unfairly. I also need to continually forgive all the people who have treated me unfairly in the past, especially the ones who do not deserve forgiveness. This is because being treated unfairly in the present will trigger my unfair memories of the past to generate unresolved pain and suffering from my past into my present life.

My mind in the present will wander to my past memories, and when it does, I need to practice forgiveness with each of my unfair memories and the people involved. Doing so will remove the power my unfair memories have over me in the present and diminish their power over me in the future.

By practicing forgiveness I remove the pain and suffering stored in unfair memories. As a little more of the negative energy in my unfair memories is released each time they come up and I practice forgiveness, the power of my unfair memories diminishes over time.

Eventually, the energy storehouse for my unfair memories will be empty of stress, pain and anger, and I can move on from the past and practice forgiveness in the present to prevent me from holding on to new unfair memories moving forward.

We all carry a bag of unresolved pain and suffering around with us. This bag is filled with all of the unfair memories that we haven't dealt with or are still in the process of dealing with. I've been carrying around my bag since I was a child and adding to it throughout my life. The weight of my bag is preventing me from being my true self because the pain and suffering inside of it is blocking the love I have to give from taking priority.

The time has come for me to empty my bag by practicing forgiveness. The process may take the rest of my life but by dedicating myself to practicing forgiveness I am diminishing the power of my unfair memories over time and increasing my ability to love everyone and everything in my life with great passion.

In order to forgive I am letting go of my need for revenge, justice and compensation. I believe that life isn't fair in any given instance but life is fair in the whole. I have been treated unfairly in the past and will be treated unfairly in the future. Every time I'm treated unfairly these unfair feelings motivate me to make the situation fair by getting the person that treated me unfairly to pay. This payment may satisfy my desire for revenge, justice or compensation but payment isn't always possible. Bad people sometimes get away with being bad. They don't always have to pay for what they've done. At least not every time they do something wrong. However, these bad people will get what's coming to them. Life is fair in the whole. But it may not be me who corrects the unfairness of the bad people who do me wrong. And good people can also treat me unfairly.

When others treat me unfairly, I am forgiving them even when they do not deserve forgiveness. Carrying around the pain and suffering they cause me won't hurt them, won't allow me to take revenge, won't cause justice to be done, and won't make them pay me back. All the effort I spend carrying around the pain and suffering they caused me generates more pain and suffering in my present life whenever I relive one of these painful memories, as my memories push this old pain and suffering back into my present life. So I am forgiving those that don't deserve it so that I can be free of the old pain and suffering that they caused me.

I am also sharing the wisdom I am learning with my loved ones. Even though my loved ones may continue to treat me unfairly, I continue to forgive them and I try to help them to realize what they're doing and why they're doing it, by helping them to understand why their negative emotions sometimes take control of their minds and motivate them to treat me unfairly.

And I am helping my loved ones to practice forgiveness so that they can empty their bag of unresolved pain and suffering they are carrying around with them. I am doing this because I love them and I am helping them to stop their unfair painful memories from controlling them so they can free themselves of their unresolved pain and suffering from their past.

By teaching, helping, and being patient I am working with my loved ones to break the cycle of unfairness on both sides. As my loved ones and I work on practicing this wisdom together, we are helping each other remove the blockages to our love.

The reward for practicing this wisdom is my increased capacity to feel and share continuous love, peace, joy, and compassion. By unloading my bag of unresolved pain and suffering I'm removing the weight that slows me down in life. My work may never be completely done, but the more I free myself from the unfairness in my past life, the more I am able to love in the present moment and in my future life."

End of My Son Wil's wisdom for increasing the love & forgiveness in his life by emptying his bag of unresolved pain & suffering that he has been carrying around with him in his adult life.

As his father, I am also determined to find creative ways to empty my bag of unresolved pain & suffering by practicing the nine steps to emotional freedom, whenever new unfair experiences enter my life and start to fill my bag with unresolved pain & suffering.

Fortunately, the reward for learning and then practicing the wisdom of forgiveness is the **continuous** love, peace, joy & compassion that enters our future adult lives, after we use forgiveness to kill the major unresolved pain & suffering that is still living inside our old unfair memories and that is still blocking the internal pathway to our childhood source of powerful unconditional love & forgiveness.

There are eight additional steps to emotional freedom that I am taking, to help me to increase my ability to kill any new pain & suffering that may enter my mind in the future, so I can replace this pain & suffering with the powerful love, peace, joy & compassion that is living inside My Internal Source of Love, a source of love which I can access at any time during the day or night, as long as I keep my conscious mind free of unresolved pain & suffering.

As you read the sections of our book containing The Nine Steps to Emotional Freedom, you will learn how to practice this wisdom, so you can kill any old or new unresolved pain & suffering in your adult life and then replace it with pure love & joy.

And you can preview the Nine Steps to Emotional Freedom from pain & suffering in Chapter 13 when you look through the Table of Contents of Our Book One.

You may also expand your knowledge of the Buddhist wisdom for taking back control of your mind from any future pain & suffering that may try to take control of you, by studying the wisdom in the book called, "Understanding Our Mind" by Thich Nhat Hanh, a Vietnamese Buddhist monk, poet, and peacemaker, who was nominated for the Nobel Peace Prize, by Dr. Martin Luther King Jr, the American civil rights activist.

Chapter 4

The Power of Love & Forgiveness

I do not know why love is being continuously created inside me during each moment of every day of my adult life, as I continue to experience the ability to love & forgive others, especially when I continue to love others who do not deserve my forgiveness.

As I try to forgive with the power of my love, I also try to kill the fear & anger that I feel whenever I think of others who hurt me unfairly as I was growing up. This choice to love & forgive is solely mine to make, as I begin to realize that The Wisdom of Children is helping me to replace this old unresolved pain & suffering with increasing love & forgiveness.

This power of love & forgiveness is a miracle that I was given when I was born. It gives me the motivation to live my life with a feeling of being worthy of living, as I look forward to sharing the power of increasing unconditional love & true friendship with everyone around me, as I look out onto the world and I try to understand the purpose of my life, whenever I think about why my life is spent living as a small speck of energy & matter on Our Precious Mother Earth inside The Milky Way Galaxy of 200+ billion stars which is a tiny part of our universe of two+ trillion galaxies and then, as I try to understand why our universe is only one of an infinite number of universes.

As I start to feel small & insignificant in this vast multi-universe of galaxies containing countless stars & planets that are capable of supporting life, I begin to realize that my love is uniting me with all the life that lives in this vastness of space & time as I share universal love with all the life forms who live interdependently with each other and with me.

And I share this powerful energy of universal love with all the life around me on Our Precious Mother Earth which occupies an infinitesimal part of this vast multiverse.

It is love that gives this vastness meaning, as Carl Sagan said, "For small creatures such as we, this vastness is bearable only through love".

And it is this love that gives meaning & purpose to my life when I decide to believe that there is a universal intelligence that gave me the ability to feel this powerful universal love when I was born. I call this universal intelligence God and I believe that my ability to love comes from God even though this belief may not be true. I also accept that God must be a spiritual being who is the source of all the love in the universe.

Since I do not understand why I was given this ability to share love with all the life around me, I just accept that I was blessed by God with the ability to love when I was born and blessed by my parents who decided to bring me into this world.

The source of love that motivates a woman & a man to create a new life may be unknowable but their love becomes powerful as it gives new meaning & purpose to their lives as they bring a child into the world. Mothers create & nurture life and fathers serve & protect their families, as each mother & father share the power of their love as they nurture their new child. So it was with my Mom & Dad who brought my brother & me into the world as they nurtured us with their love when we were sad and who shared our joy when we were happy, as they helped us share love & forgiveness with each other and with our friends & family. And for this wonderful gift of sharing love & forgiveness, I will always be grateful to my parents.

Chapter 5

Overview of the Wisdom in Our Book Series

The four books in The Wisdom of Children series help us to increase the Love, Peace, Joy & Compassion in Our Lives until it becomes continuous.

Our Book One "Learning to Understand My True Self" helps us to increase the love, peace, joy & compassion in our daily lives by teaching us how to kill the unresolved pain & suffering that is buried in our old unfair memories that many of us keep reliving each day of our lives, as we try to fully reconnect to the Internal Source of Unconditional Love of our childhood that we were born possessing and that many of us have diminished or lost, to enable us to experience the continuous love, peace, joy & compassion that we remember experiencing when we were children.

My Son & I will help you to understand The Wisdom of Children which helps us to fully reconnect to this continuous love, peace, joy & compassion and we will help you to realize the benefits of practicing this wisdom as we tell you stories of how we successfully applied this wisdom to our lives to increase the unconditional love that we share with our friends & family.

Our Book Two "Understanding How My Mind Works" helps us to learn meditation & mindfulness techniques to enable us to understand how our minds actually work and to enable us to understand how our minds should work, to help us correct the errors in our thinking, as we use our reasoning ability to control our thinking energy that we use to power our motivation to accomplish the goals for our lives.

Our Book Three "Learning to Choose My Feelings" helps us to practice choosing all our feelings, especially the feelings that nurture & protect our continuous love, peace, joy & compassion, as we learn to kill the control that our Egos have over our lives, as we stop our bad habits & our procrastinating that diminish our opportunities for increasing the life enhancing feelings that nurture happiness & success in our future lives.

Our Book Four "Increasing My Love for All Life" helps us to learn how to maximize the love, peace, joy & compassion in our lives by helping us to learn how to embrace & forgive those who hurt us, so we can remove all the pain in our hearts that prevents us from fully loving our friends & family, once again, as we learn to pass on our wisdom for increasing the happiness & success in our lives, to our children & our grandchildren, by learning to understand what is motivating them as they grow up, so we can help them to live in continuous joy & happiness and not make the same mistakes that we made when we were young, because we did not know how to protect our childhood ability to fully love & fully forgive our friends & family.

Unfortunately, many of us diminished or lost our childhood ability to love our life when our passion started to hide under all the memories of the unresolved pain & suffering that we experienced growing up.

In summary, the wisdom in Our Books helps us to kill all the major unresolved pain & suffering that is buried inside our painful memories and to kill the errors in our thinking, to enable us to fully reconnect to The Internal Source of Unconditional Love of our childhood that we were born possessing. This reconnection enables us to feel an increasing love for all life, especially for our friends & family and to feel loved by all the life that surrounds us, an ability that we possessed when we were young. As children we felt intense love for our friends & family until we were treated unfairly, at times, and we did not know how to stop this unfair pain from hurting us, when our offers of love & friendship were rejected by the neurotic people in our childhood, who were unable to accept our love and who treated us unfairly by lying to us, manipulating us, stealing from us, or abusing us.

Fortunately, The Wisdom of Children helps us to understand how this unresolved pain & suffering is generated inside our minds when we relive these unfair memories and this wisdom helps us to kill this old pain & suffering, so we can replace it with feelings of continuous love, peace, joy & compassion that motivate us to share new adult fun & adventures with our friends & family.

Please ask yourself these questions,

Is it possible to believe that The Wisdom of Children may help me to increase the joy & happiness in my adult life? Why? Q-11

How does The Wisdom of Children become a belief structure that anchors itself to my real childhood ability to unconditionally love all the life around me and to my adult ability to love my friends & family? Q-12

"Belief structures create a filter through which the chaos of our external perceptions about life are sifted into a mental reality that becomes a stable & loving presence inside our human minds." (Modified quote from Frank Herbert's Dune series)

"Our belief structures help us to realize that we are not just our bodies, as we try to understand the feelings, thoughts & images that enter our minds from the outside world, as they live with us for a while and then disappear from our minds each day. They help us to define who we are as human beings, as our Free Will helps us to use these feelings, thoughts & images to create our mental perceptions of the real world that exists outside our minds & bodies.

As this is happening, there still remains inside our minds, a quiet sanctuary that is free of the feelings, thoughts & images of the outside world, a sanctuary where we can go and where nothing lives except the knowledge we were given when we were born, that each of us is an eternal spiritual being who is loved by all creation, as we wait for our feelings, thoughts & images to help us define who we are as spiritual beings living inside human bodies on Our Precious Mother Earth.

Only when we realize that this innate knowledge is true, can we begin to understand why we were born with a powerful desire to love everyone in our lives, as we try to fully reconnect to this universal love of our childhood in our adult lives and as we try to forgive those in the outside world who do not deserve our forgiveness." (Modified quote from Terry Goodkind's Sword of Truth series)

Chapter 6

Learning to Understand My True Self

Please ask yourself this question,

Can I remember a childhood experience when I felt connected to a source of unconditional love that lived inside me and powered my motivation to learn to walk, talk & play and nourished my sense of wonder & delight when I shared fun & adventures with my friends & family? Q-13

If you do not remember sharing unconditional love with your friends & family when you were a young child, then we will help you to remember and we will help you to understand why many adults have diminished or lost their ability to connect to the source of the pure & unlimited unconditional love of their childhood, which prevents them from sharing the full power of this nurturing love with their friends & family, today.

My Son & I call this childhood gift of knowing how to connect to our powerful source of unlimited unconditional love, The Wisdom of Children.

As young children, we embraced The Wisdom of Children when we used our gift to share unconditional love with our friends & family as we bonded with their love for us, such as when I cherished my unconditional love for My Mom as I looked into her eyes and felt the love in her heart, as we shared the hopes & dreams of our future together as mother & child, as our desire to nurture mutual love & friendship grew, a desire that was expressed eloquently by Saint Aelred when he said, "A truly loyal friend sees nothing in his friend but his heart."

Now, I use this quote in my adult life when I say "I see nothing in my true friend but his heart" which helps me to share love & forgiveness, especially when my friend does not deserve forgiveness.

As a child, I looked back on my childhood experiences at school & at play, to determine what was true in my life. I knew the truth of my feelings when I felt unconditional love for everyone in my life and when I felt loved by all the life around me. This is how I embraced the truth of my childhood experiences. Truth to me as a child was the quality of being genuine, actual & factual that I could judge from my past experiences, as opposed to being false & fake, when I realized someone had lied to me on purpose, to become able to manipulate me for their personal gain.

In contrast to the truth of living the fun & adventures of my childhood, My Mom told me stories that she said were not true, but fun & enjoyable to hear and imagine in my mind, as I pretended to be the hero or the villain in a story. I tried to picture these stories in my childhood imagination, as my feelings of adventure & excitement carried me along as My Mom read to me, as I begin to live a story in my imagination. I imagined true friends who loved & supported me and I imagined fake friends who lied to me & tried to steal from me when I began to trust them with my valuable possessions, which were my toys.

In this way, my mother helped to prepare me for the world of my future, when I went outside our home to play with children from other families, who I did not know, as I learned to play with potential new friends by sharing fun & adventures, as I tried to offer them my love & friendship.

As a child, whenever other children offered me their love & support, I considered them my true friends, when I began to feel an emotional attachment to them as we played together and I started to feel affection & personal regard for their future well-being, as the love for my new friends started to blossom in my heart.

When I thought about the future, I felt an implicit trust that all the life around me, especially the lives that my friends & family were living, would offer me challenges that would be fair to me, though I did not always know if this would turn out to be true or if my friendships would last.

As a child, fairness to me was a life that was free of dishonesty & injustice when I played with my friends & family, such as the love & friendship I shared with My Mom that I felt was true & fair and that it would last. This belief was the solid rock of my childhood, as I offered all new human beings who came into my life my unconditional love, with the hope & trust that they would become my true friends and would not betray my belief in their fairness towards me.

My love for My Mom motivated me to share unconditional love, emotional openness & vulnerability with my family, as I learned to share honesty and a sense of fair play with my friends. With My Mom's encouragement, I eagerly explored the new fun & adventures that my childhood kept offering me, when I realized that My Mom would protect me when I made mistakes or got into trouble.

As we shared unconditional love to nurture & protect our true friendship, My Mom helped me to feel the love from all the life in my external world of fun & adventures and she helped me to feel my internal love for all the life surrounding me, a love that I was born possessing, as I learned to share love & forgiveness with my friends & family.

My desire to share unconditional love & nurture true friendship was generated by my Internal Source of Unconditional Love that began to nourish me with powerful feelings of love, peace, joy & compassion, when I was born and that I learned to accept as my natural state of being as a young child. These elements of unconditional love continuously supplied me with abundant passion for enjoying my life and with powerful motivation to fill each day of my childhood with new fun & adventures.

Please ask yourself this question,

As I look back through my childhood memories, can I remember when I was able to embrace my childhood wisdom for sharing unconditional love & nurturing true friendship, by opening my heart and offering my unconditional love to potential friends, with my innocent expectation that we could share fun & adventures and become true & loving friends? Q-14

Unfortunately, I and many of my childhood friends, started to lose our innocence when we begin to realize that some of our potential friends had lost their ability to share unconditional love & to nurture true friendship because they felt unloved. They were unhappy children, who we felt compassion for, who would not allow us to help them rediscover the love, peace, joy & compassion of their childhood, once again, by accepting our unconditional love & becoming our true friends, and who used us as an opportunity to vent their anger that the life all around them was being unfair to them because we were happy & having fun, and they were not. We began to realize that some children felt unloved for long periods of time when their parents, guardians or siblings kept treating them unfairly.

As we grew from childhood to become teenagers and then adults, many of us began to lose our ability to offer unconditional love & true friendship, as we started to lose our sense of wonder & delight in exploring our world of challenges & opportunities, as our once powerful motivation to learn & achieve started to decline, as our offers of unconditional love & true friendship were rejected, as our eagerness to share fun & adventures was reduced, as we encountered increasing fear, anger, worry & stress in our lives, as the unfairness in our lives continued to increase the number of unfair memories of unresolved pain & suffering that were being stored in our subconscious minds as we grew up, which increased the amount of pain we felt each day, whenever we relived these unfair memories as the pain from these unfair memories reduced our passion for enjoying our lives during each day of our childhood because we did not know how to stop this remembered pain from hurting us again & again each day, whenever we relived one or more of these painful unfair feelings.

Please ask yourself these questions,

Why did I diminish or lose the passion of my childhood by the time I became an adult? Q-15

What can I do as an adult to increase my passion for living and increase my eagerness to share new fun & adventures, so I can fully enjoy my life again, as I once did when I was a young child? Q-16

How do I fully reconnect to the internal source of love, peace, joy & compassion of my childhood, so I can start to feel & then share this powerful unconditional love with all the life that is surrounding me, especially with my friends & family? Q-17

I asked My Son to help me to answer these questions, to help me to rediscover my childhood ability to share unconditional love & nurture true friendship with our friends & family.

My Son became my true friend when he offered me his unconditional love as a young child, when he was is in love with all the life around him and he felt the love being generated by all this life. His ability to continuously love all the life around him inspired me to remember when I felt this way, when I was a young child.

This is how My Son enabled me to become his true friend, as we shared fun & adventures together, as I slowly relearned The Wisdom of Children, as I answered the fourth question that was crucial to my future well-being as a happy & successful adult.

How do I kill the unfair fear, anger, worry & stress in my mind that is being generated by my unfair painful memories and that is blocking my connection to the source of unconditional love of my childhood and diminishing my ability to increase the love, peace, joy & compassion in my adult life? Q-18

My Childhood

The earliest memories of my childhood contain the powerful passion I felt for exploring all the life around me. I do not have many painful memories of my childhood because my parents protected me from harm. Life was good to me as my parents filled my life with fun & adventures and their love. When I remember the joy of my childhood, my mind becomes filled with the love I felt as I grew up in a farming community that nurtured & protected its children, when many of our neighbors did not lock the doors to their homes because they felt safe & secure in our small town, that nestled in a land of rolling hills & valleys filled with farms that backed onto gently flowing rivers that meandered through a picturesque landscape on the way to the sea.

Our home was situated on a hillside overlooking one of these valleys. I remember looking out the kitchen window of our home across the field in our backyard past the trees that run down to the edge of the river that fed our valley with fresh water and supplied the well in our back yard with drinking water. These images remind me of one of the beautiful scenes from my childhood, when I woke up in the morning as the sun rose in the sky as it painted our land with shades of gold, as I began a new day of my childhood anticipating the start of new fun & adventures at school.

I also treasure the memories of the sunsets, when I was back home from school, as I started to get ready for bed and I looked out my bedroom window across the miles of the valley floor at the cultivated fields of the farms and the river running through our valley, as the sun painted the sky with the colors of the rainbow, as it started to descend below the horizon of the hills on the far side of our valley, as it waved goodbye to our land and our home, until it greeted us again when I woke up the next day to the possibility of new fun & adventures.

Many of my childhood memories are of the wonderful outdoors, as I breathed the clear fresh air, felt the caress of the warm sun on my body when it appeared brightly from behind a cloud that was drifting slowly across the sky, as I heard the laughter and felt the joy of my childhood friends that combined inside our minds & bodies to generate our wonderful warm feeling of unconditional love for the land & its people, on warm sunny afternoons, when the view of the valley was breathtaking, as we felt spiritually united with the land and the people who lived in our town, as our town played host to the wildlife, the buzz of the insects, a humming bird dancing from flower to flower gathering nectar, the sight of a hawk or an eagle circling high up in the sky, or a deer looking at us from the woods, as we played sports or explored the beautiful land surrounding our town, as we appreciated its wildlife or worked on the farms to help the farmers to bring in the crops or do chores around a farm, such as when I was asked as a young child to feed milk to a baby lamb who had lost its mother, to nourish it, to help the lamb grow big & strong so it could live with us as a member of our extended family, as we loved the land, the animals, the wildlife and the farmers who nurtured & protected the land.

I remember the vigorous pull of the lamb as it sucked milk from the bottle through the nipple made out of the finger of a rubber glove. The lamb was full of energy with such a vigorous desire for the life giving milk that I had to hold onto the bottle with all the strength of my four year old body to keep the bottle from being pulled from my hands by the lamb that weighed almost as much as me.

Many of the memories of my childhood I relive inside my adult mind & body in full color with the sights & the sounds of the farmers who enjoyed watching me share the life of the animals that lived on the farms. The farmers loved the children of our town and wanted us to share in their love of the farming life and their love of the land.

Wonderful memories of my childhood continue to bless my adult life when I start to remember where I began my journey through life on our precious mother Earth, when I was born as an unconditionally loving baby who was given the opportunity to experience a wonderful childhood growing up in a small town where the residents openly expressed their love & appreciation for the children living there, as they shared in the joy of our childhood. The adult residents of our town nurtured the children who filled their adult lives with the unconditional love and the fun & adventures of childhood. I was truly blessed to be a loving member of this large extended family of parents, teachers, town officials, store keepers, postal workers, volunteer workers, church members, school friends and loving neighbors, especially the farmers & their families.

Living in our small town also felt good for the adult members of our community of families who actively spent quality time together at church or at community social events and felt the love & friendship of their neighbors. Minor disputes between neighbors were resolved by our elected town council or the justice of the peace who lived in our town that contained about one thousand people.

I learned to fish in the river behind our home and I learned to build tree houses in the woods owned by the local farmers. In the winter I played hockey on many of the frozen ponds & lakes. In the summer I swam in the rivers & lakes and picnicked in the beautiful outdoors as our family cooked over an outdoor fire or boiled corn from one of the local farms. Many of the families in our community planted gardens and our mothers preserved vegetables, made pickles, and took great pride in the jams & jellies they made and then offered to the outsiders who visited relatives living in our town. Our community associations such as the legion of war veterans sponsored local events including community fairs and baseball & hockey leagues. Our outdoor public skating rink was run by volunteers such as my father during the winter months. My father volunteered for many community activities such as our volunteer fire department.

We lived in a lower middle class community that could not afford to hire sufficient help to satisfy all our needs, so the adult members of our community volunteered to work together on different projects of their choosing to help create a wonderful loving environment to bring up their children. The children of our community benefited greatly from this sense of community spirit that had evolved slowly over the last hundred plus years of the history of our incorporated town.

When a boy from our town grew up and married a local girl, many newlyweds decided to bring up their future children in the loving atmosphere of our town and they chose to build homes near their parents. When I grew up in this community of family love, our hard working parents were able to fund one public school and fund a public library that was housed on the second floor of the volunteer fire department. Our school contained an auditorium where I learned to dance and play basketball. I have wonderful memories of the school plays, singing in the school choir and attending the class graduations when I received my report card that summarized the work I had accomplished in school that year. Our school auditorium was the home of many school activities such as school dances and basketball & badminton games, as well as being the center for many community events such as the Friday night dances when a local band came to play.

As I walked to our school from my home each day of the school year, from the age of five until I was sixteen, I met many friends & neighbors on the way to school. I spent my time before classes talking to my friends about the latest hockey game on TV or to the girls who I sometimes walked home from school. I enjoyed many friendships during my childhood. My older brother helped protect me when I was a young child at school, until I learned to defend myself whenever an older kid got upset with the jokes we played on our unsuspecting school mates and my brother helped me to participate in the fun & games that my friends & I were learning how to play.

As a child I played outdoor sports, baseball in the summer, soccer in the fall and hockey in the winter. My childhood was filled with fun & adventures at school and many community events that my family enjoyed.

My Mom & Dad were loving & supportive and tried to answer my many questions about the meaning of my life, as I grew up in this farming community, when I asked,

Why I was born? Q-19

To help me to answer these questions my parents sent me to church each Sunday, to Sunday School when I was a young child and then to the regular church services when I was older. There were three churches in our small town, Baptist, Presbyterian, and the United Church. There was no Roman Catholic Church, no synagogue & no mosque within twenty miles of our town, so I did not have the opportunity to participate in these religions on a regular basis when I was a child. I sampled the religions that were available in our town, whenever a friend invited me to attend one of the three churches.

When I was fourteen, I was invited to an adult initiation course and I became a member of the United Church of Canada. I have many wonderful memories of attending Sunday School and other church activities, especially at Christmas & Easter.

When I was a young child I started to believe in a loving God who had made me in his image when I was born and who continued to help nurture me & my family, as I grew up. By the age of fourteen I had a loving personal relationship with God, as I learned to become a young Christian growing up in our rural farming community.

My Teacher & Role Model Bradley James Slauenwhite

In Grade Eight, my elementary school teacher Bradley James Slauenwhite, to whom Our Book is dedicated, helped me to analyze my memories of the unconditional love that I felt during my childhood. This help was generated by Bradley's love of learning which inspired his students to remain after regular school hours to learn the wisdom that he was passionate about, such as The Method of Outlining that was not part of the school curriculum. With Bradley's help & inspiration, I acquired a new way of looking at my life experiences, as a student, to become able to understand how my mind works and to become able to apply the wisdom from the modern & ancient sages that I was researching, to my life experiences, to gain a personal understanding of why I desired to continue sharing the unconditional love of my childhood with my friends & family, even when they were unfair to me & hurtful at times, as I grew from childhood on my way to becoming a teenager.

Bradley's teaching helped me to find answers to my questions about why I felt a spiritual connection to the unconditional love that I was receiving from all the life in the universe, as I felt the beauty & wonder of the natural world around me on my walk to school each day, as I looked at the stars at night, or as I participated in the community activities of our small town.

Ever since I was a baby, I felt love for everything in my life and I felt the reciprocal love from all the life around me. The source of these feelings had always been a mystery to me, a mystery that I had tried to solve but was unable to do so, until Bradley helped me.

With this new approach to learning that Bradley inspired me to adopt, I began to study the writings of our ancient prophets & sages with more enthusiasm, as I looked inside my mind to find a way to understand the causes of the unresolved pain & suffering that were buried inside my memories of the unfair events in my life that were created whenever someone treated me unfairly, by lying to me, by bullying me, by manipulating me, or by stealing from me. This did not occur very often during my childhood, but I had been running away from my memories of this unresolved pain & suffering for many years because I did not know how to stop the memories from hurting me whenever I relived one of them and I wanted to learn how I could kill this unfair pain & suffering and then become able to fully reconnect to my internal source of unconditional love for all the life around me.

As I explored and tried to understand these painful experiences, I enjoyed learning from Bradley as he shared his unconditional love for all the life in the universe with his students, a love that was fueled by his passion for experiencing new adventures in his life, as he helped us to develop our intellectual abilities. Bradley's students felt his love for learning and his belief in our potential to grow into happy & successful adults. This sharing of his love of new adventures & his over whelming desire to learn new ways to motivate us to share our newly acquired knowledge with him, encouraged us to ask Bradley questions about the meaning of life, to help us understand the potential opportunities that life held for us in the future, as we increased our desire to learn about and experience new opportunities for personal growth.

Then, we began to spiritually bond together as we shared Bradley's love of teaching us and his love of watching us learn, as we expressed our many desires about how to make our future opportunities successful, which inspired Bradley to offer us extracurricular fun & adventures that he was not paid for and that cost him personally, when he sacrificed his private family time to be with us after school, when he could have been spending more quality family time with his loving wife & their baby daughter. Bradley was in his twenties and married to a beautiful compassionate woman who understood his need to sacrifice some of his family time to be with his students, to be able to teach us important ideas & knowledge that he felt we needed for our future success and that he did not have sufficient time to share with us during regular school hours.

As I mentioned previously, an example of this is The Method of Outlining that Bradley taught us after school, which describes how we can analyze an idea by breaking it into its component parts to become able understand how each part supports the whole idea and how the whole idea cannot exist without the support of its parts. This approach enabled us to the get rid of any parts that may be attached to an idea but which are not necessary for the idea to exist as a whole, by itself. Once we understood which parts worked together to support the whole idea then we could combine these parts, and only these parts, back together to create the whole idea. Only then could we say that we truly understand how the idea works because we had proven how each part relates to the other parts and how they support each other to support the whole idea and how other parts, which do not support the whole idea, makes them unnecessary for the whole idea to exist, by itself.

For example, this logical approach can be used to understand the idea called "family". A family is a functioning unit made up of two or more human beings who work together for the well-being of each other and for the real life existence of the whole functioning unit called the family. The idea of family cannot be applied to someone like Robinson Crusoe who lived alone on an island in the ocean because it requires two or more human beings to make the idea of a family become a true idea. Fortunately for Robinson, someone joined him on the island who he named Friday, who became his friend and who learned how to work with Robinson to become two human beings who worked well together as a whole functioning unit for their mutual well-being & survival on the island, as a family, as described in the famous book by Daniel Defoe called Robinson Crusoe.

This example shows how the Method of Outlining works. The method requires a minimum of two functioning parts, to support each other and to join together, to become a whole idea that becomes true. In our example, it took the two parts of Robinson & Friday to work together as a functioning whole unit to make the idea of a family become true. If Friday were to leave the island then Robinson would be living alone again and the idea of a whole functioning unit called a family existing on the island would become false because one of its parts called Friday, is now missing.

Bradley helped us to practice The Method of Outlining by analyzing the truth of the ideas described in our school books, by breaking each of these ideas into two or more components parts and then looking at each part, to determine if each part was true or not, in our experience, or true or not, in the experience of someone in the world, such as a scientist who had tested this idea for truth. Bradley helped us to realize that we should be able to prove that an idea is true or not true by looking at how its parts work together to support the whole idea and that an idea becomes false when one of its supporting parts goes missing or becomes untrue.

Then, Bradley tried to convince us to not accept anything that a teacher may tell us is true in the future, until we can prove this new idea is true or false by looking for the truth in the parts that support this new idea that we experience for the first time in our lives, especially when someone tries to explain a new idea to us or we read about a new idea in a book that triggers our imagination, that contains a new idea that may help us understand the potential opportunities for new adventures in our future lives.

This is why Bradley started a science club after school so we could practice using The Method of Outlining. He allowed each of us to pick out a science experiment that we could conduct on our own that allowed us to use The Method of Outlining and then he encouraged us to share the results of our experiments with each other, as we tested the truth or falsehood of the science principles that we were being taught at school

In addition Bradley used school funds to buy a life science encyclopaedia that he put on a desk in the hall outside our class room for students to use during recess, lunch breaks or after school. He wanted the encyclopaedia to be a source of new ideas for us to explore that were an extension of the school curriculum.

Bradley also asked us to use The Method of Outlining to understand the truth of what anyone told us in our personal lives when we were not at school, such as when we were with our friends & family, or watching television, or reading a newspaper article about what our politicians were trying to make us believe was true & necessary for our future well-being, by checking the facts that were supporting the ideas that others were trying to get us to accept as true.

Bradley taught us these logic skills because he felt they were crucial skills for our success as students & future adults, skills that we did not have the opportunity to learn without his help. He was always trying to find new ways to inspire us to learn new ideas that we could test for truth in our life experiences, or test for truth by conducting a science experiment, or test for truth by reading how our wise ancestors & sages proved these new ideas, were true or false.

When we looked into Bradley's eyes, we could see the intensity of his personal excitement when he was trying to teach us a new idea or a new concept. We could observe that his passion was real because he was emotionally open with us. If he did not like what I was doing, he told me the reasons why. He was a genuine source of inspiration for me because he was honest with us and truthful when he made a mistake, which he did not try to hide. He was someone we could trust and we started to believe in the values about life & learning that he tried to instill in us. He was an embodiment of what our future reality could become if we decided to use our abilities to work hard to accomplish our dreams, as he was trying to do by fulfilling his dream of becoming a great teacher who inspired his students to learn new ideas that would help them to become successful in life. There was no bullshit or fakery about Bradley.

Bradley told us that we have great potential for success, but a student needs to become highly self-motivated & self-disciplined, to be able to use his intelligence & his learning ability to become successful in life. Bradley used his powerful passion for learning to supply him with the wisdom for success that he tried to instill in us.

In my opinion, Bradley was a rare & precious teacher, which became apparent to us, when he shared; his wonderful unconditionally loving heart, his love of exploring new ideas, his curiosity, his sense of wonder, and his wisdom & knowledge, with us, as he tried to inspire us to learn new ideas and to test these ideas for truth in our personal lives.

His love for all the life in the universe gave Bradley his special ability to inspire his students, an ability that was empowered by his passionate & determined nature, that we observed as his students, as he searched for the answers to his questions about finding better ways to inspire us to learn. Bradley talked to us about his desire to refine his teaching methods by increasing his understanding of how to motivate his students to learn, with passion, with curiosity, and with an appreciation for the wonders that knowledge holds for the learner.

This is why I loved Bradley as my teacher and my friend. I believe that he & I were born from the same mold that gave us an incurable, insatiable desire to find answers to our many questions about the meaning of life. When I met Bradley, I realized that for the first time in my life I had found someone who shared the same intense curiosity about life that I had. I was no longer alone on my journey to understand all there is to know about life. Bradley became my spiritual brother as we shared our journey of curiosity and then as we shared our wonder & our delight as we found some of the answers to our many questions about the meaning of life.

This was the passion for learning that Bradley & I were given in large measure, as a special gift when we were born. A passion I observed in Bradley's teaching methods, as he expressed his powerful desire to learn and as he offered to share his passion for science, literature & art with his students, to inspire us to become as passionate about learning as he was. Bradley told us that he was not content with his level of understanding of how to motivate students to learn. He planned to go to university someday, to acquire the extra wisdom that he felt was missing from his life as a teacher.

Eventually, Bradley did leave us after years of encouraging us to realize our true potential for success. I hope his graduate work at university helped him to fulfill the unique purpose and to experience the special meaning of his life.

Unfortunately, I lost touch with Bradley and I did not fully realize his important contribution to my future success, until many years later.

The Dedication of Our Book to Bradley is my way of saying "Thank You", even though I know that Bradley did not require my thanks because he felt privileged to be our teacher, as he shared his knowledge, his wisdom, his passion for living & learning, and his true friendship with us.

As a result of sharing his wisdom with me, Bradley became a rare & precious role model in my life. I can never repay Bradley for the many gifts that he gave me free of charge, without conditions attached to them, as he shared his love of learning with the students at our public school when I was a child.

It is appropriate to say that without Bradley's positive impact on my life which helped to inspire me to continue learning the wisdom of our prophets & sages, Our Book would not have been written.

DISCLAIMER – This is my recollection of our student / teacher relationship and does not necessarily reflect a full & correct understanding of the views & motivations of my teacher, Bradley James Slauenwhite, during my elementary school years.

The experience of sharing unconditional love & true friendship with my teacher Bradley helped me to develop my personal understanding of the compassion that human beings share with all sentient life, especially with our friends & family. This human ability to feel love & compassion for others supports my vision of a future when all the people on our precious Mother Earth use the motivational power of love & compassion to become true friends, by helping each other, by respecting each other, by treating each other fairly, and by working hard to end sickness, starvation, war & disease, so that by working together we are able to save our endangered cultural heritages & languages, so that our traditional ways of living do not disappear and we can save our endangered wildlife & the natural fauna on our planet, by becoming more environmentally friendly, as we learn to respect & safeguard more of the natural wonders of Our Precious Mother Earth for the benefit of our children and our grandchildren.

A Major Tragedy in My Teenage Life

Up to this point in my life, I had not experienced a major painful event, so I had no reason to question my belief in God or to question the meaning & purpose of my life as a young Christian, until My Mom died from a heart attack when I was a teenager.

I could not understand why God allowed My Mom to die. I blamed God for not helping My Mom to recover. I started to feel that our current life had suddenly become very unfair to me and my family.

I did not realize at the time that I was beginning to feed the painful memories of My Mom's death with the energy of my thinking that her death was so unfair. This unfair energy from my thoughts was keeping the unfair painful memories of My Mom's death alive & active in my mind each day of my teenage life. It took me many years to realize that I must stop thinking that my life was being unfair to me, before I could begin to kill the pain in these memories and start to reconcile my feeling of loss for My Mom with my memories of the love, peace, joy & compassion that filled so much of our life together as mother & son. I wanted to allow more memories of our shared love into my life by learning how to kill the unfair pain buried in the memories of My Mom's death that was preventing me from feeling this love without also feeling the pain of her death.

Learning to Overcome Feelings of Sadness & Loss

The process of learning how to kill the unfair pain in my memories was very painful for me to learn, as I asked for help from everyone that I knew and then searched the books of the wise sages of the past, such as Buddha, Mohammed, Lao-tzu & Jesus, for answers.

During this process of learning how to kill the unfair pain that I was feeling each day, I realized that I needed to express the wisdom that I was learning in my own words so I could more easily explain it to myself and to my friends & family. The Method of Outlining that was taught to me by Bradley, my elementary school teacher, enabled me to look for the foundations of truth or falsehood in the wisdom I was studying.

Then, after reading hundreds of books on wisdom that describe how the human mind works, I begin to understand four important mental concepts about the way my mind works that enabled me to start killing the unfair pain in my memories and enabled me to start bringing more love, peace, joy & compassion into my life.

1) I am the spiritual energy of unconditional love that is living inside my mind & my body that I have decided to call My Compassionate Watcher. It is My Compassionate Watcher who looks outside my mind into the external world, as I feel pain or joy in my life and who controls my thinking energy that enables me to use reason to make the correct decisions on how to act properly in my relationships with other human beings.

2) I am not My Feelings and I can learn to choose my feelings with the help of My Compassionate Watcher so they can no longer control my mind & my actions without my consent.

3) I was born as an unconditionally loving human being. I have proven this is true by remembering when I felt my unconditional love for everyone in my life, when I was a young child.

4) I have the ability to fully reconnect to the internal source of the unconditional love of my childhood, so I can start to generate the internal motivation and the mental power that I need, to allow My Compassionate Watcher to become able to stop my unfair painful memories from hurting me again in the future, whenever I relive one of them, so I can start to fill my future adult life with feelings of continuous love, peace, joy & compassion as I learn to Choose My Feelings instead of allowing My Feelings to Control Me.

I used these four mental concepts to begin to practice the wisdom that My Son & I have decided to call Living The Wisdom of Children to bring more love, peace, joy & compassion into our lives, as I learned how to feel the unconditional love of my childhood once again, as an adult, a love that I remember sharing with my friends & family when I was a young child, as I grew up in our small town in the heart of a rural farming community, when I felt love for everyone in this wonderful land of fun & adventures, during my childhood.

A Spiritual Journey with My Son Wil

The Wisdom of Children that My Son & I learned to understand & appreciate, by sharing unconditional love and fun & adventures together as father & son, we want to share with you, as we take you on a journey of discovery, as we help you to remember your childhood abilities to love all life unconditionally, especially your memories of your childhood friends when you played together in joy & happiness, as we explore the true source of The Wisdom of Children in Our Book, as we help you to learn how to increase the love, peace, joy & compassion in your adult life that you can share with your friends & family, as you help them to rediscover their diminished or hidden childhood ability to live life passionately with you.

Then, we will help you to eliminate the fear, anger, worry & stress in your adult life that may be reducing your passion for living and minimizing your ability to enjoy your future life.

We will also help you to rediscover and use your childhood abilities, to live your adult life with increased passion and help you to fuel your desire to share new fun & adventures with your friends & family.

With My Son's help I have been able to rediscover the powerful love, peace, joy & compassion of my childhood that now streams through my mind & body each day of my adult life, as I feel the powerful passion for life that I first experienced as a child, that I have fully reconnected to as an adult and that I am now using to motivate me to help my friends & family to rediscover the true source of the unconditional love that they first experienced when they were children and which now as adults, many may have diminished or lost.

Our Book describes our journeys of discovery, as we learn to apply The Wisdom of Children to all aspects of our lives and it provides **A Shortcut** for the adult readers of Our Book to use, to rediscover and to experience the full power of the source of unconditional love of their childhood, in their adult lives.

My Son used The Wisdom of Children to grow from a happy baby into the wise, compassionate & hard working young man that he is today. In doing so, My Son has exceeded my expectations as his father.

His successful life enhancing experiences that occurred when he applied The Wisdom of Children to his life, as he grew up, are examples of why I believe that all parents can use this wisdom, as my loving wife Linda & I were able to do with the help and enthusiasm of Our Son, to nurture & protect their children's ability to share unconditional love & nurture true friendship, an ability that all children are born possessing, so their children will not lose this ability, when they encounter unfair pain & suffering in their childhood and when their offers of unconditional love & true friendship are rejected by the negative unloving people that they meet in their lives, as they grow up.

The Wisdom of Children enables all parents to learn how to help their children to grow into joyful, fun loving & compassionate teenagers, as the parents experience increased peace, joy & happiness in their adult lives as they share increasing fun & adventures with their children.

And this wisdom will help their children to build on the growing joy, happiness & success in their lives, as they become adults and as they live their lives with increasing passion & unconditional love that they generously share with their friends & family.

Our modern & ancient sages have taught us that the source of the wisdom of our childhood is generated inside of us when we are connected to the source of the unconditional love that we were born possessing, as this love automatically generates powerful motivation inside each of us, to help us to nurture & protect all the life that surrounds us, as we grow from childhood to become adults.

And as we experience this ancient ability to love all life, we start to wonder about the source of this love.

Where does this continuous love for all life, come from?

This childhood desire to understand where our love comes from generates other questions that all children ask their parents & guardians and it is the same questions about the meaning of human life on Earth that our philosophers have been asking for thousands of years,

Who am I? Q-20
Where did I come from? Q-21
Why am I here on Earth? Q-22
What is my life's purpose? Q-23

Please ask yourself these questions.

The answers to these questions have generated an understanding of the purpose of human life on Earth that My Son and I share.

The purpose & meaning of your life may be different from ours. It is as if each of us is born as a unique human being with a particular skill set of abilities, that no one who has ever lived has had and that no one in future will have. It is as if each of us is an experiment for living life successfully that will never be created in the same way again. Your unique set of skills is inspiring you, to fulfill the unique purpose and to experience the special meaning of your life. You are unique, special & blessed to be given the opportunity to experience life as an unconditional loving human being on our precious Mother Earth.

Please allow My Son and me to help you to explore the many gifts that you were given when you were born, as we continue our exploration of the meaning & purpose of human life on Earth.

Many of my teachers have inspired me to find the wisdom of the meaning of my life, to enable me to experience increased joy & happiness, as I journeyed from childhood to become the adult that I am today. As one of my teachers, My Son continues to teach me the true meaning of life & love, whenever I observe his unconditional love & true friendship that he continues to share each day of his life.

He was born with the marvelous ability to love all life and to be joyous & happy, as he expressed his love which he eagerly tried to share with all life, as he grew up. His wise teachings have inspired me to reconnect to the unconditional love of my childhood, to become able to recapture my childhood ability to love all life unconditionally, as he is able to do.

With this understanding of My Son's love for all life, when he was a baby, I started to observe the unconditional love shown by the adults within my circle of friends & family and I began to realize that many human beings lose their connection to the source of the unconditional love of their childhood, when it becomes hidden under their memories of the unfair pain & suffering that all human beings experience, as they grow up. I realized that many adults try to hide from the unresolved pain & suffering buried in their memories because they do not know how to stop it from hurting them.

I also realized that true friendship can only occur between two human beings who are connected to their internal source of unconditional love.

Unfortunately, many adults do not know how to find the source of this unconditional love, once again.

Then, I realized that if I could help my friends & family to learn to fully reconnect to their internal source of unconditional love and to learn to practice sharing unconditional love, they would become true friends.

Our Book contains stories of how My Son & I learned to understand the meaning & purpose of our lives, as we practiced using The Wisdom of Children to help our friends & family to fully reconnect to their internal source of unconditional love, to become able to share unconditional love & nurture true friendship with us and to increase the joy & happiness in their lives.

Chapter 7

My Son Wil's Wisdom from The Child Living Inside Him

"In my father's introduction to Practicing The Wisdom Of Children, which we also call Our Book, my father explains that we all experienced unconditional love as children. Direct connection to unconditional love is our natural state of existence. Unconditional love is an energy source that powers positive emotion. It is "the source of peace, joy, happiness and compassion." All human beings have a permanent connection to unconditional love. The flow of its energy is never turned off but instead blocked by my ego. In childhood I began to accumulate memories of rejection, of being hurt & unfairness. Throughout my life I've collected these memories. They cause me pain. This pain blocks my connection to unconditional love. As a result, my "peace, joy, happiness and compassion" is diminished.[1] I've become fearful and angry. Since I value happiness, it is important that I learn to fully reconnect with unconditional love. Reconnection with unconditional love will improve my existence.

My father has taught me the wisdom of how to maintain my connection to my internal source of unconditional love, when the worry and stress in my life becomes intense. As a result of trying to help me to practice this wisdom for over 20 years, from my childhood to the beginning of my adulthood, my father decided to write a book, with my literary help and encouragement, to be able to summarize and explain the wisdom that we learned together as I grew up, because of his unconditional love for me and his desire to leave a legacy of wisdom for his grandchildren, which he is hoping I will pass on to my future children.

Helping to write Our Book and summarizing its wisdom are helping me to rediscover my true mode of existence. I am removing the blockage caused by my painful memories, with the wisdom that my father has been trying to get me to apply to my life. To do so, I am learning to meditate.

Typically, my mind is engaged in a constant stream of thought that continually tries to distract me from working on the goals for my life that will enhance my future well-being. These thoughts are typically ego driven and block my connection to unconditional love.

In order to experience unconditional love, I am using Meditation to practice Detachment to create a state of Mindfulness. My father defines Mindfulness as "knowing, what is happening inside my conscious mind in the present moment, while it is happening, no matter what it is" and he defines Detachment as "asking my mind to disengage my mental awareness of being inside a feeling, thought or image, to become aware of moving outside of it, and then of becoming aware of looking back at it from outside of it. Practicing Detachment is also asking my mind to stop me from becoming lost inside a feeling, thought or image when it tries to take control on my mind". Mindful breathing meditation is a means of achieving Mindfulness. When breathing mindfully, I focus my mind on my breathing. Focusing on my breathing causes my mind to perceive my body. Perceiving my body interrupts my feelings, thoughts and images. This pause allows me to disconnect from my distractions and perceive my thoughts objectively.

My father defines Meditation as "practicing detachment from all the feelings, thoughts & images in my mind that are preventing me from achieving a state of Mindfulness. Whenever I achieve a state of Mindfulness, I become able to perceive all the feelings, thoughts & images in my mind clearly & correctly without distraction or falsehood, I become able to choose to live in the present moment without accepting distractions from the past or the future, and I become able to choose to feel the continuous love, peace, joy & compassion emanating from all the life in the universe as I fully reconnect to my internal source of love that lives inside me."

My father defines Practicing Non Distraction as "stopping any distracting mental activities that diminish my state of Mindfulness, to become able to increase my ability to perceive the feelings, thoughts & images in my mind clearly & correctly."

To explain how the distractions contained in my memories affect my thoughts, to prevent me from perceiving my thoughts objectively, I am quoting from an email that I sent to my father.

"My mind, body and feelings all produce sensations that are perceived by my mind as mental formations that become my future thoughts, feelings and images. These mental formations are thus created by mental, physical and emotional experiences. Mental formations affect my state of consciousness while my conscious mind perceives them. After they diminish in prominence they are not erased but instead are stored in my subconscious mind within memories.

Memories are packages of past experiences that are stored within my subconscious mind. Each memory contains a thought and a feeling. Each thought and feeling combination compose a snapshot image of my mental and emotional experience of the sensations produced by my mind, body and feelings during a specific event in my life.

Memories are filed away in a subconscious directory. They are carefully organized into groups based on likeness. Each memory is tied to other memories in its group as well as to my conscious mind. When my conscious mind experiences new mind, body and feeling sensations as new mental formations, my old memories that are similar are pulled out of my subconscious directory, opened and experienced again.

In this way memories are triggered and relived by my conscious mind. Thus my present is deeply associated with my past. At any given time I may be living my life, as I think about the past or future rather than living in the present moment. When I do this, I am most likely only living a small portion of my life in the present and instead reliving a large portion of my past or rehashing past ponderings of the future.

When I allow my memories to control my thinking and perception I am spending my life time lost in the distractions of unoriginal content and missing the fun and adventures, which life, living all around me, is offering me in the present. This can be enjoyable if the thoughts and feelings in the memories I am experiencing are positive. Worse, this can cause me needless pain and suffering if the thoughts and feelings are negative. Although reliving thoughts and feelings through memories can be positive, doing so is not necessarily right because doing so involves egoic thinking and a loss of connection with the potential fun of living in the present moment.

Thus, memories I must seek to control to the best of my ability. My ability to do so is growing with my dedicated mindful breathing meditation to create a state of mindfulness, which is allowing me to manage the amount of control memories have over me. Thus I am able to filter out negative memories that produce negative feelings, thoughts and images and this allows me to be more aware of my positive objective thoughts." (Quote from an email to my father containing my answer to his Assignment Question # 31, How are my thoughts, feelings and images generated, stored & then relived inside my mind?)

Perceiving my thoughts objectively is useful when my thoughts and memories are negative. Negative thinking generates pain which blocks my connection to unconditional love. Mindful Breathing Meditation allows me to achieve Mindfulness that allows me to gain control over the distractions of my negative thoughts and memories. Mindfulness automatically reconnects me with unconditional love. Unconditional love replaces the pain of negative thinking.

Empowered with Mindfulness, I can perceive my negative thoughts and memories as negative and choose not to reinforce them by thinking about them. I acknowledge their existence and then I stop focusing on them each time they reappear. When I refuse to obsess over negative thoughts and memories, they lose their energy and diminish. By using Mindful Breathing Meditation to achieve Mindfulness, I am replacing the pain and suffering of my ego driven thinking, with the joy and happiness of Mindfulness, produced by my reconnection to my internal source of unconditional love.

To help explain this wisdom, I am quoting from an email to my father again.

"Mindful breathing is a form of meditation during which I focus my awareness on my in-breath and out-breath. I use the experience of my breathing to quiet my thoughts. Mindful breathing provides a center for my existence in the present moment and an anchor to which I can return, when I am distracted by excessive thoughts about the past or the future, that are disconnecting me from the fun and adventures of living in the present.

Practicing meditation and entering a state of mindfulness creates mental space between my thoughts. These gaps provide zones in which negative thoughts cannot hide behind positive thoughts. I am able to get into the gap to identify my negative thoughts for what they are, when they arise from the memories that are stored in my subconscious mind, from my imagination, or from my perceptions of the external world. Then when I understand the nature of the negative thoughts, I disengage from them and I do not feed them energy to keep them alive. My Compassionate Watcher simply observes them until they run out of energy and then disappear from my mind.

I am not my feelings, thoughts or images. I become My Compassionate Watcher as I observe them, learn to understand them, and then choose what I want to experience.

Thus, meditation practice creates mindfulness which empowers me with the ability of My Compassionate Watcher to choose which thoughts I power." (Quote from an email to my father containing my answer to his Assignment Question 29, How does meditation and mindfulness work to clear my mind of negative thoughts & feelings, to allow more peace & joy to enter my mind?)

"Using meditation and mindfulness to choose my feelings allows me to remove my suffering. In its place I receive two forms of joy.

The first form of joy is the positive feelings and thoughts that I experience in greater measure. My Compassionate Watcher filters my positive feelings from my negative feelings, allowing my positive feelings into my conscious mind while stopping my thinking energy from feeding my negative feelings, so they cannot remain alive in my mind. When my mind is cleared of negative clutter, vast spaces are opened up for new positive feelings and thoughts to fill in the gaps, left by the negative thoughts that have disappeared from my mind.

The second form of joy is awareness. By experiencing my life with awareness, I live in the present moment. The present moment is eternal and filled with the possibility of experiencing exciting fun and adventures. The ability to savor and appreciate the beauty and love contained in what the present moment has to offer is the second reward of meditation.

When living in the present moment, aware and meditating, I return to the state of joy and happiness I experienced as a baby. Babies are born aware of the present moment. Their thinking apparatus and ego have yet to take over. As babies mature through childhood their mind develops in the egoic environment of modern human society. Their life experience moves from the present moment into the fantasy land of their ego, as they grow older and become children and eventually adults.

As I matured, my excessive thinking and my ego took over control of my mind. Now, I spend much of my day trapped inside my mind that is full of thoughts, that is shutting out my awareness of what is happening around me in the present moment in the real world. Whenever my mind's thinking slows down, my ego starts to get bored and my mind searches for entertainment to fuel its thinking to keep me anchored to my imaginary fantasy world that is anchoring me to the past or the future.

Now I realize that I am not the thinking that is controlling my mind. I am not my memories. I am not my ego laden with emotional baggage from the past and worrying about the future. I am not the thinking apparatus that has taken over my life experiences and disconnected me from living in full awareness of what is happening around me in the present moment, so I can no longer fully enjoy the fun and adventures that life, living all around me, is trying to offer me.

By meditating I am bypassing all my excessive thinking and my ego that is currently controlling me. I am turning back the clock to when I was a baby, halting psychological time and living with clock time in the eternal present moment, to give me the opportunity to have more fun and adventures in my life." (Quote from an email to my father containing my answer to his Assignment Question 35, How do I use Meditation & Mindfulness to choose my feelings, to become able to live in the present moment?)

My connection to unconditional love is blocked by my accumulated painful negative feelings that are buried inside my memories stored inside my subconscious mind. Meditation and Mindfulness allows me to become A Compassionate Watcher, who is able to immediately spot the distractions of painful feelings from my newly sprouted negative memories, before they can gain control of my mind and actions, to stop them from increasing my pain & suffering.

My Compassionate Watcher uses Meditation and Mindfulness to choose which feeling I focus on. Thus I manage a negative feeling by choosing to focus on understanding why it is generating pain in mind by making it my friend and getting it to confide in me, as I try to convince my negative memory that is generating the negative feeling, to stop causing this pain again in the future, when I relive my negative memory again. By doing this for all my negative painful memories that are stored in my subconscious mind, I am starting to remove my pain blockage forever.

Meditating and Mindfulness is choosing to live a better life. I prefer happiness to sadness. I manifest my preference by undertaking the process of Meditation. Living in Mindfulness is increasing my happiness, productivity and fulfillment in the present moment as I learn to practice the Wisdom of Children to remove my pain blockage, to fully reconnect to my internal source of unconditional love for all life.

This is a brief overview of why it is important for you to join us, as a member of our extended family of friends & adventurers, as my father and I explore The Wisdom of Children contained in Our Book One."

(End of My Son Wil's summary of The Wisdom of Children that he practices each day. I marvel at My Son's accomplishments and I continue to love him dearly for becoming the unconditional loving adult human being that he was born to be)

This understanding of how the human mind works was written by My Son to encourage the readers of Our Book to practice The Wisdom of Children to enable them to experience continuous love, peace, joy & compassion in their daily lives.

My Son is living proof that this wisdom can be taught to our children and he is living proof that our children can teach us wisdom, as long as we are willing to listen to our children and ask them what is important to them as they grow up.

My Son offered me wisdom when he asked me not to give him advice unless he asked me for advice. I am eternally grateful to My Son for this wisdom, the importance of which you will understand when you read the Parents & Teenagers section of Our Book One.

And Wil continues to help me today in my continuing quest to fully understand why we have been given the opportunity to live as unconditional loving human beings on Our Precious Mother Earth and he continues to help his family & his friends, by being the unconditional loving adult human being that he was given the opportunity to become, as he grew from childhood to adulthood, which is the same opportunity that you the reader were given when you were born.

However, your life story, which I hope you will pass on to your friends & family someday in a written or video format, may have been harder or easier than Wil's struggle to become an unconditionally loving adult, an adult who is able to forgive those who do not deserve his forgiveness. And if you are not as unconditionally loving as you want to become, then, please allow My Son & me to offer you The Wisdom of Children which will help you to become more unconditionally loving in the future. The choice of practicing this wisdom is yours to make, or not to make.

Chapter 8

The Essence of The Wisdom of Children

Wisdom is a wise act or saying that improves the future well-being of our lives.[2]

As you read this summary of The Essence of The Wisdom of Children, you will realize that we need to provide you with a detailed explanation of the meaning of the terms & phrases we use in Our Book, such as meditation, mindfulness, unconditional love, true friendship and Choosing My Feelings, for you to fully appreciate the power of this wisdom. In Our Book One we will explain this wisdom and the terms you need to fully understand, in more detail. Please be patient as you strive to understand this wisdom and then as you apply this wisdom to your life, to prove that it works and that it is a true wisdom that will help to benefit your future well-being as an unconditionally loving human being, as this wisdom helps you to increase your unconditional love that generates increasing feelings of love, peace, joy & compassion in your daily life and helps you to eliminate any unresolved pain, suffering, fear, anger, worry or stress that may come into your future life.

Practicing The Wisdom of Children is acting wisely when I use my childhood ability to fully reconnect to my internal source of unconditional love for all life, to become able to generate a powerful passion for living and a compelling motivation to share unconditional love & nurture true friendship with all human beings, especially with my friends & family. The Wisdom of Children is also the wisdom of accepting the love from all the life around me & feeling love for all this life.[3]

The Wisdom of Children is composed of a mental & physical practice. The mental practice is the nurturing & protecting of the love, peace, joy & compassion that lives inside me and the physical practice of sharing this unconditional love when I offer true friendship to another human being.[4]

True Friendship starts with nurturing my feelings of affection & personal regard for a friend and then nurturing my desire to protect this unconditional love for my friend which generates feelings of love, peace, joy & compassion that I share with my friend, as I start to feel my unconditional love for my friend and for all human beings who are my spiritual brothers & sisters. (Please refer to The Nature of True Friendship section in Chapter 22 of Our Book One)

True friendship is nurtured between us when we share love, peace, joy & compassion with each other and we practice forgiving each other for the mistakes we make in our relationship.[5]

To apply The Wisdom of Children to my adult life, I am using Meditation to practice Detachment to create a state of Mindfulness when I require help to start liberating my mind & my memories from any unfair pain & suffering that I may experience in my daily life that may be blocking me from reconnecting to the full power of my internal source of the continuous unconditional love of my childhood that is living inside me, to enable me to increase the amount of love, peace, joy & compassion that I can offer my friends & family.

Chapter 9

Practicing Meditation & Mindfulness

"As I start applying The Wisdom of Children to my adult life each morning, I begin to practice Meditation & Mindfulness as soon as I wake up from sleep to the start of a new day.

Meditation is practicing Mindfulness to maintain my connection to the continuous present moment, which enables me to feel the continuous love, peace, joy & compassion that is flowing inside me, as this unconditional love flows through me from all the life in the universe.

And Meditation is practicing detachment from all the thoughts feelings & images in my mind that are preventing me from achieving a state of Mindfulness.

A State of Mindfulness occurs when I begin to know what is happening inside my conscious mind in the present moment, while it is happening, no matter what it is. (Modified quote from What is Meditation by Rob Nairn)

As I achieve a state of Mindfulness, I become able to perceive all the thoughts, feelings & images in my mind, clearly & correctly, without distortion or falsehood, as I become able to choose to live in the present moment without accepting distractions from the past or the future.

Achieving a state of mindfulness is made possible by following The Middle Path (or The Middle Way) of Meditation that Buddhists practice when they meditate. As Buddhists practice meditation, they simply observe, without additional mental effort and without striving for meditation results, as they observe all the mental activities inside their conscious minds without trying to control them and without trying to change them, as they concentrate on their breathing which helps to calm the mind by reducing the energy & speed of the mind's mental activities, similar to taking one's foot off the gas pedal when driving a car.

In this way, the meditator stops giving thinking energy (similar to cutting off the gas supply to the car's engine) to the feelings, thoughts & images in the meditator's mind by not thinking about them so they run out of the thinking energy that they need to continue living inside the meditator's mind. When they run out of this energy for living, they have no choice but to leave the mind which results in the mind's activities slowing down, as the mind starts to calm, as the number of feelings, thoughts & images in the mind is reduced.

When I follow The Middle Path of Meditation, I realize that I am not my feelings, thoughts & images because I can kill them by not feeding them the thinking energy that they need to stay alive inside my conscious mind, as I become a watcher of the activities in my mind and as I become mindful of them, as I begin to know what is happening inside my conscious mind in the present moment, while it is happening, no matter what it is.

Unfortunately, I sometimes find meditating extremely difficult to practice, when the pain inside my mind becomes intense, whenever I start to relive a powerful unfair memory that starts to generate new pain inside my mind, as my desire to run away and hide from this intense pain becomes overwhelming, as this pain tries to take control of my mind away from me.

Fortunately, I was born with an equally powerful stubborn streak which makes it difficult for me to give up and run away from pain, when I decide to continue meditating until the pain runs out of energy and disappears from my conscious mind. So, I just wait and feel the full intensity of the pain as I continue to observe it, as I strengthen my resolve to continue waiting for the pain to go away, by telling myself that the pain will eventually end. This painful waiting practice is part of the price that I am willing to pay to become able to gain the benefits that Practicing The Wisdom of Children will bring into my future adult life. These benefits far outweigh any pain that I am required to endure. They are my reward for continuing the meditation practice, as they enable me to increase the love & friendship that I share with everyone in my life.

In this way, I become A Compassionate Watcher as I observe my mental activities, as I learn to understand them and then as I sympathize with their desire to take control of my mind, as I remain in control of my mind, by taking control of the thinking energy in my mind to become able to choose the feelings, thoughts & images that I want to experience at this present time.

Once my mind calms and enters a state of mindfulness & bliss, I start to give new thinking energy to the feelings, thoughts & images that I want to experience, as I watch the unwanted feelings, thoughts & images disappear from my mind because I am no longer giving them the thinking energy that they need to feed on, to be able to stay alive inside my conscious mind. As these unwanted feelings, thoughts & images run out of the thinking energy for living that I am no longer supplying them, they start to disappear from my conscious mind, as my mind becomes calm and becomes focused on the mental activities that I want to experience inside my conscious mind.

How I Practice Meditation Each New Day of My Life

1) As I wake up from sleep in the morning and I start Practicing The Wisdom of Children, I begin to observe all the mental activities in my conscious mind as I become A Compassionate Watcher who is the embodiment of my unconditional love as I start to become aware of the present moment, as I begin to practice Meditation which stops me from living inside the past, the future, my feelings, my thoughts, my imagination, or my dreams. Then, as I achieve Mindfulness I begin knowing what is happening inside my conscious mind in the present moment, while it is happening, no matter what it is. This practice enables me to reconnect to My Internal Source of Unconditional Love which connects me to the continuous love emanating from all the life in the universe, after a night of sleep & dreams.

Next, I begin to practice Choosing My Feelings by detaching from all the feelings in my mind that are trying to control my mind, as I become able to determine which feelings are harmful or beneficial to my future well-being before I choose to indulge in feeding new thinking energy to a feeling to increase its energy & prolong its life, as it lives inside my conscious mind. I am choosing to increase the energy of a feeling, only if, it will help motivate me to work on My Goals for Today.[6]

2) As I continue to practice Meditation & Mindfulness during the day, I am experiencing the benefits of choosing to increase the love, peace, joy & compassion that I am feeling, as I feel these benefits intermittently at first when I wake up in the morning and then for longer periods of time during the day, as my Meditation & Mindfulness allows me to continuously Choose My Feelings, as my connection to my internal source of unconditional love for all life becomes continuous, as my internal source of love supplies me with powerful love, peace, joy & compassion and with powerful motivation to accomplish My Goals for Today.

3) Then, when I take a relaxing break from my work during the day, I embrace the benefits of applying The Wisdom of Children to my life by realizing that, I am practicing Meditation continuously in the present moment of today, to manage my Mindfulness, to be able to say, "no" to blindly following the desires of my pleasant or painful feelings, to become able to detach from all my feelings by not feeding them any new thinking energy that will keep them alive, until I am able to determine which ones are harmful and which ones are beneficial to my future well-being, and only then am I deciding, whether or not to say, "Yes" to feeding thinking energy to a beneficial feeling, to indulge in it & keep it alive & active inside my conscious mind.

In this way, I enable my Meditation & Mindfulness to help me to practice Choosing My Feelings, as I work on My Goals for Today, as I increase the amount of unconditional love that I am generating, as I spiritually connect with all human beings in the world who have become my spiritual brothers & sisters, and as I start to share increasing love, peace, joy & compassion with all human beings that I meet today, especially with my friends & family." (Quote the Practicing Meditation & Mindfulness section in Chapter 9 of Our Book Two)

Controlling my thinking energy so I can choose my feelings during the day is expressed concisely by My Son Wil, when he says,

"It is important for me to remember that I am not my feelings. I am not my mind either. I am the compassionate watcher that exists before thought. I am who I truly am when I'm not thinking. This primacy means that I have control over what I think about and how I feel. Life is entirely experiential. It flows through the filter of perception. Nothing exists for me divorced from how I perceive it. Thus, I can control my existence, make it pure, by controlling how I think so I can choose how I feel. This is free will." (Quote from My Son Wil's Wisdom for Choosing His Feelings section in Chapter 26 of Our Book One)

Chapter 10

My Childhood Ability to Feel Continuous Love

Please write in your own words, the answer to this question after you have relived at least two memories from your childhood, when you felt unconditional love for one of your childhood friends as you played together or when you felt unconditional love for your mom, dad or a guardian who shared fun & adventures with you, when you were a young child.

Was I born with an internal source of unconditional love that nourished me with continuous love when I was young child and can I use this internal source of love, now that I am an adult, to enable me to share increasing love, peace, joy & compassion with all human beings, especially with my friends & family, until it becomes continuous? Q-24

If my answer to this question is Yes, Why is it Yes? Q-25

If my answer to this question is No, Why is it No? Q-26

The Storage Room of Feeling Energy

To help you understand how you can relive the joy & happiness of your childhood, please imagine a Storage Room of Feeling Energy located inside your subconscious mind as it stores all the feeling energy that you receive during your lifetime from your life experiences starting with the love energy you were given when you were born.

The Storage Room of Feeling Energy inside my subconscious mind stores the energy of pain & joy, fear & love, anger & peace and suffering & happiness that I experience during my lifetime. For example, whenever I relive a memory of a childhood experience, my childhood memory takes its feeling energy out of storage and transports this energy into my conscious mind where it uses this energy to generate a new feeling in my conscious mind to enable me to relive this childhood experience, once again, during my adult life. My challenge as an adult is to learn how to relive the positive joyful feelings of my childhood that will enhance the quality of my adult life and to stop reliving the negative painful feelings that diminish my adult life.

For example, when I was a baby, the storage room was completely filled with the love energy that I was given when I was born. I was also given the ability to automatically fill the storage room with new love energy from My Internal Source of Unconditional Love to replace the love energy that I used to love someone or something in my life, such as when I offered love to my parents.

The love energy I gave to my parents flowed out the top exit of the storage room and then new love energy automatically entered through the bottom entrance of the storage room to replace the love energy I had used to love my parents.

The love energy I use flows out of storage

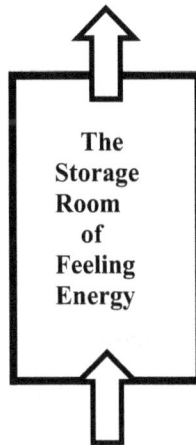

```
        ↑
    ┌───┴───┐
    │  The  │
    │Storage│
    │ Room  │
    │  of   │
    │Feeling│
    │Energy │
    └───┬───┘
        ↑
```

New love energy automatically flows into storage to replace the love energy I used

This system generated a continuous source of love energy for me to use when I was a child. It worked well until I experienced pain for the first time in my life and I did not know how to get rid of the pain energy that had entered The Storage Room of Feeling Energy and refused to leave.

Unfortunately, whenever I relived this unfair memory of the first painful experience in my life, the memory took the pain energy that it had in storage and then used it to generate new pain inside my conscious mind. This reduced the amount of pain that was stored inside The Storage Room of Feeling Energy. Eventually, the memory would deplete all the pain energy that it had stored, as long as I did not feed it new thinking energy that it could use to generate new pain into my life, whenever I relived this unfair memory again in the future.

What I did not realize as a child was that I was keeping pain energy alive inside my storage room by feeding it new thinking energy every time I told myself that life was being unfair to me, whenever I relived a painful unfair memory, such as when someone took one of my toys and would not give it back to me. I did not understand why my childhood friends treated me unfairly at times and I did not know how to stop painful memories, like this one, from hurting me again, whenever I relived them. I just told myself that life was being unfair to me and I started to expect that life would become unfair to me again in the future, especially when I started to relive one or more of these unfair painful memories each new day of my life because I did not know how to stop the remembered pain from hurting me again.

When My Son & I learned how to kill this unfair pain & suffering by stopping our thinking that life was being unfair to us, we were able to clean out the unfair painful feeling energy from our storage rooms by letting our unfair painful memories gradually deplete their pain energy supplies that they had in storage, as they used this pain energy to create new pain in our conscious minds whenever we relived one of our unfair memories, again & again, in the future.

Eventually, there was no pain energy left in storage for the unfair memories to use to generate any new pain into our lives, as long as we did not start thinking that life was being unfair to us, again, whenever we relived one of these unfair memories in the future.

To help you to understand how to kill the unfair pain energy that is generated by the memories of your childhood whenever you relive one of them, please accept that each of us has a Storage Room of Feeling Energy attached to our memory retrieval system that is located inside The Room of Memories in our subconscious minds. An unfair painful memory retrieves its pain energy from storage and then uses this energy to generate new pain in our conscious minds whenever you or I relive a painful unfair memory. Similarly, a joyful memory retrieves its joy energy from storage and then uses this energy to generate new joy in our conscious minds.

My Memory Seeds

The feelings, thoughts, & images of my life experiences are stored inside my subconscious mind as memories. The thoughts & images of each experience are stored in a memory seed and the energy of the feelings from this experience is stored inside The Storage Room of Feeling Energy. When I relive this memory in the future, my memory takes the feeling energy out of storage to generate a new feeling of pain or joy inside my conscious mind. When I finish reliving this memory, the thoughts & images return to their memory seed located in My Room of Memories, where they live, until they are triggered back into my mental awareness in my conscious mind by a new thought, my imagination, my ego or a new external event in my life that is similar to the past experience being stored inside the memory in my subconscious mind.

When there is no energy left in storage, the memory cannot generate any new joy or pain into my conscious mind, whenever I relive this memory in the future.

My future challenge is to help my unfair painful memories to deplete all the energy supplies they have in storage in The Storage Room of Feeling Energy, so I can relive these unfair memories without feeling any pain.

And I want to help my fair joyful memories to store as much energy inside The Storage Room of Feeling Energy as they can, so I will feel intense joy whenever I relive one of these fair memories about the fun & adventures I experienced in my life. (Please refer to My Room of Memories section in Chapter 24 of Our Book One)

To help your unfair painful memories to deplete their energy supplies to empty, you will need to understand how a memory creates pain in your life before you can learn how to kill any unfair painful energy that remains stored inside The Storage Room of Feeling Energy. Once you understand how this process works you will become able to replace this pain with love, as you clean out your storage room of all the unfair pain energy that your memories have been using to hurt you, so you can relive the unfair memories in your future adult life without feeling pain.

Understanding this process begins with exploring the nature of the unfairness that we all experienced when we were young children.

Chapter 11

Continuous Love Requires Freedom from Unfair Pain & Suffering

When I was a baby, I felt loved, nurtured & protected in our home when my parents offered me smiles, words of love, caresses, kisses, cuddling, food, drink and warmth, as I felt their continuous love for me, when I was hungry, thirsty or cold, or when I enjoyed the excitement of accepting new challenges in my life as I learned to walk, talk & play.

My desire for shelter & safety entered my young life when I ventured outside of our home for the first time, as I searched for new fun & adventures to bring ever increasing joy & excitement into my life. I made the decision as a young child to explore this new world when my mother told me that I would be safe because she would protect me when I made mistakes or got into trouble. Then, I started to view our home as a place of shelter & safety.

My new adventures helped me to gain confidence as I felt the love **from** all the life surrounding me whenever I ventured outside our home and I felt a powerful feeling of love **for** all this life, a love that I was born possessing that is still living inside me now in my adult life.

The Unfairness in My Childhood

However, the first time I was hurt by someone in the outside world, I asked my mother why this had happened and I asked her what I had done wrong to experience this pain in my life. My mother helped me to understand that I can decide to seek joy in my daily life by playing with friends who love & respect me or I can experience pain when I choose to explore the world outside my home with someone who is hurting inside and who cannot love me because he is feeling pain.

As I grew older, I realized that the outside world was full of immense joy and very little pain, as long as I choose adventures which included friends who loved me and treated me fairly, as we played together and explored the exciting world outside of our homes.

These experiences helped to improve the decision making process inside my mind to increase my ability to choose between feeling joy or pain in my life during each moment of every day of my life as a young child.

When I got out of bed each morning, I continued to look for new ways to add more joy to my life and whenever someone hurt me I tried to understand why they hurt me whenever I experienced unfair pain in my life as a young child.

Fortunately, I realized that I could not feed on pure joy each moment of everyday of my life because my friends did not always want to play the games that I enjoyed and I realized that I needed to learn how to motivate them to play the games I wanted to play or I had to learn how to enjoy the games they were playing, when they allowed me to play with them.

Unfortunately, I did not know how to stop the unfair suffering I experienced whenever I relived a painful memory of when someone hurt me, so I asked my parents for help, but they could not provide me with an answer that enabled me to understand why people sometimes hurt others.

As the years went by and I accumulated more painful memories that hurt me whenever I relived one of them, I decided to find a way to stop my memories from hurting me again in the future, especially the memories that I kept reliving each day of my life. So, I asked my friends, teachers & religious leaders for help and I read books of wisdom written by our wise ancestors such as the Christian Bible.

It was not until my son was born that I was able to perfect the method to remove the unfair pain energy from The Storage Room of Feeling Energy where it lived, so I could start to experience continuous love, peace, joy & compassion, once again, as I did when I was a young child. This occurred when I became able to convince my memories to stop generating more unfair pain into my future life, whenever I relived a painful memory, when I realized this pain was blocking my ability to feel continuous unconditional love.

This understanding slowly dawned on me as an adult, when I watched the continuous unconditional love in my son's eyes when he was a baby and I began to realize that the answer to my dilemma of not knowing how to stop the unfair pain in my memories from hurting me had always been inside me. I just did not know where to look to find it.

And I realized that my quest to experience the continuous love, peace, joy & compassion of my childhood in my adult life, was now possible.

The answer to my quest, to eliminate the unfair pain energy from my life, occurred to me when I watched my young son and I realized that he was born feeling powerful love for all the life surrounding him and also feeling the never ending love being generated by all this life. "His ability to continuously love all the life around him inspired me to remember when I felt this way, when I was a young child." (Quote from the Learning to Understand My True Self section in Chapter 6 of Our Book One)

As an adult, I had forgotten how to love life as intensely as my son was able to do. So, I became determined to search my childhood memories to find out how to feel this powerful love, once again, as I tried to re-experience my childhood ability to love all the life around me in my adult world with the great passion of my childhood.

This revelation inspired me to ask & answer many more questions about how to start reliving the joy of my childhood that enabled me to start continuously loving everyone in my adult life.

Then, I decided to write down this revelation in my own words to enable me to share this wisdom with my friends & family and my future grandchildren, so I wrote The Nine Steps to Emotional Freedom with the help of My Son Wil.

Practicing The Nine Steps to Emotional Freedom enables me to feel continuous love, peace, joy & fairness in my life, once again, after someone treats me unfairly or after I experience the unfair suffering of someone I love, as I learn to control these negative feelings to stop them from overwhelming my mind with fear, anger, worry, or stress whenever I start reliving the unfair painful memory of one of these life diminishing experiences.

To understand the concept of Emotional Freedom, please answer this question,

How do I use The Wisdom of Children to achieve Emotional Freedom from unfair painful feelings that enter my mind and try to control me, as they start to destroy the love, peace, joy & compassion that I am feeling at the present moment? Q-27

This question refers to "The Wisdom of Children which is composed of a mental & physical practice. The mental practice is the nurturing & protecting of the love, peace, joy & compassion that live inside me and the physical practice of sharing this unconditional love when I offer true friendship to another human being." (Quote from The Essence of The Wisdom of Children section in Chapter 8 of Our Book One)

The practice of this wisdom unlocks our ability to fully reconnect to our Internal Source of Unconditional Love that we felt when we were young children and that many adults no longer feel very often and do not know how to fully reconnect to, as they wonder why they no longer feel the immense passion they felt as children when they shared their love with all the life around them, especially their friends & family.

Fortunately, the wisdom in Our Book helps our adult minds to fully reconnect to the internal source of our childhood love that will start to feed our adult minds with continuous feelings of love, peace, joy

& compassion and increasing fairness, during each day of our future lives.

Please ask yourself this question,

How do I start to experience continuous feelings of love, peace, joy & compassion in my adult life? Q-28

I realized this was possible, when I was able to kill all the major fear, anger, worry & stress in my mind that was being generated by my memories that I kept reliving each day of my life, unfair feelings that were preventing me from fully reconnecting to my internal source of love.

What I did not realize, until these painful unfair feelings were gone from my mind, was that my internal source of love was automatically starting to fill my conscious mind with feelings of continuous love, peace, joy & compassion, as soon as there was no unresolved pain & suffering left in my conscious mind to block the pathway to my internal source of this unconditional love.

Then, I realized that I was beginning to experience continuous love, peace, joy & compassion during each day of my future life, starting when I woke up each morning and I greeted the new day, as I began to feel an enhanced love **from** all the life around me, especially the love from my friends & family and as I began to feel immense love **for** all the life in the universe that I had not felt since I was a child.

I did not know that this unconditional love would remain in my conscious mind for long periods of time, until I started to experience this love without also feeling a sense of unresolved pain & suffering in my mind, because the major fear, anger, worry & stress from the memories, that I been reliving each day of life, had finally disappeared from my mind. Then, experiencing continuous love for long periods of time during the day became a wonderful realization for me.

Now that I was able to fully reconnect to the internal source of love of my childhood, I realized that the effort that I had expended to kill all the major fear, anger, worry & stress being generated by my memories, was worth expending, as the long term battle between the pain and love inside my mind came to an end, when love won the final battle of the war for control of the feelings in my mind and the resulting continuous uninterrupted love became my reward, as lasting peace & joy entered my mind to stay with me as my best friend & companion. This was a marvelous reward and a confirmation that The Wisdom of Children works and is a true wisdom that will work for all human beings who are willing to practice it each day of their future lives.

When I realized that this wisdom had worked for me and I started to feel a continuous stream of positive feelings of love & joy during each moment of every new day of my future adult life, I also started to feel a powerful passion for living my life to the full and I became eager to share new fun & adventures with my friends & family,

Please ask yourself this question,

How do I prove that this wisdom works? Q-29

Unfortunately, I cannot prove it to you.

Fortunately, you can prove this wisdom works in your life, by looking inside your mind and by learning how to kill the energy source that your memories are using to create new unresolved pain & suffering inside your mind each day, so your memories will no longer be able to generate new fear, anger, worry & stress in your adult life, as you learn how to kill the unfair energy that a memory uses to create new pain & suffering, whenever you start to relive a painful memory.

Please realize that my memories also feed my ego with the fear & anger that keeps my ego alive inside my mind. So, once my memories run out of this unfair energy of fear & anger and I am no longer thinking that life is being unfair to me, I will stop feeding my memories the new thinking energy that it needs to keep my ego alive inside my mind.

Then, my suffering, my unfair memories & my ego will disappear from my mind and I will start to feel continuous love, peace, joy & compassion in my future life automatically, as I become able to fully reconnect to my childhood source of unconditional love, which becomes my living proof that this wisdom works.

Unfairness in Our Adult Lives

FEAR, ANGER, WORRY & STRESS is UNFAIR when the love, peace, joy & compassion in my life is diminished by the unfairness that enters my conscious mind when I keep reliving the same unfair memory each day, and I do not know how to stop the unresolved pain & suffering that is being generated by a memory from hurting me, each time I relive an unfair memory. I am being punished needlessly by an unfair memory of a real or imaginary experience from my past that may have no relevance to my present or future life. It is like being sentenced to life long punishment with no possibility of parole for good behavior, unless I can learn & then practice the wisdom to kill all the major fear, anger, worry & stress that is being generated by the unfair memories that I am reliving each day of my adult life. [7]

Fairness in Our Adult Lives

Fairness is the state, condition, or quality of being free from bias or injustice in my relationship with my feelings, thoughts & images or with another human being.[8]

Fairness requires:

Speaking the truth
Honesty when trying to convince someone to adopt a proposal
Keeping my word and my agreements even if it hurts to do so
Sharing unconditional love with all the life around me
Thanking friends, family & co-workers for their love & support
Rewarding others with praise / compensation for a job well done

Admitting mistakes & shortcomings when relating to a true friend
Freedom from bias when selecting between alternative proposals
Correcting an injustice when I treat someone unfairly
Demanding justice when someone wrongs me
Forgiving others when they do not deserve it, to become able to kill
the unresolved pain & suffering in my heart
And
Respect for another human being's right to live their life as they
choose to do so, as long as they do not hurt another human being or
Our Precious Mother Earth, in doing so.

When I was a child, I believed that all the future events in my life
would work out for the best because I believed that my friends &
family would treat me fairly, with love, honesty, respect, truth &
forgiveness, and they would compensate me for any pain & suffering
they created in my life.

Unfortunately, as I grew up, I started to lose my belief in this
fairness in my life, when I was treated unfairly by others, who would
not ask for my forgiveness and would not offer compensation for
hurting me.

By the time I became an adult, I begin to realize that I needed to start
believing in fairness, once again, so I could believe that the life
existing all around me would allow me to succeed at whatever I
choose to do, which would enable me to become worthy of living as
I accomplished the goals for my adult life. Fairness required me to
believe that other human beings would treat me with love, honesty,
respect, truth & forgiveness, whenever we worked together to
achieve mutually beneficial goals.

Without believing that fairness could exist in my future adult life, I
would not have been able to kill the unresolved pain & suffering in
my memories, especially my fear of future failure, whose death
enabled me to fully reconnect with my internal source of
unconditional love that enabled me to share increasing unconditional
love and enabled me to nurture true friendship, with my friends,
family & co-workers, as we accomplished the goals we shared.

Now, I use this concept of fairness with all my friends, family & co-workers, as I try to treat each human being with honesty, justice & respect, as I keep the agreements that I make with others or willingly pay the penalty for failure, if I cannot do so.

However, I may treat others more than fair when I play favorites with my friends & family, especially when I play favorites with the children in my life, who I love so much that I will sacrifice my time, my money and sometimes other priorities, as required, so they will have a better chance to succeed in their personal endeavors.

And I may be treated more than fair in the future, whenever My Wife Linda forgives me for not completing all the tasks on her "Honey, Please Do This for Me List", a list she gives me each week to help us to generate more love & joy in our lives that we can share with our friends & family, as we continue to support our loved ones, especially when they request our assistance.

Then, even when my life is fair, other human beings may still hurt me or treat me unfairly at times in the future, so I try to forgive unfairness when I realize that another person is genuinely sorry for the pain & suffering they created in my life.

It is not always easy to forgive unfairness but I try very hard to do so, as I try very hard to treat others fairly.

However, to become able to treat others fairly while maintaining my commitment to continue working on the goals for my life, I need to become able to manage the balance between joy & pain inside my mind.

The Balance between Joy & Pain inside My Mind

When my fear of future unfairness starts to increase, such as when pain is generated by my thoughts, images or my dreams of someone or something treating me unfairly in the future, the flow of energy from my internal source of love to my mind starts to become blocked by this new pain and the amount of joy inside my mind starts to decrease as my joy runs out of the energy it needs to stay alive inside my mind.

Fortunately, when I stop thinking about the potential future unfairness in my life, I stop feeding new thinking energy to the pain in my mind so it no longer receives the energy that it needs to stay alive. This pain could also be receiving energy from an old memory which I started reliving when I started thinking about the unfairness in my life. Even so, my old unfair memory will also run out of the available energy that it has stored inside The Storage Room of Feeling Energy that it needs to continue feeding energy to the pain in my mind

Then, when the pain in my mind runs out of energy, it starts to disappear from my mind and when this happens, my internal energy of love automatically starts to flow faster as it travels from my internal source of unconditional love to my mind because pain is no longer blocking my mind's pathway to my internal source of love.

Then, the balance between joy & pain inside my mind shifts over to joy as I fully reconnect to my internal source of unconditional love, when the pain inside my mind has dissipated and new joy fills the empty space in my mind that was created when the pain disappeared.

Now, joy becomes the predominant feeling in my mind for as long as the pathway to my internal source of love remains fully open to allow the energy of joy to continuously fill my mind, until I start to think about a new or imaginary unfair event in my life that triggers another old memory or triggers my fight or flee warning system, to create new pain inside my mind, once again.

Then, the pathway to my source of unconditional love becomes blocked once again by this new pain, as pain becomes the predominant feeling in my mind, once more, when the joy inside my mind starts to disappear from my mind, once again. This is how the balance between joy & pain inside my mind shifts from pain to joy and back again.[9]

When I was a child, I realized that I needed to find the source of this pain so I could learn how to kill this unfair pain, so it would not be able to hurt me again in the future whenever I began to relive another one of the old painful memories of my childhood that began to generate new pain into my mind and started to reduce my motivation to experience new fun & adventures in my future life.

Unfortunately, it was not until I became a teenager that I learned the source of my pain was genetic in origin and that pain was originally created in my life as a young child by my fight or flee genetic warning system to warn me that I should fight or flee from real events in my life that could hurt me.

This understanding of how my mind works helped me to realize that I needed to make all the pain that was living inside mind, my new friend, so I could understand what was causing it and then learn how to kill the unfair pain in my mind and banish it from my future life.

Unfortunately, it took me many years to learn how to kill the pain that entered my mind each day when I relived old painful unfair memories or when I became afraid of the potential future unfairness in my life.

My Conscious Mind's Limited Capacity to Feel

On my journey to discover the origins of my pain & joy, I learned that my mind has a limited ability to be aware of the feelings inside my mind during each moment of time. For example, when an intense powerful feeling enters my mind, the other weaker feelings disappear from my awareness, such as when someone holds a gun to my head and threatens to kill me.

Then, my mind becomes filled with this intense powerful fear as a result of my genetic predisposition to fight or flee from fear. The other feelings inside my conscious mind quickly disappear from my awareness as the intense fear takes over control of my mind's limited ability to be aware of the feelings inside my mind at this present time.

This example of how intense fear is able to maximize my mind's limited ability to be aware of the feelings inside my mind is in sharp contrast to an example of when I experience holding a baby in my arms, when my mind's ability to be aware of its feelings is filled to capacity with joy, as I marvel at the miraculous creation of this new life that is now living on Our Precious Earth and I start to imagine the baby's potential to bring tremendous love & joy into our world, as I begin to shower my love on this wonderful baby that I am holding in my arms.

During a typical day when I am working of my goals, my mind's limited ability to be aware of its feelings is filled with a combination of pain & joy, with joy being the predominate feeling that is feeding my motivation to continue working on my goals.

Feeling My Life is Worth Living

The total combined feeling of joy & pain inside my mind tells me that my life is worth living or not worth living. When the balance between joy & pain shifts to pain and this pain remains in control of my mind for long periods of time, I no longer feel that my life is worth living and I may become depressed. This is in contrast to when joy controls my mind for long periods of time and I feel worthy of living because of my ability to feel this joy that helps me to feel happiness as I share continuous joy with loved ones.

My Feeling of Self-Worth is the emotional assessment of the value of the joy & fairness or pain & unfairness in my life at the present time. This feeling of self-worth may be, or may not be, an accurate emotional assessment of how much joy & fairness or pain & unfairness I will receive in my future life. [10]

Please ask yourself this question,

What is the balance between joy & pain inside my mind and what causes this balance to change inside my mind? Q-30

Please answer this question after you have observed how your mind works for several days as the balance between joy & pain in your mind shifts from joy to pain and back again.

To Fight or Flee from Pain & Suffering

Unfortunately for me, I had an extreme reluctance to look at the pain that lived inside my mind because I had developed a strong habit of running away from this pain. A habit I developed over many years when I did not know how to stop this pain from hurting me, so I ran away from the pain so I would not have to feel it any longer, as I tried to fill the limited feeling capacity of my mind with distractions, such as talking to friends, watching TV, eating food or playing games, when I should have working on the goals for my life.

Please do not allow this habit of running away to stop you from observing the pain in your mind.

Now that I have learned how to kill any new worry & stress that may enter my mind in the future, I can reduce this suffering by telling my mind that this feeling will pass, as all feelings do, and I tell my mind that this pain will be replaced by joy sometime in the future, when the energy that is feeding my worry & stress diminishes, such as when I stop reliving a painful memory or when I stop thinking of potential future loss or failure, because I do not want these negative thoughts to feed new thinking energy to my worry & stress, to keep it alive inside my mind.

And to reduce any new fear & anger that enters my mind, I am learning how my ego works inside my mind, so I can learn to control my ego, when it tries to take control of the fear & anger inside my mind, to enable my ego to start using these new negative life diminishing feelings of fear & anger to convince me to treat another person as my adversary when another person treats me unfairly. This occurs when I allow my ego to convince me to follow my desire for revenge or my need for justice, without understanding the full impact of the life diminishing consequences of my future actions against the new adversary that my ego has created inside my mind, as it tries to convince me to punish the person who treated me unfairly.

For example, I was born with a strong desire to fight or flee from other human beings whenever I was treated unfairly as a young child. When I was young and someone treated me unfairly, I often became enraged and lost my temper, as my new fear & anger took over control of my mind. I usually decided to fight instead of fleeing away from this unfairness because I wanted to stop this unfairness from reoccurring again in the future. I realized that if I did not stop someone from bullying me or treating me unfairly now, they may continue to do so in the future, so I decided that fleeing away from unfairness was not an option for me when was I was a young child.

Please ask yourself this question,

Did I fight or run away from the cause of the unfairness in my childhood whenever someone treated me unfairly? Why? Q-31

Unfortunately, when I became enraged at the unfairness that I experienced in my childhood, I sometimes lost control of my mind and I would try to hit my new adversary with my fist or I would pick up a stick or some other weapon and try to strike my new adversary. I felt justified in my action until the rage of unfairness subsided inside my mind and I started to automatically reconnect to my internal source of unconditional love. Then, when I realized that I had physically tried to hurt one of my friends or a family member who I had just treated as my new adversary because he was trying to bully me or treat me unfairly, I became remorseful, as I started to reconnect to my unconditional love for the person who I had just tried to hurt.

Was my rage generated by my innate ability to fight or flee from danger? If so, Why?

Please ask yourself this question,

Is my childhood ability to fight or flee a genetic endowment from my ancestors as Charles Darwin & Carl Sagan suggested in their books about human evolution?

I do not know. What I do know is that my ego used this ability to fight or flee to convince me to fight my new adversary when I was a young child, when I allowed my ego to take control of my mind, because I had not learned how to detach from this fear, anger, rage, insecurity and the desire for revenge which filled my young mind and convinced me to try to hurt my new adversary, in an effort to stop this person from hurting me again in the future as I tried to seek fairness & justice for my new unfair pain & suffering.

Unfortunately, as a result of losing control of my mind & actions to my ego, I became a temporarily insane child.

"My Ego is the name I give to my feelings of fear & anger that live inside me when I allow them to take control of my mind & actions as I start to become lost inside these painful feelings, when I cannot stop them from controlling me.

Fear, Anger & Despair

Fear is my anticipation of the possibility that something unpleasant will occur in my future life. It is a feeling of impending pain & suffering that can overwhelm my mind and motivate me to run away from the perceived cause of my fear. The cause of my fear may be, another person threatening me, reliving the nightmare of an unfair painful memory, the possibility of a future loss, or the future failure of my plans for success in life.

Anger is my desire to stay & fight for justice against those who are creating unfairness in my life when I believe that I should be treated fairly.

Despair is a feeling of helplessness when I believe that fairness is no longer possible in my life and I start to believe that my life may no longer be worth living because I am losing something or someone precious to my future well-being or because I have given up the hope of accomplishing the goals for my life.

When I experience these painful feelings for long periods of time, I start to feel like a failure and I begin to realize that I need to convince my mind to not run away from fear & anger, but to stay & fight the pain by looking for wisdom that will help motivate me to believe that my life will become worth living, once again.

When I cannot stop my feelings of despair from growing inside me, they will eventually lead to depression and thoughts of suicide, unless I find a way to start believing that my future life will become fair to me, once again, so I can acquire the motivation to re-start working on the goals for my life.

Unfortunately, my ego uses the residual fear & anger that lives inside my mind to feed itself and to keep itself alive. It does not want me to learn how to destroy the hidden fear & anger that is buried inside my unfair memories that I keep reliving each day because my ego realizes that it will start to die when its self-sustaining energy of fear & anger starts to diminish, when I become able to start killing the hidden fear & anger that is being generated by the unfair memories that I am reliving each day of my adult life.

I now realize that I can start to kill my ego by starving it of the fear & anger that it needs to continue living inside my mind by learning how to convince my unfair memories to not generate any new fear & anger inside my mind in the future." (Quote from Our Book Three)

Because it does not want to die, your ego may lie to you by telling you that this wisdom of fairness will not work, even before you start to practice this wisdom, or your memories may generate great pain when you start to look inside your mind at your unfair memories. How much fear, anger, worry or stress you feel, will be determined by how many & how intense were the unfair memories that you have acquired & stored in your subconscious mind, from the beginning of your childhood until now.

Please do not give up trying to practice this wisdom of fairness that we are about to describe for you in more detail, so that you can learn how to stop any new fear, anger, worry & stress from hurting you whenever you start to relive an old unfair memory or your ego tries to use your residual fear & anger to take control of your mind.

Never Giving Up the Fight for Emotional Freedom from Unresolved Pain & Suffering

It is your mental decision to fight or flee from feelings of fear & anger that are living inside your mind.

If you choose to flee, you are mentally deciding that you are presently incapable of future success in life as you flee from battling the unfair pain inside your mind and you are deciding that obtaining peace & joy in your present life is no longer worth fighting for, at this time.

If you choose to stay & fight, you are mentally deciding that you are capable of killing the fear & anger inside your mind because you believe that your life will become fair to you, as your decision to fight helps you to increase the feeling that you can regain control of your mind, your life & your future destiny.

And when your feelings of fear & anger are gone, you will realize that your feelings of love, peace, joy & compassion are entering your mind more often & more powerfully because you have killed the unfair pain that was blocking your internal source of unconditional love and preventing it from feeding you with continuous feelings of love for everyone in your life. You will realize that you have been rewarded for believing that the wisdom in Our Book may work for you because you started to practice this wisdom and allowed it to improve the quality of your daily life by increasing the joy in your life and reducing the fear & anger.

Please realize that the mental decision to fight or flee from any new pain & suffering in your future life is totally yours alone to make. No one can make this decision for you. If you run away today because the pain & suffering are too great to bear, hopefully, you will decide to stay & fight for your emotional freedom tomorrow.

Losing a battle for control of your mind & your feelings does not mean you have lost the war.

When you begin to believe, once again, that the hidden fairness in your present life will reappear and will help you to battle for your emotional freedom from unresolved pain & suffering, then you will become motivated to start fighting for emotional freedom, once again.

Always believe that you can fill your mind with continuous feelings of love, peace, joy & compassion, as you learn how to kill the unresolved unfair painful feelings that may enter your conscious mind in the future. Please work hard as you practice this wisdom and please be patient with your progress!

Unfortunately, it took many years for My Son & I to formulate this wisdom of fairness, through trial & error and through many setbacks, as we learned why it was important to kill all the major fear, anger, worry & stress being generated by the unfair memoires that we were reliving each day of lives, memories that we did not know how to stop hurting us, until we started Practicing The Wisdom of Children which contains the wisdom of fairness that protects & nurtures our future lives.

Fortunately, we are able to describe this wisdom of fairness for you in sufficient detail that you should begin to experience continuous love, peace, joy & compassion and increasing fairness in your life, in less time, then it took us to accomplish. And hopefully, you will become able to use this wisdom of fairness to minimize any future unresolved pain & suffering that you may experience, such as when someone disappoints you or when you start to feel that someone no longer loves you, as this wisdom of fairness helps you to start increasing the love, peace, joy & fairness in your future life, once again, as you learn to kill any new pain or suffering in your future life by practicing,

Killing Unfairness to Achieve Emotional Freedom

This is a brief summary of The Wisdom to Kill Unfairness in our lives that we will explore in more detail. This wisdom will help us to learn how to choose our feelings, so we can minimize any pain & suffering that we may have in our present lives, as we master learning how to kill this pain & suffering permanently, whenever it appears in our lives in the future. This practice also enables us to experience increasing love, peace, joy & compassion in our daily lives as we start to fully reconnect to our childhood source of unconditional love.

Eventually, as you continue to practice this wisdom of fairness, your increasing love, peace, joy & compassion will become continuous, when you have killed the energy source of all the major fear, anger, worry & stress being generated by the unfair memories that you are reliving each day of your life, such as feeling guilty about something you did, feeling unfair pain from someone you love, feeling that the people around you are being unfair to you, or believing that your future life will contain increasingly pain because the events in your future life will continue to be unfair to you, as your memories tell you that the events in your past life have been unfair to you.

This wisdom of fairness will also help you to kill any new pain & suffering that may enter your future life, so when you experience new unfair pain from your memories or from a new unfair event in your future life, you will be able to kill these new feelings of unfairness quickly, by practicing The Nine Steps to Emotional Freedom.

Unfortunately, learning this wisdom is a painful process, so you will have to acquire enough motivation to fight & then kill the major pain & suffering that is buried in your memories, pain & suffering that is blocking your pathway to the possibility of achieving continuous love, peace, joy & compassion in your future adult life.

Please realize that the path your life has taken, from being a child to becoming the adult that you are today, has been all about finding & then using powerful motivation to live your life courageously, to enable you to attain the goals for your life each day, as you try to enhance the well-being of your life and the lives of your friends & family. This struggle to succeed started as you learned to walk, talk, run & play, when you were a child and this is the same struggle to succeed that flows inside you today.

Fortunately, you were born with the motivation to succeed, as all newly born babies are, as evidenced by the loud cry that you & I made as we struggled to take our first breath of life, shortly after we were born.

Unfortunately, many of us have severely diminished our motivation to fight for what we believe is important for our future well-being, as the unresolved pain & suffering from the unfair memories that we acquired as we grew up, continues to diminish our motivation to succeed in the future whenever we relive these unfair memories.

Fortunately, practicing The Nine Steps to Emotional Freedom becomes a major struggle for a better life that pays huge benefits, as we re-acquire the powerful motivation of our childhood, as we use this renewed motivation to help us to succeed in our adult life, as we acquire increasing love, peace, joy & compassion until it becomes continuous in our daily lives, and as we become Masters of The Wisdom of Children.

Chapter 12

The Ruler of the Feelings in My Mind

I become "The Ruler of the Feelings in My Mind" when I imagine my feelings to be my subjects that I require to wear medallions engraved with the words "Life is Being Fair to Me" or the words "Life is Being Unfair to Me".

Then, I can look at a feeling's medallion to determine if it will treat me fairly or not, whenever it is inside my conscious mind.

In my imagination, a feeling can only live inside my conscious mind by depleting "The Energy for Living Consciously" that has been given to it by a memory in my subconscious mind, by the real events in my life as they occur, or by my ego, as these feelings are energized with this energy of life and then transported into my conscious mind. When a feeling runs out of its living energy, it will die unless it can obtain more living energy from me, when I give the feelings in my conscious mind additional living thinking energy, when I tell them that "Life is Being Fair to Me" or that "Life is Being Unfair to Me".

When I say that life is being unfair to me, I re-energize the feelings of fear, anger, worry & stress that are living in my conscious mind and when I say that life is being fair to me, I re-energize the feelings of love, peace, joy & compassion that are living in my conscious mind.

So, I have a choice to make as I become "The Compassionate Watcher" who observes all the feelings in my conscious mind and as I choose the fair or unfair words of living thinking energy to give to my feelings or as I decide to not give a feeling any additional living thinking energy so it begins to die and disappear from my conscious mind, as it runs out energy.

However, to be able to choose the feelings that I want to energize or not energize, I need to be in control of my mind.

Mind Controlling Feelings

And when I am not in control of my mind, whenever A Mind Controlling Feeling takes control of me, I am using my reasoning ability to decide to detach my mental focus from this feeling, so it can no longer control me. Detachment is the first of the nine steps that I am taking to achieve emotional freedom from all the feelings in my mind that are trying to control me.

A Mind Controlling Feeling is any feeling that becomes so intense that it starts to control my mind's ability to think & act, as I indulge in this feeling and allow it to take control of me as I begin to live inside this feeling and as I begin to fully indulge in the pain or the joy that this feeling brings into my life in the present moment.[11]

Fair Feelings that I Allow to Control My Mind

When I allow the intense fair feelings of love, joy, peace & compassion to take control of my mind & body, I may start to:

Indulge in an intense feeling of love for someone as I automatically reach out to hug & kiss this person, as my overwhelming desire to share my life with this wonderful person starts to control me during this moment of time.

Or I may indulge in the joy of my favorite music that fills my mind & body with the intense love for life that this music instills in me during this moment of time.

Or I may indulge in the sights & sounds of enthusiasm, laughter & love emanating from a group of young children that I am watching, as they play together and as I start to feel their intense passion for living in this moment of time.

When I feel the intense love, joy & ecstasy of living in the present moment, I am no longer living inside my memories of the past or living in my imagination of what may happen to me in the future. I am living totally in the present moment of time and sharing my love of this moment with all the life around me, which my Buddhist teachers call "Living Fully In The Present Moment" without worry or stress, as I live with the continuous feelings of love, peace, joy & compassion of this moment that are flowing through every part of my mind & body, as I fully connect with the universal love from all the life that surrounds me, which lives with me inside My Internal Source of Unconditional Love that I was born possessing. To continue feeling this love I need to maintain my connection to my internal source of love and not allow any unfair feelings of fear & anger to start blocking my connection to this love.

Unfair Feelings that I Allow to Control My Mind

Unfortunately, when I experience intense feelings that life is being unfair to me or to someone that I am observing, I may begin to:

Indulge in the intense imaginary fear & anger emanating from a life threatening situation that I am watching on TV as this fear & anger begins to take control of my mind as I begin living inside the actor's feelings, as he tries to find a way to escape this unfair situation as his intense fear & anger begins to take control of me in this moment of time.

Or I may indulge in the intense real feelings of helplessness when I feel that I can no longer cope with life's challenges and I start to dull my mind with drugs or alcohol as I try to escape from the stress in my life, or I become angry because life is treating me unfairly, or I start crying when I feel that I can no longer cope with the unfairness in my life during this present moment of time.

Fortunately, I am learning to regain full control of my mind & actions as I learn to kill the intense feelings of unfairness in my life by practicing The Nine Steps to Emotional Freedom.

The nine steps enable me to kill all the feelings of unfairness in my conscious mind that I no longer want to experience as I starve them of the unfair words of living energy that they need to continue living inside me.

Then, I become able to stop living inside my memories or inside my imagination of future fear, anger, worry & stress that may bring more unfairness into my conscious mind.

And when new unfair painful feelings enter my future life, they are not able to live with me for long periods of time and they are not able to take control of my conscious mind for long periods of time because I have learned how to detach from them and then starve them of living energy, so they have no choice but to die and disappear from my conscious mind.

Living Fully in The Present Moment

As I practice the nine steps to emotional freedom from feelings that are trying to control me without my consent, I start to experience the continuous feelings of love, peace, joy & compassion that begin to live inside my conscious mind in the present moment, as I fully re-connect to "My Internal Source of Unconditional Love" where wonderful life enhancing feelings live continuously, as they provide me with the love that I share with friends & family in my adult life.

Chapter 13

The Nine Steps to Emotional Freedom

Practicing the nine steps to emotional freedom enables me to choose the life enhancing feelings that I want to experience in my daily life as I learn to control my mental distractions when they contain life diminishing feelings, thoughts & images of the fear, anger, worry & stress that are created inside my conscious mind by unfair memories, my ego, or new external unfair events in my life.

First, we will explore how to kill the life diminishing feelings of worry & stress and then, we will discuss how to kill our ego driven feelings of fear & anger.

Step 1 of The Nine Steps – Practicing Detachment

Detachment occurs when I disengage, separate or remove something from something else that it is connected to (Cambridge English Dictionary)

Practicing Detachment is to disengage, separate & remove my mental awareness of being inside a distracting feeling, thought or image to become aware of moving outside of it, and then to become aware of looking back at it from outside of it. Practicing Detachment is also asking my mind to stop me from becoming lost inside a distracting feeling, thought or image when it tries to take control on my mind.[12]

As I practice detachment, I begin to realize that "I Am Not My Feelings" when I detach from all the feelings, thoughts & images in my mind, as I allow them to just be, without trying to control them and without allowing them to distract me from working on My Goals for Today.

Even though Buddhists call a fully detached mind, as achieving the mental state of An Eternal Mind, I prefer to call a fully detached mind as achieving the mental state of Becoming A Compassionate Watcher who has the ability to detach from & then control all the feelings, thoughts & images in my conscious mind to enable me to choose the life enhancing feelings thoughts & images that I want to experience in my life and to enable me to kill the life diminishing feelings, thoughts & images in my conscious mind that I do not want to continue experiencing. (Please refer to a Buddhist text, such as Complete Enlightenment by Ch'an Master Sheng-yen, for a more detailed understanding of the concept of An Eternal Mind)

The first step I am taking to achieve emotional freedom from unresolved pain & suffering is to learn how to detach from the pain that a repetitive reoccurring feeling, thought or image generates inside my conscious mind, each day, whenever I relive this unfair painful experience and then I am learning how to kill this pain so I can replace the pain with joy.

The process starts with learning how my memories use living energy from The Storage Room of Feeling Energy in my subconscious mind to generate new pain inside my conscious mind.

When I attach to a painful feeling being generated by an unfair memory, I start to mentally concentrate on the fear, anger, worry or stress being generated by the memory and I start to lose my mental concentration on the positive & joyful feelings, thoughts & images in my mind, as I start to become lost inside the unfair painful feeling.

Unfortunately, when I attach to an unfair painful feeling, I start to feed thinking energy to this feeling about how unfair my life has just become, thinking energy that my memory uses to generate additional unfair pain into my conscious mind.

Obviously, I want to minimize the amount of thinking energy that I am feeding my memory, instead of increasing it, so I try to detach from thinking that life is being unfair to me and I try to learn how to kill my memory's ability to generate any new unfair pain in the future, so I will not feel this unfair pain again, whenever I relive this memory in the future.

Detaching from thinking that life is being unfair, helps me to detach from all the feelings in my mind, not just the unfair ones. As I continue to practice detachment, my mind becomes a completely un-attached mind that is not being controlled by any feelings, thoughts or images.

For example, when I detach from an unfair painful feeling in my mind, I become able to start searching for the energy source that is feeding energy to this feeling because I can now look outside of the pain for its energy source, because I am no longer trapped inside the painful feeling, such as when I start looking for the source of the pain that is being generated by an unfair memory that is using a painful feeling to tell me that my present life is being unfair to me, as the memory uses my thinking energy about this unfairness to keep the painful feeling alive & active inside my conscious mind, as it tries to get my mental attention and then tries to take over my mind so it can convince me to fight or flee from this real or imagined unfairness in my life.

Fortunately, when I decide to no longer think about the unfairness of this painful experience, I stop creating any new thinking energy of unfairness, which stops the memory from getting the new energy that it needs to create more unfair pain in my conscious mind.

Then, when I become able to remember the details of the unfairness of the past experience in my life that created this memory, so long ago, I can stop the memory from feeding new energy to the painful feeling in my conscious mind by convincing the memory that life is no longer being unfair to me and then I can feel the unfair painful feeling decrease in intensity as my memory stops feeding new energy to the pain to stop keeping it alive inside my conscious mind.

Then, when the pain in my conscious mind runs out of new thinking energy about the unfairness in my life, it has no choice but to disappear from my conscious awareness, when it uses up all the energy of the unfairness that my memory has stored inside The Storage Room of Feeling Energy in my subconscious mind and it can no longer get any new energy from my conscious mind because I have decided not to feed it any new thinking energy about the potential unfairness in my future life.

I am telling each unfair painful memory that I relive in the future, that there is no need to create new unfair pain in my mind to get my attention so it can tell me that life may be unfair to me again in the future because I now believe that my future life will be fair to me, as I start to believe in The Law of Karma and as I start to use this new belief in a wonderful future for me and my friends & family to motivate me to work on My Goals for Today that will help me to create this wonderful future. (Please refer to the Overview of The Buddhist Law of Karma section in Chapter 23 of Our Book One)

Please ask yourself these questions,

What is detachment? Q-32

How do I detach from unfair pain & suffering? Q-33

The next section will help you to understand how memories are able to create pain inside our minds without our approval.

My Memory Recorder & Playback System

To help you to conceptually understand the process of detachment from a painful memory, so you can visualize this process working inside your mind, please think of a TV video recorder that is attached to your TV at home, where you can choose to record the shows that you desire to watch again in the future. You can use your video recorder to play back your favorite shows as often as you want. You are 100% in control of what shows to record and the date & time at which you will playback one of your favorite shows.

Now, think of Your Memory Recorder that lives in your subconscious mind. It has been recording your life experiences as memories, from the time you were a child until now. The sights, sounds, smells & feelings of all your past life experiences are recorded by Your Memory Recorder as memories that are stored in Your Room of Memories inside your subconscious mind.

Unfortunately, like you, I am not in full control of when these experiences will be played back in my mind as I start to relive one of these memories. And I cannot choose to relive only my favorite experiences from my childhood. Since I am not 100% in control of when these memories will be played back into my present life and since I am not always able to stop the replay of the unpleasant & painful experiences from my past life, I have decided to practice using the wisdom in Our Book to cut off the energy supply that is keeping the unfair painful memory recordings active, as they continue to live inside the memory library in my subconscious mind, especially the unfair painful ones that are currently being replayed inside my conscious mind each day of my life, memories that I cannot stop hurting me when I relive them.

So, I want to convince My Memory Playback System that is attached to My Memory Recorder to replay these past experiences but not to replay any intense unfair pain that may be attached to the memories of my painful life experiences whenever I relive them. This is similar to being able to turn down the sound volume on a TV Video Recorder when I am playing back one of my favorite TV shows. I turn down the intensity level of my painful feelings, whenever I relive a painful memory, by killing the energy source of the unfair pain, by not thinking that my life is being unfair to me, whenever I relive one of these painful experiences. This enables me to replay an unfair experience from my past life on my memory recorder without feeling intense pain because I am slowly depleting the energy source that the memory is using to generate new intense pain in my life, each time I relive this memory.

And I am reprogramming the memory with the truth that life has become fair to me, when a memory holds false unfair information or I am reprogramming the memory with forgiveness for whoever created this pain in my life, in an effort to convince the painful memory that there is no longer any need to generate new intense pain in my future life, to get my attention, so it can tell me that life has been unfair to me in the past and may be unfair to me again in the future. I already know that life has been unfair to me in the past and I am telling the memory that I can live with this unfairness because I believe that my future life will be fair to me.

Then, when I relive this unfair memory again in the future, the memory will realize that there no need to generate new pain into my mind to get my attention to tell me that life may be unfair to me in the future because I have convinced the memory that my future life will be fair to me.

Fortunately, The Practice of Detachment is slowly killing the intense pain that is buried inside all of my painful memories, each time I relive one of my unfair memories, as each memory uses up its energy reverses until it has no energy left to generate new unfair pain into my life in the future.

A memory can only get new energy supplies when I think about how unfair my life has become when I relive a painful memory. So, I am stopping the flow of new energy to each memory by practicing detachment from my desire to think that life is being unfair to me whenever I relive an unfair memory, to prevent me from feeding new thinking energy to the unfair memory which will allow it to generate new unfair pain into my life in the future, whenever I relive this unfair memory again.

In this way I am depleting the energy reserves of all the unfair memories that are stored inside my subconscious mind, by slowly killing the energy source of unfairness that my memories use to generate new painful feelings into my conscious mind when I relive one of them.

When the energy reserves of all the major unfair memories that I have been reliving are depleted, my pathway to the source of the unconditional love that lives inside me, becomes fully open and I start to automatically receive a continuous stream of love, peace, joy, & compassion from my internal source of unconditional love, love energy that begins to flow into my conscious mind during each moment of every day of my future life because the pathway to this source of unconditional love is no longer being blocked by unfair pain from the memories that I have been reliving.

Now, when new unresolved pain & suffering tries to enter my life in the future, I am able to stop this pain from hurting me for very long, by practicing the nine steps to emotional freedom, beginning with the practice of detachment from this new pain & suffering.

Parents & Teenagers

To help you to better understand the benefits of practicing how to detach from feelings that try to control you, please remember when you were a teenager and then ask your memories to tell you if you became angry & upset when your family would not stop giving you advice & suggestions about how to manage the choices you were making in your teenage life, Advice that you did not need and did not want.

And did you decide to become a rebel by telling your family that you did not want to hear any more advice from them?

If you were not a rebellious teenager, please imagine a thirteen year old girl who rebels when her mother asks her to clean her room. The teenager wants her room to be her private sanctuary, where she can leave her clothes & books on the floor if she wants to, so she rebels when she becomes tired & frustrated after her parents keep asking her to tidy up her room.

Now, please imagine a seventeen year old son, who refuses to go on vacation with his parents, even though his parents want to take him to a place where he can have fun & adventures. He rebels because he wants to be his own boss and he wants to choose his own vacation destination, without his parents giving him advice on the best place to go with his family. He is tired of compromising for the good of the family because he is tired of the continuous advice he is receiving from his parents. So he tells his parents that he wants to stay at home alone, while they are on vacation, because he believes that his parents will boss him around with more unwanted advice & suggestions on what to see & do, while he is on vacation with his parents, even if the vacation destination is a place he would enjoy visiting someday.

Please ask yourself this question,

Why do many parents continue to give their children advice, when their children tell them that they do not need or want their advice? Q-34

The answer to this question helps us to realize that many parents of teenage children are unable to detach from their feelings of worry & stress about their children's uncertain future, which fosters the parents' compelling desire to continue giving their children advice, to help protect their children in the future, especially when the parents worry that their teenage children may get into trouble, when they are at school or when they are socializing with other teenagers, who may be experimenting with drugs, sex or alcohol.

Unfortunately, these parental fears & feelings of insecurity may not be based on true facts, especially when the parents believe that future events may be unfair to their children.

When parents continue to be afraid that their children may get hurt in the future or when the parents are afraid that their children may make the wrong choices or exhibit bad behavior in the future, many parents are not able to detach from worrying about their children.

Unfortunately, this unfair worry & stress diminishes the happiness & joy in their family life, as the parents continue to alienate their children, who become tired of listening to their parents, who continually nag them about the potential unfairness in their future lives or the negative consequences of making the wrong choices in life and who continue to give their children advice about how to make the right choices in their life, to protect them from potential future harm.

These parents could start to fix their deteriorating relationship with their children by deciding to allow their children to make their own decisions without parental advice, unless a child asks a parent for help, by adopting,

The Parents' Credo for Teenage Children.

We define a Parents' Credo as a parental doctrine, tenet or philosophy for relating to a child.

Please repeat this credo to yourself if you are the parent of a teenager.

"I will only give my child advice or offer my suggestions, when my child asks for help! And when I offer advice, I will offer it only once. Then later, I will not ask if my advice has been useful.

I will not be a bossy & controlling parent and I will not nag my child to do better, when my child does not live up to my expectations or my desires."[20]

Unfortunately, many parents are unable to stop giving advice or unable to stop trying to control their children because they are unable to detach from their continuous worrying about their children's uncertain future. When this happens, many children stop confiding in their parents about what is happening in their teenage lives, to prevent their parents from trying to control their lives and to prevent their parents from giving them additional advice that they do not want to hear & do not need, whenever they tell a parent about a new event that is about to occur in their teenage life

This happened to one of My Son's best friends. Both his parents continually nagged his best friend because they were afraid his best friend would get hurt or get into trouble in the future. As a result, the son stopped confiding in his parents and eventually he decided to run away from his parents by choosing to go to a university that was far away from his family home. Then, when he graduated, he moved to another country, where he now lives & works, which is many thousands of miles away from his parent's home.

And when he comes back home each summer to visit his friends, while he is on vacation, he refuses to stay with his parents. He says that he still loves his parents but since they will not change their habit of continuously giving him advice, he has decided to see them once a year, when he goes out for dinner with his parents. He refuses to spend additional time with his parents because when he does, he starts to relive the unfair painful memories from his teenage years, when his parents continually nagged him, in an effort to get him to follow their advice, which they hoped would prevent him from getting hurt or getting into trouble in the future.

This estranged parent & child relationship started when the parents were not able to stop worrying about their son's uncertain future, because they were afraid of the potential unfairness that the future may hold for their son, which resulted in their continuous attempts to interfere in their son's life with unneeded & unwanted advice, when he was a teenager, to help keep him safe from potential harm.

Unfortunately, the parents did not know how to practice detachment from their worry & stress about their son's uncertain future life, so their deteriorating relationship with their son became a sad, but true story!

Fortunately, the child still visits his parents each year because of his unbreakable bond of love with his parents, a bond he acquired in childhood. When he was a child his powerful ability to love motivated him to emotionally reach out to his parents as he bonded with them forever inside the core of his heart.

Unfortunately, his unfair memories of teenage angst still continue to diminish his ability to love his parents unconditionally. And his parents' fear of an uncertain future for their son still continue to diminish their ability to love their son unconditionally whenever their love for him is reduced by their fear of his potential future failure or loss. They could kill this fear but no one has taught them how.

Fortunately, the love for their son can potentially be fully restored and their son can destroy his teenage angst, when they both realize that they are keeping this worry & stress alive inside their minds and when they learn how to stop this suffering forever by Practicing The Wisdom of Children as they nurture,

An Unbreakable Bond of Love

Please ask yourself this question

How does an unbreakable bond of love develop between children & their parents? Q-35

The nurturing of the bond of love between parents & their children occurs "when young children look to their mothers for nurturing & comfort which becomes the secure foundation of their lives. To their fathers, they look for judgment & fairness, hoping for his approval & fearing his condemnation. It means that fathers are just as powerful in their children's lives, but no matter how loving and nurturing a father is, there is almost always an element of fear in the relationship, for the father is the focus of the child's fear of failure, as he grows up, when he does not meet his father's expectations for success.

Not that there aren't exceptional single fathers, who are also mothers to their children. And there are many single mothers who play the disciplinary role of the father, even though being a single parent is difficult at the best of times because single parents have little or no private time away from the children, unless their extended family of relatives & friends are willing to help bring up the children.

However, when there is both a mother & a father in their lives, many children realize their love for their mother is the strongest & brightest, while their love for Dad is not quite as bright because of the fear of father's discipline and sometimes the fear of unfair pain & unjust punishment." Such is the traditional model of family life that does not exist in many dysfunctional families today. (Modified Quote from Earthfall by Orsen Scott Card)

Hopefully, you do not have unfair painful memories of being estranged from your parents, when you were a teenager. And if you do, we will help you to kill this unfair pain in your memories, so that you will become able to reconcile with your parents. This happened to me, when I was a teenager, so I had to learn to detach from my painful teenage memories before I was able to reconcile with my parents, which I will describe to you, as we continue to explore how to achieve emotional freedom by learning to kill the fear, anger, worry & stress that is created in our adult lives by our unfair painful memories of our childhood that we keep reliving each day.

Now, please stop reading the wisdom in Our Book about detachment and go back to the beginning of Step 1 and start re-writing the essence of this wisdom in your own words to it make it easier for you to practice this wisdom and to make it easier for you to explain this wisdom to your friends & family as you become a Master of Detachment as a result of practicing detachment from the unfair feelings of fear, anger, worry or stress that you may experience during new events in your future life or that you may relive from inside old memories of your past life.

As you practice using this wisdom of detachment, please expand your understanding of this wisdom to include new insights into what your relived memories are trying to tell you and include new insights into how your mind tries to keep these memories alive inside your conscious mind, especially after you complete the next challenge.

A Challenge I Hope You will Accept

Please do not read the next section of Our Book until you practice detaching from all your feelings for one week, so you can practice learning how to stop your feelings from controlling your mind, when you realize that you should not allow a joyful or painful feeling to start controlling you, whenever it tries to stop you from working on the goals that you are trying to accomplish during the day.

I have allowed feelings to control me in the past, feelings I should not have allowed to control my actions, such as when I purchased something I desired but could not really afford, as I maxed out a credit card or when I went on a date with someone I was attracted to, but who I knew was not good for my future well-being & mental stability, but who was fun to be with at a party.

Practicing detachment will prove to you that the wisdom in Our Book can become extremely valuable to you, when it helps you to understand the feelings that are motivating you each day of your life and when it helps you to understand the memories that may be generating unfair fear, anger, worry or stress in your life, whenever you relive an unfair painful memory.

After you have practiced detachment for a week, please read the next section of Our Book, which describes Step 3 on the path to emotional freedom, which will help you to learn how to practice controlling your mind whenever your painful memories start to generate new fear, anger, worry or stress in your life. You will learn why this unfairness is being generated and you will learn how to kill these painful feelings, so you can stop them from hurting you again in the future, so you can start to relive only painless memories of the unfair experiences in your life, when you or your friends & family were hurt unfairly.

Learning How to Choose My Feelings

Unfortunately, many of us have 100s or 1000s of painful memories that we do not know how to stop from hurting us, when we relive them, until we learn How To Achieve Emotional Freedom by learning How to Choose Our Feelings to enable us to kill this unfair pain, by practicing the wisdom in Our Book.

I am quoting from the "It Is not About Doing, It Is About Being" section of Our Book Three, to help you to understand How to Choose Your Feelings, as you practice detaching from all your feelings during the day to prevent them from controlling your mind without your permission, so you can continue being in control of your mind, so you can complete the goals that you are trying to accomplish each day, by learning how to leave your feelings alone and by learning how to allow your feelings to just be.

"I am visualizing my mind learning how to choose my feelings, so when a new powerful feeling enters my mind it cannot distract me from working on My Goals for Today. I am listening to what all my feelings are telling me and then I am saying, "no" to each feeling that tries to get me to act in a certain way, by detaching from it, unless I become convinced that the feeling is trying to help me to accomplish My Goals, so I can complete more of my goals and so I can savor more feelings of accomplishment at the end of each new day of my life, as I realize that I am generating renewed feelings of being worthy of living as an unconditional loving human being who is a source of love, peace, joy & compassion for my friends & family.

During the day, as different types of feelings enter my conscious mind, stay for a while and then disappear, I am not trying to control my feelings. I am leaving these new feelings alone and allowing the feelings to just be until they disappear from my conscious mind.

The process of allowing my feelings to just be is helping me to understand what is causing each feeling, by identifying each memory in my subconscious mind that is generating each new feeling inside my conscious mind that is being triggered into existence by a new event in my life such as,

Listening to a street musician as I head to the subway as the music generates pleasurable feelings of joy in my mind, as I recognize the music that is being played from a memory of when I danced to this music with a loving friend.

Observing a parent scolding her son & daughter for coming home late from school, without notifying her, which triggers a memory of my mother scolding me when I was a child.

As I begin to observe the new feelings that enter my mind and I practice detaching from them, I begin to understand why these feelings want me to follow them and to act to satisfy the desire that each feeling contains, such as the desire to eat ice cream or the desire to call a friend and talk about tonight's baseball game

Then, I ask each feeling, who is now my new friend, to help me to determine what is generating the feeling and if it is a memory, then I ask if the memory is based on true events in my life or if it is based on untrue events that I have created in the fantasy world that I sometimes create in my mind.

When a memory is **untrue** and the feeling is painful, I am reprogramming my memory with the truth to stop the memory from generating new unfair pain in my life, when I relive the memory in the future.

When a memory is **true** and the feeling is painful, I am reprogramming the memory with forgiveness so I can convince the memory that this forgiveness will make my life fair, once again, in the future and there is no need for the memory to generate new pain into my life in the future to warn me that life may become unfair to me, once again.

And then, when I stop thinking about the unfairness in my life, that I am now feeling, these painful feelings that are being generated by the memories will start to run out of the energy of unfairness that I am giving them, energy that they need to stay alive inside my conscious mind and then they will start to disappear from my conscious mind when they run out of this energy that I have stopped giving them.

When a true feeling is peaceful & joyous, I am leaving the feeling alone and not trying to control it. I am making the decision to feed new thinking energy to my feeling about how fair life is being to me, as the life all around me helps me to feel that my life is worth living, and as the life all around me helps me to prolong the duration that the joyful feeling remains in my conscious mind before it decides to leave me and disappear, to hopefully be replaced with new feelings of joy. Feeding new thinking energy to my feelings of being worthy of living is helping me to keep positive feelings of love, peace, joy & compassion alive & active in my conscious mind.

This is how I choose my feelings during the day by managing the amount of new thinking energy that I feed to a new feeling when it enters my mind, whenever I start feeding thinking energy to the feelings of love & peace to prolong the time they spend in mind or I stop feeding thinking energy to the feelings of pain & suffering so they run out of energy for living inside my mind and then disappear from my mind.

As I observe my feelings during the day, I am not trying to change my feelings, as I allow my feelings to just be without my interference and as I allow my feelings to use up their energy reserves that they brought with them from The Storage Room of Feeling Energy in my subconscious mind, when they receive the energy from a memory, energy they need to become able to sprout into my conscious mind and then use to motivate me to follow their desires by creating joy or pain inside my mind.

As I practice being at peace with my feelings instead of trying to control my feelings while they are in my conscious mind, I am deciding to become willing to endure short term worry or stress during the day which may also include fear or anger in my present life, as I accomplish My Goals for Today, to become able to achieve the long term rewards that accomplishing My Life Enhancing Long Term Goals will bring into my life, both now and in the future.

When I am able to continuously choose my feelings by not allowing my feelings to distract me from working on my goals, I am no longer feeling worry or stress about my commitments to my family, friends & co-workers because I am not longer choosing to procrastinate about working on my goals because I am no longer afraid that I will not be able to accomplish my goals and because I am no longer afraid that unfairness will bring new pain & suffering into my future life that will kill my motivation to succeed.

Choosing my feelings enables me to feel worthy of living in the present moment during each day of my life, as I become an unconditional loving human being, as I feel the continuous love, peace, joy & compassion being generated by my internal source of unconditional love, as I use My Free Will to take control of my mind, my life & my future destiny, as I begin to choose all the feelings that I want to experience, as I work hard to accomplish My Goals for Today, and as I Realize That I Am Not My Feelings.

I become the observer of all the feelings in my mind as I practice being A Compassionate Watcher who is in continuous communication with my internal source of unconditional love, as I observe my feelings and as I do not do anything to try to control my feelings while they are in my conscious mind during the day.

Instead of trying to control my feelings, as I observe my feelings, I am deciding how long to keep my feelings alive & active in my mind, by deciding how much new thinking energy to feed a new feeling when it sprouts into my conscious mind from its memory that is stored in My Room of Memories in my subconscious mind.

This enables me to allow worry & stressful feelings to just be without trying to control them, so they eventually disappear from my mind when they run out of energy." (End of quote from Our Book Three)

Relieving Worry & Stress

Activities that increase my future well-being and reduce my worry & stress:

Exercising each day

Going for long walks or riding a bicycle with a loved one

Working on a project with children, friends & family members

Talking confidentially to a friend, who only gives me advice when I ask for help

Playing computer games or card games with those I love

Sharing a hobby with someone who enjoys sharing the same hobby with me, such as: collecting antiques or memorabilia, model building, photography or wood working

Playing sports with friends

Gardening with a family member

Doing housework, trying new cooking recipes or washing the car with someone I love

Sewing, knitting or crocheting with friends as we share stories about our lives

Reading books for pleasure, intrigue, mystery & excitement, when I am alone

Watching romance, comedy, action & adventure movies with those I love

And continuing to share love, peace, joy & compassion with all the life around me

Activities that reduce my future well-being and increase my worry & stress:

Eating food to excess & becoming fat

Taking mood altering addictive drugs

Gambling until it becomes an addiction

Promiscuous sex without sharing love

Abusing a friend or family member

Abusing Friends & Family

This section on abuse will help us to realize the need to become a Master of Detachment from the feelings in our minds that try to control us and motivate us to hurt our friends & family unfairly.

Abuse occurred in my life, as I grew up, when I treated another human being in a harmful, injurious, or offensive way, by verbal abuse such as speaking in an insultingly, harshly or unjust manner or by physical abuse when I tried to physically hurt someone, whenever

I allowed the fear & angry in my mind to start controlling me, fear & anger that was generated inside my mind whenever someone treated me unfairly.

And then, I decided to learn how to control my abusive desires when I realized that I hurt others unfairly when I became abusive.

Unfortunately, some of my friends did not learn how to control their desire to abuse and they allowed this desire to grow in intensity & power, as they grew up, until the desire to abuse others became a re-occurring daily habit in their adult lives, whenever someone treated them unfairly.

Fortunately, I learned that when I became abusive to my friends & family during my childhood, I was trying to relieve the stress of not getting what I wanted or I was trying to get justice & revenge when someone treated me unfairly, by blaming another person for the fear & anger that these disappointments created in my life.

I blamed others with my verbal or non-verbal antisocial behavior and then I tried to avoid these abused people in the future, because this helped me to stop being reminded about how unfairly I had treated others when they disappointed me.

And I continued to abuse others to relieve new feelings of fear & anger that were being created in my daily life, as I continued to use my internal coping mechanism that I was born possessing, a coping mechanism that is part of My Subconscious Fight or Flee System that my mind uses to help me to fight, such as, when I fight someone who treats me unfairly or when I flee from a painful feeling of disappointment when I do not get what I want from a relationship with someone.

So, I decided to learn how to stop my abusive behavior whenever it tried to take control of me during the day, when I began to realize that I should take responsibility for the consequences of my actions when I hurt others with my words or actions and when I began to realize that I should not allow my feelings of fear & anger to take control of me, whenever I desired to blame others for creating new disappointments in my life.

And I began to stop playing the role of the victim whenever I was treated unfairly in my life, when I realized I could live with this unfairness without allowing my desire for justice & revenge to take control of my mind during the day as this desire tried to motivate me to start abusing my friends & family, once again, whenever they disappointed me when I did not get what I wanted from them.

Then, I realized that I was feeding my abusive desires with the energy they needed to stay alive inside my mind, when I told myself that life was being unfair to me, whenever I relived a painful unfair memory.

So, I realized that I needed to learn how to forgive others so I could stop my memories from generating new fear & anger into my life and I needed to learn to stop thinking how unfair my life becomes whenever I feel this new pain & suffering.

Unfortunately, I did not know how to ask my mind to help me to forgive others when I was a young child, even though, an understanding of forgiveness was offered to me & my childhood friends when our parents or guardians they took us to a Church, a Mosque, a Synagogue or a Shrine, where we heard stories about the power of forgiveness from our religious teachers, such as when my parents sent me to church, first to Sunday School and then to regular church services as I grew older.

However, I was not able to implement the power of forgiveness into my daily life on a consistent basis until I became an adult after I had studied the wisdom of our wise ancestors, such as Buddha, that enabled me to fully understand how my mind works, an understanding that allowed me to acquire the extra power of forgiveness that I needed to kill the pain that I felt whenever I remembered how another person had treated me unfairly, as I used this power to forgive others in my life who did not deserve my forgiveness.

Then, I realized that once I was able to forgive another person, I became able to love this unfair person once again, whenever I thought of this person, because the act of forgiveness had enabled me to fully reconnect to my internal source of unconditional love for all life, especially to my innate potential to feel love for everyone in my life. This internal source of unconditional love started to automatically fill my mind with love as soon as I was able to use forgiveness to kill the pain of unfairness that was blocking my pathway to becoming able to feel the full power of this love.

Unfortunately, some of us grew up in homes where there was little fairness in our lives and we did not learn that our future lives would be filled with fairness, as described by The Law of Karma. We grew up to become abusive adults who developed an automatic habit of relieving our daily stress by verbally or physically abusing our friends & family. A habit that is still controlling our adult lives and diminishing the potential love available to us in the present moment, as the members of our friends & family shun us or are reluctant to be part of lives, because we continue to abuse them.

Bad Habits that Create Abuse in My Adult Life:

When I make fun of a friend and then I tell my friend it was just a joke.

When I physically hurt someone when I am feeling angry because I have been treated unfairly and I want revenge.

When I tell a loved one about the qualities that he does not possess whenever he does not treat me fairly or whenever he does not do the things that I ask him to do, things that are important for him to do for me or for the future well-being of our friends & family.

When I automatically find fault with what a friend is saying whenever I start to feel stress about what my friend is talking about, instead of listening respectfully to what my friend is saying and then asking questions to show my friend that I am trying to understand the wisdom that my friend is trying to share with me.

When I tell someone that I want in be alone, whenever I start to feel the stress from a memory that this person triggers in my mind, when she comes into a room where I am trying to relax, when I am trying to generate some peace & quiet in my life.

When I try to find a fault or find a negative quality about another person, so I can feel superior to that person, especially when I am jealous, because this person has something that I want, such as a more prestigious position at work or a romantic relationship with someone special, who I also desire to share romance with.

Unfortunately, these are examples of the coping mechanisms of abuse that I may use to relieve the worry & stress of my perceived unfairness in life or to relieve the worry & stress of feeling that I may not be as worthy of living as another person, when a feeling of unworthiness enters my mind as I start to feel that someone is better or more successful than me.

Help for an Abusive Adult

Fortunately, for those of us who have become abusive adults, I can learn to understand the abusive habits that support my abusive behavior and then I can learn how to stop these bad habits from hurting my friends & family in the future, when I begin to learn how to control my mind to enable me to detach from my desire to abuse another whenever I am treated unfairly in the future.

Even though my abuse may cause minor pain inside my victim, it will still be damaging to our relationship and will prevent us from increasing the love & friendship that we share. Being able to control my mind will help me to stop abusing my loved ones. I need to realize that I am fully responsible for my abuse and I am fully capable of killing my abusive habits.

Then, I become willing to go past the wall inside my mind that is blocking my ability to look at the painful unfair experiences from my childhood that created my desire to abuse others in my adult life, so I can begin to understand my need to abuse others.

I built this wall inside my mind when I was a child so I would not have to look at my memories of unfair abusive events in my childhood when I was a victim of abuse, when someone lied to me, stole from me, bullied me, or manipulated me unfairly, resulting in memories that I did not know how to stop hurting me when I was a child.

These old memories of the painful unfair experiences of my childhood are being kept alive inside my subconscious mind by the mental energy that I feed them every time I say, "It is Okay" "It does not matter" or "I do not care" when I hurt another person in my adult life because I feel justified as I hurt this person who has treated me unfairly, as I experience my unresolved desire for justice & revenge for being treated unfairly during my childhood, unfair experiences that I am now reliving in my adult life in the form of an increased desire to abuse someone because I have not been able to forgive the old friends & family members who treated me unfairly when I was a child.

Unfortunately, this unfair pain from my old memories plus the pain from new memories of unfairness in my adult life are blocking my connection to my internal source of unconditional love and preventing me from killing the pain that is living inside these memories of unfairness.

So, until I begin to understand how I am feeding my adult desire to abuse someone with my new thinking energy that life is being unfair to me again, I will continue to abuse others in my adult life because my desire to abuse enables me to obtain a sense of relief from the worry & stress that life will continue to be unfair to me.

The cycle of abuse starts with the build-up of intense worry & stress inside my mind, then I feel the need to find someone to abuse so I can release this worry & stress from my mind, then I use the worry & stress to power the physical and/or verbal abuse that I force on my victim, and then I feel the calming effect on my mind that occurs when the pain leaves my mind and when some of the pain goes to live inside the new memory created inside the person I just abused. This ends the cycle of abuse, until new worry & stress starts to build up inside my mind again, worry & stress that is continually being generated by the partially hidden memories of the unresolved pain & suffering from my past life. Then the cycle of abuse starts again.

Unfortunately, many of us choose abuse as a worry & stress relieving action that is harmful to our future well-being and to our friends & family. Learning to control my mind to become able to detach from the desire to engage in these abusive activities is an acquired skill that may be hard to accomplish, even when I understand the abusive activity is harmful, after it has become a strong habit & a mental addiction in my life.

When I am able to understand how my mind becomes controlled by the desire to abuse another person in the future, I begin to realize the need to become a Master of Detachment, so I can maintain control of my mind and prevent my desire to abuse from ever gaining control of me, my mind & my actions, again.

And hopefully, when I realize that I am unable to control my mind enough to be able to stop my abusive behavior, I will seek the professional help of a psychologist or a healer.

Help for an Unwilling Victim of Abuse

And when I have a friend or a family member who gets upset with me on a regular basis or blames me for things that are not my fault on a regular basis, then I have become an unwilling victim of mental abuse and I am a victim who may need professional advice on how to stop providing stress relief for a habitual abuser.

And if someone physically abuses me, I will call the police immediately, even if I am willing to forgive my abuser. Then I will try to get professional help on how to stop this physical abuse from ever happening again in the future, even though asking for help may be very emotionally difficult for me to do.

I am not allowing myself to be a willing victim of mental or physical abuse. I am fighting for my personal dignity and fighting for fairness in my life. I am not running away from abuse by forgiving the habitual abuser, as the negative painful & unfair consequences of this ongoing abuse reduces the future joy & love that I share with the habitual abuser, when he is not being abusive.

True & lasting forgiveness for a habitual abuser, who does not deserve my forgiveness, can only occur after the abuser has learned to stop his abusive behavior in the future and I have stopped being a willing victim of his future abuse.

I am becoming an unwilling victim of abuse who fights for fairness in my life whenever someone tries to abuse me in the future. (Please refer to the Killing the Worry & Stress in My Life section in Chapter 23 of Our Book One)

Step 2 of The Nine Steps - Practicing Friendship

Friendship is a relationship between people & feelings that is based on mutual trust, attachment and common interests.

Practicing Friendship is asking my mind to make friends with the painful feelings, thoughts & images that are generated inside my mind when life is being unfair to me.

And Practicing Friendship is asking my mind to make friends with the joyful feelings, thoughts & images that are generated inside my mind by the unconditional love from all the life surrounding me, as this joy flows into my heart, when life is being fair to me.[13]

Painful feelings started to occur in my childhood when I became afraid of the future, when I realized that I was vulnerable and could not protect myself from my older siblings when they bullied me or when I was treated unfairly by an adult who was bigger, stronger and more experienced than me. As a young child I wanted to feel safe & secure, so whenever I became afraid of someone or whenever some future event in my life became unfair to me, I asked my parents or a guardian to protect me, especially when someone treated me unfairly or when I got into trouble in my neighborhood or at school.

Unfortunately, my parents & guardians were not always available to protect me from such events as bullying at school or the unfair treatment by my sometimes neurotic friends. The pain & suffering these unfair experiences created in my life, I filed away in my memories as negative life diminishing experiences that I did not know how to stop from hurting me in the future whenever I relived one of these unfair memories. So, I spent my childhood running away from this remembered pain by suppressing the unfair memories whenever I started to relive one of them because I did not want to feel this unfair pain any more. This process of reliving painful memories that I could not stop from hurting me, started to generate my fear of the future, a fear that someone would come into my future life and create more unfair pain. Gradually, this fear of future unfairness started to generate a new fear of the future loss of my happiness, such as when I became afraid to ask other people for help because I was afraid they would treat me unfairly or I was afraid they would reject my cry for help.

Fight or Flee

Each day of my childhood, I made a choice to run away from the new fear & anger being generated by my unfair painful memories or to stay & fight the unfairness in these feelings, to become able to understand why I was reliving these unfair painful feelings and to become able to find a way to stop these unfair memories from hurting me again in the future.

On some days I ran away, when I believed that life would continue to be unfair to me and on other days I stayed to fight, when I believed that my future life would start to become fair to me, once again.

Childhood Memories from Our Ancestors

How we react to the primordial fear & anger that we feel, when we are children, may be built into us by our genetic makeup. As Charles Darwin said in his second book on evolution, The Descent of Man,

"May we not suspect that the vague but very real fears of children, which are quite independent of experience, are inherited effects of real dangers and abject superstitions during ancient savage times? It is quite conformable with what we know of the transmission of formerly well-developed characters, that they should appear at an early period of life, and afterwards disappear—like gill slits in human embryology."

Or as Carl Sagan, who agreed with Darwin, said in his book, The Dragons of Eden,

"Could the pervasive dreams and common fears of "monsters," which children develop shortly after they are able to talk, be evolutionary vestiges" from our ancestors?

Killing Unfair Pain & Suffering

Each of us is born with the ability to kill the fear & anger that is generated by our memories.

Unfortunately, many of us did not know how to use this innate ability to stop the fear & anger when we were very young, so many of us ran away from the fear & anger, into the arms of someone we love, someone who protected us by providing us with physical safety & emotional security.

In contrast to running away, some of us stayed and tried to fight the fear & anger, by enduring it, so we could begin to understand what was causing it, in the hope that we could learn how to stop it from hurting us again in the future.

For example, when I was two years old, I decided to stay & fight the monsters in my dreams, until I was able to stop the monsters whenever they tried to hurt me in a future dream.

Please ask yourself these questions,

When I experience unfair pain & suffering, am I spiritually alone in the universe and does my consciousness live solely inside my head, or am I spiritually connected to a universal consciousness that lives outside my body, a universal consciousness that I can use to help me to kill future pain & suffering, so I can start to live my life more fairly & successfully? Q-37

Where do my thoughts & feelings come from? Q-38

Scientists do not know for sure where our thoughts come from, though they are continuing to look for the source of human thoughts & feelings.

And I do not know for sure where my thoughts & feelings come from, except those that come from my memories.

Do you know where your thoughts & feelings come from or are you puzzled about the process, like me?

Fairness or Unfairness in Life

This mystery started to puzzle me when I was a young child and I wanted to understand where thoughts & feelings came from. I also wanted to understand why my friends would sometimes lie to me and treat me unfairly, so I decided to find the wisdom that would help me to understand how we create thoughts & feelings that motivate us to treat others fairly or unfairly.

When I was a young child, I loved everyone in my life and I wanted others to love me & be fair to me, so I was motivated to understand why others would love me most of the time and treat me unfairly, at other times.

As a result of many years of trying to understand how I create or destroy my thoughts & feelings, I developed The Nine Steps to Emotional Freedom with the help of My Son Wil and with the help of the wisdom of our ancestors, especially Buddha.

Even though I still do not fully understand where my thoughts & feelings come from, I have learned how to choose my thoughts & feelings when they appear inside my mind so that I can experience clear & true thoughts about my past & present life experiences and I can feel continuous love, peace, joy & compassion in my life by Practicing The Wisdom of Children for sharing unconditional love & nurturing true friendship with my friends & family.

When I was a child, I continually reminded myself that,

My Pain Needs to be Embraced

I began to realize that I had to stop running away from the feeling of pain & suffering that was being generated by my memories, whenever I started to relive one of these unfair memories. Instead of running away, I learned to stay and feel the pain, so I could learn to understand what was causing it and then become able to kill it.

By the time I became an adult I had learned that:

As frightening as the pain may seem, it is enduring the pain that makes me mentally strong.

When I allow my mind to feel the full power of the pain, by embracing it, my mental courage makes me stronger than I could have ever imagined in the past, when I ran away from my pain.

This is one of the greatest human qualities that I possess. It is the ability to bear my pain without breaking.

Now, I use this ability whenever my life becomes unfair to me, when I bear my pain without running away, until my life starts to become fairer than it is now.

Just because I may stumble and lose my way when I try to bear the pain being generated by my memories, it does not mean that I am lost forever because I am embracing my renewed childhood ability to kill the pain & suffering in my adult life, as I imagine my reward of sharing a wonderful future with my friends & family, when I have been able to kill all the major pain & suffering in my life.

Now, my renewed childhood ability to love all the life around me with renewed passion is continuing to motivate me to face new pain & suffering whenever it enters my future life, until I become a Master at Killing the Unfair Pain inside My Mind, as I learn to protect myself from any pain that may be generated by my unfair memories, both now and in the future.

As an adult, whenever I feel a desire to run away from new fear & anger, I tell my mind that I will not live my life continually running away from fear & anger, because when I do, this fear & anger will try to stop me from working on my goals for living a wonderful life because I will become more & more afraid of failure.

To motivate myself to continue working on the goals for my life, I must choose to bear & endure my fear, anger, worry & stress, my fear of potential failure, my desire to start procrastinating about working on my goals, my uncertainty of success and my pain of disappointment whenever I make mistakes on my road to success. I tell my mind that I will not give up accomplishing the goals for my life and I will continue to bear the fear & anger that I may feel in the future and I will not run away from this suffering, until I learn how to kill it, because this will enable my future life to become filled with love & joy and with filled with friends, family & co-workers who will share a wonderful life with me, a life that is filled with great passion for living life to the full, instead of a life filled with increasing fear, anger, worry & stress.

Now, when I start to relive a painful memory, I try to stand mentally still and I try to feel the full power of my pain, so I can fully detach from this pain as I try to make the pain my friend, so it will help me, as a friend, to find out what is causing this pain whenever I relive an unfair painful memory again in the future.

When I am able to make the pain my friend, then I try to convince the unfair memory that is generating the pain to become my friend also, when I ask my memory,

What are you trying to tell me, each time I relive your pain?
Q-39

Your answer to this question will be different from mine, however, your answer will probably include one of these phrases, "life is being unfair to me, life has been unfair to me, or life is going to be unfair to me."

If this is true for you, please answer the next question,

How do I use friendship to understand an unfair memory, so I can find the source of this unfairness and learn how to kill the unfairness, so my memory will not hurt me again in the future, when I relive it? Q-40

Then, my memory retrieval system will begin to realize that I already know that life may be unfair to me in the short term, but it will also begin to realize that I now believe that my future life will be fair to me in the long term.

When my memory retrieval system realizes that I now believe that my future life will be fair to me and to my friends & family, it will stop generating new pain whenever I relive an unfair memory in the future because I have taken away its reason for generating new pain into my life, pain that it no longer needs to generate to warn me that I am in danger of being hurt because I will no longer be unfairly hurt in the future because my life will be fair to me.

Please ask yourself this question,

How do I convince an unfair painful memory that life will be fair to me in the future, so it will stop generating new pain in my life, the next time I relive this memory, because it now realizes that it no longer needs to use pain to warn me that l am in danger of being hurt? Q-41

Please write the answers to these questions in your own words to make it easier for you to understand this wisdom and to enable you to use this wisdom to start killing the unfair pain inside your memories. Once the major pain is gone from your memories, the path to your internal source of unconditional love will no longer be blocked by the pain & suffering that your unfair memories may be generating into your life each day, as you continue to relive these memories, until you become able to kill this pain & suffering and you start to automatically feel enhanced love, peace, joy & compassion in your daily life, as your life becomes more fair to you & your loved ones because you allow your life to be fair to you.

Step 3 of The Nine Steps - Controlling My Mind

When I achieve the mental state of a fully detached mind, I become A Compassionate Watcher who has the ability to detach from & then control all the feelings, thoughts & images in my conscious mind, as I choose the actions that I will take today, as my memories, my ego & the external events in my life generate the ever changing feelings, thoughts & images that will enter my conscious mind today, as they live with me for a while, and then as they disappear from my conscious mind & body, later today.

As these feelings, thoughts & images try to influence the choices that I am making during the day, I begin to detach from all of them unless one of them offers to help me to work on the goals that I am trying to accomplish today, as I maintain Control of My Mind to work on my goals, as my motivation flows from my internal source of unconditional love that is living inside me.

I am able to keep control of my mind during the day by practicing meditation & mindfulness to stop the distractions that enter my mind during the day, such as when someone treats me unfairly during the day and my desire for justice & revenge tries to take control of my mind and tries to stop me working on my goals, so it can start to control my actions, as it motivates me to confront the person who just treated me unfairly so we can acknowledge the unfairness and set things right.

Meditation is practicing detachment from all the feelings, thoughts & images in my mind that are preventing me from achieving a state of Mindfulness. Whenever I achieve a state of Mindfulness, I become able to perceive all the feelings, thoughts & images in my mind clearly & correctly without distraction or falsehood, I become able to choose to live in the present moment without accepting distractions from the past or the future, and I become able to choose to feel the continuous love, peace, joy & compassion emanating from all the life in the universe as I fully reconnect to my internal source of love that lives inside me.

Mindfulness is knowing what is happening inside my conscious mind in the present moment, while it is happening, no matter what it is. (Modified quote from What is Meditation by Rob Nairn)

Mindfulness helps me to connect my mind to the universal source of love that is powered by all life in the universe. This love has been continuously flowing through me since I was born and this love helps to empower my ability to use reason to control my mind and it helps motivate me to work on my goals. When I start to feel my connection to this universal love, my mind automatically starts to become calm & peaceful. (Please refer to the Practicing Meditation & Mindfulness section in Chapter 9 of Our Book One)

How does meditation & mindfulness help me to keep control of my mind? Q-36

Practicing Control of My Mind also occurs when I use my decision making ability to order, limit, rule or choose some activity that is occurring inside the thinking process in my conscious mind, by choosing what physical action I should take in the external world or by choosing what mental actions I should take to understand what is happening inside my feelings, my thoughts, my mental images, my mind, my body & my relationships with my friends & family. (Modified quote from the Cambridge English Dictionary)

Now that I am an adult, I start to practice control of my mind after I wake up from sleep each morning when I ask my mind to mentally review the long term goals for my life to help me prepare a list of the short term goals that I want to accomplish today. I keep this list in my conscious awareness as I get out of bed and walk to the exercise room to start my aerobic exercises. When I start my exercises, my list of goals recedes from my awareness to the back of my conscious mind and stays there until I need to review it during the day as I select the next goal on my list to start working on.

Then, when I start working on this new goal and I become distracted, I practice detachment to help me to remove this distraction from my mind, so I can get back to working on my goal.

Later in the day, after I have been working for a long period of time, I may start to become mentally tired and I may need a short rest to help my mind recover from the prolonged mental concentration on my work. As I rest, I often choose the feelings that I want to experience such as listening to music or I may decide to talk to a friend, as I wait for my mind & body to recover from the stress & fatigue of working on my goals.

Even when I am resting and my mind is in a state of calmness & peace that my meditation & mindfulness provides, I still have my list of goals for today resting at the back of my mind, waiting for me to review this list so I can start working on my next goal when my mental fatigue disappears and enthusiasm for my work returns.

Being able to use meditation & mindfulness to keep full control of my mind during my adult life is a skill that that took me many years to perfect because I had developed a powerful habit of losing control of my mind during my childhood, whenever I relived a painful childhood memory of someone treating me unfairly, by lying to me, manipulating me, bullying me or stealing from me.

Because I did not know how to stop this unfair pain from hurting me when I was a child, whenever the unfair pain took control of my mind, I started to mentally run away from the unfair pain & suffering in my life and I spent a lot of time each day waiting for this unfair pain to go away, as I tried to think of enjoyable things to do that would help me to get rid of the pain.

As a result, I was not always able to choose the feelings that I wanted to experience during my childhood because I was not in full control of my mind, whenever the unfair pain & suffering in my life became intense, as this pain started to kill the motivation that I needed to fully enjoy my life or to work on my goals for the day.

So I asked my parents, my teachers, my friends and the religious leaders in our community to help me to understand what was causing this pain and how to get rid of it.

Unfortunately, the help I received was not enough to kill the pain being generated by my unfair memories. As I continued to relive these painful memories of the unfair events in my life and I thought about how unfair my life had just become when I started to feel the pain that was living inside those unfair memories, I became even more determined to find a way to stop this unfair pain from hurting me again in the future. So, I started to read books on philosophy, religion & psychology to help find out how to kill this pain. Unfortunately, I was not able to find the answers when I was a child but I did not give up searching for a solution.

By the time I became a teenager, I was living with a fractured mind that often contained unfair pain that I was trying to run away from and my mind also contained my desire to work on new goals, only if they were enjoyable, such as playing sports & reading books. The unfair pain in my mind also made me afraid of the future because I knew my memories would start to generate new pain in my life at any time during the day or night and this prospect made me afraid to work on new goals because I knew the future pain would start to rob me of my motivation to complete these new goals. So, I spent much of my teenage life procrastinating when I had goals to accomplish that I knew I would not enjoy working on, such as some of my school projects that I had to complete that did not interest me . This habit of procrastination I carried with me into my adult life.

I wanted to become able to kill this habit of procrastination, so I could take back full control of my mind and stop running away from the pain that I did not know how to stop hurting me.

However, to become able to do this, I had to learn how to make the unfair pain become my friend, so it would help me to understand why this suffering was being generated in my life.

Step 4 of The Nine Steps - Practicing Fairness

I am asking my mind to help me practice fairness by treating all human beings equally with the same love & forgiveness that I offer my friends & family.

And I am asking My Mind to help kill any unfairness that is living inside me to restore the long term fairness in my life.

The Power of Fairness is the ability that I was born possessing which enables my adult life to be fair to me in the future, as long as I practice The Nine Steps to Emotional Freedom. [14]

This feeling of fairness is based on the understanding that I am loved by all the life the universe, as shown by the love & forgiveness that my friends & family continue to offer me each day and it is the reason why I continue to succeed as an adult today, when I face the daily challenges in my adult life and I succeed with the help of the fairness of other people in my life.

And fairness requires that I be fairly punished when I break the rules for treating all human beings equally, with love, forgiveness, honestly, respect & keeping my agreements with others.

For example, when I allow the fear, anger, worry or stress in my life to motivate me to treat another person unfairly, I deserve to be punished for my bad behavior.

My punishment may start when the person I have hurt no longer trusts me with friendship & believes that I have lost my honesty & integrity.

Or my punishment may start when the person I have hurt demands compensation from me that may include money or it may require the use of my time & effort to repay this person for the damage I have created in this person's life.

And my punishment may also require me to the show person I have hurt that I am genuinely sorry & remorseful for the pain I have created in this person's life.

And when I hurt someone severely, then I may deserve to be punished with time in jail and/or behavior modification training, etc.

The prospect of receiving this type of punishment in the future will motivate me to treat other human beings fairly in the present.

However, this motivation is based on the fear of future punishment, so I have decided to use love to motivate me to learn how to treat others equally with love & fairness.

Loving with Fairness

Practicing the fairness of love kills any new fear, angry, worry or stress that may enter my life in the future. This will clear my mind of the negative unfair feelings and it will prevent the feelings from motivating me to start abusing another human being, whenever I blame another person for creating a new unfairness in my life.

Abuse may occur when a new unfairness in my future life triggers the fear & anger that is living inside my old unfair memories and triggers a desire for justice & revenge to be generated by my Fight or Flee ability that I was born possessing, to enter my conscious mind with the energy that they need to grow in power until they become intense, which motivates me to start looking for a way to clear these painful feelings from my conscious mind. This desire for release from the new intense pain & suffering may motivate me to abuse the person who created the new unfairness in my life, even if this is a minor unfairness.

Then, I may act abusively to release these intense painful feelings from inside my mind, so they will leave my conscious mind and go to live in my victim's mind as new unfair memories of abuse.

This abuse is not the fault of the person I abused. I am 100% responsible for my abusive behavior, whenever I create new unfair pain & suffering in a victim's life. (Please refer to the Abusing Friends & Family section in Chapter 13 of Our Book One)

And then, sometime in the future, I will pay a just & fair price for the new pain & suffering that I created in my victim's life. The Law of Karma will ensure that I pay for my crime of abuse. (Please refer to the Overview of The Buddhist Law of Karma section in Chapter 23 of Our Book One)

So, to prevent my abusive behavior from re-occurring in the future, whenever any new fear, angry, worry or stress tries to live inside my mind, I am using detachment from these painful feelings, as I wait for them to decrease in intensity, until I become able to ask this pain to become My New Friend, so I can ask My New Friend why my memory, my ego or a new external event in my life is generating this new unfair pain into my life.

If a memory is creating this new unfair pain in my life, then I am using the knowledge I have just gained from My New Friend to help me convince my memory to not generate any new unfair pain & suffering into my conscious mind in the future, by telling the memory that it no longer needs to be afraid of my past unfair experiences because my future life will be fair to me in the future.

When this memory starts to believe me that my future life will be fair to me, the memory will stop feeding its energy to any pain & suffering that may be living in my conscious mind. Then, as these unfair feelings run out of this energy for living, they start to disappear from my mind, which leaves a new empty space in my mind, that automatically starts to fill with love, peace, joy & happiness from my Internal Source of Love, love that I can use to help motivate me to treat other human beings with fairness, as I encourage them to treat me equally with their love & fairness.

And Practicing Fairness enables me to live with any new unfair feelings of fear, anger, worry or stress that may occur in my future life, because I have learned how to make each new painful feeling My New Friend, who will help find out why this pain is being generated inside my mind and then I can use this knowledge to kill this new pain.

This is how The Wisdom of Children enables me to understand why it is important for me to believe that my future life will be filled with fairness whenever someone treats me unfairly in the future.

Now, when I remember my fights with the monsters in my childhood dreams, I realize the need for a young child to believe that life will be fair in the future because this belief will help motivate the child to continue fighting for fairness & justice in his personal life.

I am still using this belief of fairness in my adult life, as I realize how powerful this wisdom of fairness is, a wisdom that I use every day to help motivate me to believe that my future adult life will be filled with the fairness & support of other people, especially my friends, family & co-workers, as they offer me their love, support & forgiveness which helps motivate me to achieve success as I endeavor to accomplish the goals for my life.

I have also learned to use this wisdom to help me to feel continuous love, peace, joy & compassion in my adult life, with the realization that I need to continue practicing this wisdom of fairness to become able to kill any new fear & anger that may enter into my future life, similar to using this wisdom when I successfully fought the monsters in my dreams when I was a young child, when I believed that my future life would be fair to me by helping me to convince my imaginary friends & family who lived with me inside my dreams, to help me kill the monsters who were being unfair to me when they tried to hurt me.

Unfortunately, many adults have lost their motivation & determination to fight the unfair fear, anger, worry & stress in their lives and do not have the knowledge to practice the wisdom of fairness. They may have started to lose their determination to be successful in life, when they were children, when they stopped believing that their future life would be fair to them. They may have concluded that there is little fairness in their lives because they falsely held a belief like this one, "No matter what I do, my future life will probably be unfair to me, just like my past life was unfair to me, which sucks!"

Fortunately, we can help our friends & family members who are suffering from the unfair pain being generated by their painful memories, to get back their motivation & determination to begin fighting for more fairness in their lives, by helping them to find a way to start believing that their future lives will become fair to them, once again.

The Wisdom of Children helps us to believe that our future lives will be fair to us and it helps us to become free of the suppressed fear, anger, worry & stress that lives in our unfair memories, as this wisdom enables us to begin to feel renewed motivation & determination to work on the goals for our lives, as we begin to share increasing love & joy with our friends & family.

Then, as a result of practicing this wisdom of fairness, we begin to realize that we have the opportunity to become better role models for our friends & family members who may be suffering from unfair memories of fear, anger, worry & stress that are robbing them of their motivation & determination, unfair memories that they keep reliving each day of their adult lives, which we can help them to learn how to kill permanently with love.

Imagining My Alter Ego

To help me to understand the concept of Practicing Fairness, I am imagining my ego becoming My Alter Ego, which I imagine as a second self who is distinct from my normal or original personality. (Alter Ego is Latin for "The Other I")

My Ego is the name I give to my feelings of fear & anger that live inside me when I allow them to take control of my mind & actions as I start to become lost inside these painful feelings, when I cannot stop them from controlling me.[21]

I realize that I need to understand my ego's ability to control my mind & actions because it is generating fear & anger in my life that is motivating me to treat other human as my adversaries, which is motiving me to treat others unfairly and which is preventing me from Practicing Fairness in my life.

And then when I understand how my ego is controlling me, I will use this information to stop my ego from controlling my mind & actions in the future.

A person who has an alter ego is said to lead a double life. And that is what I do when I allow the fear & anger being generated by my unfair memories to start controlling my mind, when I allow my alter ego to start making decisions for me as it starts to control my life.

Then, I become relegated to being A Compassionate Watcher who takes no future actions, as I allow my alter ego to lead me in this double life.

When I am experiencing the fear & anger being generated by an unfair memory that I am reliving in my conscious mind, I am imagining an exact copy of my mind & body standing beside me. I imagine it looking exactly like me, as it talks to me, as it begins to tell me what actions to take in the next few minutes of my future life, as my alter ego whispers in my ear with suggestions on how to run my life, as it tries to convince me to allow it to start controlling my mind and my future actions, by telling me that it can manage my suffering for me, since I do not know how to stop the fear & anger on my own.

And when I am suffering, I have a strong tendency to allow my alter ego to take control of my mind. A habit that I have acquired over many years of repeated suffering, whenever new suffering was generated in my life by unfair painful memories that I started reliving, suffering that I tried to run away from whenever I relived a painful memory because I did not know how to stop this unfair pain from hurting me.

I am imagining my desire to run away from this suffering becoming stronger as a result of allowing my alter ego to take control of my mind so many times, over a period of many years, because I did not know how to stop this unfair suffering from hurting me and all I wanted to do was run away from this suffering that I did not want to feel anymore, so I let my alter ego take control of my mind, so I could run away and hide from my painful feelings, thoughts & images.

To stop this double life from re-occurring in the future, I am practicing The Nine Steps to Emotional Freedom by detaching from any new unfair fear & anger that may be generated by my unfair memories and by putting my mental arms around this new pain as I tell it that I am your friend. Then, I stop thinking about how unfair this new pain feels, which prevents my alter ego from acquiring any new unfair thinking energy that will help to keep it alive inside my conscious mind, as it tries to maintain control of my mind and my future actions.

Then I imagine my real self, who is A Compassionate Watcher, putting its mental arms around my alter ego and telling it that I have decided to take back control of my mind so I can learn how to reduce my future suffering on my own, without your help.

As I imagine My Compassionate Watcher starting to work with the fear & anger that is filling my mind, as I start to relive a new unfair painful memory, I imagine myself making this new pain my friend as I work with my new friend to find the reasons for my suffering that are buried inside my painful memory that I am now reliving.

And when I find out the reasons for my suffering, I imagine myself using these reasons to stop the suffering from occurring again in the future, by practicing The Nine Steps to Emotional Freedom to convince this unfair memory & my ego that my life will become fair to me in the future, so there is no longer any need for this unfair memory or my ego to generate new unfair pain into my conscious mind in the future, so they can get my attention, so they can warn me that my future life may become unfair to me, once again.

Personally, the main reason I suffered for so many years was my belief that someone would come into my future life or some event would occur into my future life that would hurt me or my family &

friends, unfairly. This fear of potential loss & fear of future failure My Son & I call Primordial Fear which we describe in more detail in Our Book Three.

I used this understanding of Primordial Fear to help me to kill the unfair fear & anger being generated by my memories & my ego, fear & anger which became my alter ego when I allowed this pain to take control of my conscious mind because I wanted to run away from any new unfair pain that occurred in my life because I could not stop this pain from hurting me.

Fortunately, I realized that my continual non-stop thinking process about potential unfairness in my future that was being generated by my primordial fear was also providing energy to my painful memories, memories that were using this unfair thinking energy to generate new pain into my daily life.

Then, I realized that if I could stop this unfair thinking energy from flowing from my conscious mind to my unfair memories, I could kill the continuous ever present fear of future loss or future failure that lived inside my conscious mind, fears that had lived in my mind for many years and which until then, I did not know how to kill, as my ego kept using the unfair thinking energy that I was continuously generating inside my conscious mind to keep generating new pain & suffering into my daily life.

When I started to stop feeding my unfair memories & my ego with any new mental thinking energy about the unfairness in my life, my future suffering started to decrease, as I begin to realize that the events & the people in my life were actually treating me more fairly than I thought they were because I started to realize that the unfairness being shown to me by my unfair painful memories & my ego was not a true description of what my life was actually like, which I realized when I started to practice The Nine Steps to Emotional Freedom which enabled me to stop creating the thinking energy of unfairness in my mind that was feeding continuous new energy to the unfairness in my memories & my ego, which was keeping the feelings of unfairness alive in my conscious mind.

When I was able to stop creating this new thinking energy of unfairness in my mind, I became able to bring more love, peace, joy & compassion into my daily life, as I started to kill the unfair pain that was blocking the pathway to my internal source of positive life enhancing energy, whenever I started to relive an unfair painful memory. I accomplished this automatic reconnection to my internal source of unconditional love by detaching from the feelings of unfairness in my mind that were blocking the pathway to this love.

So, if you are feeling a great deal of remembered pain & suffering in your life that you try to run away from because you do not know how to stop this pain & suffering from hurting you and as a result, you decide to allow your ego to start taking control of your mind so you can run away and hide from this pain & suffering, then, I recommend that you start practicing The Nine Steps to Emotional Freedom, as I & My Son have done, to become able to kill this remembered pain & suffering whenever it appears in your future life.

Then, as you practice the Nine Steps to continue killing this pain & suffering each day whenever it appears inside your conscious mind, you will start to feel increasing love & joy as you automatically begin to fully reconnect to your internal source of unconditional love, as My Son & I have done, when the pain & suffering is no longer blocking the path to this unconditional love, which forces your ego to give you back full control of your mind as the increasing love inside your conscious mind starts to motivate you to take back control of your life, as you begin to share increasing fun & joy with your friends & family, as you reduce the pain & suffering in your mind each day by not feeding new unfair thinking energy to your unfair painful memories, energy that they require to stay alive in your conscious mind so they can generate new pain, suffering & feelings of unfairness into your daily life.

Banishing your ego from you mind, will enable you to Practice Fairness in your life each day as you start treating all human beings equally with the same love & forgiveness that you offer to your friends and family because your ego is no longer able to convince you to treat other human beings as your adversaries.

To understand why your ego tries to convince you to do this, please refer to the Practicing The Wisdom of Children is Hazardous to My Ego! Section of Our Book One.

Questions to Ask My Mind when Practicing Fairness

Please ask yourself these questions,

1) Why did I start running away from my memories of pain & suffering when I was a child? Q-42

Answer: I ran away because I did not know how to stop the pain from hurting me, so I tried to not think about the pain whenever it appeared in my mind and I tried not to look at it, because I was afraid of the pain

2) Does a memory use up its store of available energy when it creates new pain & suffering in my mind Q-43

Answer: Yes it does, which I realize when I detach from the pain and then observe it for long periods of time. The pain reduces in intensity and eventually disappears.

3) How does a memory obtain new unfair energy to become able to create new pain & suffering in my mind in the future? Q-44

Answer: I give the memory new unfair energy whenever I tell the memory that life has been, or will be, unfair to me.

4) Why does a memory create new pain in the future whenever I feed it new energy of unfairness? Q-45

Answer: The memory creates new pain to get my attention, so it can tell me to fight or run away & hide from the unfairness in my life whenever it believes that my life will become unfair to me in the future, once again.

5) Can I learn why a memory thinks my future life will become unfair to me, once again? Q-46

Answer: Yes, I can learn why by making the painful memory My New Friend so it will tell me why it is thinks that way. My memory will help me to understand why I am afraid of the future, such as, when I have not been able to forgive those who treated me unfairly during my childhood because they do not deserve my forgiveness or when I think that I may not be able to forgive those who may treat me unfairly again in the future.

6) When I learn why the past was unfair, can I convince a memory to stop generating new unfair pain in the future, with the unfairness energy it has stored in its energy reserve? Q-47

Answer: Yes, I can learn to stop new future pain from occurring by convincing the memory that my life will start to become fair to me in the future and that it no longer needs to cause me pain to get my attention, so it can tell me that my future life may be unfair to me.

7) What happens when I cannot convince a memory that life will become fair to me in the future? Q-48

Answer: The memory eventually runs out of the available unfair energy that it has stored in The Room of Feeling Energy in my subconscious mind, that it uses to create new unfair pain in my life and when this energy reserve is fully depleted, then it will be unable to create any more pain & suffering in my life, as long as I do feed the memory new energy by telling the memory that my life will become unfair to me, once again, in the future.

In summary, when all the unfair memories in my conscious mind run out the energy they need to keep themselves alive, my conscious mind becomes totally clear of feelings of unfairness.

Then, my conscious mind totally fills up with continuous feelings of fairness that my life is worth living and with continuous feelings of love, peace, joy & compassion.

8) What is fairness and how may I create more fairness in my life, today? Q-49

Please write the answer to this question in your own words

Step 5 of The Nine Steps - Practicing Forgiveness

Forgiveness occurs when I stop feeling anger or resentment toward someone, for an offense, a flaw, or a mistake made against me and forgiveness occurs when I no longer desire to punish or expect compensation from this person because I have killed my desire for justice & revenge and replaced this desire with renewed unconditional love & forgiveness for this person. (Modified quote from the Cambridge English Dictionary)

And Practicing Forgiveness is asking my mind to help me to convince a painful memory that I am forgiving those who created this painful experience in my past life and as a result of this forgiveness, that my future life will become fair to me.[15]

Forgiveness takes away my unfair memory's need to generate new pain in my future life, because it no longer needs to use pain to get my attention, because it no longer needs to tell me that my future life may be unfair to me, as it has been in the past.

To convince a true unfair painful memory & my ego to stop generating any new pain & suffering in the future, I am forgiving me or anyone who caused an unfair experience in my past life that created the painful memory that I am now reliving.

I realized that I needed to learn to forgive me FIRST, before I could forgive anyone else, because I have been feeding my painful feelings the thinking energy of how unfair life has been to me, an untrue thought that was keeping my painful feelings alive & keeping them hurting me, as they have done so, for so many, many years of my life, all because of my mistaken belief that my future life will continue to be unfair to me, as it has been in the past.

When I realized that I needed to forgive myself first, I started to cry because a great sadness overcame me when I realized that I suffered this unfair pain needlessly, for so many years of my life from childhood to adulthood. I could have stopped this pain long ago, if I had stopped thinking that life has been unfair to me in the past and will continue to be unfair to me in the future. This thinking about the unfairness in my life was feeding energy to my painful memories which allowed them to keep generating new unfair pain into my life, as they had done so for so many years with the thinking energy that I kept giving them every time I told myself that my life will continue to be unfair to me.

When I forgave myself, I automatically started to feel increased peace in my life, as my daily feelings of unfair pain started to disappear from my life.

Then, I realized that I was clearing away the unfair pain from my conscious mind that was blocking my pathway to my childhood source of unconditional love, which allowed me to start loving everyone in my life more often, including loving my new found ability to make my painful memories my friends, so I could convince them to stop hurting me again in the future, whenever I started reliving a painful memory.

From that moment onwards, forgiveness became **The Key** that I used to convince a true memory that there is no longer any need to generate new unfair fear & anger in my future life.

And I began to convince my ego that it no longer needs to be afraid of any future unfairness in my life because I am now interconnected with all the life in the universe that will treat me fairly in the future because The Law of Karma will make sure that my future life is filled with fairness, though I may still experience unfairness for short periods of time until I kill the source of this unfairness. (Please refer to The Law of Karma section of Our Book One)

Please remember an experience in your life when you forgive a family member for treating you unfairly. Then, please write down this experience in your own words as you try to understand the thoughts that went through your mind as you remember the reasons why you forgave, even though the friend or family member may not have deserved your forgiveness.

Your answer will most likely include the realization that your desire for this person's future well-being motivated you to forgive them because you loved them enough to believe that they would not hurt you in this way again.

Then, after you have written down this experience in your own words, please ask yourself these questions,

Is there anyone in my life who will benefit from my forgiveness, today? Q-50

How will my forgiveness reduce the pain that I feel, whenever I relive the unfair experience that this person created in my life? Q-51

What is forgiveness and how does it stop unfair pain from reoccurring when I relive a painful memory? Q-52

Step 6 of The Nine Steps – Choosing My Feelings

The mental process of enabling my feelings of childhood love, peace, joy & compassion to live inside my mind today occurs when I ask my mind to help me choose the joyful feelings that I want to experience today and then I prolong their life expectancy inside my mind by feeding them thinking energy about how life is treating me fairly by enabling me to feel this joy.

I am **not** telling my unfair memories or my ego that life is being unfair to me, so I can stop feeding my memories the unfair thinking energy about unfairness that they need to continue generating new painful feelings into my mind.[16]

Then, when these painful feelings completely ran out of the unfair thinking energy that I am no longer supplying them, they have no choice but to disappear from my conscious mind.

I realize that the hard work of killing the major unfair fear, anger, worry & stress being generated by my memories & my ego is worth the effort when they have disappeared from my conscious mind and are no longer able to block my powerful childhood feelings of love for everyone in my adult life.

I also realize that I can choose to detach from a feeling of pleasure by getting outside of the enjoyable feeling, by not thinking about how I want to stay inside the pleasure and become lost inside the joy, so I can indulge in savoring all of it, as I allow it to control my conscious awareness by excluding all other feelings that are not as enjoyable to feel. When this happens, I try to detach from the feeling of pleasure, whenever I realize that I should not allow this pleasure to distract me from working on My Goals for Today.

In this way, I begin to realize that I can choose to, prolong or cut short, the life of any one of my feelings or all of my feelings by controlling the amount of thinking energy that I decide to feed or not feed to a feeling, when it enters my conscious mind from a memory, my ego, or from the external world of people or events that occur in my daily life.

What do I ask my mind to do to help me choose my feelings of Childhood Love, Peace, Joy & Compassion? Q-53

(Please refer to the Choosing My Feelings section in Chapter 19 of Our Book One)

The Qualities of a Hero

When you become a Master of Choosing Your Feelings, you will acquire the qualities of a hero who is able to choose positive internal feelings to motivate you to be successful in your endeavors, no matter how much pain & suffering you may endure in the external world, as you accomplish the goals for your life.

A hero is defined as a person of distinguished courage & ability, who is admired for brave deeds and noble qualities.

A hero with these qualities is described by Ayn Rand in this modified quote from a draft she made for her novel, The Fountainhead, in which her hero Howard Roark succeeds against almost impossible odds in his quest to become a successful architect, while maintaining his principles & his integrity.

"He has the quiet, complete, irrevocable calm of an iron conviction. No dramatics, no hysteria, no sensitiveness about it—because there are no doubts. It is a quiet, almost indifferent acceptance of an irrevocable fact of his existence.

A quick, sharp mind, courageous and not afraid to be hurt, which has long since grasped and understood completely that the world is not what he is and which has long since grasped just exactly what that world is. Consequently, he can no longer be hurt. The world has no painful surprise for him, since he has accepted long ago just what he is to expect from the world....

He does not suffer, because he does not believe in suffering. Defeat or disappointment is merely a part of the battle. Nothing can really touch him. He is concerned only with what he does. Not how he feels.

How he feels is entirely a matter of his own, which cannot be influenced by anything and anyone on the outside. His feeling is a steady, unruffled flame, deep and hidden, a profound joy of living and of knowing his power, a joy that is not even conscious of being joy, because it is so steady, natural and unchangeable....

He will be himself at any cost—the only thing he really wants of life. And, deep inside of him, he knows that he has the ability to win the right to be himself, consequently, his life is clear, simple, satisfying and joyous—even if very hard outwardly."

Hopefully, this description of a hero will help to inspire you to choose your feelings, to help you maintain your connection to your internal source of unconditional love, peace, joy & compassion and will help you to maintain your personal integrity & principles, even in the face of adversity & setbacks in your future life, as you continue to create your future happiness & success and as you continue to share your love of being alive, with your friends & family.

What are the qualities of a hero that are living inside me, waiting to re-born? Q-54

Step 7 of The Nine Steps - Practicing Self-Discipline

Self-discipline is the ability to make myself do things that I know I should do even when I do **not** want to do them. (Cambridge English Dictionary)

I am practicing Self-Discipline to enable me to continuously think that my life will be fair to me in the future, to enable My Internal Source of Unconditional Love to motivate me to continuously share unconditional love & nurture true friendship with everyone in my life.

And practicing Self-Discipline enables me to detach from all the feelings, thoughts & images that are trying to control my mind, so I can use My Free Will to choose the feelings that I want to experience.[17]

Then, I am killing any new harmful pain that may enter my future life, from an unfair painful memory that I may start to relive, from my ego, or from a new event in my life as I maintain a continuous connection to My Internal Source of Unconditional Love and as I practice Self-Discipline to become a Master of Emotional Freedom, so I can continuously choose the feelings that I want to experience in my future life, such as choosing the motivation that I need to start a new fun filled adventure in my adult life with those I love.

The habit of Self-Discipline can only be acquired by learning to do what I do **not** want to do, a wise saying that I shared with my loving son when he was a young child, when he did not want to do something that was important for his future well-being.

I helped My Son to understand this wisdom, when I asked him to explain his understanding of the meaning of self-discipline.

We talked about how he learned to do things he did not want to do, so that he could do the right thing, such as being honest with his friends, admitting his mistakes & asking for forgiveness, so he could practice fairness & honesty when he played games with his friends, such as hockey, soccer & softball and we talked about how My Son practiced self-discipline as he learned to skate when he was three years old.

In his "Learn to Skate Class" he would take two skating strides, fall down, get back up, try a few more strides, and then fall down again. This would go on for an hour and then he would come off the ice, smiling and filled with excitement about how he had learned to improve his skating, as he learned to skate without falling down so much.

When we were children, many of us may not have realized that we were learning self-discipline because we were having fun, as we practiced self-discipline to learn the skills to play new games or go on new adventures.

For me, self-discipline enables me to enjoy each new day of my adult life, as I use self-discipline to start my aerobic & strength exercises each morning when I wake up, as I thank The Wisdom of Children for reconnecting me with my internal source of love to enable me to receive the powerful motivation that I may need to complete the goals for my life during each new challenging day of my wonderful life, as I live on Our Precious Mother Earth, as an adult human being who has the ability to love everyone in my life.

This is why practicing detachment from the pain & suffering in our lives is so important for us to learn, so we can kill the unfair painful feelings in our minds that may be blocking our connection to our internal source of unconditional love, a connection which provides us with all the motivation that we need to practice the self-discipline required to create & enjoy new fun & adventures with our friends & family.

Is there a new adventure that you have always wanted to experience, but which you keep procrastinating about by telling yourself that you do not have the money, the motivation or the opportunity to learn the skills required, so you can start this new adventure?

And if so, can you imagine yourself practicing the self-discipline that you need to overcome the obstacles that stand between you and the start of your new adventure, as you begin to motivate yourself by choosing to feel the excitement of sharing this new adventure with someone you love?

Please imagine what it takes to create this adventure in real life and then please write down your answer to this question in your own words,

How does self-discipline help me to continuously share unconditional love & nurture true friendship with everyone in my life? Q-55

Step 8 of The Nine Steps - Practicing Thankfulness

I am thanking the members of my friends & family who have been supporting me with encouragement, hope, sympathy, forgiveness & unconditional love, as I start to fully appreciate how much I love them and how much I owe them for their support, as I use my re-acquired childhood ability to share increasing love, peace, joy & compassion with friends & family, feelings that are being continuously generated inside my conscious mind by the internal source of unconditional love that is living inside me, when painful unfair feelings are no longer blocking my mind's access to this love, whenever I am able to convince my memories & my ego to stop generating new fear, anger, worry & stress into my adult life, both now and in the future.[18]

I am thankful for The Practice of Detachment which has enabled my adult mind to fully reconnect to my childhood ability to feel the powerful unconditional love from all the life in the universe, which filled each moment of everyday of my life when I was a young child.

Now, this powerful universal love lives inside my adult conscious mind, continuously, as it nurtures me, as My Compassionate Watcher detaches from all the new feelings, thoughts & images that enter my conscious mind each day, so it can determine which ones have value for my future life & the lives of my friends & family and which ones have no value because they are potentially harmful to our future well-being.

My renewed connection to this universal love is telling me that my life is worth living in this present moment and that I am of great value to my friends & family, as my present life continues to give me opportunities to fill each new day of my life with increasing peace, love & joy because I am practicing The Nine Steps to Emotional Freedom from fear, anger, worry & stress, as I decide to take responsibility for my future happiness and as I decide to stop blaming others for the unfair events in my life or for my failures.

As I practice detaching from any new fear, anger, worry & stress in my life, I am also attaching to the feeling that all the life in the universe loves me and wants me to be happy, as do my friends & family.

"It is as if I was born as a unique human being with a particular skill set of abilities, that no one who has ever lived has had and that no one in future will have. It is as if I am an experiment for living life successfully that will never be created in the same way again. My unique set of skills is inspiring me, to fulfill the unique purpose and to experience the special meaning of my life, which is to share unconditional love & nurture true friendship with all human beings in the world, especially my friends & family. I am unique, special & blessed to be given the opportunity to experience life as an unconditional loving human being on our precious Mother Earth." (Modified quote from A Spiritual Journey with My Son Wil section in Chapter 6 of Our Book One)

As I learn to choose my feelings and as I learn to stop any fear, anger, worry or stress that my memories or my ego may want to generate inside my conscious mind, I am beginning to realize that I am gaining mastery over my unfair memories & my ego.

As I acquire the ability to manage my unfair memories & my ego, I am acquiring the opportunity to express my thankfulness to those who have loved & supported me in the past, when my unfair memories & my ego were preventing me from expressing my love & support for my friends & family because my ego had convinced me to treat them as my adversaries and my unfair memories were blocking the pathway to my internal source of love that was generating my desire to express my gratitude to those love ones who supported me & forgave me when I messed up.

An example of my need for thankfulness occurred when my ego convinced me to treat my parents as my adversaries, when I was a teenager, when I decided that their advice was not helping me and I stopped thanking them for their love & support.

When I became an adult, I began to realize that my parents kept giving me advice when I was a teenager because they were worried about me, as I kept making mistakes and making bad choices during my life as a teenager, when I was becoming a rebel at home and at school.

And when I became an adult, I learned to forgive myself for my bad behavior and then I asked my parents for their forgiveness, before I could kill the pain that I had created in my memories during my teenage years that was feeding fear & anger to my ego and keeping it alive inside my adult conscious mind, whenever I relived the painful memories of my teenage years when I lived at home with my parents and I treated my friends & family unfairly.

Unfortunately, My Mom died when I was a teenager, so I was an adult when I prayed to her to ask her for forgiveness. My Mom loved her children who became the focus of her life as a stay at home mom. She spent her free time involved in community activities and shared a close personal relationship with the mothers & the children of our community.

I knew My Mom would forgive me because her love & forgiveness for her children never waned during her lifetime, and to this day, I keep the wonderful memories of the love & friendship that we shared as mother & son, alive in my heart.

Fortunately, My Dad was alive when I asked him for forgiveness and now, I keep my wonderful memories of My Dad alive in my heart as I think about him as a loving father. I did not visit My Dad, as often as I should have, after I left home to go to university and then went on to start my career, but I treasure the memories of the times we spent together before he died a happy grandfather, who enjoyed celebrating with his friends & family, especially his grandchildren.

My Dad did not remarry after My Mom died, so I asked My Dad many years later, why he did not ask a new loving woman to share his home. He humorously told me that he was still looking for that special loving woman who would keep him in the lifestyle that he would like to grow accustomed to.

I concluded that My Dad loved My Mom so much that he cherished his love for her during his remaining life after she died and he felt that this was enough love for him, even though I thought that he must have been lonely, coming home each day from the work that he enjoyed to an empty house that was re-energized whenever his friends came to visit him.

My Dad spent much of his leisure time outside of his home enjoying his friends and his volunteer work in the community where I grew up. And on special occasions he celebrated at home whenever his sons, his adopted daughters & his grandchildren came to visit and he celebrated again whenever he travelled to visit them.

This is how I practiced forgiveness & thankfulness to become able to reconcile with my family, which enabled me to share increasing love, peace, joy & compassion with my family, once again, as I used to do, before I became a rebellious teenager.

My rebelliousness generated many of the thousands of painful memories that I accumulated as I grew up, from the days of my childhood until I became a teenager, when I began to realize that my ego was using the energy of the fear & anger that was buried inside these painful memories, to feed itself and to keep itself alive each day of my teenage life. I began to realize that I needed to learn how to kill the pain being generated by these powerful childhood memories, to become able to gain mastery over my ego which tried to take control my mind & my future actions whenever I relived this fear & anger and I started to think how unfair my life had become, once again, as I started to feel this unfair pain, and I unknowingly allowed this unfair pain to feed my ego and keep my ego alive & active inside my conscious mind.

Now, I practice thankfulness for the unconditional love that I am sharing with my friends & family and for the love that I am receiving from all the life in the universe, an unconditional love that is motivating me each day of my future life to maintain mastery over my ego & my unfair memories, by making sure that I I do not feed them any new unfair thinking energy to keep them alive inside my mind. And when they disappear from mind, I become able to live my adult life with abundant passion that my source of unconditional love automatically provides me, free of charge, when fear & anger are no longer blocking the pathway to this love.

How does thankfulness help me to cherish my friends & family as they keep loving me & keep forgiving me, especially when I do not deserve their continuing love & forgiveness? Q-56

Step 9 of The Nine Steps – Sharing All the Love in The Universe

I am maintaining a continuous connection to all the love in the universe that is flowing through me during every moment of every day of my adult life, as I feel this powerful love automatically recharging My Internal Source of Love that lives inside me, as I share this newly acquired love with all the life that is surrounding me on Our Precious Earth, especially with my friends & family.[19]

And I am using this love to kill any new Unfair Pain that may enter my future life, by not thinking about how unfair my life has just become, when I start to feel this pain, so I do not feed this pain with new thinking energy about this new unfairness in my life that enables the pain to stay alive inside my conscious mind, as I watch this pain run out of energy and then disappear from my mind.

Then this unconditional love becomes continuous as long as I am able to kill any new unfair pain that enters my conscious mind, when it tries to block my internal connection to this love, as I practice being a Master of Choosing My Feelings during each new day of my adult life.

End of The Nine Steps to Emotional Freedom from the unresolved pain & suffering that is living inside My Unfair Memories & My Ego.

How do I maintain a continuous connection to all the love in the universe during each moment of every day of my future adult life? Q-57

Practicing Requires Suffering

A lot of suffering may be waiting for you, as you begin to confront your painful memories when you begin killing their ability to hurt you in the future.

The challenge of learning the wisdom in Our Book starts with your decision to look inside your mind and take personal responsibility for your future happiness, as you become willing to endure all the pain & suffering that you will find in your memories, to enable you to locate and then fully embrace your internal source of unconditional love for all life, that you were born possessing and that may become hidden inside you, whenever you experience new fear, anger, worry or stress in your adult life or when you start to relive painful memories that you may not have learned how to stop hurting you because no one has taught you how to stop feeding these memories the energy that they need to continue generating unfair pain inside your conscious mind.

I hope & pray that you will make the decision to study this wisdom by practicing The Nine Steps to Emotional Freedom to enable you to Continuously Choose Your Feelings, as you practice killing the Unfair Pain being generated by Your Unfair Memories and to enable you to gain Mastery over your ego, so you can fully reconnect to your Internal Source of Unconditional Love for All Life, which will start to increase the love, peace, joy & compassion that you experience each day of your future life, until this love becomes a continuous affirmation that your life is worth living because of your renewed ability to share increasing unconditional love and nurture true friendship with your friends & family.

(Please refer to the Killing the Worry & Stress in My Life section in Chapter 23 of Our Book One so you can practice the steps to emotional freedom by killing the unfair pain inside your unfair memories)

(And please refer to the Becoming a Master of The Wisdom of Children section in Chapter 25 of Our Book One for additional wisdom on freeing your mind of pain & suffering to become able to feel continuous love, peace, joy & compassion)

Chapter 14

What am I Asking My Mind to Do, When I Practice The Nine Steps?

The answer to this question empowers my mind with the mental tools that I need to practice The Nine Steps to Emotional Freedom from unresolved pain & suffering, which enable me to experience continuous love, peace, joy & compassion during every moment of every day of my adult life. (Please refer to Question 58 in the Questions to Answer in My Own Words section in Chapter 31 of Our Book One)

Today, my first challenge to achieve emotional freedom started this morning when I decided to detach from my dreams, so I could wake up and use the understanding of how my mind works to choose to fully reconnect with the continuous love, peace joy & compassion flowing through me from all the life in the universe, and then use these life enhancing feelings to help motivate me to share new fun & adventures with those I love, today.

My second challenge was to get out of bed and start my Aerobics, Yoga & Strength Training Exercises to help my mind & body function at their full potential.

After exercising, I observed how my mind & body were feeling by measuring the level of my mental & physical energy that is available to me today, as I began enjoying my feelings of well-being that my morning exercises have helped bring into my life.

Then, I started thinking about the goals for my life as I reviewed my mental list of potential goals for today before showering, as I gauged how many of the goals I could accomplish today.

After breakfast, I started working on my first new goal and I started adding thinking power to my desire to accomplish all my goals for today, as I began to look forward to increasing my feelings of being worthy of living as I accomplish each goal during the day.

Now, I am spending the rest of today working on my goals and continuously loving my friends, family & all the life on Our Precious Mother Earth, which is made possible by the enhanced wisdom of our ancestors, as I continue to practice The Nine Steps to Emotional Freedom to enable me to choose the feelings of love & inspiration that I want to experience today.

To continue my challenge of achieving emotional freedom today, I am asking my mind to help me to choose the feelings that I want to experience instead of allowing unfair painful feelings or other distractions to gain control of my mind, as I continue practicing The Nine Steps to Emotional Freedom, as my understanding of how my mind works helps me to fully reconnect to my internal source of continuous love, peace, joy & compassion that is living inside me.

When I Ask My Mind to help me practice The Nine Steps to Emotional Freedom during each moment of every new day of my life:

1) I am Practicing Detachment to stop my distractions from trying to control me.

I am asking my mind to help me practice meditation & mindfulness, so I can calm my mind enough to become able to **spot** any new distractions that may enter my mind, as these new feelings, thoughts & images try to distract me from working on my goals.

And then, I am asking my mind to use my reasoning & decision making abilities to find a way to **detach** from these new distractions, as quickly as possible, so I can stop them from trying to control me, to enable me to return to using the full power of my mental creativity to accomplish my goals.

Even though Buddhists call a fully detached mind, as achieving the mental state of An Eternal Mind, I prefer to call a fully detached mind as achieving the mental state of Becoming A Compassionate

Watcher who has the ability to detach from & then control all the feelings, thoughts & images in my conscious mind, to enable me to choose the life enhancing feelings thoughts & images that I want to experience in my life and to enable me to kill the life diminishing feelings, thoughts & images in my conscious mind that I do not want to continue experiencing. (Please refer to a Buddhist text, such as Complete Enlightenment by Ch'an Master Sheng-yen, for a more detailed understanding of the concept of An Eternal Mind)

2) I am Practicing Friendship with my feelings, thoughts & images to understand why they are living inside my mind.

I am asking my mind to help me make friends with the powerful feelings, thoughts & images that I will experience today, so each feeling, thought or image will be encouraged by this new friendship to tell me why a memory, my ego, or an event in my life created this powerful feeling, thought or image to live inside my conscious mind.

Then, I am using the understanding of why these powerful feelings, thoughts & images are being created and why they are living inside my conscious mind, so I can empower the life enhancing feelings that are motivating me to work on my goals and so I can kill the life diminishing feelings that are beginning to hurt me.

3) I am Controlling My Mind to accomplish my goals for today.

I am asking my mind to help me achieve the mental state of a fully detached mind as I become A Compassionate Watcher who controls all my feelings, thoughts & images, as I choose the actions that I will take today, as my memories, my ego & the external events in my life create the ever changing feelings, thoughts & images that will enter my conscious mind today, as they live with me for a while, and then as they disappear from my conscious mind & body, later today.

As these feelings, thoughts & images try to influence the choices that I am making during the day, I begin to detach from all of them unless one of them offers to help me to work on the goals that I am trying to accomplish today, as I maintain Control of My Mind to work on my goals, as my motivation flows from my internal source of unconditional love that is living inside me.

4) I am Practicing Fairness to enable my future life to be fair to me.

The Power of Fairness is the ability that I was born possessing which enables my adult life to be fair to me in the future, as long as I practice The Nine Steps to Emotional Freedom.

I am asking my mind to help me practice fairness by treating all human beings equally with the same love & forgiveness that I offer my friends & family.

And I am asking My Mind to help me kill any unfairness that is living inside me to restore the long term fairness in my life.[14]

So, when my memories, My Ego or new external events in my life generate new unfair anger, fear, worry & stress inside my conscious mind because they believe that life may be unfair to me in the future, I tell them that they are wrong and I tell them that my future life will be filled with fairness, because I believe that fairness is only way that human beings can work together successfully, so that all human beings can benefit from our accomplishments, as this desire for increased fairness in our lives motivates us to stop any neurotic unfair human beings who may try to prevent us from working together as their neurosis begins to create pain & suffering in our lives.

All human beings are born with the desire to create fairness as shown by our collective desire to elect politicians, who we give our trust, to help pass new laws that will bring increased justice & fairness into our lives.

Even though there is a lot of unfairness in the world, my mind has the ability to convince my memories, My Ego or new external events in my life that my future life will be fair to me and to my friends & family.

So, when I am able to convince a memory, My Ego or a new external event in my life that my future life will be fair to me, it will stop generating new feelings of unfairness inside my conscious mind, such as anger, fear, worry or stress and my mind will start to become peaceful, once again.

In other words, a memory, My Ego or a new external event in my life will believe that life will be fair to me in the future, as long as I can convince it that the unfair experience that was created in my past life, will not occur again in the future.

Though new unfair events may still create pain in my future life, I am learning what is creating this new unfairness when it enters my life, so I can kill this unfairness quickly to help restore the long term fairness in my life that will bring feelings of increasing love, peace, joy & compassion back into my life.

5) I am Practicing Forgiveness to unblock the pathway to my internal source of love, peace, joy & compassion.

I am fully re-connecting to my internal source of unconditional love by asking my mind to help me forgive those who created painful experiences in my past life.

Forgiveness takes away my mind's need to generate new pain into my future life because it no longer needs to use pain to get my attention so it can tell me that my future life may be unfair to me, as it has been in the past, because it now accepts that my future life will be fair to me for long periods of time in the future because I have forgiven those who created this pain in my past life and because my mind now believes that these previously unfair human beings will not hurt me again in the future.

So now that I have used forgiveness to convince my mind that my life will be fair in the future, my mind will no longer be motivated to generate new pain into my life that will block the pathway to my internal source of unconditional love.

Then, as this pathway becomes clear of the unresolved pain & suffering that was living inside my conscious mind, I begin to feel continuous love, peace, joy and compassion which is being generated inside my subconscious mind, a powerful unconditional love from my childhood that I was born possessing and that has been flowing inside me during every moment of every day of my life, from childhood until now.

6) I am Choosing My Feelings that I want to experience & I am killing my feelings that try to hurt me.

As I fully reconnect with My Internal Source of Unconditional love that lives inside me, I become able to ask my mind to help me choose my feelings that I want to experience in my life, as I observe all my feelings that live inside me, as I choose to feel the childhood love, peace, joy and compassion which is being generated by my internal source of powerful unconditional love, feelings that I can use to increase the power of the living thinking energy in my conscious mind to help me kill any negative feelings, thoughts or images that may try to hurt me or block the pathway to the source of my life-enhancing feelings of unconditional love, friendship & forgiveness.

7) I am Practicing Self-Discipline to share unconditional love & forgiveness with everyone in my life.

Self-discipline is the ability to make myself do things that I know I should do even when I do **not** want to do them. (Cambridge English Dictionary)

I am practicing Self-Discipline to enable me to continuously think that my life will be fair to me in the future, to enable My Internal Source of Unconditional Love to motivate me to continuously share unconditional love & forgiveness with everyone in my life.

And practicing Self-Discipline enables me to detach from all the feelings, thoughts & images that are trying to control my mind, so I can use My Free Will to choose my feelings that I want to experience.[17]

8) I am Practicing Thankfulness to nurture true friendship with everyone in my life.

I am asking my mind to help me thank the members of my friends & family who have been supporting me with encouragement, hope, sympathy, forgiveness & unconditional love, as I start to fully appreciate how much I love them and how much I owe them for their support, as I use my re-acquired childhood ability to share increasing love, peace, joy & compassion with them, feelings that are being continuously generated by the internal source of unconditional love that is living inside me.

9) I am Sharing All the Love in the Universe to recharge my internal source of unconditional love.

I am asking my mind to help me to use meditation & mindfulness to maintain a **continuous** connection to all the love in the universe that is flowing through me during every moment of every day of my adult life to enable this powerful love to continually recharge My Internal Source of Unconditional Love that lives inside me.

As I practice the nine steps, I see nothing in my friends & family but their childhood ability to love everyone in their lives with great passion, no matter how diminished their ability may be at the present time, as I prepare to embrace their love today, as I prepare to love them, and as I prepare to forgive them for any unfair pain & suffering they may create in my life.

Then each morning, after I mentally review the Nine Steps, I ask myself three additional questions:

1) Can I remember when I felt immense love for all the life around me, when I was a young child, as I shared new fun & adventures with my family & friends? Q-1

The answer to this question helps me to realize that I was born to live my life with great passion, which increases my motivation to fully reconnect with this childhood ability to feel immense love during each moment of every new day of my adult life.

2) Will I pay any price that is required to fully reconnect to the passion of my childhood, to enable me to feel continuous love, peace, joy & compassion in my adult life? Why? Q-5

The answer to this question helps me to realize that there may be temporary adversity & pain in my life as I accomplish My Goals for Today, as I begin to realize that the price of this suffering is worth paying, to be able to continue loving everyone in my life with great passion, as I accomplish my goals which will help me to serve & protect those I love.

Practicing the wisdom of The Nine Steps to Emotional Freedom "helps us to learn meditation & mindfulness techniques to enable us to understand how our minds **actually** work and then enables us to understand how our minds **should** work, to help us correct the errors in our thinking, as we use our reasoning ability to control the thinking energy that we use to power our joyful life enhancing feelings, especially to empower the motivation to accomplish the goals for our lives."

And I believe that the Primary Goal for our lives as human beings living on Our Precious Mother Earth is "to increase the love, peace, joy & compassion in our daily lives by learning how to kill the unresolved pain & suffering that is buried in our old unfair memories that many of us keep reliving each day of our adult lives, as we try to fully reconnect to the Internal Source of Unconditional Love of our childhood, a connection that we were born possessing and that many of us have diminished or lost.

When we fully reconnect to our childhood ability to live our lives with great passion, we start to experience the **continuous** love, peace, joy & compassion that we remember experiencing when we were children." (Modified quotes from the Overview of the Wisdom in Our Book Series section in Chapter 5 of Our Book One)

3) What have I learned from practicing The Nine Steps to Emotional Freedom?

The answer to this question helps me realize that I have practiced the wisdom in Our Book One, well enough, to learn how to detach from all the feelings, thoughts & images that will go through my mind during each new moment of today, as I observe all the events that are happening in my life, such as the activities of my friends, family, co-workers, and other human beings, who I will share love & friendship with today.

As I detach, I am looking at the new feelings, thoughts & images that are being created by the new events in my life today, as these feelings, thoughts & images enter my conscious mind, stay with me for a while, and then eventually disappear from my mind, later today.

I do **not** try to change them or control them as they pass through my mind.

However, I do decide which ones will help motivate me to work on My Goals for Today and I am adding my living thinking energy to the life promoting feelings to prolong their lives as they sojourn inside my mind, by telling myself that life is being fair to me, as I try to fully understand how they will benefit me before they leave my mind.

The unwanted feelings, thoughts & images, whose nature & purpose I can identify, I leave alone without trying to change them or control them, until they run out of the living energy they brought with them when they entered my mind.

And I do **not** give them any new thinking energy that will keep them alive inside my mind, by **not** telling myself that life is being unfair to me, whenever one of these unwanted feelings, thoughts or images generates new worry, stress, pain, suffering, fear or angry inside my mind, whenever someone treats me unfairly or when I start to relive a painful unfair memory.

I am refusing to indulge in feeling the unfairness or the pain by mentally detaching from these unwanted mental distractions, as they try to control me, until they run out of the energy they are using to stay alive inside my mind.

Then, I begin to feel increasing **peace**, as these unwanted, distracting and sometimes hurtful feelings, thoughts & images stop diminishing my motivation to work on my goals today, as they start to die from lack of energy and begin to disappear from my conscious mind.

As these unwanted distractions disappear from my mind, empty space is created inside my conscious mind, which starts to fill up with the unconditional love that lives in my subconscious mind because the pathway to this love is no longer being blocked by the unresolved pain & suffering that these unwanted feelings, thoughts & images brought into my conscious mind, unwanted distractions that are no longer living inside me.

In summary, asking my mind for help is a continuous ongoing mental process that starts each morning, when I wake up, as I start to receive the 60.000 + feelings, thoughts & images that will go through my mind each day and as I start practicing Step One of The Nine Steps to Emotional Freedom by using my living thinking energy to detach from all my feelings, thoughts & images that are living inside my conscious mind, so I can begin to understand each new life enhancing feeling, thought & image and I can begin to understand each new life diminishing mental distraction, as each one of them enters my mind and then tries to get my mental attention; so it can convince me to do something, to observe something, to feel something, or to help me understand the message which it brought with it, when it entered my conscious mind.

And when I make mistakes during the day, as I try to implement the nine steps into my life, I do **not** tell myself that I am unworthy of living. Instead, I tell myself that I am worthy of living because I was born with the ability to correct my mistakes, to learn from my mistakes, and then choose to use this new learning to **not** make the same mistakes again in the future.

In this way, The Nine Steps to Emotional Freedom enable me to choose the feelings, thoughts & images that I want to experience each day and enable me to Kill those that are of no help to me, especially the ones that try to hurt me, de-motivate me, or distract me from working on my goals during each new day of my life, goals which are important to me, such as working of projects that help me earn a living, or help me to love friends & family more, or help me to share new fun & adventures with those I love."

Chapter 15

My Son Wil's Wisdom for Practicing The Nine Steps to Emotional Freedom

I'm a sailor in a boat of my own construction, riding on a sea of uncontrolled feelings. I can continue to drift aimlessly with the current from wave to wave of changing feelings, hopefully enjoying my feelings or just surviving the pain of whatever negative feeling comes my way. Or I can upgrade my boat, install a motor, pull out a map, and navigate through the waves of feeling until I reach a new destination where the sea gently rocks my boat with continuous undulating waves of love and joy.

What defines my life in this sea of feelings? What sets my direction? What controls the nature, speed and direction of the waves of feeling?

To a great extent my life on this sea of feelings is defined by my fears that are given strength by the pain I've accumulated in my memories. What would it be like to be fearless? To set my direction without worrying about what might happen? Truly unlocking my potential for increasing the love and joy in my life requires me to kill the pain in my memories. I can kill the pain carried by the waves of feeling that are created inside my memories by following nine steps:

Step 1 - Practicing Detachment

Everything I've ever not wanted to do, I've not wanted to do because of the pain present in my memories related to that thing I've not wanted to do. They say there's a reason that work is called work and play is called play. Work isn't supposed to be fun. It's just something that I don't want to do but do anyway because it's necessary for me to do so. But what if that wasn't the case? What if I at least was indifferent about what work was and at most was allowed to become excited about it by learning to kill any pain associated with doing it.

Thus, it's evident that everything material in my life forms a blank slate onto which I project my feelings. My bias towards things, the way I feel about them, is dictated by my past experiences with them. My preconceptions and misconceptions are made by assuming that future experiences will be exactly like past experiences, and that furthermore, my past experiences, and the ways I felt about them, were completely valid and true. Believing, in this way, that the future will be just like the past, and that my memories of the past are completely accurate, means that I'm doomed to take life like I always have, repeating the same mistakes, and accepting positive change very slowly, if at all.

Freeing me from the rigidity caused by my fear of the waves of pain that I may encounter on the sea of my feelings requires that I practice detachment. Detachment is the process through which I separate me from my feelings. Doing so allows me to realize that the way I feel about a situation has little to do with my present reality and more to do with the pain present within my memories. When my present situation reminds me of painful memories of similar situations in my past, I make the emotional connection and thus magnify and intensify my negative thoughts and feelings. To remove this mechanism's power over me I must detach from my feelings and realize that I can control how I feel.

Step 2 - Practicing Friendship

After practicing detachment, my next step to emotional freedom is practicing friendship. Making friends with the pain in my memories allows me the opportunity to gain the knowledge to improve my ability to practice detachment. When I find myself in a situation in which my memories are causing me excessive pain, rather than allow the pain from those memories to overwhelm me, I take the opportunity to understand where the pain is coming from and why my memories are causing me pain. Detaching and understanding my pain from an emotional distance allows me to further realize and reinforce that the pain from my memories needn't control me. I can control the way I feel about any situation by making my feelings my friends because how I feel about a situation is up to me.

Step 3 - Practicing Control of My Mind

The easiest way to detach from distractions that may try to take control of my mind is to practice meditation when I work on my goals for today. Meditation is practicing detachment from all the distractions in my mind that are preventing me from achieving mindfulness. Mindfulness is a state of awareness in which I'm aware of everything that's happening around me. I spend most of my life daydreaming, wrapped up in my feelings, constantly thinking, and unaware of the present moment. My feelings control me the most when I'm daydreaming.

When I meditate and achieve a state of mindfulness I detach from my thoughts and feelings. This creates mental space in which I can start practicing control of my mind by using my reasoning ability to control how I feel and act towards my present situation. Thus, when presented with a difficult situation, I withdraw from it by hitting my meditative trigger. For me it's taking notice of the objects around me that I had been previously ignoring. A meditative trigger can be anything that allows me to achieve a state of mindfulness. Hitting my meditative trigger and meditating for a moment allows me to detach from any distractions that may enter my mind and try to stop me working on my goals for today.

Step 4 - Practicing Fairness

By practicing control of my mind I am able to treat all human beings equally with the same love and forgiveness that I am offering my friends & family. As I think about the situations I face in life, I can build a positive habit of facing pain with detachment by believing that my future life will become fair to me. Thus, I become better and better at practicing fairness and friendship as I gain emotional knowledge and meditative experience. My memories cause me less pain and my feelings control me less.

Step 5 - Practicing Forgiveness

Unfairness is the most powerful negative feeling that stems from my memories. Thus, practicing forgiveness is very important when assessing the situations I find myself in, in life and when evaluating the validity of the feelings I feel when reliving my memories. When I experience unfairness in a present situation, I detach from my feelings of anger or fear. When a present situation reminds me of a past situation where I was treated unfairly, I detach from the feelings of fear or anger that I feel as a result of my memory. Detaching in this way requires me to forgive those people who have treated me unfairly in the past and to forgive the forces of nature that may be treating me unfairly in the present. I realize that my emotional reaction has little relevance to reality and little impact on outcomes. Detaching from my emotional response to unfairness by forgiving the cause of that unfairness allows me to diminish my pain both now and in the future.

Step 6 - Choosing My Feelings

The key benefit of detachment is realizing that I am not my feelings. Going through life, it is very easy for my feelings to dictate my every action. Emotionally, I will strive with all my actions to pursue pleasure and to avoid pain. Living emotionally in this way causes me to settle in a physical state that resonates with my emotional state. Thus, I can find myself statically indulging my pleasures while avoiding work that may be painful that would lead to improvement.

Long term improvement in my life comes from achieving my goals. This is because achievement allows me to move to a higher level of physical and emotional resonance as I learn to choose the feelings that I want to experience.

Step 7 - Practicing Self-Discipline

Enduring the pain of physical exercise improves my body and allows for me to experience higher levels of physical achievement and greater levels of physical pleasure in the future. While detaching from pleasure is important in order to maintain emotional control, it is possible to enjoy pleasure while detaching. This is because detaching while experiencing pleasure allows me to control, yet still experience, positive feeling.

After exercising, my entire being is enhanced. The benefits far exceed the costs of the work I put in. However, I often don't exercise because I have negative feelings towards work. By detaching through meditation and mindfulness when my negative feelings are preventing me from exercising, I realize that the work I put in is minimal and the benefits I receive in return are great in the long term. I accomplish my goals by making my negative feelings my friend and by allowing them to teach me about my emotional mechanism. I forgive myself for having negative feelings and treating me unfairly in the past when I allowed my negative feelings to prevent me from exercising.

By taking these steps I choose my feelings and allow myself to achieve my goals, such as exercising. Practicing Self-Discipline to achieve my goals pushes me to higher and higher levels of physical and emotional resonance. In this way I can improve my existence, minimize my emotional costs, and maximize my emotional benefits.

Step 8 - Practicing Thankfulness

Practicing thankfulness helps me to become inherently joyous and loving. Once I've detached, befriended, forgiven, and managed the negative feelings in my memories that were preventing me from accomplishing my goals, I'm ready to thank. Being thankful is the exercise through which I strengthen my connection to the universal source of love and joy. Similar to how exercising by doing squats helps me to run faster; being thankful helps me to be more loving and joyous.

There are many things to be thankful for and they are easy to recognize once my mind is free of negativity. Being alive is wondrous and on top of that is celebrating my love for living in a world filled with unconditionally loving people.

Step 9 - Sharing All The Love in The Universe

I possess within me a permanent connection to the universal source of love and joy. I was born with an uninterrupted connection to this source. However, over the years I've been increasingly cut off from it by the accumulation of pain in my memories through negative experiences.

The ultimate goal of gaining freedom from my painful feelings is to allow me to reignite my permanent connection to the universal source of love and joy.

Taking The Nine Steps to Emotional Freedom allows me to free myself from my emotional prison of negativity. Like a prisoner behind bars, I can't realize what I'm missing in the world outside until I take steps in the right direction towards increasing the love, peace and joy in my life, as I walk outside of my self-imposed prison of negative painful memories that I have been allowing to control my life and keep me in prison, afraid to work on new challenges and afraid to makes changes in my life because I may fail. Now I am becoming fearless, as I practice Choosing My Feelings, as I bring continuous love, peace and joy into my life from all the life in the universe that I share with my friends and family, by taking control of my feelings to enable me to choose my future life and my future destiny." (End of Quote from My Son Wil)

Please use Wil's wisdom to help you write a summary of the Nine Steps and then use your own words to explain this wisdom to your friends & family, to enable their positive feedback or constructive criticism to help you to master this wisdom as you practice the nine steps.

Chapter 16

A Last Word at The Beginning

"The Wisdom of Children is composed of a mental & physical practice. The mental practice is the nurturing & protecting of the love, peace, joy & compassion that lives inside me and the physical practice of sharing this unconditional love when I offer true friendship to another human being." (Quote from The Essence of The Wisdom of Children section in Chapter 8 of Our Book One)

Hopefully, when you read My Son Wil's wisdom for practicing the nine steps, you began to confirm inside your mind that you were born with the miraculous ability to feel love for all the life around you and to feel the love being generated by all this life, an ability which enables you to practice The Wisdom of Children.

For many of us, our adult ability to love all life has become hidden by our memories of the pain & suffering that we experienced in our lives. If this has happened to you, then I am challenging you to work with My Son & me to reclaim your childhood heritage, to become able to abundantly love all life once again, as you did when you were a child, so you will become able to experience continuous love, peace, joy & compassion during every moment of every day of your future adult life.

Please allow us to help you to start accomplishing this challenge, by realizing that deep inside you, at your core, You Are Perfect. As Buddha says, you are like an unpolished diamond that has become hidden inside your mind & body. A diamond that is waiting for access to the light of the universe to start shining brilliantly again, as it once did when you were a young child, when you were in love with all life and felt loved by all life.

There is nothing wrong with you at the core of your being, except that you may have surrounded your core of love with memories of fear, anger, worry & stress. We will help you to kill this unfair pain

& suffering to enable you to find & then polish your diamond of love, as you enable your renewed love to shine with brilliance, as you enable your friends & family to experience your renewed powerful passion for living and your renewed motivation to share unconditional love and nurture true friendship with all human beings, especially with your friends & family.

When you decide to accept our challenge, your study of The Wisdom of Children will begin in earnest. Please join us as we begin our exploration of this wisdom, as you learn to understand why it is important to nurture & protect your childhood ability to feel intense love for all life, especially for your friends & family.

And please remember A Last Word of Wisdom before You Begin the challenge of reclaiming your birthright. Please remember that you are perfect because your ability to unconditionally love all life is perfect.

Why is my ability to unconditionally love all the life that surrounds me, so perfect? Q-59

The answer is, "Because I was born with this perfect ability".

Why was I born with the perfect ability to unconditionally love all life? Q-60

You may decide to ask for help when you answer this question, help from your friends & family, help from the wise sages who understand your cultural heritage, or help from the religious leaders in your community. Our discussion on faith in Our Book One may also help you to answer this question.

Personally, I do not know the answer to this question. However, I have decided to accept on faith that my perfect ability to love all life is an unconditional gift of love from My Creator, who I call God. Your answer may be different from mine. What is important is for you to answer this question to the best of your ability and then become able to live with your answer in a state of acceptance, a state of love and a state of peace & joy, as I have learned to do with my answer.

Now, I am going to ask you two questions that I want you to answer in your own words before you read the next section of Our Book. To answer these questions, please look inside your mind and try to get in touch with your childhood memories of the fun & adventures that you shared with your friends & family, when you were a young child. Try to remember the games you played and then compare the intense passion of your childhood love of fun & adventures with your adult passion for sharing fun & adventures with your friends & family. Then, when you are able to compare the passion of your childhood to your adult passion, please answer these questions,

Do I want to increase the passion in my adult life by fully reconnecting to my intense childhood desire to seek new fun & adventures, by fully reconnecting to the internal source of unconditional love & motivation of my childhood? Q-61

When I decide to increase the passion in my adult life, how do I start to fully reconnect to my childhood source of unconditional love & motivation? Q-62

Personally, I have asked these two questions and I have decided to practice The Wisdom of Children, to become able to fully reconnect to my childhood passion for living a life filled with new challenges and new fun & adventures, by learning how to kill all the major unfair pain & suffering in my memories that are blocking my pathway to my childhood source of unconditional love & motivation. Once my pathway has been cleared, the love, peace, joy & compassion that is living inside me will start to automatically flow into my conscious mind as I begin to feel new powerful childhood motivation to share new fun & adventures with my friends & family.

And if your answers to these questions are similar to mine, then please practice using your childhood ability to feel loved by all the life surrounding you, a love that has been flowing into your mind & body from all the life around you, during all the days, months & years of your past life, to help you use your childhood ability to love all the life around you and to help you dramatically increase your passion for new fun & adventures in your future adult life, as you continue Practicing The Wisdom of Children.

Chapter 17

My Childhood Ability to Share Unconditional Love

The Four most important statements about my childhood ability to feel immense unconditional love for all the life around me and to feel powerful supporting love from all this life are:

1) I was born as an unconditionally loving baby, who loved everyone in my life and who felt loved by all the life that surrounded me, when I was a young child.

2) My childhood ability to feel spiritually connected to all life by unconditional love started to diminish as I grew up, as I experienced unfair pain & suffering that I did not know how to stop from hurting me, whenever I relived the memories of the painful experiences that occurred whenever someone treated me unfairly, by manipulating me, by lying to me, by stealing from me, or by abusing me.

3) Unfortunately as a child, no one taught me how to stop this unfair pain & suffering from hurting me, whenever I relived a painful memory, by teaching me how to practice detachment and by teaching me how to fully reconnect to my childhood ability to love all life passionately once again, whenever I felt unfair pain, so I could convince an unfair memory to become My New Friend and convince it to stop hurting me in the future.

4) This unfair pain had disconnected me from my childhood source of unconditional love by the time I became an adult. I no longer felt loved by all the life that surrounded me and I was no longer able to love all life passionately because of the painful memories that I kept reliving each day of my adult life, that I did not know how to stop hurting me.

Are these statements about my childhood also a true description of your past life? Q-63

If these four statements do not describe your past life, then you may not need to increase the childhood passion in your present adult life because you may still be fully connected to your perfect childhood ability to passionately love all the life that surrounds you, especially being able to love your friends & family passionately.

And if you are still fully connected to your childhood ability to share unconditional love & nurture true friendship with your friends & family, then you are indeed a rare & precious human being who is able to share an immense passion for living with those you love.

Unfortunately for many of us, we have diminished or lost our connection to our childhood ability to love all life passionately and we need to learn how to kill the pain that is buried inside our painful memories that is hiding our connection to our childhood ability, a process that will enable us to live our adult lives more passionately, as we learn to rediscover & fully reconnect to our childhood ability to feel an immense love for all life and to feel powerfully loved by all this life, as we once did when we were young children.

You will soon begin to realize that accepting the challenge of rediscovering your childhood ability to love all life passionately may sometimes require hard work, when you decide to practice the Courage & Self-Discipline that will be required to answer each question in Our Book, as soon as you read a question for the first time.

Please do not delay answering a question by saying to yourself that you will answer this question later. Answering each question will help you to understand the wisdom in Our Book and will help you to implement this wisdom into your life, faster. So please do not read the next section of Our Book, until you have answered all the questions in the section you have just read, to the best of your ability. You may not be able to answer a question fully, the first time you try to answer a question. That is OK. Even a partial answer will help you.

To help you to get started on your journey of rediscovery & reconnection to your childhood ability to love all life passionately, please answer these questions in your own words,

What is my written description of two memories of my childhood, when I played with friends and I felt our mutual love for the fun & adventures that we shared? Q-64

Will these memories help me to rediscover & embrace my childhood ability to love all life passionately, to help me to bring more love, peace, joy & compassion into my adult life? Q-65

What is the next step that I must take, to be able to continue on my adult journey to fully rediscover my childhood ability to feel increasing love from all the life that is surrounding me and to feel increasing love for all this life? Q-66

Chapter 18

Practicing The Wisdom of Children is Hazardous to My Ego!

In the Chapter 7 section of Our Book One entitled, My Son Wil's Wisdom from The Child Living inside Him, Wil briefly mentioned the Ego and how it prevents us from fully reconnecting to our childhood source of unconditional love & true friendship.

An Ego is a person's sense of self-esteem or self-importance.

"My Ego" is the name I give to my feelings of fear & anger that live inside me when I allow them to take control of my mind & actions as I start to become lost inside these painful feelings, when I cannot stop them from controlling me. I started to experience these painful feelings of fear & anger during my childhood and I started to store these painful feelings inside my memories, whenever someone rejected my offers of love & friendship when I was a young child. [21]

When I was a young child and I saw my physical body reflected in an external mirror hanging on a wall, I began to perceive myself as a human being who is separate from other human beings, who are external to my body.

This separateness became the basis for my ego, who is the make-believe being that I create in my conscious mind and store in my memories each day of my life, whenever someone rejects me.

My ego believes that I am spiritually separate from other human beings.

My ego also believes that the love, peace, joy & compassion that I want to feel continuously in my life, are only found outside of my body

And my ego believes that I must compete with other human beings to obtain this external joy & happiness.

Unfortunately, I began to falsely believe what my ego was telling me, when I was a young child, when I started labeling the external things that existed outside my body as mine, such as my toys.

I made the mistake of not realizing that I should be using My Internal Source of Love for everyone in my life to motivate me to label all the external things in my life as ours because I was sharing my toys with friends & family who loved me and who would not take my toys away from me.

Unfortunately, I started to become possessive about my toys when I started to feel the primordial fear that my ego was feeding me, fear that made me afraid that someone or something would come into my life and hurt me, by taking away my toys. (Please refer to the Childhood Memories from Our Ancestors section in Chapter 7 of Our Book One)

I did not understand why I was born with this primordial fear and I did not want to feel this fear any longer, so I started to run away from this fear because I did not how to stop it from hurting me.

As I started to believe what my ego was telling me. I allowed my ego to convince me that I must protect my toys & other things that I valued in my life or I would lose them, when they were taken away from me by other human beings who did not love me and who would reject my offers of love & friendship. So, I started to believe that I should treat these unloving human beings as my adversaries, so I could protect the valuable external things in my life from being lost to me.

Then, I started to label this primordial fear of potential future loss in my life as "unfairness". I started to lose my belief that I would be treated fairly and I started to lose my belief that my friends would continue to love me. I became afraid they may try to steal my toys, lie to me, bully me, or refuse to allow me to play with them.

Then, as I grew older, I started to experience more pain, rejection & unfairness in my life when external things were taken away from me or opportunities for new fun & adventures were denied me.

This was why I allowed my primordial fear of potential future loss to motivate me to start believing that all my friends were potential adversaries who I should compete with by lying, cheating or stealing from them, as some of them were doing to me. I started losing my love for some of friends when I was not able to kill my primordial fear that was growing stronger inside my conscious mind.

Unfortunately, this primordial fear started to disconnect me from My Internal Source of Unconditional Love that I was born fully connected to. I no longer felt spiritually connected to all life around me and I no longer loved everyone in my life, as intensely as I once did when I was a baby because I was feeling increasing fear of future rejection in my young life.

By the time I became a teenager, my mind was fractured as I felt my fear of future loss or failure competing with my desire to share love & friendship, for control of the feelings in my mind.

Now as an adult, when I look back at my memories of growing up, I realize that I may have lost my spiritual connection to my unconditional love for all the life around me, when I started to falsely view other human beings as my adversaries, who I felt were spiritually separated from me by the unfairness they created in my life and who my ego convinced me to compete with to obtain my share of the scarce resources in the world that would provide me with external joy & happiness, when my offers of internal love & friendship were rejected by potential new friends during my childhood.

I blamed myself for many of these rejections because I felt there was something wrong inside me, a wrongness that was preventing other human beings from loving me.

And I allowed my ego to convince me to obtain external joy & happiness, such as fame & fortune, so I would no longer need to feel internal love for the unfair human beings in my life who I believed were now spiritually separate from me and who I believed may reject me & my offers of love & friendship in the future.

Fortunately, I was able to learn how to kill my primordial fear of future loss or failure that lived in my mind for so many years and I was able to fully reconnect to My Internal Source of Unconditional love that I was born with, by practicing The Nine Steps to Emotional Freedom. This allowed me to love everyone in my life, once again, with the powerful passion of my childhood that I had not felt since I was a young child.

To accomplish this I had to learn how to stop my ego from controlling my mind with feelings of fear & anger.

I want to share this wisdom with you to help you understand The Nature of Our Egos, so I will quote from Our Book Three which is devoted to understanding how Our Egos try to take control of our lives, to make us falsely believe that we are spiritually separate from other human beings, who we need to compete with to get our share of the scarce resources in the world, to become able to experience continuous external joy & happiness in our lives.

"Unfortunately, as I grew up, my painful memories increased as I experienced more rejection & unfairness in my life.

Fortunately, many human beings accepted my desire to love them during my childhood and I felt secure when I was with them because I knew they valued my friendship and they would not reject me. When a new friend accepted my love, I started to feel the love from my new friend & I started to feel secure, as I started to feel the expectation that we would share fun & adventures as our mutual love & friendship for each other continued to grow.

Unfortunately, I created my ego in my mind for the first time when I was very young, when other human beings rejected me, when I realized that I did not know how to stop the fear & anger that was created by this rejection, from hurting me. Then, whenever I relived these memories of rejection, I became afraid that I would not obtain lasting external joy & happiness in my life because others were continuing to treat me unfairly, as they continued to reject me, when they tried to manipulate me, lie to me, steal from me, or abuse me.

I started to think that these unfair people were my adversaries who were spiritually separate from me because they did not love me when they rejected me. I constructed my ego in my mind to help me to understand why I was being treated unfairly because I was afraid someone would treat me unfairly again in the future.

From the time I was a young child until I became an adult, I mentally ran away from my fear & anger because I could not stop it from hurting me.

Unfortunately, turning to my ego for help has become a powerful addiction in my life that I am beginning to realize is difficult for me to break because I have been allowing my ego to automatically take control of my mind for many years, whenever I start to feel fear & anger in my life.

As a result of allowing my ego to manage my fear & anger, my ego has become a powerful make believe person in my mind, whose advice I automatically follow.

My ego uses its power over me, to lie to me, so it can maintain control of my mind & actions, by telling me that I am spiritually separate from the human beings in the world, who become my adversaries whenever they reject me.

My ego continues to lie to me, when it tells me that I can reduce my feelings of fear & anger by treating other human beings as my adversaries.

My ego tells me that when I gain power over my adversaries, I can begin to control them, so they will no longer be able to reject me and they will no longer be able to generate new fear & anger in my future life.

Then, I began to realize that my ego was being created & controlled by my fear of rejection, my fear of being hurt in human relationships and my fear of potential loss or failure in all other activities that I may undertake in the future. This knowledge helped me to learn how to stop my ego from controlling me, so I could stop the fear & anger that is buried inside my unfair memories of rejection, from hurting me again in the future.

I have learned that in all areas of my life, as I work, study, socialize or play, my ego is afraid that I will fail when I try to obtain control of the scarce resources in the world, such as the love & friendship of another human being that will generate external joy & happiness in my life, so my ego tries to take control of my mind & actions by trying to convince me that its FALSE beliefs about my life are true.

My Ego FALSELY believes that I should not try to reconnect to My Internal Source of Unconditional Love because my ego is afraid that it will start to lose control of my mind and it will no longer be able to help me, as I begin to stop feeding it the energy of fear & anger from my memories that is keeping it alive & active inside my conscious mind, as I start to replace this fear & anger in my conscious mind with feelings of love, peace, joy & compassion, when I start to fully reconnect to My Internal Source of Unconditional Love that automatically starts to feed me these life affirming feelings.

This is the source of unconditional love that I was born possessing when I first appeared on Earth as a beautiful helpless baby, who needed love, food, clothing, shelter, protection & safety to survive and then prosper in my new life, as I became a loving child who was encouraged to learn to laugh, talk, walk, run & play by my parents & guardians.

Unfortunately, My Adult Ego is afraid of dying and it is afraid of my ability to take back control of my mind, so it tries to convince me that I will not be able to find a way to reduce my feelings of fear & anger without its help, as it tries to convince me to continue allowing it to control my mind & actions.

My Ego FALSELY believes that I must obtain the scarce resources in the world that generate external joy & happiness in my life, so I can reduce my feelings of fear & anger, when I feel spiritually separate from other people, when they treat me unfairly, by using these external resources to persuade other people to help me to feel friendship & emotional security, such as when I obtain the scarce resources of love & support from my friends & family.

My Ego FALSELY believes that when I lose control of these scarce resources, when someone treats me unfairly, I will start to feel fear & anger again because I feel spiritually separate from other people who I can no longer persuade to comfort me, until I have regained control of the scarce resources that will give me power over other people. My power is based on my control over the scarce resources that other people want. I will give other people a share of these scarce resources that I control, only if they do what I want them to do, such as when I become a multi-millionaire and I use my scarce resource of money to buy a large family home on an estate and a vacation villa on a tropical island and I use the power of my money to persuade the staff, that I hire to maintain these properties for me, to comfort me so I no longer feel afraid & insecure.

Other Scarce Resources that my ego craves to become able to provide me with feelings of external joy & happiness are:

Driving an expensive car so I can feel superior to others who do not have one

Wearing expensive clothes that make me feel attractive & desirable to others

Travelling in luxury to exotic destinations for fun & adventures

Being married to an attractive desirable spouse who makes others jealous of me

Maintaining a high level of financial success that makes me feel secure

Having sex with anyone I feel attracted too that can be bought with money or my ability to provide them with help & support

Seeking revenge on those who have treated me unfairly

Mingling with the rich & famous to feel worthy of living

My Ego FALSELY believes that many people will not offer me friendship just because they like me or love me. When I become rich, many people will offer to become my friends because they hope to gain a share of my wealth & security when I party with them or offer them money or protection.

My Ego FALSELY believes that my fake friends will try to use me to get what they want from me and then when they have what they want from me, they will dump me and no longer be my friends. This is why my ego wants me to become financially secure by obtaining control over the scarce resource of money, so I can use my money to control other people, who will try to use me & abuse me by faking friendships that are full of lies.

Other scarce resources, such as becoming famous & adored by the general public, are harder to obtain and my ego realizes that I may not be able to get a share of these scarce resources when they are controlled by other people.

My Ego FALSELY believes that I will not be able to obtain continuous external joy & happiness unless I can maintain my control of the external scarce resources which I FALSELY believe I need for my external joy & happiness.

My Ego FALSELY believes that when another human being does not give me control of a scarce resource in the world that I believe will help to provide me with continuous external joy & happiness, then, I should manipulate this person to get control of the resource by lying, cheating or stealing from him.

My Ego FALSELY believes I should feel no remorse for my bad behavior because this person is my adversary who deserves my unfair treatment when he does not give me a share of the scarce resource that I need for external joy & happiness, when I ask for control of a share of the resource.

My Ego is a defense mechanism that my mind created when I was very young, when I faced obstacles in my life and I did not have success in obtaining external joy & happiness with my offers of love & friendship. It is the mechanism that my mind uses to try to understand why I have not succeeded in obtaining the scarce resources that my ego wants for me, to be able to enjoy my external life. It is the mechanism my mind uses to justify me taking control of the source of a scarce resource when the person controlling a resource says, "NO" to me, when I ask for a share of this resource. Then, I start treating this person as my adversary who I must compete with to gain control of the scarce resource that I falsely believe I need for external joy & happiness.

An example of this occurred in my childhood when another child rejected me when I asked to be allowed to play with his friends on a baseball team. Then, my ego started to look for ways to control this child, so I offered him a bribe and then I asked an older child to threaten him with harm when he rejected my bribe.

My Ego is Created by Errors in My Thinking

The errors occur, when I allow my ego to convince me that I need scarce resources to obtain external peace & joy in my life, when I falsely believe that other people are in control of my life, and when I falsely believe that I will become a victim, unless I can get control of the scarce resources that my Ego wants to make me feel happy & secure.

All of my ego's false beliefs are based on my fear of rejection, my fear of being hurt, my fear of failure, and my fear of potential future loss of something that I FALSELY believe is precious to me, such as my desire to obtain fame & fortune that I mistakenly believe will provide me with continuous external joy & happiness.

Unfortunately, the fear & anger that is buried inside my memories will continue to enter my conscious mind and stop the external joy & happiness that comes from fame & fortune from comforting me for long periods of time because I will continue to relive the unfair painful memories of the fear & anger that have accumulated during my lifetime from when I was a child until now as an adult, because I have not learned how to prevent these painful memories from hurting me, as they automatically reappear in my mind, time & time again, when I cannot stop these memories from hurting me whenever I relive them.

My challenge is to keep my ego from controlling my mind & actions because that will lead to more pain & suffering in my future life, as I continue to relive these unfair painful memories of fear & anger and as I alienate other people, as I start to compete with them to obtain the scarce resources in the world that my ego craves.

Fortunately, I have learned that I can make a choice when I get out of bed each morning of my future life, either to allow my ego to take control of my mind as I feed it new fear & anger from my memories of the unfair pain & suffering that I experienced in my past life, **OR** I can ask My Compassionate Watcher to control my ego by becoming My True Self, as I decide to fully reconnect to My Internal Source of Unconditional Love, which is living inside of me, to become able to experience continuous internal joy & happiness in the present moment, instead of trying to gain control of the scarce resources in the external world, such as fame & fortune, that will supply me with inconsistent & unfulfilling external joy & happiness in the future.

I am learning to control my ego by reducing the amount of new fear & anger that is being fed to my ego from the painful memories that I am reliving each day of my life, by learning to practice killing the Unfairness in My Memories, so my memories will not be able to feed new fear & anger to my ego when I wake up in the morning, to enable me to begin my morning without feeling the fear of potential loss or failure during this day, and instead, to enable me to wake up each morning with feelings of internal love, peace, joy & compassion when I think about the challenges that I will face today.

Now, my ego is starting to die because I am no longer feeding my ego any new feelings of fear & anger from my memories, as this lack of energy prevents my ego from controlling my conscious mind, as I continue to work on My Goals, as I embrace the new challenges in my life that are helping ne to share increasing unconditional love with my friends, family & co-workers." (End of quote from Our Book Three on The Nature of Our Egos)

Becoming My True Self

To become My True Self, without the influence of my ego in my daily life, I am reminding myself that I am Pure Eternal Spiritual Energy of the Universe who I call My Compassionate Watcher who is fully reconnected to my internal source of love, peace, joy & compassion that provides me with powerful motivation to accomplish My Goals for Today.

When I experience this energy of internal unconditional love that has been given to me by the vast limitless source of universal unconditional love that permeates the universe in which we all live, I realize that I am not alone. I am connected to all life in the universe by these energy strings of love. (Please refer to The Energy Strings of The Universe section in Chapter 22 of Our Book One)

And I realize that I do not need to acquire scarce resources in the external world to make me happy because my internal source of love provides me with all the love that I need to share with my friends & family which will enable us to share happiness when we are together, when we share our love & forgiveness with each other. I realize that my ego is wrong when it tries to motivate me to treat other human beings as my adversaries so I can obtain control of these scarce resources of external joy & happiness. With this realization I have decided that I will not allow my ego to seductively gain control of my mind so that it can sucker me into following its demands to obtain external joy & happiness that I do not need in my life.

Unfortunately, I now realize that many adults are unable to fully reconnect to their internal source of unconditional love, to become able to experience increased love, peace, joy & compassion in their daily lives because they are afraid to look inside their minds at their painful memories, which are hiding their internal source of unconditional love that they were born possessing and which is still alive inside them.

When I read the spiritual books of the wise sages, I learned that anyone who does look inside his mind at his painful memories is considered to be a rare & precious person, for having the courage to endure the pain & suffering that he finds, when he looks inside his mind and then starts to experience his unfair painful memories, as he searches for his internal source of unconditional love, as he begins to learn how to stop the unfair pain & suffering, to enable him to replace the unfair pain & suffering from his memories with continuous feelings of love, peace, joy & compassion, when he is able to locate and fully reconnect to his internal source of unconditional love.

My Ego realizes that when I reconnect to my internal source of love, I will use this love energy to convince my memories to stop generating the fear & anger that is keeping my ego alive and I will stop treating other human beings as my adversaries because I no longer need to compete with other human beings for external joy & happiness that I no longer need in my life.

Now that I am reconnecting to this love, I am trying to treat all human beings equally with honesty & respect as I offer to share with them the powerful unconditional love that is continuously flowing through me to them from my unlimited internal resources of unconditional love, without requesting anything from them.

And my ego is beginning to realize that it is starting to lose control of my mind & actions as I fully reconnect to my internal source of unconditional love for all human beings in the external world. So my ego is trying to prevent me from fully reconnecting to my internal source of unconditional love that is generating my internal love, peace, joy & compassion because my ego feels threatened, as it becomes afraid of dying.

Please answer these questions in your own words:

Do I have an Ego and if so, how do I learn to control my ego so it will no longer be able to control me, when I feel that the life all around me is being unfair to me and when I start to feel afraid of the future events in my life? Q-67

Does every human being in the world have an Ego, such as the one that is trying to control my mind & actions as it motivates me to feel separate from other human beings, so it can convince me to start competing with other human beings by lying, cheating & stealing from them, to become able to obtain my share of the scarce resources in the world that I mistakenly believe will bring me continuous external joy & happiness? Q-68

What is my ego trying to convince me to do and what impact will this action have on my life, today? Q-69

My answers to these three questions have helped me to learn to understand the nature of my ego and how to prevent it from hurting me and those I love, in the future.

My Ego's Belief in Separation

I realize that my ego has been trying to isolate me all my life.

My Ego wants me to think that I live separately from all the life surrounding me, because with that belief, it can rationalize grabbing as much for me to become mine, as it can, by treating other human beings as my adversaries.

However, My Internal Source of Unconditional Love does not want me to treat other human beings as my adversaries. It wants me to share unconditional love & nurture true friendship with all human beings that I know.

To help you to understand how Our Egos try to separate us from other human beings, please review our human history when human beings with large egos treated others as their adversaries when they passed laws to enable them to enslave other people. Even today, enslaving other human beings continues as billions of dollars are being made in illegal human trafficking around the world each year because many countries do not have the financial resources or the political will power to stop human trafficking.

So, if you have an Ego that is trying to gain control of your mind & actions to convince you that other human beings are your potential future adversaries, who you must complete with, to enable you to obtain the scarce resources that are necessary for your external joy & happiness, please realize that your ego is afraid of the wisdom in this book because it realizes that as you learn this wisdom and apply it your life, your ego will start to lose its control over your mind & actions, as you begin to stop chasing things in the external world that you hope will make you feel happy & secure, as you start to embrace your Internal Source of Unconditional Love that lives inside of you, as it starts to nourish you with internal love, peace, joy & compassion, as you start to remember the wisdom of your childhood when you felt powerful love for all human beings, especially your friends & family.

It took me many years to learn how to stop feeding my ego the unfair thinking energy that was keeping it alive, before I was able to say that I have become The Master of My Ego by learning how to kill my ego's attempt to take control over my mind whenever I started to feel new fear & anger being generated by an unfair painful memory that I was starting to relive or by a new unfair external event in my life that had just occurred.

Now that I am The Master of My Ego, I am fully reconnected to the internal source of unconditional love of my childhood that is automatically generating continuous feelings of love, peace, joy & compassion into my adult life because I have learned how to kill the fear, angry, worry or stress that I may start to feel in my life, whenever I relive the unresolved pain & suffering that is buried inside one of my unfair painful memories.

Fortunately, my ego no longer receives sufficient fear & anger from my memories to energize itself back into my life for long periods of time, to enable my ego to start blocking my connection to my internal source of unconditional love, once again. (Please refer to Killing the Unfairness in My Memories section in Chapter 26 of Our Book One)

Your ego will try to stop you from learning this wisdom by distracting you, as you read the wisdom in Our Book.

For this reason, we have repeated the wisdom in Our Book many times, in slightly different ways, to help you to overcome your ego's resistance to The Wisdom of Children.

We could have written Our Book in fewer pages, but we do not believe that this approach will provide sufficient repetition, that may be necessary for many readers of Our Book, to become able to kill the control their ego has over their lives.

I hope & pray that you will be able to gain control over your ego, quickly.

Unfortunately, it took me many years to gain control over my ego, as I slowly learned all the tricks that my ego was using to control me. The wisdom in Our Book One will help you to do this in less time. However, please do not jump to Our Book Three and start reading about how to gain complete control over your ego. You will need to learn the Meditation & Mindfulness techniques that helped us to understand The Science of The Mind that you will write about in your own words as you read the wisdom in Our Book Two, wisdom that will enable you to become a Master of the Meditation & Mindfulness techniques that you will need to practice to become able to win all your battles with your ego for complete control of your thinking energy, as you learn how to master your ego.

So, please be patient with your progress as you practice the wisdom in Our Book One that will teach you the basics of how to gain control over your ego. I hope that you will learn to become a master of this wisdom, quickly. Other readers of Our Book One may proceed slowly like me, and it will take them years to master this wisdom.

Fortunately, when we were born we were given the gift of Free Will that enables us to become wise by deciding to learn The Wisdom of Children which enables us to increase the love, peace, joy & compassion in our lives, when we make the conscious decision to continue practicing, even when the pain in our memories makes it difficult to do so. All we have to do is to decide to continue Practicing The Wisdom of Children, by making the effort to apply this wisdom to our lives and by being patient with our progress, whether it is fast, slow, or somewhere in between.

And, I am asking you to practice forgiving My Son & me for all the repetition of the wisdom in Our Book that we believe will help you to overcome the resistance of your ego, to enable you to regain full control of your thinking energy & actions, to enable you to kill all the major unfair pain in your memories, and to enable you to kill any unfair pain, suffering, worry & stress that may try to enter your conscious mind when you wake up each morning, as you start thinking about the challenges you will encounter during the day.

Once you acquire mastery over your ego, you will wake up each morning with a song in your heart, as you start to feel continuous internal love, peace, joy & compassion, as you begin to take on the challenges of each new day of your life, with eagerness & anticipation, as you think about the fun filled adventures that your new day will offer you, as you once did when you were a young child, when you woke up each day excited about life because you were in love with all the life around you and you felt loved by all this life. The wisdom in Our Book will help you to recapture these childhood feelings.

I cannot prove that you are capable of renewing your powerful childhood passion for living and renewing your compelling childhood motivation to share unconditional love & nurture true friendship with your friends & family. You have to prove this is true for yourself, by practicing the wisdom in Our Book and by continuously forgiving your friends & family for the unfair pain that they may create in your future life.

You will learn to kill the control that your ego has over your life, as you become able to increase the internal love, peace, joy & compassion that you feel each day of your life, as you kill the pain buried inside your painful memories of the unfairness from your past life that unfortunately you may be reliving each day of your life, as you remember your past regrets, the people who hurt you, or the loved ones you have lost.

Please answer these questions in your own words, as you learn to detach from your ego. These answers will help you to understand how your ego tries to control your mind & your actions,

How does my ego try to make me feel spiritually separate from my friends & family, at times, when I become upset with the unfairness in my life and I start to treat those I love as my adversaries when I start to crave fairness, justice or revenge because of the unfairness they are generating in my life? Q-70

How do I learn to Choose My Feelings so I can choose to forgive those who treat me unfairly and then, so I can start to offer them unconditional love, once again, when I am able to kill my ego's desire to treat my love ones as my adversaries? Q-71

(Please refer to Imagining My Alter Ego section in Chapter 13 & Killing My Ego's Ability to Hurt Me section in Chapter 27 of Our Book One)

Chapter 19

Choosing My Feelings

"To prevent my ego from controlling my mind & my life, I start my daily practice of Choosing My Feelings each morning when I get out of bed, as I walk to the exercise room to start my aerobic exercises and I begin to concentrate on feeling my breath move in & out of my lungs, as I start continuous control meditation to maintain my awareness of my breathing throughout the day.

Then as I exercise, I start continuous release mediation to enable me to expand my awareness outward from my breathing to all the revealed activities in my conscious mind to become able to see and then detach from any new distracting feeling that may enter my mind during the day, by saying, "no" to following its desire to get me to act to bring more pleasure into my life or to avoid potential pain, when this desire tries to stop me working on My Goals for Today.

And whenever a distracting desire, my ego or a new event in my life gains control of my mind and stops me from working on My Goals during the day, I am restarting continuous control & release meditation once again, to regain control of my mind, to enable me to restart working on My Goals for Today." (Quote from Learning to Choose My Feelings section of Our Book Three)

Then at the end of the day, when I look back at each hour of the day and I review my successes and my failures during the day, I can say that I have tried to choose my feelings throughout the day.

And as a result of being able to choose the feelings that have motivated me to work on My Goals during the day, I am able to congratulate myself, as I reaffirm that I have had a successful day and as I reaffirm that I am an unconditional loving human being who feels worthy of living because I am able to Choose My Feelings throughout each new day of my future adult life, as I continue to accomplish my goals for increasing the love, peace, joy & compassion in my life and in the lives of my friends & family.

(Please refer to The Key to Choosing All My Feelings, Thoughts & Images section in Chapter 23 of Our Book One)

Chapter 20

The Battle for Improvements is the Battle against Relapses

"As I improve my adult ability to Choose My Feelings, I often relapse back to being controlled by painful feelings that motivate me to treat others as my adversaries. My relapses were many when I started to practice Choosing My Feelings, but now they are less frequent. Each time I relapse, I reaffirm that I was born as a human being who is prone to making many mistakes when I allow my ego to control me.

Fortunately, I was born with the ability to use my Free Will to correct my mistakes by stopping my ego from controlling me in the future, to become able to successfully choose my feelings and to become able to generate continuous love, peace, joy & compassion in my life, instead of allowing my ego to generate new fear & anger into my life.

It is Okay to make a mistake, as long as I try to learn from my mistake and as long as I try to prevent the same mistake from re-occurring. Each time I make a mistake, I say that I am an unconditionally loving human being who is entitled to make a mistake, as long as I do not hurt other human beings when I do so. I do not say that I am unworthy of living when I make a mistake. I say that I am worthy of living because I have the ability to correct my mistakes and to become successful, when I recover from my mistakes.

I realize that I am entitled to make mistakes and then correct them, as part of the challenge of evolving into a more unconditionally loving human being, a challenge that I realize I was born to accept and I was born to successfully accomplish, as I practice believing in The Law of Karma which tells me that my friends & family will ultimately be fair to me, as we try to increase the love & compassion that we share with each other.

I view each mistake that I make during the day as an opportunity to evolve, as I learn to choose more of my feelings and as I learn to continuously forgive myself for continuing to make new mistakes. As I correct each mistake, I am reaffirming that I am an unconditionally loving human being who is worthy of living my life successfully. I am proving this is true, by learning to continuously choose my feelings to help motivate me to fulfill the unique purpose & to experience the special meaning, of my life." (Quote from Learning to Choose My Feelings section of Our Book Three)

"It is as if I was born as a unique human being with a particular skill set of abilities, that no one who has ever lived has had and that no one in future will have. It is as if I am an experiment for living life successfully that will never be created in the same way again. My unique set of skills is inspiring me, to fulfill the unique purpose and to experience the special meaning of my life, which is to share unconditional love & nurture true friendship with all human beings in the world, especially my friends & family. I am unique, special & blessed to be given the opportunity to experience life as an unconditional loving human being on our precious Mother Earth." (Modified quote from A Spiritual Journey with My Son Wil section in Chapter 6 of Our Book One)

Chapter 21

Who Loves Me Enough to Save Me?

Who loves me enough to save me, when I am danger of being hurt?
Q-72

The answer:

When I was a child it was my mother & father

Now that I am adult, it would be my friends & family who share
unconditional love & nurture true friendship with me, a love that
motivates them with a powerful desire to preserve and nurture my
life & well-being.

For example, my wife & son share their love with me each day and
they also scold me whenever I attempt to do something stupid, in
order to prevent me from getting into trouble, so they will not be
compelled by their love to save me from my folly.

Please list the names of your friends & family who would try to save
you when you get into trouble and then ask each one of them
privately, why they value you enough to try to help you when you
are in danger of being hurt.

And if you do not have anyone in your life at the present moment
who would try to save you from being hurt, then please realize that
your increasing ability to love others more powerfully will begin to
motivate others to love you enough to help save you from being hurt
in the future.

And there are many others out there in the world who you do not
know, who are already preparing to save you from future hurt, such
as the nurses & doctors in our hospitals, the police, the military
protecting our nation, our religious & cultural leaders and believe it

or not, our politicians when they are not acting in their own self-interest.

And who would **not** be willing to save me from being hurt?

The answer:

Anyone whose mind is being controlled by his ego when his ego motivates him to treat me as his adversary, will not be willing to save me, whenever he feels that I am preventing him from gaining access to a potential source of external joy that he wants in his future life.

This could be a friend who I refuse to lend money to or a child who wants me to buy him a new toy, when I say "No" to each of them, as their egos start to feel anger and start to treat me as an adversary, when they tell me that I am treating them unfairly.

Please list the names of your friends & family who may not be willing to save you from being hurt because they are being controlled by their egos.

Please realize that the control their egos have over their lives is temporary and that they will reconnect to their internal source of love & joy in the future, a love that will motivate them to kill their egos control over them as their desire to love & protect you from harm fills their minds once again, as this love motivates them to rescue you whenever you get into trouble.

Answering these questions will help you to understand why we desire to help one another when they are trouble and why saving another person's life is important to our future well-being as human beings because we were born to share unconditional love with everyone in our lives and the answers to these questions will help you to understand how our egos sometimes try to prevent us from helping others whenever our egos motivate us to treat others as our adversaries.

Chapter 22

The Desire for Unconditional Love & True Friendship

My Son & I believe that all human beings want to share unconditional love & nurture true friendship with everyone in their lives. This includes those who have created unfair pain & suffering in our lives. Please allow this desire for love & friendship that all human beings possess to bond us together as you read Our Book, as we describe our childhood ability to share love & friendship, an ability that we were given when we were born. Your childhood experiences may be different than ours, but they are also similar to ours because we are human beings who share the same ability to love, to forgive, to make mistakes & to ask for forgiveness.

When we were young children we felt the unconditional love emanating from all the life around us and we felt love for all this life, as we tried to share our love with everyone in our lives, with our innocence expectation that we would become True Friends, as we enjoyed sharing fun & adventures as we played together with our friends & family.

Unfortunately, as we grew up we started to carry the memories of having our love rejected by the negative people in our lives, who were in pain & suffering and who were not able to offer us love & friendship, when we offered them our unconditional love.

Unfortunately for many of us, by the time we became adults our painful memories of rejection and of being hurt with unfairness started to hide our connection to our internal source of love, peace, joy & compassion that we felt as children.

As a result of these negative experiences, many of us lost our ability to love other people unconditionally because our love became hidden under all the memories of the pain of unfairness in our past lives, which many of us are still reliving each day of our future lives because we have not learned how to stop these painful memories from hurting us.

When this happens to us, our love becomes conditional as we start making demands on other people for their love, commitment & security before we are willing to offer them our love. We are afraid of being rejected & hurt unfairly, as we have been so many times in the past. We have lost our courage to love other people without making demands on them, to not betray our love, before we are willing to offer them our love.

Even though we are afraid, we have not lost our childhood desire for unconditional love & true friendship. We are still searching for the wisdom of how to love other human beings unconditionally and how to manage the pain that we feel when we relive our memories of rejection, of being hurt, and of being treated unfairly.

As we realize that there is something important that is missing from our adult lives, we begin to understand that we need to reconnect to the full power of the source of unconditional love that lives inside us, to a love that we used to feel when we were young children and a love that will enable us to live our adult lives with more passion, without the fear of future rejection & unfairness, so we can love our friends & family more affectionately without making demands on them and so we can use the immense power of the unconditional love of our childhood to become able to forgive our friends & family more easily, when they hurt us again in the future, even though this new unfairness may be unintentional.

When our need to feel this unconditional love becomes an insatiable burning desire, each of us starts trying to find answers to this question,

"How do I fully reconnect to the internal source of love, peace, joy & compassion of my childhood, so I can start to feel & then share this powerful unconditional love with all the life that is surrounding me, especially with my friends & family? Q-17"

(Quote from the Learning to Understand My True Self section in Chapter 6 of Our Book One)

To help you answer this question, so you can start to fully reconnect to the sources of unconditional love that you felt when you were a young child, My Son & I offered you the wisdom of The Nine Steps to Emotional Freedom that enables you to stop your unfair painful memories from generating any new worry & stress in your daily life and we helped you to understand of how The Wisdom of Children will help you to kill any new fear & anger that your ego may generate in your life.

Practicing this wisdom will enable you to fully reconnect to your internal source of unconditional love that you were born possessing but which may have become diminished in power or completely hidden from you, by your memories of unfair pain & suffering that you are reliving each day or your life.

Now, we will continue to offer you stories of how My Son & I practiced the wisdom of the unconditional love of children, to be able to rediscover the sources of love, peace, joy & compassion that we felt as children.

As each of us grows older, hopefully, we learn to become wiser. Wisdom is the ability to discern or judge, what is true, right & lasting. Wisdom becomes an insight into the meaning of life, which becomes a search that each of us takes to find the purpose of our life. Understanding the wisdom of the meaning of our life enables us to share increasing unconditional love & true friendship with our friends & family, which helps us to fully reconnect to our sources of unconditional love that give us a powerful desire to fulfill the purpose & meaning of our life.

My Son & I will help you to rediscover The Wisdom of Children that you experienced when you were a child, as you discover or reconfirm your purpose in life as we describe how we learned to use this wisdom to fully reconnect to the internal source of powerful unconditional love for all life that all human beings are born fully connected to, and that now, many of us have diminished or lost.

The Wisdom of Children is the mental practice of nurturing & protecting the love, peace, joy & compassion that lives inside me and the physical practice of sharing this unconditional love when I offer true friendship to another human being." (Modified Quote from The Essence of The Wisdom of Children section in Chapter 8 of Our Book One)

When I was a young elementary school student and I studied the nature of unconditional love from the sages who are venerated for their possession of wisdom, judgment & experience, such as Buddha, Mohammed, Lao-tzu & Jesus, I began to realize that I was learning to nurture & protect the love, peace, joy & compassion in my life as I studied how the sages were able to live their daily lives with powerful unconditional love. As I grew up, this knowledge helped me to recover from the many mistakes that I made, to recover from the pain of rejection, to recover from being hurt, and to recover from the unfair experiences of my childhood.

As a young student, I slowly began to realize that the unfair events in my life were generating opportunities for me to learn how to unconditionally love all life with an increased understanding of and compassion for all the new suffering & setbacks in my personal life that required me to learn how to stay motivated, so I could continue to accept the many opportunities for new fun & adventures in my life that were being offered to me each day, as I tried to fully understand why I was continuing to lose the full power of my unconditional love & motivation, as I grew older.

It was not until I became an adult that I was able to fully understand the wisdom of the sages that enabled me to add more power to my ability to share unconditional love & nurture true friendship. And it was not until I fully understood the source of the unconditional love that My Son shared with me, when he was a baby, that I was able to fully reconnect to the full power of the unconditional love for all the life around me, a full power that I used in my daily life when I was a child.

Then, I finally understood that the major purpose of my life is the sharing of unconditional love & the nurturing of true friendship with all human beings and it was my love for My Son that motivated me to start writing Our Book which tells stories of how we shared our journey through life together as Father & Son, as we used the wisdom of the sages to increase the love, peace, joy & compassion in our daily lives, so that we could learn to protect our ability to share unconditional love with our friends & family. Then, I asked My Son to help me to write our new book in his own words, so his stories about life would encourage our readers to rewrite the wisdom in Our Book in their own words, as My Son has done.

Hopefully, the stories of our spiritual journey together will inspire you to benefit from the wisdom of the sages that we describe in Our Book. Thousands of years ago, our ancient sages looked inside their minds to understand the source of their wisdom of unconditional love. This is the same universal source of unconditional love of our childhood that you & I are now beginning to understand will benefit our adult lives, as we start to remember when we were very young, when we felt this unconditional love that was powering our motivation to learn to talk & walk and run & play with our friends & family when we were children.

As My Son & I learned the wisdom of the sages and begin to share it, as adults, our friends & family started to benefit from the increased love, peace, joy & compassion that we felt each day, as we used our renewed compassion to help end the unfair pain & suffering in their lives, as we helped to increase the love & forgiveness that they shared with each other, and as we begin to share new fun & adventures with our friends & family.

I know that the love you experience in your daily life will start to increase because I am now experiencing the increased unconditional love that this wisdom has brought into the lives of my friends & family. This experience has given me a deep personal satisfaction, that I feel each day, as I use my connection to the powerful sources of unconditional love that lives inside me to help love all life on Earth, as My Son & I offer this wisdom to all human beings that we know, to help them to increase the love that they feel & share with their friends & family, as they become more motivated to nurture &

protect all the life on our environmentally fragile planet and as they become increasing able to live their lives with greater passion.

Please answer these questions in your own words,

Who do I want to share unconditional love with today? Why? Q-73

Who do I want to nurture true friendship with today? Why? Q-74

Our Book describes how I lost my connection to the sources of unconditional love that I first experienced when I was a child and Our Book describes how I was able to rediscover the wisdom of this love, to become able to share unconditional love & nurture true friendship with all human beings, once again, as I became able to fully reconnect to my childhood sources of unconditional love with the help of My Son.

The Energy Strings of The Universe

My ability to understand the wisdom of my childhood, as I became able to discover the meaning of my life and as I became able to experience continuous love, peace, joy & compassion during each day of my adult life, started to develop long before I was born, with the creation of the atoms that make up all life in universe, after the universe was formed 13.8 billion years ago, long before the first human beings walked on Earth.[22]

Way back then, the energy of the universe arose from a primordial state in The Big Bang, when the universe started expanding at the beginning of universal time from a dense core of primordial energy the size of a dime. The universe is continuing to expand at an increasing rate today. Scientists tell us that the energy of The Big Bang was made up of tiny strings of energy that were connected to each other and that each energy string was aware of what the other strings were doing. These tiny strings of energy are still connected to each other today and each string still has the awareness of what the other strings of energy are doing, even when two strings are separated by vast distances in space & eons of time.

The evidence of the ability of the tiny strings of energy to communicate & work with each other can be observed when we look at the stars at night and realize that the laws of the physical universe are being maintained by the tiny strings of energy, as they provide energy to keep the planets orbiting around their stars, as they have been doing for billions of years.

As human beings, we have this primordial energy inside of us. Each of the atoms in our bodies is made up of these tiny strings of energy. The smaller atoms in our bodies were made by these infinitesimal energy strings in the immense heat & pressure of stars, like our sun. The heat & light that is created inside a star is a byproduct of the nuclear fusion of hydrogen atoms into helium atoms in the center of the star. When a star, the same size as our sun, runs out of its supply of hydrogen, that it needs to fuel its nuclear reactor, the star starts to collapse onto itself as the forces of gravity increase the heat & pressure inside the dying star. As the star dies, the increased heat & pressure at its core creates atoms heavier than helium up to the size of a large iron atom.

The atoms in our bodies larger than iron, such as selenium, were made during the collapse of stars even bigger than our sun, stars that were at least nine times more massive than our sun. The violent collapse of these huge stars, when they ran out of their supply of hydrogen to burn as nuclear fuel to keep the star alive, resulted in explosions that generated the extreme heat & pressure that is necessary to create atoms heavier than iron. Our planet Earth benefited from these supernova explosions that spread the newly created heavy atoms throughout the universe. It is these heavy atoms that helped to create our Earth when it formed 4.5 billion years ago, and after billions of years on our Earth, it is these heavy atoms that helped the organic life on our planet to evolve into the first human beings. It was the supernova explosions of gigantic stars, billions of years ago before the Earth was born, that created the heavy atoms that now live in our human bodies that enable you & me to live on Earth today.

The tiny primordial energy strings from the Big Bang, that created our universe, continue to power the atoms in our bodies that were created in these supernova explosions. This primordial energy keeps the electrons spinning inside each of the trillions of atoms inside each of us. The atoms in our bodies which we acquire from the food we eat, the air we breathe, and the water we drink, are billions of years old.

Inside each of the atoms in our human bodies, electrons have been spinning around the atom's core for billions of years and have not slowed down, as our desire to understand this process creates obvious questions in our minds,

Were electrons designed by a creator or by random chance, to keep spinning forever? Q-75

Where does an electron's continuous self-sustaining energy come from? Q-76

Present day scientists do not understand the source of the energy strings that power the electrons spinning around the cores of the trillions of atoms living inside each human being. All we can do for now is to accept that they exist and that they are powering our lives, as they provide us primordial energy free of charge.

Man has been trying to reconnect to this primordial energy for thousands of years by looking for its source inside our minds & bodies. Also mankind has been looking outside of our minds & bodies at the universe, for evidence of the primordial energy of The Big Bang in our celestial observations of the stars. Now, we are using our understanding that we have derived from these observations to try to recreate the processes which powered The Big Bang that created our universe.

The major finding of this search for knowledge about the evolution of the universe and the evolution of human beings, so far, is that the primordial energy exists and that the forms it takes are impermanent. The forms such as our bodies & the stars arise due to secondary causes and remain for a limited time, years or eons, and then disappear. None of the energy strings are lost in this process. The primordial energy of the atoms is not lost as expressed in Einstein's equation $E=Mc^2$. Matter is not lost. It is converted into energy by processes such as nuclear fission and the reverse is true, with nuclear fusion scientists are creating matter from energy.[23]

Questions about The Meaning of My Life

As human beings, when we explore inside our minds & bodies and feel the power of this primordial energy, as we work with this energy to allow our bodies to function as human beings, we begin to wonder where this energy comes from, and then we begin to ask the questions that philosophers have been asking for centuries, to begin to understand why this energy powers our lives, as unconditionally loving human beings.

> Who am I? Q-20
> Where did I come from? Q-21
> Why am I here on Earth? Q-22
> What is my life's purpose? Q-23

Our Book is dedicated to developing answers to these questions that are based on our life experiences of applying the wisdom of the ancient & modern philosophers to our daily lives. Doing this enables us to adopt a true wisdom that works to improve the well-being of our lives and enables us to reject any false wisdom that diminishes our life experiences.

My life has become filled with challenges & setbacks as I continue to search for answers to these questions. My Son helped me to answer these questions about my life's purpose, when he taught me to remember the unconditional love I felt as a child and he helped me to become a child of love, once again, as he began to share his love for all life with me when he was a baby.

With our answers, we will be able to take you on an amazing journey, as you participate with us in trying to find the answers to these questions, as we give you the opportunity to practice the wisdom of children in your life, as you begin to realize that this wisdom is working for you, as it increases the unconditional love in your life. Then this wisdom will become our shared wisdom, as we continue to explore this wisdom together, as you answer additional questions that we have asked, and then as you compare your answers to mine & My Son's.

As you continue to apply this wisdom to your life, you will become able to share this wisdom with your friends & family, as you help them to apply this wisdom to their lives, so they can increase the love, peace, joy & compassion that they share with each other & you.

The personal wisdom that you acquire on your journey of discovery will be similar but also different than ours, because you were born with unique & special skills.

"The purpose & meaning of your life may be different than mine. It is as if each of us is born as a unique human being with a particular skill set of abilities, that no one who has ever lived has had and that no one in future will have. It is as if each of us is an experiment for living life successfully that will never be created in the same way again. Your unique set of skills is inspiring you, to fulfill the unique purpose and to experience the special meaning, of your life. You are unique, special & blessed to be given the opportunity to experience life as an unconditional loving human being on our precious Mother Earth." (Modified quote from A Spiritual Journey with My Son Wil section in Chapter 6 of Our Book One)

Was my birth as a human baby the result of random chance? Q-77

Or divine creation? Q-78

Is there a divine intelligence that helped create the universe & all human beings? Q-79

Fifty years ago many scientists did not believe in God because no irrefutable evidence of God's existence could be found. In the last fifty years our understanding of the universe has increased, to the point where our scientists are starting to conclude that a divine intelligence must have guided the creation of the universe. The chances of the universe being created by random chance are becoming mathematically impossible, as our understanding of the complexity of the universe increases.

For example, the evolution of human beings on our planet Earth may be a rare event in the universe. For human beings to evolve on Earth, a number of random chances or divine occurrences within our Solar System had to occur, for Earth to be able to support complex life. Our Sun had to have a long life that many stars do not have. Our planet had to be the right distance from our Sun so that it would not be too hot or too cold for water to exist as a liquid and for complex life to evolve in this water environment. Our Earth had to be large enough to have enough gravity to keep our atmosphere from escaping into space as happened on the planet Mars. We needed our Moon to regulate the wobble of our Earth to keep the temperatures from fluctuating between extreme highs & lows to keep temperature changes moderate. We needed the huge gravitational pull of the planet Jupiter to attract the majority of random asteroids & comets in our Solar System, so they would not threaten Earth and wipe out the fragile life on our planet, as happened when the dinosaurs became extinct 65 million years ago.

The concept of how rare & remarkable our planet Earth is to support our unconditional love for all life is explained by Dr. Iain Stewart in the BBC series, Earth The Power of the Planet. Please watch this series so you can begin to appreciate that you have been given the random chance or divine opportunity, to continue to evolve as a complex life form on Earth, as part of the complex life system that our Earth, our Solar System, and the physical laws of our universe maintain, to give us the opportunity to enjoy our lives as unconditionally loving human beings and the responsibility to protect Our Precious Mother Earth.

In support of a Universal Intelligent Design for all life, scientists have recently acknowledged that Darwin's Theory of Evolution cannot explain how the intricate molecular machinery, that enables our cells to work, was created by random chance. Even though this new understanding tells us that the intricate molecular machinery in our cells may have been created with the help of an unknown universal intelligence, Darwin's Theory of Evolution is still highly regarded by scientists for its ability to explain The Evolution Of Human Life on Earth over the thousands of years of our known history after our unknown date of creation as intelligent human beings. Please watch the PBS television series by Nova on Evolution to help you to understand the important social & scientific impact that Darwin's theories have on our understanding of the history & evolution of human life on Earth, after human life's unknown creation date when a universal intelligence may have helped human life to get its start on Earth.

On the last page of his famous book, On The Origin of Species published in 1859, Charles Darwin summarizes his theory of the evolution of life of Earth when he writes,

"To my mind it accords better with what we know of the laws impressed on matter by the Creator that the production and extinction of the past and present inhabitants of the world should have been due to secondary causes, like those determining the birth and death of the individual. When I view all beings not as special creations, but as the lineal descendants of some few beings which lived long before the first bed of the Cambrian system was deposited, they seem to me to become ennobled. Judging from the past, we may safely infer that not one living species will transmit its unaltered likeness to a distant futurity. And of the species now living very few will transmit progeny of any kind to a far distant futurity; for the manner in which all organic beings are grouped, shows that the greater number of species in each genus, and all the species in many genera, have left no descendants, but have become utterly extinct. We can so far take a prophetic glance into futurity as to foretell that it will be the common and widely-spread species, belonging to the larger and dominant groups within each class, which will ultimately prevail and procreate new and dominant species. As all the living forms of life are the lineal descendants of those which lived long before the Cambrian epoch, we may feel certain that the ordinary succession by generation has never once been broken, and that no cataclysm has desolated the whole world. Hence we may look with some confidence to a secure future of great length. And as natural selection works solely by and for the good of each being, all corporeal and mental endowments will tend to progress towards perfection."

Unfortunately, Darwin's theory is not able to explain The Arrival of the Fittest Life Form, or how a new life form is created to start its evolutionary life on Earth. The evidence for a divine intelligence is shown by the complexity of the intelligent information encoded in the DNA in the cells of our body. Scientists do not know how it was created, but scientists are now starting to realize that it may not have been created by random chance.

Darwin supports the concept that there may be a divine intelligence, or a Creator, who started the evolution of all life on Earth, in the last line of his book, when he writes,

"There is grandeur in this view of life, with its several powers, having been originally breathed by the Creator into a few forms or into one; and that, whilst this planet has gone cycling on according to the fixed law of gravity, from so simple a beginning, endless forms most beautiful and most wonderful have been, and are being evolved."

The Choice to Acquire Faith

When I physically die, does my spiritual essence that is contained in My Soul, live on, because there is a Creator or a God that gives human beings eternal spiritual life or is my life at an end with no possibility of a future life for me? Q-80

I have never met anyone who has come back from the dead to tell me that there is life after death, so I do not know the answer to this question. However, I can use Faith to imagine & believe that my current life in my body is not my only opportunity to enjoy life. I can imagine what life after death is like.

I can also believe in reincarnation that tells me that my body will die, but My Spirit will live on and that someday in the future, I will be

254 Coulson/Practicing The Wisdom Of Children Our Book One

given the opportunity to live in a new body and experience a new life on Earth again.

I have chosen to live my current life based on this Faith that I will be reincarnated in a new body on Earth. My Faith may be wrong, but I no longer have a fear of death. Instead, I have Faith in a divine intelligence living in the universe that is giving me the expectation of rebirth in a new body and a new life in the future.

This belief in reincarnation supports my belief that I have an eternal soul and that My Soul is the container for My Karma, my memories of my past lives & My Eternal Mind-Stream of divine universal consciousness which I call My Compassionate Watcher, who continuously observes all the sentient life surrounding me and who I refer to every time I say the words, "I am."

Killing My Fear of Death is worth The Price of My Faith

Dr. Wayne Dyer describes Faith in his book, Your Sacred Self, when he says,

"I understand that faith is a decision that I make intentionally. Then as my decision becomes a knowing, I am beginning to sense the sacred energy that flows through everything in the form of divine intelligence in the universe. It is a mental decision to know that everything is on purpose. Faith is becoming an energy that resides within me at all times." [24]

I studied many philosophical & religious concepts that support My Faith in a divine universal intelligence who I call God. The simplest and most fundamental one that I have been able to accept is,

God is the source of all unconditional love in the universe, including mine. [25]

I have Faith that God gave me an Internal Source of Unconditional Love when I was born that is supplying me with a never ending stream of spiritual energy containing an abundance of love, peace, joy & compassion.

I know that My Internal Source of Unconditional Love is real because I experience continuous unconditional love each moment of everyday of my adult life. In this way I am experiencing my concept of God each day of my life, as I experience the unconditional love that I share with my friends & family.

I do not try to understand why I given this wonderful gift of being able to continuously connect to a never ending source of unconditional love that lives inside me. I do not have the means or the knowledge to understand why I was given this gift. I would like to know the answer, but I have decided to accept the truth that this gift is real, and to be at peace without knowing why.

I do not know where My Internal Source of Unconditional Love comes from. I have Faith that it comes from my creator, who I call God, to nurture me with love, peace, joy & compassion each day of my life. It is there inside me. It has always has been inside me since I was born. I just accept it and rest in love, peace, joy & compassion, as I realize that it will still be there inside of me tomorrow, to energize me with motivation to accomplish My Goals and to help me to enjoy my life tomorrow, as it is doing today.

It is a very satisfying personal experience. I feel blessed as I experience being fully connected to my internal source of unconditional love because many adults that I know are disconnected from their internal source of unconditional love, because all the unresolved pain & suffering in their lives is hiding it from them and they do not know how to find it again.

Unfortunately, these disconnected adults can no longer experience the unconditional love from all life that they felt as children. Being disconnected makes them feel lost, alone & afraid and that no one truly loves them, as they feel spiritually separate for all human beings. Our Egos foster this false belief. (Please refer to Studying the Wisdom in Our Book is Hazardous to My Ego! section in Chapter 18 of Our Book One)

Fortunately, when these disconnected adults begin to remember that they were connected to the love from all the life in the universe when they were young children, then they start to feel the love from all this life once again. Then, by practicing the wisdom in Our Book, they become able to experience continuous love, peace, joy & compassion in their daily lives, as they start to kill their memories of the unresolved pain & suffering in their lives that is preventing them from feeling loved by their Creator.

As Eben Alexander says in his book, Proof of Heaven, "Without recovering the memory of our larger connectedness, and of the unconditional love of our Creator, we will always feel lost here on Earth." [26]

Other human beings have different concepts of their Creator, who I call God, that are as real to them, as my understanding of God is real to me. I accept that there is not a uniform concept of God that is accepted by the religions of the world.

Fortunately, simpler concepts of God such as mine, that describe God as a God of love, fit in quite well with the majority of the concepts of God that are accepted by the world religions.

It is my belief that the most important purpose & meaning for our lives is to develop a continuous loving connection with God, who is our Creator, who gave us our ability to feel love for all the life around us, so we can fully utilize our internal source of unconditional love that we were born possessing, to share unconditional love & nurture true friendship with all human beings, especially our friends & family.

The American lyrical poet & playwright and the first woman to receive the Pulitzer Prize for Poetry, Edna St. Vincent Millay described Faith in God when she wrote,

> "Man has not invented God
> He has developed faith
> To meet a God already there" [27]

Edna St. Vincent Millay also described the joy of reincarnation in her poem Renascence,

> "O God, I cried, give me new birth,
> And put me back upon the earth!
> Upset each cloud's gigantic gourd
> And let the heavy rain, down-poured
> In one big torrent, set me free,
> Washing my grave away from me! "
>
> "I know not how such things can be! --
> I breathed My Soul back into me.
> Ah! Up then from the ground sprang I
> And hailed the earth with such a cry
> As is not heard save from a man
> Who has been dead, and lives again.
> About the trees my arms I wound;
> Like one gone mad I hugged the ground;
> I raised my quivering arms on high;
> I laughed and laughed into the sky,
> Till at my throat a strangling sob
> Caught fiercely, and a great heart-throb
> Sent instant tears into my eyes;
> O God, I cried, no dark disguise
> Can e'er hereafter hide from me
> Thy radiant identity!" [6]

When I Do Not Believe in God

And when I become an atheist because I no longer believe in the concept of a Universal Creator, then The Wisdom of Children that I describe in Our Book will still help me to increase the love, peace, joy & compassion in my daily life because I am an unconditionally loving human being, who was born with an internal source of unconditional love that I can fully reconnect to.

I will help you to prove this is true, so please read on for a few more pages, until we discuss how an adult can start to fully reconnect to his internal source of unconditional love, by reliving the unconditional love that he experienced as a child.

Then on this solid base of true childhood experience, we will start to build our concept of The Wisdom of Children, that we can use as adults to increase the amount of unconditional love that we feel each day, so we can increase the amount of love, peace, joy & compassion that we share each day with our families & friends, whether you believe in God or not.

We will no longer explore where our ability to offer unconditional love to other human beings may have come from, other than to ponder this question,

Does my ability to love come from a creator or from the random chance of evolution? Q-81

What we will do instead is try to except that our ability exists because we were born with the perfect ability to love all life, without knowing why we were blessed with this ability.

A Shortcut to The Wisdom of The Meaning of Life

Our Book describes stories from my life, before My Son was born, before I married his wonderful Mom.

When I was a child I was fully connected to My Internal Source of Unconditional Love, but then I lost this connection. I will describe to you how I became lost & confused, when I no longer had access to my internal source of immense love, to help motivate me to accomplish My Goals each day. I will describe how I found the wisdom that I needed, to enable me to fully reconnect to this source of unconditional love, to become able to increase the love, peace, joy & compassion in my life, as I started to reduce and then eliminate the unfair pain & suffering in my life.

Understanding how I have done this by learning the wisdom of the sages, that has been available to human beings for thousands of years, will give you a shortcut to the wisdom of the meaning of life, which is to share unconditional love & nurture true friendship with all human beings, and this will make it easier for you to begin to apply this wisdom to your life, so you can increase the amount of love, peace, joy & compassion that you experience and share in your daily life.

When I was a child I used my internal source of unconditional love to nurture true friendships with my friends & family, to enable me to share love, peace, joy & compassion with those I loved.

Unfortunately, I did not understand the need to protect my connection to my internal source of unconditional love when I was a child.

As a teenager, when I studied the wisdom of the wise sages, such as Mohammed & Buddha, I began to understand how My Body, Energy & Mind were using my internal source of unconditional love to generate love, peace, joy & compassion in my daily life.

Unfortunately, I did not learn how to protect my connection to my internal source of unconditional love from being shut off from my conscious awareness by the major unfair pain in my memories that was starting to block my connection to my internal source of unconditional love, as I relived some of my painful memories each day of my young life.

This partial blockage occurred whenever I started to relive the unfair pain from my memories which I did not know how to stop hurting me. I had to learn how to make these memories pain free, by not feeding them new compulsive thinking energy about the worry & stress in my teenage life, to stop keeping the unfair pain fed & alive, by not compulsively thinking about how life was being unfair to me, as a teenager.

It was not until I became an adult that I learned to kill the major unfair pain in my memories, after I completed my study of the wisdom of the sages. This wisdom taught me how My Mind created, stored and relived the unfair pain in my memories and then I learned how to choose my feelings to stop any existing painful memories &

any new painful experiences in my life, from creating new unfair pain that would try to block my connection to my internal source of unconditional love, once again.

I learned to kill any new unfair pain by not feeding it thinking energy to stop keeping it alive, so new unfair pain would not block my connection to unconditional love. Killing all the new unfair pain enabled me to maintain my full connection to my internal source of unconditional love that automatically started to begin generating continuous feelings of love, peace, joy & compassion in my adult life each day, when I woke up each morning.

This is why it important for you to begin to understand your nature as an unconditionally loving human being by learning to understand the spiritual nature of your Body, Energy & Mind, so you can learn to nurture & protect your connection to your internal source of unconditional love, so you do not lose it again once you have been able to fully reconnect to it, so you can keep it generating continuous love, peace, joy & compassion into your conscious mind during every moment of every day of your future adult life.

This may not be easy for you to learn because your ego will try to prevent you from learning this wisdom because your ego does not want you to start killing the control that it may have over your life.

My Adult Love for All Life

As a young child I was not taught about My Awareness of My Connection to All Life in day care or preschool. As I grew up I was taught this concept by my religious leaders who described My Awareness of My Connection to All Life as my awareness of God, who is the embodiment of all the unconditional love in the universe, who is the divine intelligence of the universe, who created me in his image, who bestowed on me my internal source of unconditional love, and who bestowed on me my ability to love all life in the universe, especially to love my friends & family who are unconditionally loving human beings who were created in God's image, as I was.

Our religious leaders spend their lives trying to teach us to understand & believe in the concepts of God's love and what our relationship to a loving God should be. Each of our world religions has a different concept of God that is based on the same simplified concept, that God is the embodiment of unconditional love, and that God's pure unconditional love lives inside each of us. This spiritual knowledge is designed to help us to learn how to connect to the unconditional love from the all life in the universe that is living inside each of us, to enable us to experience a loving relationship with God.

Understanding The Awareness of My Connection to Life

To understand the concept of My Awareness of My Connection to All Life as an adult, I began to realize that this experience is real when I am feeling continuous love, peace, joy & compassion and when I am feeling the unconditional love emanating from all life in the universe.

To be able to understand the truth of this statement, please look inside your mind at your earliest memories of when you were a baby and ask yourself these questions,

What is my earliest memory as a baby, when I was aware of the unconditional love living inside a family member or a guardian? Q-82

How did I express my unconditional love for all life when I was a child by expressing my love & joy when I played games or went on adventures with my family, by laughing, singing or shouting my excitement & delight to everyone, so they could share in my joy of being alive to experience these wonderful feelings of new fun & adventures? Q-83

The Meditation & Mindfulness techniques that we will learn, as we study the wisdom in Our Book Two, will enable you to relive your earliest memories as a young child.

When you are able to access your earliest memories, please write a description of your love for your family or your guardians and their love for you. This writing experience will help you to fully reconnect to your internal source of unconditional love for all life that you were born fully connected to and that you experienced continuously each day of your life as a baby and then as a young child. Writing about your childhood love for all life will help make you aware of your spiritual connection to all life in the universe as an adult.

As you study the next few sections of Our Book, you will begin to fully understand the concept of My Awareness of My Connection to All Life in the universe and this knowledge will help you to feel the unconditional love from all life in the universe and will help you to apply The Wisdom of Children to your life, to increase your ability to share unconditional love & nurture true friendship with your friends & family, to enable you to increase the love, peace, joy & compassion that you feel each day of your adult life.

So, to help you to reconnect to your childhood memories let us explore,

Becoming an Unconditionally Loving Human Being

When I was a young child and I asked the question, Who am I?

 I started to realize that,

I am Spiritual Energy who lives inside My Mind & Body, who has the ability to observe the revealed feelings, thoughts & images in My Mind and who has the Free Will to manage My Mind & Body to use my ability to reason to choose to act as a human being, to enhance or diminish the well-being of my human life.[28]

I began to realize as a young child that my human life is impermanent because My Body is impermanent. I was told by my parents that someday My Body would die from natural causes and then become ashes when it was cremated in a fire at my funeral.

Now as an adult, when I look inside My Mind and I ask the question, "Who am I?, I become aware of three aspects of my nature as an unconditionally loving human being, consisting of My Mind, My Spiritual Energy & My Body, as I confirm as an adult that I am still the same spiritual entity that I was when I was a child. My Spirit is the same pure spiritual energy of my childhood who I cannot see or touch. My Spirit is still observing My Body from inside My Mind. Nothing has changed in the relationship between My Body and My Spirit since childhood, except that I am getting closer to the day of the death of My Body.

I do not know what happens to My Pure Spiritual Energy after My Body dies.

However, I have Faith that after My Body dies; I will be reborn into a new body to be able to live again in a new life. I have decided to believe that I have Eternal Life even though I do not know if this is true, so I will have to wait until My Body dies someday to find out for sure.

Until I die, I am accepting on faith that I am Pure Eternal Spiritual Energy of the universe who is living inside a body that is impermanent.

1) My Mind

My Mind is my spiritual awareness of my existence as Pure Eternal Spiritual Energy of the universe

My Mind is the pure base of My Awareness of My Existence as a human being. I am aware that My Mind is filled with primordial energy which is beyond time, creation & destruction that is connecting me to My Awareness of My Connection to All Life.

My Mind is made from the energy strings of the universe that manifest in all life in the universe. These energy strings manifest in My Body as atoms and in My Mind as mental energy. The universe including My Mind is made up of the interaction of the energy strings of the primordial state of the universe which is the basis of all existence.

As I experience The Pure State of The Primordial Awareness of My Mind, I experience being connected to all life in the universe. I become aware of all the love in the universe and the universe becomes aware of all the love in me. I become all life and all life becomes me. This connection automatically generates powerful feelings inside me of love, peace, joy & compassion for all life, especially my own life. This realization is not knowledge about the universe. It is a living experience of the nature of the universe that is supplying me with unconditional love from all life that I first experienced when I was a baby.

As a baby and then as a young child, I accepted my unconditionally loving nature, although I was not able to fully understand or to put into words that I was aware of my existence as Pure Eternal Spiritual Energy of the universe or that I was aware that I was using the energy strings of the universe to connect me to my awareness of the unconditional love emanating from all life in the universe or that I was aware that the energy strings of the universe were connecting me to all the revealed aspects of My Conscious Mind, as my mind connected me to the external world and kept me anchored in the NOW, as I tried to maintain my connection to my internal source of unconditional love for all life that I was born fully connected to, as my internal source kept supplying me with unlimited unconditional love and a powerful motivation to challenge the opportunities for fun & adventure in my young life, which the external life outside my body kept offering me. (Please refer to My Love From All Life & My Love For All Life Mantra sections of Our Book Four)

When I was born and then as I grew into a young child, I did not ask to love all life in the universe that contained my love for my parents, my siblings, my friends, my pets, my home, my toys, my clothes, and my daily experiences, such as eating food, listening to music, taking a bath, playing, talking, walking, having fun & adventures and feeling warm & loved, as my mother cuddled with me, and as my life felt good.

As a baby and then as a young child, I just accepted & used my ability to share unconditional love & nurture true friendship with all life, especially with my friends & family.

When I was a baby and then as a young child, I continuously experienced My Awareness of My Existence inside My Mind as an unconditionally loving human being as I continuously experienced My Awareness of My Connection to the external unconditional love from All Life, and as I continuously experienced My Awareness of My Connection to My Internal Source of Unconditional Love for All Life.

What is My Awareness of My Connection to All Life in the universe? Q-84

2) My Spiritual Energy

The primordial spiritual energy of the universe powers My Mind, My Body and the energy reserves in My Room of Memories that generate joy or pain in my life when I relive my memories. Learning how I power these memories with thinking energy helps me to understand how I keep the feelings from my memories alive inside my mind or how I can kill these feelings.

What is Pure Eternal Spiritual Energy? Q-85

Is the primordial spiritual energy of the universe powering the energy of My Mind & Body? Q-86

I have Faith that it is. (Please refer to The Energy Strings of The Universe section in Chapter 22 of Our Book One)

3) My Body

My Body is the impermanent material form which ties me to the Pure Eternal Spiritual Energy that lives inside My Body that enables me to become an unconditionally loving human being. I am an impermanent human being because when My Body dies, My Body parts will be transformed back into the individual atoms & energy that are made from the primordial energy strings of the universe. Nothing will be lost. However, I do not know where my Pure Eternal Spiritual Energy goes when My Body dies.

Will I be united with a new body when my spiritual essence goes to Heaven? Q-87

Will I be reincarnated into a new body and start a new life on Earth? Q-88

Or, Will I cease to exist because My Spirit dies when My Body dies? Q-89

I do not know the answers to these questions.

The Mirror in My Mind

The concepts that describe our minds are complex, so please try to understand these concepts by visualizing them working in your mind, as you read the description of how our minds work. We will elaborate on this overview of how our minds theoretically work and then you will be asked to write a description of how your mind should work at the end of Our Book Two, after you have practiced The Wisdom of Children to get to know the inner workings of your mind. During this process, the description of how your mind actually works will become real to you & understood by you, as you observe your mind working in your daily life in the future. It will take time, maybe weeks or months, to learn the concepts of how your mind theoretically works as you use this wisdom that lives in your mind to make choices about which actions to take in your future life. Please be patience with your rate of progress as you begin to understand the complex subject of how your mind actually works as you start to compare it to our description of how our minds theoretically work.

My mind experiences the uninterrupted flow of 60,000 + feelings, thoughts & images, which arise in my mind each day, stay for a while and then disappear from my mind. My mind has the ability to judge, to reason & to imagine, within the limits of space & time.

When I am not thinking, my mind is resting in its ability to reflect my feelings, thoughts & images in The Mirror in My Mind.

This uninterrupted flow of feelings, thoughts & images, which arise in my mind each day from my mind's perceptions of my daily experiences as I live my human life, from the time I get out of bed in the morning until I go back to bed at night, do not arise from outside of me but are merely reflections of the external world that are living inside my mind.

The Mirror in My Mind reflects the way my mind works as it processes the perceptions of my life experiences each day that come, from the external world, from my memories, from my ego & from my imagination.

To help me to understand this process, I am visualizing my mind & body being powered by the Pure Eternal Spiritual Energy of the universe, which I call by several names including My Compassionate Watcher, who is sitting inside The Mirror in My Mind watching all my revealed feelings, thoughts & images being reflected as they go by the surface of The Mirror in My Mind as these reflections are processed by my mind each & every moment of my life as a human being.[29]

Please try to visualize yourself sitting inside a mirror inside your mind as you watch the reflections of your life pass by The Mirror in Your Mind.

My mirror is on a movable stand connected to an energy outlet which supplies my mirror with The Energy of My Mind which is generated by the Pure Eternal Spiritual Energy of the universe to power a search light attached to The Mirror in My Mind to be able to shine a powerful light on the contents in each room of My Mind [30], such as the room that contains all my memories, as I watch selected memories and as I choose to ignore the reflected images in other rooms in my mind, such as the room containing my desire to eat chocolate ice cream, as I use The Light of My Mind to make the contents of a room of my choosing to appear bright & clear [31]

The contents in a room of my mind become bright & sharply defined, as My Compassionate Watcher decides if the reflections living in this room in my mind are a true description of my life experiences or are not a true description of my life experiences, at this moment in time.

My Compassionate Watcher also looks at other reflections as my mirror reflects the contents of the 60,000 + new feelings, thoughts & images that pass through My Mind each day, and observes if these reflections are a true description of my life experiences or if the reflections are false, such when my ego or my imagination reflect a make believe experience about my life.

Then, My Compassionate Watcher labels the true reflections in my mind as The Clarity & Truth of My Mind which are the clear & true reflections of the feelings, thoughts & images in my mind that My Compassionate Watcher uses to create new possible future actions that I may take that will improve my life [32], as it continues to judge the truth or untruth of all the new reflections that are entering my mind, at this time, as it continues to use the new feelings, thoughts & images of possible future actions that it creates inside my mind to help me to accomplish the goals for my life & to help me to judge the outcomes of these possible future actions, to help me to choose the best possible action to take in next few minutes to help me accomplish My Goals for Today.

This is The Creativity of My Mind which is the mental process that My Compassionate Watcher uses to create potential new actions & outcomes for my future life [33], to help me to decide which of the possible futures I should try to create in my life, a life that My Compassionate Watcher wants me to fill with joy & happiness that I can share with my friends & family.

Then, as I take many more mental steps in my thinking that I use to choose the physical actions that I will take today, as I work on my goals, My Compassionate Watcher rests in a state of internal unconditional love for me, a love that I was born possessing and that I first experienced when I was a baby. My adult ability to love all life that comes from this source of unconditional love that lives inside me, powers my innate ability to reflect my feelings, thoughts & images in The Mirror in My Mind. This innate ability is called The Primordial Awareness of My Mind that I use to reflect the brightness, clarity, energy & truth of the reflections of the feelings, thoughts & images in my mind, as I realize that I am not the content of my feelings, thoughts & images, I am only the processor of this mental information, a processor who I call My Compassionate Watcher.

That is why I process the content of the feelings, thoughts & images in my mind like a mirror does. I reflect this ever changing content in my mind all day, but at the end of the day I have not changed, just like every mirror in the external world does not change after reflecting the images of whatever or whoever looks into one of these mirrors during the day. All the mirrors in the world remain unchanged. They are still just reflecting mirrors. None of the images that they reflect are stuck to them. None of the images have become part of any of these mirrors by the end of a long day of reflecting all sorts of images of the external world. That is why I am like a mirror; I reflect all the feelings, thoughts & images that pass through my mind all day without being changed by any of them. My Pure Eternal Spiritual Essence has not changed as a result of reflecting all the feelings, thoughts & images in my mind. And that is why I can safely say that I am not my feelings, thoughts or images. They are not part of My True Self, who is My Compassionate Watcher, who is My Pure Eternal Spiritual Energy, who is a perfect being of pure unconditional love as Buddha described, and who I believe was created by the eternal universal energy field of pure unconditional love who I call My Creator or God.

What is The Mirror in My Mind? Q-90
What is The Energy of My Mind? Q-91
What is The Light of My Mind? Q-92
What is The Clarity & Truth of My Mind? Q-93
What is The Creativity of My Mind? Q-94
How does The Mirror in My Mind work to reflect the truth of the contents of my mind? Q-95
Why am I not my feelings, thoughts or images? Q-96

(Please refer to the Living as My True Self section in Chapter 27 of Our Book One for an expanded understanding of how The Mirror in My Mind works)

The Primordial Awareness of My Mind

The Primordial Awareness of My Mind is my mental Awareness of My Existence as an Unconditionally Loving Human Being.[34]

The Primordial Awareness is a combination of;

The Awareness of My Existence as pure eternal spiritual energy of the universe that is living inside a human body

The Awareness of the revealed activities of my mind including all my feelings, thoughts & images

The Awareness of the revealed activities of My Body from the tips of my toes to the hair on top of my head

The Awareness of My Connection to All Life in the universe

My Awareness that I am receiving a continuous stream of unconditional love from all life in the universe [35]

The Awareness that my internal source of unconditional love is generating a continuous stream of love for all life in the universe [8]

The Awareness that the universe is feeding me 60,000 + new feelings, thoughts & images each day, that come into my mind, stay for a while and then return to the universe from which they came, when they disappear from my mind

The Awareness that I am not the content of my feelings, thoughts & images in my mind

The Awareness of my ability to become The Compassionate Watcher of my feelings, thoughts & images that I choose to reflect in

The Mirror in My Mind, to enable me to use my Free Will & my reasoning ability, to clearly observe them, to fully understand them, and to think about using them to enhance or diminish the well-being of my life

The Awareness of my life promoting desire, as an adult, to fully reconnect to my internal source of unconditional love for all life that I was born fully connected to, to enable me to rest in continuous love, peace, joy & compassion, as My Compassionate Watcher manages all my thinking energy, to become able to control all the revealed activities of my mind & body

And when I am practicing Meditation & Mindfulness to manage the combination of each type of awareness of my mind, I become fully connected to My Primordial Awareness of The Universe which provides me with spiritual energy to cleanse my mind of all the mental distractions that may be trying to prevent me from fully reconnecting to My Internal Source of Unconditional Love & True Friendship.

What is The Primordial Awareness of My Mind? Q-97
What are the different types of Primordial Awareness of My Mind? Q-98

Definitions of My Feelings, Thoughts & Images

My thoughts are the products of my mental activities that contain the words & symbols that flow through my mind, as I think & reason. My thoughts are being fed by what I perceive through my five senses, my memories, my feelings, my images & my sense of My True Self.[57] (Please refer to Our Book Four to explore Becoming My True Self)

Each of my feelings contains a pleasant, neutral or painful desire to act in a certain way. My feelings are stored inside My Room of Memories along with the thoughts & images of my life experiences, my dreams & my fantasy worlds that I create in my mind.[58]

Each of my desires is a pleasant, neutral or painful mental energy that is contained inside a feeling that is telling me to attain or possess something in the real external world or in my imagination that is within reach of my potential future mental & physical actions.[59]

E.g. My desire to create in my imagination a mental video of me skippering a sailboat in an ocean race, or my desire to physically act to purchase chocolate ice cream and enjoy its cool refreshing taste on a hot summer day.

My images are my mental creations of the physical likeness of the real external world, or the representation of my mental pictures & videos of my real life experiences, my memories, my dreams & my fantasy worlds that I create in my mind.[60]

My feelings, thoughts & images enter my mind, stay for a while and then disappear. When they disappear from my mind, a copy of the feelings, thoughts & images is stored in my subconscious mind, as a memory.[61]

A memory is the mental capacity or faculty for retaining and reviving information that is stored in my subconscious mind inside My Room of Memories which stores the feelings, thoughts & images that I experience during the day. [62]

I am not the contents of my mind. I am The Compassionate Watcher who is sitting inside The Mirror In My Mind, who is choosing which feelings, thoughts & images to reflect in The Mirror In My Mind, to enable me to clearly observe them, think about them, and understand them.[63]

My External World consists of all the revealed activities in The Real External World, outside my mind & body that I am reflecting in The Mirror in My Mind at the present time.[64]

My Internal World consists of all the revealed mental & physical processes inside my mind & body that I am reflecting in The Mirror in My Mind at the present time.[65]

What are My Definitions of the feelings, thoughts & images in my mind? Q-99

Questions about My Mind, Spiritual Energy & Body

As we continue to explore The Wisdom of Children and our nature as unconditional loving human beings who are made up of the three aspects of My Mind, My Spiritual Energy & My Body, we become able to answer these questions,

Am I a Mind without a spirit & a soul and am I destroyed when My Body dies? Q-100

And

Are love, peace, joy & compassion only found outside of My Body and not inside me? Q-101

OR

Am I pure primordial spiritual energy called My Spiritual Being who is absolutely connected to all living things in the universe and do I exist forever? Q-102

And

Are love, peace, joy & compassion found inside of My Body and will this internal unconditional love continue to stay connected to My Spiritual Being after My Body dies? Q-103

(In Our Book Two we will increase our understanding of How Our Minds should Work when we explore the abilities of the mind in more detail.)

How I Stopped Being Connected to Unconditional Love

When I looked into a mirror on a wall in our home when I was a child, I realized that my mind & body were physically separate from other human beings. However, I still felt spiritually connected to every human being that came into my life by my unconditional love for all life, that I was born with and that I felt each moment of every day of my life as a child. I offered my unconditional love to all human beings, that I met, only to have it rejected on many occasions by human beings who were not connected to their internal source of unconditional love. These disconnected human beings could not offer me love when I offered them my love. As these experiences of rejection, of being hurt & of unfairness in my childhood increased, I started to feel the fear that any new human being, who came into my life, may reject or hurt me.

Unfortunately, my parents & my school teachers were not able to teach me how to kill this fear of future pain & suffering or how to kill the pain contained in my memories of the unfairness in my life. When I was a child I started to suppress these painful memories that refused to die and I started to become afraid of looking at these painful memories because I did not know how to stop the unfair pain from hurting me, when I relived these memories.

As I grew up, I started to look outside my mind into the external world to find the joy & happiness that I was missing inside me. As I looked for more love in the external world, I started to feel separate from other human beings when I relived the memories of my feelings of unrequited love & unfairness that were created by the disconnected unloving human beings who treated me unfairly during my childhood. I continued to lose more of my continuous awareness of my internal connection to unconditional love as my internal connection became increasingly diminished by my accumulating painful memories.

As the years continued to roll on by, I struggled as I tried to learn how to kill the unfair pain in my memories and I continued to feel increasing unfairness each morning when I woke up, as a generalized feeling of unfair pain & suffering continued to hurt me during the day. So, I continued to suppress my painful memories, as they accumulated from a few, to hundreds, and then to thousands of painful memories.

By the time I became an adult, I acquired the habit of becoming fully disconnected from my internal source of unconditional love for many hours each day and I realized that I did not want to look inside my mind to try to find my internal source of unconditional love. I was afraid to look inside my mind because when I did, I triggered painful memories that generated intense feelings of fear & anger. So I made a conscious effort to stop looking inside my mind to try to find the internal love, peace, joy & compassion of my childhood because I was afraid of the pain I would find in my memories.

During this period of intense suffering in my life, whenever I met a new person in my life, I started to distrust my feelings of love & friendship for this new person because of my fear that my love may not last and that this new person may reject me, someday in the future. I continued to feel spiritually separate from anyone that I associated with because of my fear of possible future rejection and because I continued to feel that the love I desired from the external world to fill the emptiness in my heart was being produced by external circumstances that I could not control.

The false belief that I was being controlled by external situations was reducing my potential future joy & happiness. I started to believe that the love, peace, joy & compassion that I felt for my friends & family were not being generated inside of me. I started to falsely believe that these feelings were being generated by circumstances outside of me, somewhere in the external world, and I started to falsely believe that these enjoyable feelings could be taken away from me, at any time, by circumstances beyond my control.

My Ego fostered these false beliefs so I would continue to feel spiritually separate from other human beings, so it could continue to convince me to look for love outside of me and so it could continue to control me by convincing me that all human beings in my personal life should be treated as my potential adversaries, who I may have to compete with, to become able to obtain external joy & happiness.

Then, I begin to falsely believe that I was not the cause of my feelings and I begin to feel that I was losing control of my life because I was not in control of my external joy & happiness. The thoughts of an external source for my feelings of joy & happiness, that I was not in control of, began to generate feelings of insecurity, loneliness & unhappiness, when I continued to falsely believe that I was spiritually separate from other human beings, who I falsely believed were in control of the amount of external joy & happiness that I would receive in my future life.

Why do I sometimes allow my feelings of being spiritually separate from other human beings to convince me to believe my ego? Q-104

How I Started to Fully Reconnect to Unconditional Love

To stop worrying about the false beliefs of my ego that kept trying to convince me that I was spiritually separate from other human beings, I applied the wisdom contained in Our Book to my life. The wisdom has shown me that I can choose to fully reconnect to My Internal Source of Unconditional Love for all human beings and for all life. The wisdom has taught me The Science of My Mind to enable me to kill all the major unfair pain in my memories that has been disconnecting me from my internal source of love, peace, joy & compassion, and the wisdom has taught me to take the control of my mind away from the mistaken beliefs of my ego, when I falsely believe that I am spiritually separate from other human beings.

Now, I realize that all the motivation which I need to live my life with powerful passion, has always lived inside of me and it is inside me now, at this moment. This realization has helped me to revitalize my spiritual connection to all life, especially with all human beings.

Other realizations about My True Self contained in the wisdom in Our Book have helped me to increase my ability to love my life & all human beings, more & more each day, as I try to maintain a continuing reconnection to My Internal Source of Unconditional Love that I first felt when I was a baby.

As I look back on my study of the wisdom in Our Book, I realize that I began to fully understand & benefit from the wisdom in Our Book when I decided to use my childhood memories of my unconditional love for all life, to kick start my reconnection to the full power of my internal source of unconditional love, which automatically started to offer me powerful motivation to become able to choose all my feelings & to kill the feelings I did not want to experience, especially the unresolved pain & suffering in my daily life and to become able to stop believing in the lies of my ego, who was using the fear & anger contained in my painful memories to maintain control of my mind & actions. This experience has made me realize that,

My childhood memories are my proof that I was born with the ability to feel love for all life and to feel loved by all life, continuously, every moment of every day of my adult life.

How do I get confused, when I start to falsely believe that the love I need to motivate me to live my life with passion exists in the external world? Q-105

Restating The Purpose of Our Book

The primary purpose and function of Our Book is devoted to understanding how I can control my internal feelings, thoughts & mental images to increase the love, peace, joy & compassion in my life, by realizing that I am spiritually connected to all life in the universe by the internal source of unconditional love that I was born possessing. This unconditional love unites all life into one big family. My continuous feelings of unconditional love for all life that I automatically feel each day, when I wake up in the morning, are evidence that I am connected to all life because I remember that I felt this way as a child and now as an adult I am beginning to realize that I am able to fully reconnect to the feelings of this love for all life being generated by this internal source of unlimited love that lives inside my adult body.

The secondary purpose and function of Our Book is devoted to understanding how I can use my external connection to all life to increase the joy & happiness in my external relationships with other human beings.

Secret Millionaires Learning to Share Unconditional Love

To help you understand the impact that unconditional love has on the lives of other people, please watch the television series called The Secret Millionaire. This show ran for many years in Britain and had separate series running in the United States, Ireland & Australia. In the television series millionaires live on a meager allowance in impoverished neighborhoods, working undercover doing charity work to get to know the local people living in the area, as they look for people they can help. Each episode portrays the emotional struggle of a millionaire as he starts to feel unconditional love for those he tries to help and as he begins to talk about the unconditional love that he is starting to feel for these new friends and for his own family. At the end of each show the millionaire gives out large amounts of his own money to care givers who are helping less privileged people to improve their lives.

What is amazing about the show is the unconditional love shown by the care givers that each millionaire meets during the days undercover. As you watch the show you will start to fall in love with the wonderful care givers who offer unconditional love to help less fortunate people. The care givers ask for nothing in return for their love. Many of the care givers have very little money of their own and they do a lot of fundraising to help the less fortunate, while sacrificing their own opportunities to improve their own lives financially. You will realize that unconditional love motivates the care givers to spend their time, their efforts and their financial resources to help others. You will be amazed as you hear the stories of the care givers and the less fortunate people they help. You may be surprised, when you start to cry tears of compassion for the caregivers or the millionaire, who is starting to reconnect to the internal source of unconditional love of her childhood, which she has forgotten or ignored for many years, as she made her millions. Please buy or borrow copies of the shows to enjoy watching them, as they will help you to fully reconnect to the immense power of unconditional love & compassion that you felt when you were a child.

You will also experience the positive impact that unconditional love has on each millionaire. At the beginning of each show the undercover millionaire expresses personal feelings about the need to help less fortunate people. Many of the millionaires have distanced themselves from less fortunate people who were not connected with their business endeavors, as they made their fortunes. By the end of their undercover charity work experience, after they have experienced the unconditional love of the care givers helping less fortunate people, many of the millionaires state in their own words that when they go back home to their families, they are determined to spend more time loving their families and less time making the next million in their business. Many are so touched by the unconditional love that they have shared with the caregivers that they come back to these impoverished neighborhoods in the future to offer more help & money to support the care givers, who they started to love when they worked with these compassionate human beings during their charity work experience. As they try to find the words to understand their renewed feelings of unconditional love for others who they do not know, a love that they last felt when they were children, many of the millionaires are asking questions, that are similar to what you and I are asking ourselves,

How do I fully reconnect to my internal source of love, peace, joy & compassion that I was born with, so I can start to feel the powerful unconditional love for all life that I felt as a young child?

And how do I nurture the true friendship that this love motivates me to share with other human beings?

How I Nurture True Friendship

When my best friend made negative unfair comments about me behind my back, I found it difficult to maintain my continuous feelings of unconditional love for him because I had to learn to challenge the fear that my ego wanted me to believe was genuine and wanted me to follow, to satisfy the desires of my ego for fairness, revenge & justice in my life, as it tried to get me to reject & suppress my feelings of love for my best friend, when I realized that my best friend had betrayed my trust in him, a trust that he would continue to treat me with love, fairness & respect.

I knew this betrayal would harm our friendship so I decided to confront my friend, but to be fair to him and to make sure that this rumor was true, I first checked with the people who had heard my friend say negative things about me. When I found out the rumor was true, my pain continued to increase, so I asked him,

Is it true that you made negative unfair comments about me?

He responded by apologizing and by saying that he said those negative things as a joke. They were not meant to hurt me. It took a while for the pain of betrayal to diminish and go away, but I forgave him and I asked him not to make any more jokes at my expense. I value the joy & friendship he brings into my life, so I decided not to allow my hurt feelings to damage our friendship, especially when the memories of my betrayal continued to sprout in my mind and urge me to indulge in the painful feelings of the unfairness of the betrayal by my friend, a betrayal that I had stored in my memories.

To help prevent the pain of betrayal from re-occurring, I accepted the challenge of keeping the memory of my hurt feelings from becoming a source of worry & stress in my daily life, especially when my friend and I are together in the future. Now, I try not to allow the painful memory of betrayal to increase in strength & power when I ask myself the questions,

Will betrayal happen again?

Will I be treated unfairly again?

When these questions enter my mind and my worrying starts, I try to manage my stress, by not feeding new unfair thinking energy to the energy reserves of the memory of the betrayal, that is stored in My Room of Memories in my subconscious mind, by not thinking about the unfairness of the betrayal to stop providing the memory with a source of unfair thinking energy and to stop it from generating new unfair pain in my conscious mind whenever I relive the memory of the betrayal in the future.

My best friend made a mistake, learned from his mistake, and then vowed never to make unfair painful jokes about me again. So I forgave him because he did not intentionally try to hurt me.

Then, I killed the unfair pain in my memory of the betrayal by refusing to feed new unfair thinking energy to my memory of the betrayal which will stop it from using new thinking energy to generate new painful feelings of the unfairness of my betrayal, whenever I relive this unfair memory.

Previously, I relived this memory of betrayal many times as the memory used up its energy reserves to generate the pain of betrayal in my conscious mind, until it had no energy left to generate any new unfair pain in my life. Then, the next time I relived the memory, I did not feel intense pain because I had not given my memory any new thinking energy to generate new pain into my mind and I had convinced the memory that I had forgiven my friend and there was no need for the memory to use pain to get my attention so it could tell me that my friend may betray me again.

Slowly, I learned to trust my friend again. Trust can take years to earn and then can be lost in one instance of betrayal.

Now, I am choosing to believe that life will be fair to me in the long run, when someone treats me unfairly in short term, which helps me to keep new unfair pain out of my relationships whenever someone hurts me unintentionally. When this happens, I try to forgive my friend immediately. I do not let the new unfair pain of the betrayal of my love or my trust to damage our friendship. Instead I cherish the love, peace, joy & compassion that my friendships offer me by killing any new unfair pain of betrayal.

Married couples are especially vulnerable, when they carry unfair pain around inside them from the unfair hurt & betrayals of their spouses because they haven't been taught how to forgive.

How can I feel romantic love for someone, when I am carrying around unresolved unfair pain & suffering in our relationship?

We are imperfect human beings, who continue to make unintentional mistakes in our relationships with our friends & family. We often need forgiveness from our friends & family to help us to reduce our feelings of remorse for our mistakes.

As we try to obtain forgiveness, we can still improve our relationships by learning how our feelings, thoughts & images work together inside our minds, either to allow Our Egos to convince us that our friends have become our adversaries who will hurt us again in the future, which will generate needless worry & stress about potential unfairness in our future lives, OR we can decide to choose our feelings and offer forgiveness to our friends when they hurt us unintentionally and we can ask for forgiveness when we hurt others, which will enable us to bring increased love, peace, joy & compassion back into our relationships.

"It is reported that over 90% of what we worry about never happens. That means our negative worries have about a 10% chance of being correct." - Dr. Susan Jeffers [36]

We worry about concerns that may be based on untrue thoughts that we do not check for truth because we believe we cannot control the thoughts generating the worry. We become compulsive thinkers who cannot stop worrying. Contrast this with the increased love, peace, joy & compassion that results from choosing our feelings, when we realize that we can kill our worry & stress, when we check the reasons why we are worrying to determine if the reasons are true or not. If they are not true then we have no need to continue worrying and being stressed out.

Parents are especially vulnerable, when they worry about their children and when they do not know how to teach their children to understand their feelings by checking their feelings for truth, instead of just allowing their children to indulge in their feelings of unresolved pain & suffering because these negative life diminishing feelings are generating a strong motivation that is saying Follow Me! to the child, instead of asking the child to check these feelings for truth and then rejecting these untrue hurtful feelings.

My example of the unfair pain that I felt when my best friend betrayed me, I learned to control, by first checking that the facts supporting my worry were true. Then I confronted the situation to reduce the unfair pain of betrayal in my life, and then remove it by forgiving my friend, so I can continue sharing increasing love, peace, joy & compassion in our relationship in the future. Our current friendship is based on trust & honesty and a desire to solve any problems that cause pain in our friendship. Our mutual goal is to increase the unconditional love that we share with each other. A friendship can only stand so much pain until the love in the friendship is destroyed by betrayal, so we are using this instance of betrayal as a lesson to learn from, so that it does not happen again. Now that we have gone through the pain of disappointment & betrayal together, we are back on the path to becoming True Friends, once again.

How do I choose feelings that increase my love, peace, joy & compassion and nurture true friendship instead of indulging in feelings that are motivating me to seek justice or revenge for a betrayal of our friendship when I am trying to forgive a friend who hurt me? Q-106

Why True Friends Support Me

True Friends are human beings, who value a friendship highly and who feel a deep sense of loss, when that friendship is threatened, when things go wrong in the friendship or when one of the friends is suffering emotional or physically.

True Friends visit me, when I am physically ill. They show their genuine friendship by showing their desire to stay by my side and just be there for me. They do not want to leave, even though they know that they can only help by offering me emotional support. They ask for nothing in return because they value the love, peace, joy & compassion that our friendship provides and they want to help me to get better.

True Friends offer me a shoulder to cry on, when I am in emotional pain. They do not give advice. They are there to help by listening and by trying to understand me. They know that I need someone who will provide me with emotional support. They know my emotional pain like a physical illness will intensify, then slowly diminish and then eventually disappear. True Friends are there to support me in times of sorrow with their wisdom that someday, hopefully soon, I will become able to experience love, peace, joy & compassion with them, once again.

I treasure having True Friends to help speed my recovery. They ask for nothing in return, as they offer me unconditional love and a willingness to share my pain, until I become better.

The Nature of True Friendship

The ability to nurture True Friendship exits between two human beings, who share unconditional love with each other, who enjoy sharing fun & adventures together, who support each other through painful life experiences, and who forgive each other for the unfair pain & suffering that they create in their friendship.

Your true friend may be a mom or dad, husband or wife, son or daughter, boyfriend or girlfriend, co-worker or playmate, child or senior citizen. The only prerequisite is their ability to love you unconditionally and to forgive you, when you mess up and betray the friendship. In return, you require the ability to accept the unconditional love, cherish it, and try not to betray it, by thoughtless acts or words that hurt your true friend.

True friendship occurs, when one human being offers unconditional love to another human being, who accepts the unconditional love and then offers unconditional love in return.[37]

Saint Aelred described true friendship eloquently he said, "A truly loyal friend sees nothing in his friend but his heart." [38]

Which I modify by saying to myself when I am with a true friend, "I see nothing in my true friend but his heart"

True friendship may occur in a few seconds in total silence, as two human beings look into each other's eyes for the first time, to see the unconditional love in each other's heart. A special bonding of true friendship starts to occur without words, as they are joined together by the primordial energy strings of the universe that are generating the energy of unconditional love for all life, that resides in the hearts of all human beings, such as the unconditional love that is merging the new friends together, spiritually. True friendship can only be offered by a human being who is connected to his internal source of unconditional love.

What is the nature of True Friendship and how can it improve the well-being of my life? Q-107

"True friendship is nurtured between us when we share love, peace, joy & compassion with each other and we practice forgiving each other for the mistakes we make in our relationship" (Modified Quote from The Essence of The Wisdom of Children section in Chapter 8 of Our Book One)

All young children are born fully connected to the universal source of unconditional love and they offer love & true friendship to all new human beings that they meet. An adult who is connected to his internal source of unconditional love can quickly bond with a young child who he meets, who becomes his True Friend as they share their love for all life, even if it is only for a few minutes. Please do not miss your opportunities to share unconditional love with young children.

Unfortunately, it takes much longer to develop True Friendship with an adult who is not fully connected to his internal source of unconditional love because a mutual sharing of unconditional love is required.

Is my life blessed with a True Friend? Who? Why? Q-108

If you do not have a True Friend, My Son & I will help you to develop True Friendship by teaching you to share the wisdom that we have learned on our journey of self-discovery, to become able to increase the love, peace, joy & compassion in our lives, to become able to share increased unconditional love with our friends & family and to become able to develop True friendship.

I learned the wisdom of sharing unconditional love from the sages of the past, such as Buddha, Mohammed, Lao-tzu, Kee Nanayon & Jesus and from the sages of the present, such as Wayne Dyer, Deepak Chopra, Byron Katie, Thich Nhat Nhah & My Son, especially when he was a young child. I am offering you the wisdom that I have proven to be true, by applying the wisdom to my own life and then experiencing the benefits of its truth. The Wisdom of Children will help you to bring more unconditional love into your life and the wisdom will help you to share your increasing love with True Friends, as the wisdom has helped me to live the experience of True Friendship in my life.

First comes a desire for belonging and then after unsuccessful attempts at learning how to be a True Friend, comes wisdom from those who have touched our lives with offers of True Friendship in a positive way. Only then does True Friendship evolve, first with trust, then with a mutual sharing of unconditional love, and then with the willingness to be emotionally open & vulnerable with a True Friend, without offering unsolicited advice or demanding commitments from your friend.

Then friendship can lead to romance.

Loving Someone for the Qualities in The Heart

My father told me when I was young, that I should marry a Fat Bald Headed Woman when I grew up. I didn't understand this wisdom until I became a teenager and went through puberty. Then, I began to realize that my father was asking me to woo a girl with a good heart, who was willing to continually forgive me when I messed up, as I tried to understand her when I was a young teenager and I did not fully understand her needs & desires. I had to go on many dates before I began to understand a girl's needs & her desires, as she grew into womanhood, and then I began to realize that many women are superior to the men in their lives because they are better nurturers of family love.

Many men are not brought up to be a primary care giver in a family relationship. Many men learn how to become family nurturers from the women in their lives, starting with some basic lessons in nurturing from their moms and then advanced nurturing lessons from the women that they end up marrying and having children with.

My father told me when I was a young boy that I should marry a girl for what is in her heart and not because the outside packaging is pretty to look at. I remembered his wisdom when I became a teenager and then I began to fully understand the wisdom of the men in our family, as I went on dates and eventually asked a girl to marry me.

When I offered this wisdom to my son in his preteen years, I made some additions to my father's wisdom to help improve my son's chances for romance & lasting love, when my son asked me for advice about the girls in his life.

"When you become an adult, I recommend that you marry a Fat Bald Headed Girl for what is in her heart and not marry her for the pretty outside packaging that she offers to the world.

In the meantime, I recommend that when you talk to a girl at school, who you are attracted to, please ask her questions so that she will begin to talk about herself and emotionally open up to you, as she begins to feel loved & understood while she is in your company. It is important for you to not talk about yourself or give her advice about her problems, that she describes when she talks about her life. And when she asks you questions about the other girls at school, that you both know, it is important for you to tell her that you keep your discussions with the other girls, private, to protect their reputations by not gossiping about them. In this way your new friend will leave her chat with you, feeling understood & appreciated by a new boy who is emotionally open & loving and who is sensitive about her social needs at school.

You must be willing to offer your love to a new girl without conditions, in the hope that she will cherish your love, and you must be willing to endure unfair pain when you are rejected by a new girl, and then you must pick up your broken heart and kill the pain of rejection & of being hurt, so you can mend your broken heart, and then try to love again, until you find an unconditionally loving girl who will bond with your love.

To help you understand the lure of romantic love in your life, please rewrite this paraphrase of a wise saying by Alison Willcocks in your own words, to help you to understand the wisdom that I learned from your granddad.

Allowing Love to Fly Free

> When I am in love, I encourage my girlfriend to be free
> Like a beautiful butterfly who is both fragile & wise
> As she flies away to share friendship with other boys
> And learns to remain true to our love
> Or she will not fly back to me
>
> If she does not return, I must find the courage to love again
> When I take my heart from my chest
> And offer it to a new girl
> With the hope that she will hold my heart next to hers
> And bond my love to the love in her heart

Even though she may throw my heart on the ground
And jump up & down on my love
To leave me with a broken heart, once again
I will forgive her, as I wash off my hurt & rejection
And put my unblemished heart back in my chest

In this way, I will keep offering my unconditional love
Until I capture the heart of a wonderful girl
Who will cherish my love with precious trust
And will help pay the price required to keep our love pure
As we start sharing our lives with romantic love

You will probably meet a thousand women in your lifetime, who have loving hearts and who are willing to forgive you, for being less than perfect, when they realize that you are less than their ideal image of the man that they want in their life. Any one of these women will embrace your love and be willing to love you for the rest of her life, when you are willing to make a commitment to her to share mutual unconditional love.

And out of these thousand women, you may be able to find one, who is both beautiful & rich and who is the only child of parents who are committed to leaving their fortune in wealth & wisdom to you & their daughter, starting with a huge donation on your wedding day, and then as often as you ask for help & advice.

Or you may fall in love with a pauper when you realize that, "Money can't buy you love", even though money certainly helps to nurture love by taking the financial stress out of your relationship with the woman you intend to marry.

Also please realize that your future wife will most likely become the boss in your relationship, when your children are born because of her superior family nurturing skills and because of her need for your extra help in taking care of the children, whether or not you want to help, as she begins to teach you the family nurturing skills that you need to learn to be able to help support the children, skills that you may not already possess.

It is well known by all the women that I know that boys & men require a lot of training by the loving girls & women in their lives.

Someday, you may meet a loving woman who will decide to take pity on you because she has fallen in love with you and she feels that you have the potential to become a man who is able to nurture love, appreciation, understanding & sensitivity in her life. She will know that you require a lot of training to mold you into the man that you have the potential of becoming, a man that she will spend the rest of her life forgiving, when you fail to meet her many future expectations. Such is the price that many women are willing to pay for a man's love.

As the years go by, you will learn to love her deeply and to beg her for forgiveness, when you do not live up to her many expectations. Hopefully, with time & her training, you will slowly improve your ability to love her, even though I am reasonable sure that you will never ever be able to be truly worthy of her love & forgiveness. Such is the magic & power of a woman that a man will never fully understand, but will always be grateful for in his life, especially when she becomes the mother of his children."

Many single men do not fully understand this fatherly wisdom on nurturing romantic love, until after they are married and become the fathers of young children. Then, they begin to realize the superiority of many of the women in their lives, who are able to nurture love in their family relationships when dealing with the worry, stress & disappointments of family members and who are able to offer powerful family nurturing skills to successfully raise young children in a family environment of unconditional love.

The Wisdom of Children that we are offering you in Our Book will help you to become a better nurturer of family love, to enable you to increase the love shared in your family and to enable you to become a better parent. (Please refer to The Evolution of Family & Social Nurturing Skills section in Chapter 6 of Our Book Two.)

This wisdom will enable you to help children to grow more self-confident, when they look to you for help & guidance, as they start to navigate through new challenges in their childhood.

For example,

Allowing Young Children to Make the Final Decisions

It is particularly difficult for parents to allow their young children to make the final decision when deciding what challenges the child should accept in life, without giving unsolicited advice, or demanding that the child follow the final decision of the parents, whether the child likes it or not. When a parent does not allow a child the opportunity to make final decisions, the child will not be given the wonderful gift of becoming able to learn from mistakes.

The old saying that, "Adversity builds character" could be re-worded as, "Mistakes help children to build character", as long as the parents encourage the child to make her own decisions, to correct her mistakes, and to try again, until the child succeeds. Then the parents & the child can celebrate, as the child's self-confidence grows from her successes, as she overcomes her setbacks & mistakes.

My Wife and I learned the wisdom of helping our son to learn to make final decisions on his own, by studying Maria Montessori's childhood development wisdom, as shown by the following quote from a letter that I wrote to My Son, thanking him for the opportunity to be his father and for the many wonderful years that we spent together, as father & son.

"Dear Wil,

A father wants to take pride in his son's accomplishments and you have given me many opportunities to be proud of you.

Before you were born, when you were in Mommy's tummy, we studied Maria Montessori's books, The Absorbent Mind and The Montessori Method.

The wisdom of Maria Montessori helped us to teach you how to nurture and protect your intellectual abilities, when you were born. You, like all normal mentally healthy children, were born to be a genius. Unfortunately, many children as they grow older start to shut down their mind's ability to learn at the high rate of speed, as they start to lose their motivation to learn due to the frustration of their desires to learn what they want to learn." [39] (Quote from Our Book Four)

Unfortunately, many parents create a home environment where a child starts to shut down his ability to learn at a high rate of speed, when the parents start making all the major decisions in a child's life. Many parents do this to satisfy their desire to give their children the opportunities & the toys that they never had, when they were children, because they believe they have the obligation to help their children to succeed when facing the challenges of childhood. This also becomes the parents' opportunity to relive their childhood, by giving their children the wonderful childhood that they never had, but they want their children to have.

Unfortunately, many parents do not realize that they should allow their child to make the final decisions for, what the child wants to learn, who the child wants to play with, and what opportunities for learning to accept, as the child grows up, to enable their child to remain highly motivated to keep learning at a high rate of speed. It is difficult for a child to remain motivated to learn, when the parents are not allowing the child to choose what motivates her, by not allowing the child to make many of the final decisions about what she wants to learn & do, when the parents make the final decision based on what the parents think the child should learn & do and not on what the child wants.

Maria Montessori taught us to provide our son with the tools that he needed to learn and then taught us to allow our son to learn, without our intervention or unsolicited advice. If you are a parent or a guardian of a young child, please read, The Absorbent Mind by Maria Montessori to help you to learn how to help your child, to continue to develop his intellectual abilities by learning at a high rate of speed.

As our son learned to make more & more of the final decisions in his life as he grew up, he became increasing self-confident & wise for his tender young years, compared to many other children his age, when he started going to school for the first time, as he practiced sharing unconditional love & nurturing true friendship with his new classmates. As a result, our son, Wil, has many friends from his childhood who make an effort to spend time together, when they are home from university or college and when they are on holiday or on vacation. I expect our son to maintain many of his childhood friendships, all of his adult life.

And I have had many opportunities to learn wisdom from our son, as he grew from childhood into adulthood, that I have tried to share with other parents that I know.

How Unsolicited Advice Can Hurt A Child

I learned from My Son that giving him advice on improving his hockey skills, during the car ride home from a hockey game, was ruining My Son's opportunity to savor his enjoyment of the game that he had just played.

My son was twelve years old at the time, and he explained why he did not want or need my advice and then he asked me not to give him anymore advice on any topic unless he asked me for advice.

It took me many months to break my habit of giving my son unsolicited advice. I had to learn to detach from my automatic desire to give my son advice, a habit that grown powerful after twelve years of giving my son help. Eventually, I was able to kill this entrenched & hard to break habit of giving unsolicited advice to my son. However, I found it both difficult & painful to accomplish. A father wants to help his son even when his son tells him that he does not want his help, unless he asks for it.

I began to realize that my son may soon become a rebel teenager, like I was when I was a teenager. I was a teenager who rejected my parents' advice, because I had decided that the advice from my parents & my teachers at school was not helping me to navigate successfully through my teenage years, when I wanted to try marijuana, drink alcohol & chase girls, so I asked my parents to stop giving me advice, just like my son was asking me to do.

When our son was young, we were taught by Maria Montessori to allow our son to make the final decisions when he was choosing which new adventures to try next, during his childhood. It was not until he started going to school that we started to give him unsolicited advice because we were afraid he would get himself in trouble at school and we would not be with him when he needed our help. Our fear of potential perils in his uncertain future was not justified and he slowly realized that our advice was not needed or wanted, as he grew up. Like many parents, we realized almost too late that our fear of an uncertain future for our son was driving him away from us because we keep giving him advice instead of allowing him to make the final decisions in his life.

Fortunately, with our son's help, we learned to stop giving him unsolicited advice, which enabled us to repair the damage in our relationship, which allowed us to enjoy his teenage years without worrying about his uncertain future, so much.

Many parents that I know, find My Son's wisdom, "Please do not give your child unsolicited advice", difficult to understand and almost impossible to practice.

Questions for Parents

Is it not a mother's right to give her children unsolicited advice, as often as a mother feels it is appropriate to do so? Q-109

Do fathers feel the same need to give unsolicited advice to their children? Q-110

When I give my children unsolicited advice, am I being a True Friend? Q-111

Is unsolicited advice harming our relationship with our child? Q-112

Questions for Adults

Should I stop giving advice to my friends when it is not asked for? Q-113

Do I find unsolicited advice from my friends, helpful? If so, When? Q-114

Is unsolicited advice hurting my friendships? Q-115

As you answer these questions, I trust you will come to the conclusion that deciding not to give unsolicited advice will help to enhance your family relationships and friendships.

How I Benefit from Studying The Wisdom of Children to Increase My Ability to Share Unconditional Love & Nurture True Friendship

Can I say that the person I love, who I want to share my life with, who I may be engaged to, married to, or in a complicated romantic relationship with, is a True Friend? Q-116

Can I bring True Friendship to my family relationships? Q-117

The answer is I can, but its takes hard work, love & forgiveness and it requires a journey of self-discovery, as I look into my past life to understand my failed relationships, as I try to apply The Wisdom of True Friendship to my current life.

Will I make a journey of self-discovery with Bill & Wil, as I read Our Book One to discover The Wisdom of Children and apply this wisdom to my life to increase the Unconditional Love & the True Friendship in my life? Q-118

If you decide to answer, "Yes" to this question, then you will soon realize as you start applying The Wisdom of Children to your life that there will be a lot of pain & suffering along the way, as you begin to remember your past hurts & past regrets.

However, when you decide that are you are willing to kill the unfair pain & suffering contained in your memories and forgive others for unfairly hurting you, your reward will become beneficial to you, as you realize that The Wisdom of Children is working in your life, as you realize that the wisdom is true, as it becomes an important part of your adult life, as it begins to improve your relationships with your friends & family, as you learn to share increasing unconditional love & true friendship, and as you realize that your painful memories are starting to lose their power to hurt you again in the future when you relive them.

You will learn to control your thinking energy to become able to choose your feelings as you begin to experience increased love, peace, joy & compassion in your life. You will become more fun loving and an inspiration to your friends, who will want to share their adventures with you because you have an increased capacity to love them, to have more fun with them, and to help them feel increasingly understood, valued & appreciated. And you will be on the path to becoming their True Friend, as you offer them unconditional love & forgiveness without giving them unsolicited advice.

The desire for friendship was identified by Dr. Abraham Maslow, the renowned psychologist, as the desire for belonging, which Dr. Maslow called the highest human social need. As human beings we have a built-in need & desire for True Friendship in our lives.[40]

As you fully reconnect to your Internal Source of Unconditional Love, you will increase your ability to offer True Friendship to all human beings.

Unlocking The Meaning of My Life

The meaning of life for each human being becomes the purpose & significance of that person's life.[41]

The meaning of my life is expressed in my personalized answer to the questions that I have been asking about my life, that connect me, to the questions about the meaning of human life on Earth that our philosophers have been asking for thousands of years.

> Who am I?
> Where did I come from?
> Why am I here on Earth?
> What is my life's purpose?

It is as if I was born as a unique human being with a particular skill set of abilities, that no one who has ever lived has had and that no one in future will have. It is as if I am an experiment for living life successfully that will never be created in the same way again. My unique set of skills is inspiring me, to fulfill the unique purpose and to experience the special meaning of my life, which is to share unconditional love & nurture true friendship with all human beings in the world, especially my friends & family. I am unique, special & blessed to be given the opportunity to experience life as an unconditional loving human being on our precious Mother Earth." (Modified quote from A Spiritual Journey with My Son Wil section in Chapter 6 of Our Book One)

What is The Meaning of My Life? Q-119

The meaning of my life is embodied in my desire to share unconditional love & to nurture true friendship with all human beings who I know & spend time with at home, at work, or at play.

In addition to this personal meaning of the purpose of my life, there is a higher level of meaning for our lives that we share with all human beings on our planet Earth. It is called The Wisdom of The Meaning of Human Life

"Wisdom is a wise act or saying that improves the future well-being of our lives." (Quote from The Essence of The Wisdom of Children section in Chapter 8 of Our Book One)

The Wisdom of The Meaning of All Our Lives is generated by our global compassion for all life on Earth and by our personal compassion for those we personally know & love in our adult life, our friends & family.

There are many keys for unlocking the wisdom of the meaning of our lives to become able to increase our love, peace, joy & compassion that we share with those we love.

Unfortunately, I may quit my journey of self-discovery to increase the unconditional love in my life soon after I start. Why?

We will learn why in the next section of Our Book One.

Making a Commitment to Understand The Wisdom of Life

When I realized that I needed to develop a burning desire to dramatically increase the love, peace, joy & compassion in my life, by learning to kill all the major unfair pain living inside my negative memories that was preventing me from fully reconnecting to the full power of My Internal Source of Unconditional Love, I asked myself this question.

Am I willing to make a commitment to perform the hard work required to find all the keys for unlocking The Wisdom of The Meaning of My Life, to be able to maximize the love, peace, joy & compassion in my daily life? Why? Q-120

To help you to answer this question, please make a commitment to continue reading Our Book and continue applying The Wisdom of Children that you discover inside its pages to your daily life. When you do, you will begin to increase the love, peace, joy & compassion in your daily life until it becomes continuous.

And as you practice this wisdom, please describe your experiences of how this wisdom is benefiting your life with increased love & forgiveness and then share these experiences with your friends & family. The best way to increase your wisdom is to tell others about what you have learned so they can tell you of similar experiences in their lives as they become your teachers. The questions your friends & family will ask you about your experiences and the wisdom of their experiences will help you to bond with them spiritually as they become your true friends.

Nurturing the Wisdom that Lives Inside Me

The love, peace, joy & compassion in my life is increasing in power & longevity as I practice this wisdom.

I do not need a degree in psychology or religion to understand this wisdom, which was given to me when I was born and which I intuitively understood by experiencing it when I was a child.

And now, I am practicing this wisdom to continuously share unconditional love & nurture true friendship with my friends & family and to prevent anyone or anything from taking this love & friendship away from me in the future.

Chapter 23

Sharing Unconditional Love

As I reconnect to my childhood source of love
I start living life with increasing passion
As I share new fun filled adventures
With those I love

And I savor the love I receive from others
As I learn to mend the hearts I break
By loving my friends & family without restrictions
And by forgiving those who do not deserve forgiveness

As I share unconditional love
With sensitivity, understanding, trust & freedom
And I honor my commitment to accepting life's challenges
Without delays or requests for leniency

As I continue to help co-create our wonderful life
When we are together
And I cherish our enduring love & friendship
When we are apart

Unlocking the Wisdom of the Meaning of Our Lives helps us to increase the love, peace, joy & compassion that we share until it becomes continuous.

The First Key for Increasing My Unconditional Love

"I am learning to fully embrace my powerful childhood ability to love everyone in my life, so I can share continuous love & nurture true friendship with my friends & family in the future."

Unfortunately, I may quit my journey of self-discovery to increase the unconditional love in my life soon after I start. Why? Q-121

I may stop looking inside my mind, when I encounter pain from my memories of the past experiences of unrequited love & unfairness in my life that cloud over my internal connection to unconditional love, that I was born possessing and that may be hidden behind a wall of pain, that I will have to break through to become able to fully reconnect to my internal source of love, peace, joy & compassion before I can share increasing unconditional love & nurture true friendship with another human being.

The Second Key for Increasing My Unconditional Love

"I am learning to become courageous by looking inside my mind at my pain & suffering, so I can transform my memories & my ego by melting away their power to inflict unfair pain & suffering on me in the future, so they cannot hurt me anymore."

Looking inside my mind at my painful memories is often too painful for me to bear, when I do not know how to understand what is causing the pain, or how to kill it. I often decide to run away from my internal pain, by becoming lost in the activities of the external world and by acquiring things & doing things that I hope will bring me external love, peace, joy & compassion because internal spiritual love is no longer available to me.

Unfortunately, I still have the unresolved pain inside me that keeps sprouting into my mind as I relive my painful memories, which diminishes the quality of my fun & adventures in the external world during each day of my future life. This prevents me from fully enjoying life's challenges & opportunities and prevents me from being honest & open in my friendships, because I am afraid to look inside me at my painful feelings that I am trying to hide from others, as I try to nurture my friendships & loving relationships in the external world in the future.

I remain afraid & insecure, as I try to acquire the courage & the motivation to look at my painful memories in the present moment. To help me to acquire the courage that I need, I am learning how the pain is generated by my painful memories that I am afraid to confront and then how to become able to kill the pain. To do this requires an understanding of how my mind works, when it stores, feeds & activates the pain from my memories that I am reliving each new day of my life.

Am I afraid to look inside my mind at my painful memories? Why? Q-122

Accumulating Painful Childhood Memories

Babies are full of joy & happiness that they readily share with those they love. Only when children start to experience unfair pain & suffering, do the memories of their negative experiences start to build up in their subconscious minds. In the future when these painful memories sprout into conscious awareness, the child does not know how to manage the pain, unless the parents have taught the child how to use Meditation, Mindfulness & The Science of The Mind to kill the unfair pain inside the child's memories, to make the negative memories painless.

As I grew from childhood to adulthood, my cycle of suffering grew, until my childhood's natural ability to feel love, peace, joy & compassion was clouded over by a large number of memories of unfair pain & suffering that kept sprouting into my mind each day, to become the negative life diminishing energies that started to cause me unfair pain & suffering during each day of my life. To understand why this was happening, I realized that I needed to understand how my mind generated the pain from the memories of my negative life experiences in the external world because I wanted to learn how to stop this unfair pain, so I could be happy again. To accomplish this, I realized that I needed to understand how I was using My Mind, to understand my internal world when I looked inside my mind, and to understand the external world when I looked outside of my body.

How do I acquire painful memories? Q-123

How many painful memories do I have? Q-124

All young normal children are connected to their internal source of unconditional love during every moment of every new day of their lives. When an adult plays with a child who is connected, the adult can observe the unconditional love that the child has for all life & for all human beings that the child comes in contact with.

Connecting to My Childhood Source of Love

My earliest childhood memory of being connected to My Internal Source of Unconditional Love for all life occurred when I was less than a year old. I had not yet learned to walk. My mother carried me outside our home on a beautiful summer's day and placed me in a sandbox with my toys. This was the first time that I had been in a sandbox and I reveled in the experience. The sky was bright & clear. A gentle breeze was blowing through the trees and there were all sorts of interesting new combinations of sounds that I had not heard before. The birds were singing, the leaves of the trees rustling with the wind, and the insects buzzing. The sand was warm to my touch as I played for the first time with my toys to push the sand around into all sorts of interesting shapes & piles of sand. I felt the love from all the life surrounding me and I felt my love for this life, as I looked over my shoulder and saw my Mom sitting in a chair watching me play. I felt her love for me and I felt my love for My Mom, as I felt cherished & secure, as I felt the special bond between us, "My Mom & I, Always Together, as We Share Fun &

Adventures!" Then, when My Dad came home from work, he picked me up from the sandbox and carried me into the house. I felt his warm embrace as I nestled in his arms feeling warm & secure.

As my conscious mind becomes filled with these vivid scenes of my childhood that flow past The Mirror in My Mind, I start to feel the love, joy, wonder & delight that are also stored inside this beloved memory.

The unconditional love of a child is a feeling of intense love, peace, joy & compassion, which we begin to understand as adults, when we look at the elements that make up this love and then recombine the elements back together again, to achieve a powerful feeling of unconditional love for all the life that is surrounding us, as we embrace our childhood ability to love intensely, an ability that we were born possessing and that, unfortunately, many of us have diminished or lost, as we try to imagine this childhood feeling of unconditional love being shared by the billions of human beings living on Our Precious Mother Earth and as we try to imagine the resulting good that this love will generate in our lives when we start to embrace the full power of this love that motivates us to work together to eliminate all the hungry, poverty, sickness & disease from the lives of all human beings living on Earth.

Sharing The Unconditional Love of My Childhood

I embrace The Unconditional Love of My Childhood as an adult, when I start to share my love, peace, joy & compassion with all human beings, especially my friends & family, without asking for anything in return for my love.

Then, I continue to share this love, even when my love is rejected or I am treated unfairly, by a member of my family or friends.

Fortunately as an adult, when I embrace my childhood ability to love unconditionally, I can sense another person's ability to love me, even when they are hurting me, when I realize they were born with the ability to love me unconditionally, an ability that they may have lost at the present time but which they will find again, to become able to share unconditional love with me, hopefully, soon.

All I have to do is help them to fully reconnect to their internal source of unconditional love that they were born possessing, so they can start to experience the powerful love, peace, joy & compassion of their childhood, as adults.

What is my earliest childhood memory of my unconditional love for a family member or a guardian? Q-125

The Elements of Unconditional Love

My unconditional love generates feelings of love, peace, joy & compassion into my life. Each of these elements of unconditional love gives me a different ability to share unconditional love & nurture true friendship with my friends & family and with all the life that is surrounding me, whenever I use my childhood ability to become a child of love, once again. This love may be for a child or a teenager, a son or daughter, a girlfriend or my wife, a mother or father, a baby or a senior citizen, a friend or a stranger, or it could be for something I enjoy doing when I bond my love of being alive with my desire to experience new fun & adventures in my life, such as sailing, mountain climbing, writing a novel, taking my pet for a walk outdoors, or sharing wisdom with a new friend who just entered my life for the first time.

The Elements of Unconditional Love are:

1) Love - is deep affection for the continuous well-being of all life. Love lives in my heart and encourages me to take actions to help create, nurture & protect life enhancing experiences, as I share my love with all the life around me, especially with my friends & family as they share their love with me, as I try to use my childhood ability to create, nurture & protect this love with the great power & passion for living that I was born possessing.[1]

My feelings of love become continuous whenever I start to think of the person that I love or the fun & adventures that I want to experience in the future, as my mind starts to imagine new ways to cherish & share the wonder & delight of being in love.

2) Peace – is inner contentment, serenity & calmness of mind.

My feelings of peace & inner contentment occur in my mind whenever I am connected to the Internal Source of Unconditional Love of my childhood, as I allow this love to manifest in my adult life.

I am using The Wisdom of Children to maintain my continuous connection to the source of unconditional love, so I can continue to help my friends & family members to bring more love into their minds, so our relationships will become more peaceful. And I am sharing this love with my neighbors to help them to bring peace to their minds & their lives, in the hope that they will teach this wisdom to others, to help bring increasing peace to our nation & to the world, so that all human beings will learn to live in peace with each other.

3) Joy - is great delight, exceptionally good & satisfying experiences, keen pleasure, elation & rapture.

My joy is a combination of the mental pleasure that promotes my well-being and the physical stimulation of my body's senses that produces physical pleasure. When I am experiencing joy, I am not feeling any pain that may be hiding inside my conscious mind.

Examples of my joy are when I experience a baby's innocent smile, a child at play, an adult's satisfaction in accomplishment, a mother's pride in her children, and hugging my wife & child.

Joy is a personal evaluation that all my feelings, thoughts & images are satisfying me at the present time. Joy is intense & short lived. It lasts for a while and then disappears. It is stopped by pain and does not return, until I experience a new joyful stimulation from my internal or external world.

4) Compassion – is commiseration, mercy, tenderness, clemency, understanding, rapport, affinity, sympathy, pity & empathy.

My Compassion is a feeling of deep sympathy for another human being who is stricken by misfortune, a feeling that is accompanied by my strong personal desire to alleviate this person's suffering and my global desire to help nurture the well-being of all human beings on Earth by helping to minimize their pain & suffering, especially their distress, sorrow & unfulfilled desires.

Sharing My Compassion

I am sharing my compassion with other human beings by writing about The Wisdom of Children, a wisdom that all human beings can use to help alleviate their suffering and then replace this pain with increasing love & forgiveness.

Unfortunately, I do not have the resources, the money, or the long life that I need, to personally help each human being who is suffering, so I am trying to help those who will listen to my words that describe the benefits of Practicing The Wisdom of Children and who will then use this wisdom to help themselves and their friends & family to generate increasing compassion in their lives.

Unfortunately, I realize that some human beings will not practice The Wisdom of Children because they are afraid of trying to embrace their unfair memories so they can become friends with the pain their memories are generating, so they can learn how to kill their unresolved pain & suffering and then, so they can replace these negative feelings with abundant feelings of love, peace, joy & compassion, when they become able to convince their memories to stop generating new unfair pain into their lives in the future.

And whenever my compassion for another human being nurtures my desire to forgive, whenever someone treats me unfairly, I am trying to forgive, even when another person causes permanent loss or injury to me or to a member of my family or to one of my friends because I am trying to find a redeeming quality in this person that will enable me to believe that this person is capable of becoming a better human being, who will someday start treating other human beings fairly, especially my friends & family.

Unfortunately, some individuals such as the terrorists who kill innocent human beings, especially young children, I will not forgive because they have no redeeming qualities, in my opinion, even though some of our religious leaders may disagree with me.

In contrast to my lack of compassion for unredeemable human beings, I have deep feelings of compassion that inspire me to help all human beings in the world to learn The Wisdom of Children, especially the children, so I can help the children to learn how to remain connected to their internal source of unconditional love, by teaching them how to relieve the suffering that painful experiences bring into their young lives, as they grow up to become teenagers and then adults.

What is my definition with an example from my personal experience of each subcomponent of unconditional love? Q-126

Happiness

Feeling unconditional love for long periods of time generates happiness inside my mind

Happiness – is contentment, exhilaration, delight, satisfaction & well-being.

Happiness is a supreme state of contentment or well-being, as I live with all the life around me, especially with my friends & family. It is a blissful state where I am resting in continuous love, peace, joy & compassion without desires, even though my every wish may not have been fulfilled.

My continuous personal feeling of satisfaction with my state of well-being in the world may be interrupted by short term pain, but my happiness returns when the pain disappears, because of my internal personal conviction that the future events in my life will continue to enhance my well-being, especially with my friends & family because The Law of Karma is working to ensure that my life is blessed with fairness in the long term that will ensure my future happiness, even though I may experience unfairness in my life in the short term.

Examples of happiness are celebrating my wedding day surrounded by my lovely bride and my friends & family, being in the delivery room to witness the birth of our son, watching My Son succeed as I feel a father's pride in his accomplishments, and sharing the love of my friends & family as they accomplish their goals and fulfill their dreams.

Fear & Anger that Create Despair in My Life

The Wisdom of Children has taught me that the Fear & Anger I sometimes feel may not be real because it is being falsely created by my imagination, my memories or my ego.

"Fear & anger is the little-death that brings total obliteration of the love, peace, joy & compassion in my mind, whenever I allow fear & anger to control me. Fear & anger is the mind-killer, so I am challenging my fear & anger, by detaching from it, to allow my fear & anger to pass through me. And as this fear & anger starts to leave me, I am observing its passing until there is no fear & anger left inside me. Then, only I remain in the present moment as my ability to share love, peace, joy & compassion with my friends & family automatically starts to return to me, when my fear & anger are gone.

Only I, The Compassionate Watcher of my internal love, peace, joy & compassion will be left to take control of my actions, as I start to navigate, once again, through life to my future destiny." (Modified Quote from the Dune series by Frank Herbert)

Unfortunately, when my imagination, my memories or my ego start to create pain inside my mind, this fear & anger starts to hide my internal source of love, peace, joy & compassion, until I cannot feel my unconditional love anymore.

Fortunately, I can learn to kill the fear & anger that lives inside my mind because this pain is produced solely by me, when I start to think that my future life will be unfair to me. When I stop thinking that my future will be unfair to me, I stop feeding thinking energy to the fear & anger in my mind, as I stop feeding it the energy that it is using to keep itself alive inside me. When my fear & anger start to run out of energy, it starts to disappear from my mind. Then, my love, peace, joy & compassion is no longer hidden from my conscious awareness and my unconditional love automatically starts to re-motivate me, so I can resume working on My Goals for Today, as my motivation returns and as I protect my mind from feeling any new fear & anger today, by continuously Choosing My Feelings in the future, so that I become able to kill any new pain & suffering that tries to enter my mind.

And to help protect me from new fear & anger entering my future life, I am asking this question,

What will maintain the fairness in my future life, so I can use this fairness to kill any future fear & anger that may try to enter my mind? Q-127

The answer to this question is contained in The Law of Karma

Overview of The Buddhist Law of Karma

The Law of Karma generates, maintains & protects the fairness in all human relationships.

My ability to experience love, peace, joy & compassion is protected by The Law of Karma, which generates the fairness in my life, fairness that I need, to become able to share The Wisdom of Children with others.

My Soul is the container for My Karma, my memories of my past lives & My Eternal Mind-Stream of divine universal consciousness which I call My Compassionate Watcher, who continuously observes all the sentient life surrounding me and who I refer to every time I say the words, "I am." (Quote from The Choice to Acquire Faith section in Chapter 22 of Our Book One)

The Law of Karma maintains & protects the fairness in human relationships by ensuring that another person will be fairly punished, when he hurts me unfairly, by manipulating me, by lying to me, by stealing from me, or by abusing me. I may not punish him, but he will still suffer for his hurtful actions.

And The Law of Karma ensures that I will be fairly rewarded for my future actions whenever I act to benefit the well-being of all the life around me, especially the lives of my friends & family.

If my actions are fair & good, the consequences will be beneficial to me later in my future life. If my actions are unfair & bad, then I will be punished in full measure for the hurt that I have caused.

The consequences I create in my present life are called My Karma which is internally stored inside My Soul with my memories of my past lives by My Compassionate Watcher. My Karma helps to generate my future desires to act in a certain way that are based on the effects of my past actions that I created in my past life. The causes of my past experiences create future good or bad desires in my future life. Cause always creates effect. My future action always creates a future consequence.

So, I am trying to create fair & good desires in my present life that will motivate me to nurture & protect the well-being of all life in the future, especially the lives of my friends & family, to ensure that my future life will be filled with the fair & good consequences of these life enhancing actions.

I have Faith that the Law of Karma works, based on my life experiences that have shown that it is working to ensure fairness & goodness in my life and in the lives of all the human beings that I know.

My Karma is generated by the primordial energy strings of the universe, that administer the universal law of fairness in all human relationships, that influence my future actions & my future well-being, and that has been determined by the consequences of my past actions.

The strength of My Karma is the strength of my propensity to act in a certain way in the future that has been programmed into My Compassionate Watcher by the good or bad consequences of my past actions.

The Law of Karma is not based on fatalism because I can still change my future actions, even though I cannot stop My Karma from influencing my future actions, which create joy or pain in my future life, depending on the consequences of my previous actions which generate either good or bad Karma in my future life. [42]

How Wisdom Balances & Harmonizes Life

To understand The Law of Karma more fully, please try to understand how your karma influences your present & future life. To help you do this, I will describe how my cycle of eternal life, which is my cycle of birth, life, death & reincarnation, is influenced by My Karma. This description will help you to understand how karma works in the life of every spiritual being, whether they are living as a human being on Earth or as a pure spiritual being in Heaven.

Let me start by telling you that I believe I am an eternal spiritual being called My Compassionate Watcher who lives inside a human body while I am living on Earth. As a human being, My Compassionate Watcher preserves My Karma and the memories of my past lives on Earth.

According to the wisdom of Buddhist teachers, my childhood ability to love all life passionately is brought with me to Earth when My Compassionate Watcher is reborn inside a precious human baby as I start a new life on Earth called "My Soul living a human life on Earth", as I become a human being who shares unconditional love & nurtures true friendship with all the life around me during my lifetime on Earth.

As I grow from a baby into a child, then a teenager & finally an adult while I am living on Earth, I create fair & good actions in my life that help other human beings and I create unfair & bad actions in my life that hurt other human beings.

The good & bad consequences of these actions are stored in My Karma by My Compassionate Watcher who observes every action that I undertake while I am living on Earth. And when I die and leave my body to go back to Heaven, My Compassionate Watcher takes the essence of my past lives on Earth & My New Karma from this life, with me, as I travel back to Heaven to live a new life inside a spiritual body called "My Soul living a spiritual life in Heaven".

Then as I rest in Heaven, I learn new wisdom from wiser souls who are already living in Heaven. This new wisdom I will take back with me to Earth when I am reborn once again, when I start a new life on Earth, so I can continue offering to help other human beings to increase the wisdom that they share with those they love on Earth.

However, as I continue to rest in Heaven until I am reborn on Earth, I am reviewing my past life on Earth as I begin to realize that I need to ask for forgiveness from those souls who I have hurt during my past life on Earth. Some of them I will meet in Heaven and I will be able to ask for forgiveness while I am still in Heaven and I will try to repay these souls in some manner to help elevate the pain & suffering that I have created in their lives. And some of them will already be reincarnated into a new human body on Earth. So, I will have to travel back to Earth to ask for their forgiveness and offer to repay them, when I am reborn into a new human body on Earth.

My cycle of birth, life, death & reincarnation continues until I reach a high level of wisdom & spiritual existence, when I have fulfilled my task of acquiring forgiveness for all my bad Karma from those I have hurt, until all my debts to other eternal souls has been fully repaid, Then and only then, will I be able to stop returning to Earth, when I am satisfied that my work on Earth is complete. The choice of whether to live on Earth or to continue living in Heaven is now my choice to make. The Law of Karma is no longer requiring me to return to Earth to pay off any more debts. I am now free & clear of the bad consequences of the pain & suffering that I have created during my past lives.

DISCLAIMER - Until recently, I did not have any evidence that this Buddhist wisdom is true, other than my own human experience during my present life on Earth, a life that is telling me that this wisdom may be true. And I do not know if I will be reborn again into a new life on Earth. I hope this blessed event occurs so I can continue my journey towards Buddhist enlightenment as I share unconditional love & nurture true friendship with all sentient beings that I meet in my new reincarnated life. However, I am in no hurry to find out if reincarnation is true because I am enjoying my present life on Earth immensely and I do not want to leave this life any time soon.

Many Lives, Many Masters by Dr. Brian Weiss

Fortunately, more evidence is being discovered about our past lives, as clinical therapists, doctors & scientists continue their work in the new field of parapsychology.

Some of this evidence for life after death is contained in the book, "Many Lives, Many Masters" by psychotherapist Dr. Brian Weiss who used hypnosis to connect a patient to her past lives and to the spirits of the dead who were waiting in Heaven to be reborn into a new human life on Earth, These spirits were able to communicate with Dr. Weiss through his patient and were able to provide him with knowledge about Human Birth, Life, Death, Reincarnation & Karma that he describes in his book.

I found this book a fascinating read, even though I do not have the ability to remember my past lives during my present lifetime. I hope to be given the ability to connect to my past lives when I die at the end of my present life on Earth, when I go to back to Heaven to live as a purely spiritual being before I am reborn again into a human body as I begin my next life on Earth.

My Son & I have used a modified excerpt from Dr. Brian Weiss's book to help us to understand how reincarnation helps us to evolve into intellectually superior, wise & unconditionally loving human beings, over many lifetimes.

DISCLAIMER - This is our interpretation of the wisdom contained in, "Many Lives, Many Masters" by Dr. Brian Weiss and does not necessarily reflect the views of the author. The quotes from the author's book have been modified to the first person singular tense to help us to relate his wisdom to our lives and certain phrases have been modified. We have also have added our words to his words to help expand the meaning of his wisdom so we can practice this wisdom in our daily lives.

Beginning of the modified quote from, Many Lives, Many Masters by Dr. Brian Weiss:

Birth, Life, Death & Reincarnation

"When I am born on Earth, my task is to learn to become God-like through knowledge. I know so little wisdom. But I am thankful for My Guardian Angel who is living with me as one of my spiritual guides & teachers of the wisdom that I need to learn to be able to live my life successfully as I learn to love all life passionately. I have so much to learn.

Fortunately, I can add to the wisdom I have acquired on Earth by approaching God on the spiritual plane of existence while I am in Heaven, before I come back to the physical plane of existence on Earth when I am reborn, where I will grow up and then begin to teach this wisdom to others, as I try to help them to improve their lives.

There are many souls in the spiritual dimension. I am not the only one. I must be patient as I learn wisdom. There are many spiritual dimensions of wisdom & higher levels of spiritual existence. I start at a lower level of spiritual existence when I die and I move to higher levels of wisdom in the afterlife, when I am living in the spiritual realm in Heaven. What higher level I reach in this spiritual dimension depends upon how far I've progressed in learning wisdom during my previous life times on Earth.

What is required for me to progress to a higher level of wisdom & spiritual existence?

To progress, I must share my knowledge with other people while I am alive on Earth. I have abilities far beyond what I normally use. Some people start using these abilities sooner than others. As I gain wisdom, I also try to correct my vices while I am alive on Earth. Only I can rid myself of the bad habits that I accumulate when I am alive on Earth. If I choose not to rid myself of these vices, then I will carry them over into the next life. But if I decide that I am strong enough to become the master of these vices while I am alive on Earth, then I will no longer have to carry them into my next life. I am also learning not to just live with people who I am comfortable living with because their wisdom is at the same level as mine. It is normal to feel drawn to somebody who is on the same level that I am. But this does not help me to evolve. I must also go to live with people at a lower level who can benefit from my wisdom. Helping these people will increase my opportunity to progress to a higher dimension of wisdom & spiritual existence, as I learn new wisdom by helping others.

I have been given intuitive powers that I should follow and not try to resist using. Those who resist may meet with new pain & suffering when they do not use their wisdom to do the right thing.

I will not be reborn on Earth with the same powers as others who are being reborn. Some of us will be reborn with powers greater than others because we have acquired additional powers during our previous lives. Thus, people are not all born equal, but eventually after many reincarnations we will reach a point where all of us become equal.

Fortunately, I can choose when to re-enter my physical state on Earth and also I can choose when to leave this state when I die. I will also know when I have accomplished what I was sent down here to do. So, I will know when my time is up and then I will be able to accept my death when I am satisfied with my accomplishments during a future reincarnated lifetime on Earth.

Coulson/Practicing The Wisdom Of Children Our Book One

This will occur when I realize that I can get nothing more out of that future lifetime. After I die, I will have plenty of time to ponder on my accomplishments and the new wisdom that I have learned on Earth, as I rest in Heaven and re-energize My Soul before I choose to be reborn into another life in the physical plane of spiritual existence on Earth or before I choose to remain on the spiritual plane in Heaven.

Unfortunately, some of the others living in Heaven may hesitate, when they are not sure of when they should return to Earth and they might lose the chance to return that was given to them, as an opportunity to reduce their debt of Karma to others so they can reach a higher level of wisdom & spiritual existence as they reduce this debt.

However, everyone's path is basically the same. We must all learn certain virtues while we are living on Earth. Some of us are quicker to accept this wisdom for living, than others are willing to accept, especially the wisdom of practicing the virtues of purity, hope, faith & love. I must learn to practice this wisdom and learn to understand the wisdom of these virtues well. It's not just one hope and one faith and one love that I need to learn. So many things feed into each one of these virtues and there are so many ways to learn them. And yet, so far, I've only tapped into a little bit of each one.

People of the religious orders have come closer than any of us have in acquiring these virtues because they've taken vows of chastity and obedience. They've given up so much without asking for anything in return. The rest of us continue to ask for rewards and justifications for our behavior, when there are no lasting rewards from acquiring power, money & other things. Lasting rewards only come from helping others, when we help others without expecting anything in return for our help, as we help in an unselfish manner.

I am being guided by my spiritual teachers & guardian angels, as they encourage me to accomplish what I have been sent back to Earth to do. Then, when I have finished my tasks, my present life will end, but not before I have completed the tasks to my satisfaction. Fortunately, I have many lifetimes ahead of me to accomplish my goals, more than enough time, because I will live forever as a spiritual being.

Patience & timing are also important for me to learn when I am on Earth. Everything, including wisdom & opportunities for success, comes to me when it is time for them to come. A life cannot be rushed, cannot be worked on a schedule as so many people want it to be. I must accept what comes to me whenever it comes to me and not ask for more.

Also, I need to realize that life is endless because I am a spiritual being who will never die. I just pass through different phases of spiritual existence as I live my life in the spiritual or physical realms, such as when my physical body dies in this life or when the birth of my new physical body occurs when I am reborn into a new life on Earth. During these phases of physical life & death, my spiritual body remains unchanged and is never ending as I continue to be a spiritual being who lives inside many physical human bodies during many life times on Earth. As a spiritual human being I have many opportunities to evolve to higher levels of wisdom & spiritual existence as I live on Earth. But time is not important to my spiritual nature as I live inside my human body. What is important to me is the wisdom that I am learning as a human being living on Earth.

New wisdom becomes clear to me, as time passes, as I learn new things. But I must have a chance to digest this knowledge that I learn with the help of my spiritual teachers & guardian angels who live with me in Heaven and on Earth.

And to become able to help other human beings, I must choose other humans who are able to stop their fear & anger from controlling their minds & future actions. It is a waste of my energy to try to help them when fear is the predominant feeling in their minds. Fear stifles them from fulfilling what they were sent to Earth to do. So I take my cues from those who I am trying to help, by helping them to obtain a level of peace that is very, very deep inside their minds, which becomes a peaceful place where they can learn the wisdom that I am offering them.

Then, I can help them because the pain & suffering that lives on the surface of their minds cannot reach them when they are deep within their minds, where their feelings of peace are being created at the present time with the help of the spiritual being living inside each of them. This state of peace gives me the opportunity to reach them, to become able to help them to kill their daily reoccurring fear & anger so they can gain my wisdom for practicing continuous love, peace, joy & compassion in their future lives.

Living inside a physical body on Earth is not my normal state of spiritual existence. When I am in my spiritual body in Heaven, I feel most natural. Whenever I die on Earth and I am sent back to my spiritual state of existence in Heaven, I enter a state of wonder, awe & contentment as I am sent back to experience eternal peace, rest & renewal of the spiritual energy that I have lost while I struggled with the challenges of living on Earth.

I can also enter into this spiritual state of peace, rest & energy renewal while I am living on Earth, when I become a more evolved spiritual being. To do this, I first have to reach a higher level of wisdom & spiritual existence. Then, I can start to mentally rest while I am on Earth as my spiritual energy is being renewed and then, I can start to live on Earth in a state of continuous love, peace, joy & compassion as I fulfill the tasks that I was sent from Heaven to accomplish.

Do I need my physical body to continue growing as I achieve higher levels of wisdom & spiritual existence?

No, I do not. I go through many stages of growth when I am on Earth. When I shed my baby's body, I grow into a child's body, then from my childhood body I grow into an adult body, then from an adult body I grow into an old person's body. Then when I die, I shed my physical body on Earth and I go to live in a spiritual body in Heaven.

That is what I do as I grow older on Earth. I don't stop growing. I continue to grow. When I get back to the spiritual plane in Heaven, I keep growing there too. I go through many different stages of development as I grow in wisdom and as I grow into higher levels of spiritual existence. When I arrive in Heaven, my living energy & my motivation to share wisdom may be low, so I go through a renewal stage when I arrive in Heaven, then a learning stage, and finally a stage of decision making, until I decide it is time to return to Earth, so I can continue sharing wisdom & love with other human beings on Earth.

Some souls choose to go back to Earth to fulfill a new purpose there. Other souls choose to go on to another stage of development in Heaven. And they stay in spirit form as they do this. This time is spent in growth and learning, a continuous growth.

My human body is a vehicle for me to use to learn new wisdom and to grow spiritually, while I'm on Earth. It is My Soul & My Spirit that is living inside my physical body that lasts forever and it is My Spirit & My Soul that carries me back to Heaven when I die on Earth, when I leave my discarded physical body on Earth.

Is learning in the physical state faster?

No. Learning in the spiritual realm is much faster, far accelerated from that in the physical realm. But I choose what I need to learn. If I need to come back to Earth to work through a relationship, I come back. Then, when I am finished with that, I go back to Heaven in spiritual form. I can always contact those that are in the physical realm if I choose to. But only if there is something important to be gained by doing this, such as telling them something that they must know.

How do I make contact?

Sometimes I can appear before a person on Earth and look the same way as I did when I was last here. At other times I just make a mental contact. Sometimes the messages are cryptic, but most often the person on Earth knows what it pertains to. They understand. It's like a mind-to-mind contact.

Karma

When I do not reach a higher level of spiritual existence while I am in Heaven, it is because I have debts that must be paid to other souls who I have hurt in my past lives. When I have not paid off these debts before I die when I am on Earth, then I must take them into my next life, in order that they may be worked through. I progress to higher levels of spiritual existence by paying off my debts. Some souls progress faster than others. This is The Law of Karma at work, making sure that we pay for the pain & suffering that we have caused others in previous lifetimes.

While I wait in Heaven for my rebirth on Earth, I continue to pay off my debts. At this time, I am also trying to kill my dominant mental traits that will create new bad karma in my future life on Earth, such as my greed or my lust that will start controlling me when I am reborn on Earth. These traits will also prevent me from paying my debts during my next life on Earth, the debts to those souls who I been greedy with or lusted after in my past lives.

So, I try to kill my mental traits of greed & lust while I am in the spiritual realm in Heaven so I will not have to carry these traits, as while as other ones, with me into my next life. If I carry them with me, my burdens will become greater in the next life, as I use these traits to create more pain & suffering and increase the debts that I owe others.

With each life that I go through when I do not fulfill my debts, the next one will be even harder. But when I fulfill my debts and I kill the mental traits that will create new future debts, I will be given an easier life. So in this way, I can choose to fill my future lives with continuous love, peace, joy & compassion as I help others, after I killed off my traits of greed & lust that were creating the suffering during my lifetimes on Earth and were creating debts that The Law of Karma required me to carry with me into each of my new lives until they were paid off.

This is How Birth, Life, Death, Reincarnation & Karma Balance & Harmonize Life as they help us to grow in wisdom, as we are encouraged by our spiritual teachers & our guardian angels to practice using love, peace, joy & compassion to help nurture & protect all life on Our Precious Mother Earth."

End of the modified quote from "Many Lives, Many Masters" by Dr. Brian Weiss

I highly recommend that you read this book. It will help you to better understand the concepts of life, death & rebirth and our need to obey The Law of Karma as we pay off our debts to others, to enable us to evolve to higher levels of wisdom & spiritual existence during our never ending life, when we are living in Heaven as spiritual beings living inside our spiritual bodies or when we are living on Earth as spiritual beings living inside our physical bodies.

The Buddhist Law of Karma in Greater Detail

Now, let us look at the Buddhist concept of The Law of Karma in greater detail. This concept is similar to The Law of Karma described in Dr. Brian Weiss's book.

I wrote this section on The Law of Karma for readers of wisdom like me, who are never truly satisfied with their understanding of the wisdom they practice in their lives, and who like me, may continually be trying to find new creative ways to test their wisdom for truth as they continue to read about the wisdom that gives purpose & meaning to human life on Our Precious Mother Earth as this wisdom is described in the books written by many different authors of wisdom.

Fortunately, my friends & family and especially Linda, the romantic love of my life, have been willing to tolerate me because I am never satisfied with my accomplishments for long, especially my understanding about the wisdom of living a fulfilled life, as I continually search for new adventures to undertake that will give me a greater understanding of the meaning & purpose of our lives as human beings, as we try to live with each other peacefully, most of the time, on Our Precious Mother Earth.

My debt of Karma to my loved ones, continues to increase in this lifetime, even though I know my friends & family are helping to reduce my debt of Karma by forgiving me for neglecting them at times, when I find it difficult to stop researching new wisdom or writing new material for our books, when my desire to continue my work is so compelling that I lose track of time & space and I have to be reminded, usually by Linda, that I have obligations to my friends & family which includes spending more time with our loved ones.

The Law of Karma is The Law of Cause & Effect

According to this law, as described by the Buddhist authors that I have read, all my actions, whether physical, verbal or mental, produce consequences and also leave imprints on My Mind-Stream. This sets up a causal chain which continues from one rebirth to another. Karmic seeds ripen when they encounter appropriate conditions. I never experience consequences without having committed a causal act.

And I cannot avoid consequences of negative actions unless I apply remedies.

(Please refer to the concept of the Mind-Stream in the Glossary section of a Buddhist text, such as, Lamdre - Dawn of Enlightenment by Lama Choedak Yuthok)

To help you to understand this Buddhist wisdom, we have included detailed definitions of the words that we are using to describe this wisdom.

For example:

Mind-Stream is a Buddhist concept which refers to the continuous, unending and unbroken flow of our individual consciousness, from the "beginning less time" until now and Buddhism considers this flow of consciousness to be indestructible.

This Mind-Stream is a flow of energy that does not have a permanent body or a permanent self because it is continually changing as the stream of consciousness adds more experiences to its stream, similar to a river of water that is continually changing as its tributaries add more water to the river before the river empties its contents into an ocean of water.

Similarly, the river of the Mind-Stream of my individual consciousness, which generates My Eternal Mind, empties into the ocean of universal consciousness, where my individual consciousness is interconnected with every other individual consciousness in the universe, including your consciousness. I am an ever-flowing, ever-changing mind-stream of consciousness that is interconnected with all the conscious life in the universe.

What we call death is the total non-functioning of the physical human body. According to Buddhism, My Mind-Stream does not stop with the non-functioning of my human body, which is death, but it continues manifesting itself in another form, producing re-existence which is called rebirth.

Another explanation of rebirth is; "When my physical body is no more capable of functioning, energies do not die with it, but continue to take some other shape or form in another life. The process of taking on another life inside a new body is called rebirth." (Modified Quote from the book What The Buddha Taught by Walpola Rahula)

Fortunately, when I practice Mindfulness I am able to detach from all the feelings, thoughts & images that are trying to control my mind which allows me to connect to The Eternal Mind of My Mind-Stream, as I decide to live continuously in the present moment. Mindfulness is the state of knowing what is happening in the present moment, while it is happening, no matter what it is.

In contrast, when I allow a feeling, thought or image to start controlling my conscious mind, I become connected to My Ordinary Mind which hides My Eternal Mind from me, when I lose My State of Mindfulness and I stop living in the present moment.

To make the concept of My Mind-Stream easier for me to understand, I think of my individual stream of consciousness living inside My Soul with My Karma. My soul is the container that houses My Mind-Stream (also called, My Compassionate Watcher, My Eternal Mind or My Buddha Mind) and My Karma in the afterlife when my physical body dies on Earth.

Then, My Soul waits in the spiritual plane of existence, until I receive a new spiritual body for My Soul to live in, when I am reborn in Heaven or when I receive a new physical body to house My Soul when I am reincarnated on Earth.

Unfortunately, I do not know if My Mind-Stream of Consciousness actually exists. I will have to wait until my human body dies to find out the truth or falseness of the Buddhist concept of the mind-stream.

However, since I am enjoying a wonderful human life on Earth at the present time, I am in no hurry to find out if My Mind-Stream of universal never ending consciousness actually exists.

Someday, My Soul that is living inside my human body will leave my body as it is transported into the afterlife. As it enters the afterlife, it carries with it My Karma & My Compassionate Watcher, which is name I give to My Eternal Mind-Stream of love as My Soul navigates my passage through the afterlife until I leave the afterlife when My Soul is reborn into a new human body on Earth.

One of the main objectives of Our Book is to help adults realize that The Law of Karma will maintain the future fairness in their lives by nourishing the source of the power of universal love that lives inside all human beings.

And The Law of Karma helps us to eliminate the unresolved pain & suffering in our lives as we practice sharing unconditional love & nurturing true friendship with all human beings that we know, a practice which will help us to achieve the enlightenment of A Continuous Buddha Mind, which is our Eternal Mind.

A Special Teaching on The Nature of Our Mind

For those readers of our book who want to gain a more detailed understanding of the Buddhist concepts of The Mind-Stream, The Eternal Mind, The Ordinary Mind, and The Law of Karma, we have included a modified version of a teaching on The Nature of The Mind by His Holiness Sakya Trizin, who is Supreme Head of the Sakya School of Tibetan Buddhism.

Please note that this wisdom may be difficult to understand fully, as it was for me, when you read this teaching for the first time.

I found the Buddhist wisdom for understanding how my mind works scattered throughout many different Buddhist teachings, so I started to compare the study notes that I made as I explored each of these teachings and then I tried to unify this wisdom into one teaching, as I tried to fully understand how my mind works. This process took me many years to accomplish and has resulted in My Son & I writing the Practicing The Wisdom of Children series.

As an example of this undertaking, I have included a modified version of the Study Notes that I made when I tried to understand the wisdom of His Holiness Sakya Trizin. I hope you find these Study Notes helpful.

And if you find this teaching on The Nature of The Mind difficult to understand, as I did when I first read it, please stop reading and then move on to the next section of the book. Please come back to these Buddhist concepts of how our minds work, at a later date, when you realize that you want to understand these concepts more fully, so they can help you to achieve the mental state of A Continuous Buddha Mind.

Start of the teaching on The Nature of The Mind by His Holiness Sakya Trizin:

"One of the main teachings of the Buddha Is The Law Of Karma, the teaching that all the lives we have are not without cause, are not created by other beings, and are not by coincidence, but are all created by our own actions. All the positive things such as love, long life, good health, prosperity and so forth are also not given by anybody else. It is through our own positive actions in the past that today we enjoy all the good things. Similarly all the negative aspects, like short life, sickness, poverty, etc. and all the undesirable things are also not created by any outsider but by our own actions, the negative deeds we committed in the past.

Since Buddhists believe that The Law of Karma is true for all human beings and since I am a human being, then, if I really wish to be free from suffering and to experience happiness, it is very important for me to work on the causes. Without working on the causes, I cannot expect to yield any good results. Each and every thing in the universe must have its own cause of creation and it must be a complete cause. Things cannot appear without a cause. Things do not appear from nowhere, from the wrong cause, or from an incomplete cause. So the source of all my suffering is the causes of my negative deeds that were created when my causes became my negative actions that created negative karma in my life.

My negative deeds result from not knowing reality, not knowing the true nature of my mind, so I mistakenly create causes that have negative effects on my future life.

For example, instead of seeing the true nature of My Mind, I cling to a make believe permanent self without any logical reason. I have a natural tendency to cling to the concept of a permanent self because it helps me to understand why other human beings appear to be separate from me, as my physical body appears to be separate from theirs. It is a kind of habit that I have formed since beginning less time that helps me to understand "other" human beings.

However, if I carefully examine and investigate, I cannot find my permanent self. If there is a permanent self, it has to be my body, my mind, or my name.

First, a name is empty by itself. Any name can be given to anybody. So my name is empty by itself. The word "empty" means that something is not permanent in nature. It lives or exists for a short time and then changes into sometime else, such as when our bodies die and then are turned into ash by the energy of fire when our bodies are cremated.

Likewise, when I say the words "my body", it is just like saying "my house, my car, my home, my country" and so forth, so the words "my body" are empty words because they are not permanent words and "I" am separate from these words. I am not these words. If I examine every part of my body, I cannot find permanence anywhere. I cannot find anything called "I" or my permanent self. It is just many organic things that are living together that form what I cling to as my body. If I investigate carefully from head to toe, I cannot find anywhere a thing called my permanent self. My body is not a permanent self because my body has many changing parts, many different parts. People can still remain alive without certain parts of the body, so my body is not my permanent self.

Likewise, My Ordinary Mind is not a permanent self. When My Eternal Mind which is generated by my ever changing, never ending & indestructible consciousness called My Mind-Stream, becomes attached to my feelings, thoughts & images, it becomes My Ordinary Mind. Then, I may think that my ordinary mind is a permanent self even though my mind is actually changing from moment to moment. All the time my mind is changing. And my past mind is already extinct, already gone. Something that is already gone cannot be called a permanent self. And my future mind is yet to arise. Something that is yet to arise cannot be a permanent self. And my present mind is changing all the time, every moment it is changing. My mind when I was a baby and my mind when I am an adult are very different. And these different minds do not occur at one time. It is all the time changing, every moment it is changing. Something that is constantly changing cannot be a permanent self.

So, since my name, my body or my mind are not my permanent self, I have no such thing called a permanent self in my possession, but due to a long standing habit of mine, I have a very strong tendency to cling to a make believe permanent self. Instead of seeing the true nature of my mind, I cling to a make believe permanent self without any logical reason. When I believe this, it is just like mistaking a colorful rope for a snake, until I realize that it is not a snake but only a rope. I have fear and anxiety of this make believe snake, and as long as I cling to a make believe permanent self, I create suffering in my life. Clinging to a permanent self is the root of all my sufferings. not knowing reality, not knowing the true nature of the mind or body, I cling to a permanent self which generates suffering in my life because I start to believe that other human beings also have permanent selves and that I have to protect my permanent self from their actions that may hurt me.

When I believe that I have "a permanent self", naturally I believe that "other" human beings also have permanent selves. "My permanent self and their permanent selves" are dependent on the same concept of "a permanent self". Just like right and left. If there is right, there has got to be a left. Likewise, if I have a permanent self, there are "others" who have permanent selves. When I have a permanent self and "others" consider their selves to be permanent, then my love for my permanent self and my attachment to my permanent self, arises in my mind and motivates me to protect my permanent self and to keep it from harm. I also want to protect my friends and relatives and so forth. Then the concept of hatred may arise in my mind when I start to disagree with another permanent self, one of the "others", who has different views or different ideas.

Unfortunately, the three poisons, which are the ignorance of not knowing how my mind works, clinging to a make believe permanent self, and attachment to my desires or my dislikes, are the main poisons that keep me inside a net of painful illusions, called samsara."

A brief pause in the teaching by His Holiness Sakya Trizin

Start of my first study note:

The Definition of Samsara helps us to understand the teaching on The Nature of The Mind,

The Definition of Samsara states that Samsara is the pain & suffering of cyclic existence, which is the recurring pattern of birth, death & rebirth in which all sentient beings are trapped, until they practice the wisdom of enlightenment that will release them from this vicious cycle which creates the illusions of a permanent self that causes pain & suffering in their lives. (Please refer to the concept of Samsara in the Glossary section of a Buddhist text, such as, Lamdre - Dawn of Enlightenment by Lama Choedak Yuthok)

When I believe that I am a permanent self, I start to view other human beings as being permanently separate from me and I allow my ego to treat other human beings who are unfair to me as my adversaries. This causes my future conflicts with other human beings and causes my future fear, anger, hatred and desire for revenge, when another human being hurts me unfairly.

In contrast, when I realize that I am an impermanent self and that I am spiritually interconnected with all human beings by love, then all human beings become my spiritual brothers & sisters, as I realize that all human beings are living with me forever in a continuous interconnected Mind-Stream of love that permeates the universe.

So, I pray that sometime in the future, all human beings will begin to live on Our Precious Mother Earth with the realization that we are spiritual brothers & sisters, as we begin to unconditionally love & forgive each other and as we begin to nurture the well-being of our future lives by working together for our mutual benefit by living in peace & harmony with each other.

To help this prayer become a reality, I am asking for forgiveness for any pain or suffering that I may have caused another human being, as I learn to forgive me for falsely believing that I have a permanent self and as I learn to forgive me for wanting to hurt another human being when I believed this person was my adversary, when he treated me unfairly.

Now, I realize that deep down inside each human being, who lives with me on Earth, is a sometimes hidden love for each other that is connected by our mind-streams to a permanent source of universal love that permeates the universe, which makes us true spiritual brothers & sisters that were born as unconditionally loving human beings on Earth with the ability to love all life, especially all human beings.

Then, when we realize that we are spiritual brothers & sisters, we can begin to use our love for each other to work together to eliminate ignorance, war, poverty, hungry & disease on Earth for our mutual benefit and for the benefit of future generations.

I pray that the realization of our shared ability to love & forgive each other will start to occur when the majority of human beings on Earth begin to realize that there is no such thing as a permanent self, when we begin to understand that all the religions in the world who believe in a God of Love & Forgiveness, such as Islam, Christianity & Judaism, have the potential to unite all human beings together into one spiritual & loving family, who will forgive each other, as often as is necessary, to become able to work together for the common good of all human beings on Earth.

Why is it important for me to learn that there is no permanent self and that my body, my mind, my name & my human life are impermanent? Q-128

The answer to this question is motivating me to practice detaching my mind & body from all things that I do not need, such as excessive wealth & possessions that I do not use, so I can concentrate on achieving the one thing that I desire above all else in my future life. That one thing is A Buddha Mind that occurs when I transform the impurities in my mind that are causing my samsara, so I can achieve a state of mind that is free of impurities, which allows me to fully reconnect my mind to the universal mind stream of continuous love, love, peace, joy & compassion for all the sentient life that surrounds me and which motivates me to share unconditional love & nurture true friendship with my family & friends, while I am living my rare & precious human life on our Mother Earth in this life time, where my mind stream will remain continuously connected to my impermanent body until my body dies, and then my mind stream will be transported by My Soul to the afterlife, where I become freed from my impermanent existence on Earth.

Unfortunately, I may not achieve the enlightenment of A Continuous Buddha Mind in my current lifetime, since it may take me many future lifetimes to kill the impurities of samsara that are still attached to My Eternal Mind and that are hiding My Buddha Nature, as My Eternal Mind-stream of love navigates my passage through the afterlife until I am reborn into a new body, after each of my future lives & deaths, until I become permanently detached from the impurities that are preventing me from achieving A Continuous Buddha Mind and I become free of the continuous cycle that starts with each rebirth into a new human body on Earth, then a short life on Earth attached to my impermanent human body, until I experience the death of my human body, once again, and then as I experience the afterlife in my spiritual form, once again, until I am reborn, once again, into a new human body on Earth, in an endless cycle of birth, life, death, afterlife and rebirth, which only stops when I achieve A Continuous Buddha Mind.

Fortunately, I am able to increase the love, peace, joy & compassion that I share with my friends & family in each of my new future lifetimes because The Buddhist wisdom promises me that "Practicing the wisdom of enlightenment results in immediate benefits during my current life on Earth and the eventual achievement of A Continuous Buddha Mind in a future lifetime".

Unfortunately, I do not know if practicing the Buddhist wisdom will enable me to achieve A Continuous Buddha Mind in this lifetime because I am still suffering from the ignorance of not knowing the truth of many of the impurities in my present life, even though I have spent my lifetime trying to understand the special meaning of my life and I am trying to understand why I was given the opportunity to live a rare & precious human life on Earth.

However, I have not given up trying to fully reconnect to My Buddha Nature that is living inside me, as I continue to learn more Buddhist wisdom so I can benefit from practicing this wisdom in this life time.

End of my first study note

Teaching by His Holiness Sakya Trizin continued:

"Basically, the ignorance of not knowing how my mind works, the clinging to a make believe permanent self, and the attachment to desire or dislikes are the three main poisons of samsara that prevent human beings from fully reconnecting to their Buddha Nature, as they try to increase their ability to love & forgive each other. And from the three poisons arise other impurities, such as jealousy, pride and so forth. And when I have these poisons, I create actions. And when I create an unfair & hurtful action, it is like planting a poisonous seed on a fertile ground that in due course will yield painful results. In this way I create Negative Karma constantly, when I am caught up in the realms of believing in a false permanent existence and the necessity of protecting this illusion.

To be completely free from the consequences of my unfair hurtful actions and the resulting future pain & suffering of samsara, I need the wisdom that can cut the root of samsara, which is the wisdom that realizes selflessness, which is the realization of the impermanent nature of my body, my ordinary mind & my name. Such wisdom also depends on a method that works to unite all human beings together into a loving & compassionate spiritual family. Without practicing this method, I cannot cause wisdom to arise. And without wisdom, I cannot find the right method to practice. Just like needing two wings in order to fly in the sky, I need to practice both the method of love & forgiveness and I need to practice the wisdom of selflessness, in order to attain enlightenment. The most important method, the most effective method, is based on loving-kindness, universal love and compassion, and from this generates the bodhicitta, or the enlightenment thought, which is the sincere wish to attain perfect enlightenment for the sake of all sentient beings. When I have this thought, then all the right and virtuous deeds that I need are naturally acquired.

And I need additional wisdom that realizes the true nature of all phenomena, and particularly of my mind, because the root of samsara and nirvana and everything else is in my mind. The Lord Buddha said: "One should not indulge in negative deeds, one should try to practice virtuous deeds, and one should tame the mind." This is the teaching of the Buddha. The fault lies in my wild mind, when I am caught up in samsara and the cycle of existence. The purpose of all the eighty-four thousand teachings of the Buddha is to tame My Ordinary Mind. After all, everything is in my mind - it is my mind which suffers, it is my mind which experiences happiness, it is my mind which is caught up in samsara and it is my mind that attains liberation or enlightenment. So when the true nature of my mind is realized, and I am able to fully reconnect with My Eternal Mind & My Buddha Nature, all other things, all other outer and inner things, are then naturally realized.

So what is my mind? If I try to investigate where my mind is, I cannot find my mind anywhere. I cannot pinpoint any part of my body and say, "This is my mind." So it is not inside my body, not outside my body, and not in between my body. If something exists, it has to be of specific shape or color but I cannot find it in any shape or any color. So the nature of my ordinary mind is emptiness, which means my ordinary mind is not permanent and I can detach my ordinary mind from all my feelings, thoughts & images to become My Eternal Mind, also called My Continuous Buddha Mind, which is indestructible & ever changing because it is generated by My Eternal Mind-Stream."

A brief pause in the teaching by His Holiness Sakya Trizin

Start of my second study note:

To help you to understand this teaching, please think of the emptiness of your ordinary mind, as a vessel that cannot possess a permanent content of feelings, thoughts & images or as a vessel that does not hold anything that has a permanent nature, because your mind & body and everything else in the universe is constantly changing. Your mind only exists as a never ending stream of consciousness that only holds ever changing feelings, thoughts & images, and it holds each one for only a short time.

End of my second study note

Teaching by His Holiness Sakya Trizin continued:

"But when I say that everything is emptiness and doesn't exist permanently, it does not mean that everything has an impermanent nature, which lasts for a short period of time, before it starts to change and become modified. Even though, it is the changing impermanent content of my mind which I use to do all the wrong things, it is also my mind which I use to do all the right things, and it is my mind which experiences the results of my actions, such as the new suffering that I bring into my life. Therefore, there is a permanent mind called My Eternal Mind of course - I am not dead or unconscious, but I am a conscious living being, and there is a stream of continuity of my consciousness which is generating My Eternal Mind, which I call my Mind-Stream, which is indestructible but whose content is impermanent and changing constantly, as do the actions that I use my mind to formulate, before I act to cause an effect that creates good or bad Karma in my future life.

Just like a candle light that is always burning, the clarity of my permanent mind is constantly continuing. The characteristic of my mind is clarity. I cannot find it in any form or in any color or in any place, yet there is clarity in my mind that is constantly continuing. This is a permanent characteristic of my permanent mind. And the two, the clarity and emptiness (or impermanent nature) of the content of my mind are inseparable, just like fire and the heat of fire are inseparable.

The clarity and the emptiness cannot be separated. The inseparability of the two is the essence, the un-fabricated essence of My Eternal Mind which is being generated by my eternal & indestructible mind-stream.

In order for me to experience such a state of mental clarity, it is important to go through the preliminary meditation practices. Also, through preliminary practices I accumulate merit. It is best to meditate on insight wisdom to find out the true nature of my mind.

For that I need to prepare my present mind, which is my ordinary mind that is constantly attached to streams of thoughts. Such a busy and agitated mind will not be a base for insight wisdom. So first I have to build a base with concentration, using the right method. Through concentration, I try to bring my mind to a very stable state as I try to detach from all my feelings, thoughts & images to enable me to become fully reconnected with My Eternal Mind. And on such stable clarity and single-pointedness, I can then meditate on insight wisdom and through this I can realize the true nature of my mind, which is My Eternal Mind. But to realize this, I require a tremendous amount of merit, and the most effective way of acquiring this merit is to cultivate bodhicitta."

A brief pause in the teaching by His Holiness Sakya Trizin

Start of my third study note:

To help you to understand this teaching, please think of merit as the consequence of performing a good deed or an "act of merit" that creates a blessing, such as creating the energy of peace, joy or happiness that begins to live inside you, both in this world and in the hereafter.

Bodhicitta is the attainment of the understanding that my mind contains only emptiness which means my mind contains no permanent content or permanent self because it is always changing.

Bodhicitta is also the desire to obtain personal enlightenment in order to benefit other sentient beings, to help them to end samsara, which is a state of suffering caused by their ignorance of impermanence, which generates their continuing cycle of birth & death and prevents their enlightenment.

End of my third study note

Teaching by His Holiness Sakya Trizin continued:

"So with the two together, the insight meditation method and the wisdom of bodhicitta, I can realize the true nature of my mind, which is My Eternal Mind. And when I begin to realize that My Eternal Mind has a true & ever changing nature and I begin understand this true nature, then, my understanding of the wisdom of the true nature of my mind will increase until I fully understand the true nature of My Continuous Buddha Mind when I attain enlightenment by achieving a continuous connection to My Eternal Mind."

End of the teaching on The Nature of The Mind by His Holiness Sakya Trizin

Start of my fourth study note:

To help you to understand this teaching, please realize that "attaining enlightenment" refers to the awaking of My Buddha Nature, an ability that all human beings possess.

When I become a perfectly awakened Buddha, who correctly understands the status of all knowable things in the ultimate reality of the universe, then I am able to use the thinking power of My Pure Eternal Mind which becomes The Mind of a Buddha, also called A Buddha Mind, that is free from impurities which enables me to understand the nature of the universe, when I become a perfectly awakened Buddha who possesses the consummate bliss of continuous love, peace, joy & compassion, which are feelings that live in my mind as I offer to share them with all human beings, especially my friends & family.

I become a perfectly awakened Buddha whenever I eliminate all stains of obscurations from my mind's vision, which enables my mind to perceive only a pure & correct vision of understanding, whenever I use my mind's vision to observe the true nature of the universe and the true nature of all the life that is surrounding me in the present moment.

A Formal Definition of My Buddha Nature

Buddha Nature is Buddha gotra (Skt); sang rgyas kyi khams/ rigs (Tib). Our Buddha Nature gives us the potential for achieving Buddha-hood which is present within all sentient beings. The

Buddha Nature of sentient beings contains The Eternal Mind which is also called The Buddha Mind, which is vast, pure and unsullied.

Beings are held back by their adventitious defilements and obscurations which become attached to their eternal minds which cause their minds to become Ordinary Minds. Once these illusions are removed, their true eternal minds, characterized by both clarity and emptiness, automatically emerge. (Please refer to the concept of the Eternal Mind in the Glossary section of a Buddhist text, such as, Lamdre - Dawn of Enlightenment by Lama Choedak Yuthok)

End of my fourth study note

DISCLAIMER - This is our interpretation of the wisdom contained in His Holiness Sakya Trizin's teaching on "The Nature of The Mind" and does not necessarily reflect the views of Sakya Trizin. The quotes of Sakya Trizin's wisdom have been modified to the first person singular tense to help us to relate his wisdom to our lives and certain phrases have been modified. We have also have added our words to his words to help expand the meaning of his words, as we try to understand this wisdom.

Fortunately, you may obtain a sacred & pure understanding of the wisdom of His Holiness Sakya Trizin & other Tibetan Buddhist Masters at The International Buddhist Academy website,

http://internationalbuddhistacademy.org/

Please realize that Buddhists have been studying the science of the human mind for thousands of years. Without their wisdom & help we would not have become able to understand the true nature of our human minds and we would not have been able to write Our Book, because we do not have the time & the resources to recreate this wisdom by ourselves, due to the short life span that we have been allowed to live as unconditional loving human beings on Our Precious Mother Earth.

Fortunately for us, the Buddhist wisdom of the mind has been acquired through great effort & sacrifice by our ancestors and is held

sacred & pure by Buddhist Masters such as His Holiness Sakya
Trizin, to whom we are forever indebted, for their unconditional love
for all life, especially their love for us that has motivated them to
become teachers of the Buddhist wisdom on the nature of the mind,
so they can offer it to us for our mutual benefit and for the benefit of
future generations of human beings.

What the teachers of this wisdom are trying to tell us is that our
future lives will ultimately become fair to us because all human
beings are connected to each other by universal unconditional love
and this love will make out future lives fair, as long as we do not
associate with human beings who are temporarily cut off from their
universal source of love by their memories of pain & suffering that
they keep reliving, as they continue to experience samsara in their
lives.

When we do associate with human beings who treat us unfairly then
our Buddhist teachers have taught us to forgive them, so we can start
to share unconditional love with them, so we can help them to
reconnect to their internal source of unconditional love, so they will
start loving themselves more and they will start to offer us increasing
love & fairness, once again.

Unconditional Love is like a Precious Coin that I Spend when Sharing Love

To help me to understand the wisdom of sharing love, peace, joy &
compassion, I use my conscious mind to imagine being given a new
coin of unconditional each day of my future life with the instructions
that I spend it today to bring unconditional love into someone's life,
even if this sharing of love only lasts for a short time.

My Precious Coin of Unconditional Love has two sides, one of love
& one of compassion. In the middle of My Coin of Unconditional
Love is the wafer of peace & joy that bonds the two sides together
into a feeling of unconditional love for all life. I am given a new
Coin of Unconditional Love each day of my life by My Internal
Source of Unconditional love that lives inside me to enable me to
spend this coin of love to nurture and protect those I love. I realize

that My Coin of Unconditional Love is empowered by the unconditional love emanating from all life in the universe that comforts & protects everyone in the world who is able to access this love that lives everywhere there is life. Then at night, when I am resting, I savor the experiences of my day, knowing that the power of My Coin of Unconditional Love has motivated me to share love & nurture true friendship and knowing that I will receive a new Coin of Unconditional Love tomorrow to help me to share love & friendship with someone new.

As children we spent our new wonderfully pure, bright & clear Coin of Unconditional Love each day as we shared our love with our friends & family.

Unfortunately, by the time we become adults, many of us are unable to receive new Coins of Unconditional Love each day, as the worry & stress in our daily lives prevents us from remembering where to find our Internal Source of Unconditional Love, which is no longer offering us new coins to spend because our source of love is hidden under our memories of unfair pain & suffering that we keep reliving each day of our adult lives.

As an adult, when I look inside of my mind and I begin to practice The Wisdom of Children, I become able to fully reconnect with my internal source of love which allows me to acquire a new Coin of Unconditional Love that I can spend today.

Only when I have convinced my memories to stop generating new pain & suffering into my life each day will My Coin of Unconditional Love start to shine brightly again, with the pure energy of unconditional love that I first experienced when I was a child.

Only then will I be able to re-start spending a new coin each day as I begin to experience increased love, peace, joy & compassion in my life, while simultaneously experiencing reduced unfair pain & suffering from my negative memories.

Only then will my friends & family start to experience & benefit from the increased love & compassion that I offer to share with them.

Only then will my new understanding of The Wisdom of Children help me to maintain my connection to My Internal Source of Unconditional Love, as I learn how to kill any new unfair pain that enters my future life and tries to block the access path to my source of unconditional love.

Only then will killing the new unfair pain in my life become my daily challenge & my quest, so that when the killing is done, I will experience pure, untarnished unconditional love continuously during each moment of every day of my future life because I am able to maintain a solid connection to the source of this love, for all time, as I live in the present moment.

Then, as I look back on my life experiences, I will realize that my happiness is built on my ability to share love, peace, joy & compassion with those I love, as I continue to receive the increased energy of healthy self-love from my internal source of unconditional love that I am learning to share with other human beings, as I help motivate them to rediscover their own internal source of unconditional love whenever they lose their connection to this love, as I have been able to do in my past life whenever I lost my connection to my source of love, as I spend My Coin of Unconditional Love each day to nurture & protect those I love by helping them to maintain their connection to the source of unconditional love for all life in the universe, by sharing unconditional love & nurturing true friendship with everyone in my life.

How often do I spend My Coin of Unconditional Love? Why? Q-129

The Compassion of Buddha, Mohammed, Lao-tzu & Jesus

The deep & all-embracing compassion of our wise prophets & sages such as Buddha, Mohammed, Lao-tzu & Jesus inspire us to live our lives with unconditional love & forgiveness for every human being that we meet during our lifetime.

I understand the Christian wisdom of love & forgiveness more intimately than the wisdom of other religions, so I will use this understanding to describe the wisdom of our prophets & sages, who teach us different but similar wisdoms, as they teach us to love all the human beings we meet during our lifetime on Earth and to forgive those who hurt us, especially those who do not deserve our forgiveness.

In the Bible, a lawyer asked Jesus,

"Master, which is the greatest commandment in the law?"

Jesus said unto him,

"Thou shalt love the Lord thy God with all thy heart, and with all thy soul, and with all thy mind. This is the first and greatest commandment. And the second is like unto it, Thou shalt love thy neighbor as thyself."[43]

As a Christian, for me to be able to practice the second commandment, "Thou shalt love thy neighbor as thyself", I have to love myself first, to be able to acquire healthy self-love, to become able to acquire a store of healthy self-love & compassion for others that I can share with my neighbors.

When I hate myself, I cannot acquire the love that I need to be able to generate feelings of forgiveness for other human beings.

My feelings of healthy self-love & compassion for others will only be renewed inside me when I feel my connection to the internal source of love, peace, joy & compassion that lives inside of me, a love that I received as a gift from God when I was born, a gift I can use to kill the unfair pain that may be generated by my painful memories or my ego that will try to stop me from experiencing continuous healthy self-love that I am using to generate compassion for my neighbors.

My Connection to All Life

When I visualize the tiny primordial energy strings of the universe powering My Awareness of My Connection to All Life and powering the energy of my mind & the atoms of my body, then I expand my view, to visualize these tiny energy strings powering the atoms inside all life in the universe, as I start to feel my connection to all life in universe. All life in the universe becomes a part of me and I become a part of all life in the universe, as I visualize the energy strings connecting me to all life, as I feel the energy of the unconditional love from all life inside of me. We are joined together inside a field of spiritual energy of love by the energy strings of the intelligent primordial awareness of the universe, who I call God, who gives all human beings our internal source of unconditional love, which connects all human beings on Earth together into one big family of brothers & sisters, mothers & fathers, and children.

My Happiness is a personal sharing in the unconditional love from God that is enhancing the well-being of my life by offering my life a continuous source of unconditional love.

My Personal Compassion is my personal desire to use my unconditional love to enhance the well-being of all human beings, especially my friends & family.

My Global Compassion is my global desire for universal unconditional love to enhance the well-being of all human beings on Earth who are members of my family of unconditional loving human beings.

My Compassion provides me with my personal motivation to use my efforts to help improve the well-being of all human beings, by offering them the wisdom in the books that I write and the services of the educational foundations that I set up, as I dedicate my efforts to helping all people on Earth to apply The Wisdom of Children to their lives. Their life force is given to them by God to motivate them to increase the joy & happiness in their lives and I empathize with the desire of all human beings to improve their lives as I feel healthy self-love & compassion for others and as I try to help all human beings, one at a time, starting with my friends & family.

Practicing The Wisdom of Children is acting wisely when I forgive those who hurt me, when I believe they are able to fully reconnect with their internal source of unconditional love, to become able to ask for my forgiveness, sometime in the future, as they become able to start sharing unconditional love & nurturing true friendship with me, once again.[44]

I desire to help all human beings to rediscover their internal source of unconditional love & true friendship, so they can become able to share joy & happiness with me, instead of pain & suffering.

This includes my friends & family whenever one of them loses the connection to their internal source of unconditional love and can no longer love me or treat me fairly, whenever a neurosis temporally takes control of their mind.

Neurotic People Blocking Their Compassion for Others

A neurotic has a personality disorder typified by excessive anxiety or indecision and a degree of social or interpersonal maladjustment.[45]

Many neurotic people block their feelings of compassion for other people. They feel that the joy, love & happiness that they want in their lives is outside of them, somewhere in the external world because they can no longer connect to their internal source of love, and they feel the need to compete with other human beings, to obtain the scarce resources of love in the external world. With this attitude they start to treat other people unfairly, as others become adversaries who they start to dislike, as they compete with other human beings for the external love in the world. This adversarial relationship makes them feel separate from other people, as their memories of the unfair pain & suffering in their lives cuts them off from their internal source of love, peace, joy & compassion.

To become able to experience internal healthy self-love & compassion for another person, once again, a neurotic person needs to learn how to kill the major unfair pain in his memories that is blocking the path to his internal source of love, to become able to reconnect to the well spring of unconditional love that is always flowing inside him. Then, he can start to share unconditional love with other people, once again, and he can start to feel respect & compassion for other people. We will explore how we can help the neurotic child who is buried inside many adults, to reconnect to his internal source of unconditional love in Our Book Four.

When neurotic children grow up, they become bad when they become cut off from their internal source of love for long periods of time, as they start to treat other people unfairly when they begin blaming others for their pain & suffering. This is in contrast to a good child who grows up sharing love with everyone and who tries to treat others fairly as he shares forgiveness with friends & family.

As Buddha, Mohammed, Lao-tzu & Jesus taught us, every single human being on Our Precious Mother Earth can help to enhance or decrease the amount of love & fairness that is being created in our lives each day.

For example, "religious faiths can help good people to make themselves better, kinder, more honest, more faithful & more responsible. This is in contrast to bad people who use their religious beliefs as an excuse to lie, cheat, steal, and murder, when they tell themselves that the other fellow isn't of their faith, and that makes it all right to treat this other person unfairly, because he is not a member of their faith.

The same beliefs of good & bad are held by all types of people, both believers & non-believers of the different religious faiths around the world.

And good people can be found everywhere in all cultures, while believing in all sorts of different religious doctrines on what is good & bad, and so can the bad people. However, what is true in all cultures & everywhere on Earth is that every religious faith makes a good person better and a bad person worse." (Modified quote from Against the Odds by Elizabeth Moon)

To experience continuous happiness & compassion I am learning to stop being bad and learning how to be good. I am accomplishing this by killing the major unfair pain inside my memories, to prevent my memories from generating pain when they sprout into my conscious mind each day, so pain does not interrupt my feelings of unconditional love, that I was born possessing, that I experienced every day of my life as a child and that I need to fully reconnect to as an adult, to provide me with the powerful motivation I need to share love & nurture friendship with the good & bad people in my life. To accomplish this, I need to practice using my childhood ability to love everyone in my adult life.

The Love & Compassion of Children

The childhood education pioneer Maria Montessori in her book, The Absorbent Mind, describes the nature of a child eloquently, when she writes,

"The child is the only point on which there converges from everywhere a feeling of gentleness and love. People's souls soften and sweeten when one speaks of children, the whole of mankind shares in the deep emotions which they awaken. The child is a well-spring of love. Whenever we touch a child we touch love." [46]

Maria Montessori also describes a child's innate sense of compassion for another child when she writes,

"One day it happened that a little one had spread out all the wooden geometric figures with their cards on the floor. Suddenly a band heading a procession was heard passing in the street right under the schoolhouse window. All the children ran to look, except the one, because he would never have dreamed of leaving so much work lying about loose. It must all be put back in its right place, and no one seemed inclined to lend him a hand. But his eyes filled with tears, as he would dearly have loved to see the procession. The others noticed this and many turned back to help him." [47]

Psychiatrist Theodore Rubin, who is a past president of the American Institute of Psychoanalysis and the author of over 30 books, states in his book, Compassion and Self Hate,

"A human infant is born with a great capacity to like and to get along fairly well with himself. It takes considerable effort to divert him from his natural affinity for a compassionate life." [48]

Psychiatrist Theodore Rubin describes compassion as, "ultimately, a state of mind in which benevolence reigns supreme and in which a state of grace is established within us." [49]

In other words, when I was a young loving child I desired to help other human beings, especially friends & family and I was forgiving of mistakes.

Accepting My Unconditionally Loving Nature

Before you read any more of this wisdom, it is important for you to remember when you were an unconditional loving human being when you were a young child.

Only when you decide to remember the experience of being connected to unconditional love in your childhood, can The Wisdom of Children start to help you to increase the passion in your daily life, as an adult. You need to remember your childhood experiences when you were unconditionally in love with all life and when you felt the love from all life inside of you. Only then will you be able to prove to yourself, as an adult, that you have proof that you understand The Wisdom of Children because you experienced unconditional love when you were a young child. Then upon this proof from your childhood you can start to build adult wisdom. This solid base of your childhood experience of unconditional love will enable you to apply The Wisdom of Children to your adult life, to enable you to fully reconnect to your Internal Source of Unconditional Love & True Friendship that you experienced in your childhood, to begin to experience increased love, peace, joy & compassion in your adult life.

What is my written description of two memories from my childhood of the fun & adventures I experienced as a young child, when I felt love for all life & I felt the love from all this life, as I enjoyed playing games with my friends & family? Q-130

I have relived the earliest memories of my childhood when I was in love with everyone. Now I accept the truth that I was born as unconditional loving human being and now I have a choice to make when I wake up each morning of my future life.

I can decide to think about using this knowledge of Who I am, as an unconditional loving human being, to improve the well-being of my life by thinking about how to use my ability to unconditionally love my friends & family, or I can decide to ignore my childhood ability to unconditional love all life, especially my friends & family.

If I decide to ignore my ability to unconditional love all human beings, I will start to suppress my memories of being an unconditionally loving human being when I was a young child, to stop me from remembering that I have this ability as an adult, to love all human beings in the world, especially my friends & family.

This is the decision that Ayn Rand made when she wrote her philosophy of Objectivism, when she said, "I am therefore I will think", when she accepted her nature as an unconditionally loving human being and she decided to work with other human beings in mutual self-interest to improve the well-being of their lives by writing her books, screenplays & monthly newsletters, to inspire us to think rationally for the benefit of our mutual self-interest and the mutual self-interest of all unconditionally loving human beings on Earth.

The motivation to help other human beings to improve their lives is generated by our innate ability to unconditionally love all life, especially all human beings. It is an acceptance of who I am as a human being, when I remember that I was born with an internal source of unconditional love for all life.

My understanding of Ayn Rand's, "I am therefore I will think" rationally is, I accept my nature as an unconditionally loving human being and I will use my rational thinking ability to work with other human beings in mutual self-interest, to nurture & protect the laws for the personal freedom of all human beings in our country, which will benefit my future well-being and the well-being of those I love, especially my friends & family.

DISCLAIMER - My understanding of the phrase, "I am therefore I will think" does not necessarily reflect the understanding or the views of Ayn Rand.

This is the opposite of the philosophy of Rene Descartes who said, "I think therefore I am." Rene may not have fully realized that many human beings do not automatically think rationally. Many human beings follow their feelings & their Ego, which allows them to doubt the true nature of their spiritual existence, when they decide not to accept the truth of their spiritual existence as unconditionally loving human beings.

A human being who follows Rene's philosophy may conclude that the concept of who he is as an unconditional loving human being is a figment of his imagination and his memories of the unconditional love that he felt during childhood are not real, so he can justify his ego driven need to feel superior to other human beings. These feelings of superiority may motivate him to take as much as he can from other people to satisfy his desire for external joy & happiness. And these feelings of superiority may motivate him to treat other human beings unfairly, by lying to them, by cheating them or by bullying them whenever he feels this unfair behavior will help him to obtain control of the scarce resources of money & power in the world that other people have and that he wants for himself. This denial of his innate nature as an unconditionally loving human being enables him to maintain feelings of superiority towards human beings who may not share his ethnic background, political beliefs or religious convictions and enables him to justify taking continual unfair advantage of other human beings to satisfy his desire for external wealth & security.

Unfortunately, this philosophy of superiority has been used to justify warfare and the slaughter of innocent human beings for thousands of years and justifies the trafficking of human slaves around the world, today, which is generates billions of dollars from slavery each year.

My understanding of Rene Descartes's, "I think therefore I am" is that I was born superior to other human beings who should treat me with respect because they are inferior to me and deserve to be told what to do, to satisfy my ego's desire for external love & respect. (Please refer to Our Book Three to explore why many human beings desire to feel superior to people who hurt them unfairly)

DISCLAIMER - My understanding of the phrase, "I think therefore I am" does not necessarily reflect the understanding or the views of Rene Descartes.

In contrast, the acceptance of our fundamental nature as unconditionally loving human beings motivates us to eliminate feelings of superiority, when we look at other people, when we realize that every human being has the ability to live in harmony with every other human being because of his unconditional love for all human beings that motivates him to protect the laws & institutions that protect every citizen's right, to vote to elect the lawmakers who will act as representatives of the citizens of the country, to pass laws to protect the rights of every citizen, to own land & material goods, to earn his own livelihood, to keep the profits from his work, to enjoy his privacy, to be allowed free speech, to bear firearms to protect his family & property, and to be allowed the freedom to pursue his personal joy & happiness, as long as he does not violate the rights of other human beings in doing so.

Adoption of the philosophy of unconditional love, as a way of living, promotes world peace as we learn to live in harmony with all human beings, as we work together in mutual self-interest to eliminate cultural, religious & racial intolerance, because we no longer feel that we are superior to other human beings who do not share our cultural history, our religion, or our racial ancestry and because we have become fully reconnected to our internal source of unconditional love which is filling us with love & compassion for all human beings.

This is a decision that each of us makes about our life, when we decide to unconditionally love all human beings, unless we make the mistake of adopting feelings of superiority to justify the demands of our Ego, when we falsely believe that we must treat other human beings as adversaries, when we falsely believe that we must compete with other human beings to obtain external joy & happiness in our lives, instead of working together in mutual self-interest to achieve common goals that benefit all human beings.

I hope & pray that all human beings accept the truth of their childhood memories that they are unconditionally loving human beings, and I hope & pray that all human beings will decide to practice using The Wisdom of Children to improve the well-being of their lives and to help improve the lives of their friends & family.

Those who decide they are not unconditionally loving human beings, or who question their spiritual existence and do not know who they are, may begin to live their lives in their imaginations, without a solid basis for understanding the truth & the reality of who they were born to be, as unconditional loving human beings. They do not possess a solid foundation of acceptance of who they are in the real world, upon which to build the future well-being of their lives and to become able to earn the respect of other human beings. Living in the world of imagination is the basis for generating feelings of superiority which results in treating other human beings with disrespect.

Unfortunately, many human beings that I know do not accept that they were born as unconditionally loving human beings and this lack of acceptance of who they are, inhibits their ability to become unconditionally loving adults and inhibits their ability to accept unconditional love when it is offered to them by other human beings.

Distilling The Main Theme of Our Book

The main theme of Our Book is that all human beings are born fully connected to an internal source of unconditional love that continually nourishes us each day, and that many human beings diminish or lose their internal connection to this love by the time they become adults.

Have I diminished or lost my internal connection to unconditional love? Q-131

If so, Why? Q-132

How do I fully reconnect to my source of continuous love? Q-133

And if you have diminished or lost your connection to the Internal Source of Unconditional Love, you will soon begin to realize, as you read Our Book, that it takes years to lose this love connection, and it may take you years to learn how to effectively kill all the major unfair pain in your memories that you started acquiring in your childhood, that may be blocking your connection to your Internal Source of Unconditional Love as an adult.

You need to kill the major unfair pain in your memories to be able to tear down the wall of pain & suffering that you may be experiencing each day of your adult life, as you relive your unfair painful memories, as you relearn how to fully reconnect to your Internal Source of Unconditional Love that is still living inside you, that is waiting for you to fully reconnect to, as you try to remember your experiences of being fully connected to your internal source of unconditional love when you were a young child.

The father of humanistic psychology Dr. Abraham Maslow touches on the love which resides in the child that is buried inside many adults, when he describes the playfulness of an adult who learns to play like a child again, which he calls learning to become self-actualized in his book, Toward a Psychology of Being.

Playfulness "could as easily be called happy, joy, or gay exuberance or delight….. It has a certain quality of triumph in it, sometimes perhaps also of relief. It is simultaneously mature and childlike." [50]

Dr. Maslow identified this desire for childlike playfulness in his observations of the peak experiences of his students in his study of 190 college students who were asked to describe, "The most wonderful …..experiences of your life; happiest moments, ecstatic moments, moments of rapture" [51]

Adults who become self-actualized are able to feel this child like playfulness on a consistent basis, as a result of what Abraham Maslow calls regression to an earlier state of being by becoming childlike again, by reconnecting to the joy and happiness of the child who is living in the heart of every adult.

As Dr. Maslow writes; "Behavior …can also come from ignorance and from childish misinterpretations and beliefs (whether in the child or in the repressed or forgotten child in the adult) …. Our depths can …. be good, or beautiful or desirable. This is …. becoming clear …. from investigations of the sources of love, creativeness, play, humor, art, etc. Their roots are deep within the inner deeper self, i.e. in the unconscious. To recover them and to be able to enjoy them and use them we must be able to regress."[52]

Unfortunately, Dr. Maslow made the observation that many adults are not able to regress enough, to experience the self-actualization of these peak experiences on a consistent basis, so they can feel the love, peace, joy & compassion of the forgotten child in the adult, each day of their future lives.

To quote Dr. Maslow; "Though, in principle, self-actualization is easy, in practice it rarely happens (by my criteria in less than 1% of the adult population)." [53]

I am hoping that now, more than 40 years after Dr. Maslow's book was written, that a larger percentage of adults in the world of today are willing to self-actualize the forgotten child inside them.

Part of the reason why many adults find it difficult to reconnect to their forgotten child who may be hiding inside them is their fear of looking inside themselves at their painful memories. Many of us try to run away from our internal pain by trying to find external joy & happiness that resides outside of us, outside of our internal unfair pain & suffering, which we then spend our adult life trying to suppress, so we do not have to feel our internal unfair pain & suffering, that we do not know how to control and that we do not know how to stop hurting us, when we relive our old memories about the unfairness in our lives that caused the painful events that are generating our continuous internal suffering, as we relive some of these memories each day of our lives. Memoires, that we try to suppress each day, so we will not have to continue feeling the remembered pain of the unfairness from our past life, such as when a friend betrayed us, when a potential lover rejected our offers of romance, or a loved one left us.

Fortunately, it has been my observation of the desires of the adults, that I have known in my life, that however much we suffer as adults, from our suppressed unfair pain & suffering, there is still hope that we will find a cure for this internal unfair pain & suffering.

The hope of rekindling the fire of love & compassion in an adult who has suffered a great deal in life is not lost.

As Psychiatrist Theodore Rubin says; "since human beings are inherently compassionate, compassion in them can be awakened and generated whatever their age and however horrendous their past experiences have been." [54]

Accumulating Painful Memories

As babies we do not have any painful memories and as adults we may have accumulated thousands of painful memories.

My first painful memory of childhood occurred when I was still in diapers, when I was tugging on my aunt's dress trying to get her attention. She told her sister who she was talking to, that it is necessary to discipline children, and then she slapped me with her hand across my face. This was the first time in my life that anyone had ever hit me and it hurt me. She then asked her sister, not to tell My Mom who would get very upset if she knew. I could not talk yet, but I understood many of the words that my aunt was saying. I was shocked when I felt the pain of the blow on my face. I did not understand why my life had so suddenly become unfair, so I filed the memory of the incident and the unresolved pain, away in my memory. It was only later in life as an adult that I was able to kill the unfair pain contained in my memory of my aunt who was so cruel to me, when I was trying to obtain help from an adult who I trusted & loved, when I received pain for my efforts.

Then, as a young child I began to realize that my life experiences may become unfair in the future. Fortunately, I realized later in my life, when I studied the wisdom of the ancient sages that the Law of Karma maintains the balance of fairness for all life. The consequences of hurting me generated Bad Karma for my aunt, though I do not know how she suffered later in her life for being physically abusive to a young defenseless child.

This incident is my first memory of unresolved unfair pain in my life. This was the start of the accumulation of hundreds of memories containing unresolved unfair pain that I accumulated throughout my childhood, which eventually clouded over my connection to my internal source of unconditional love by the time I became an adult, when I had accumulated thousands of unfair painful memories.

Unfortunately, whenever I relived these painful unfair memories during my childhood, I lost the connection to my internal source of love, peace, joy & compassion and I started looking for love & happiness outside of me in the external world to compensate for my loss of internal unconditional love.

Unfortunately, painful memories may re-surface in our conscious adult minds each day. When we were children, no one taught us how to kill the unfair pain in these memories, so they kept accumulating year after year. Now, as adults we need to learn how to kill this unfair pain when we realize that it may be hiding our connection to the internal source of unconditional love that we felt as children. As adults we need to feel this childhood unconditional love so it can provide us with the powerful motivation that we need to renew our positive thinking energy & our reasoning ability that will help us to understand how to kill any new unfair pain that may come into our lives in the future.

And unfortunately, Our Ego may use the negative thinking energy that is generated by our unfair painful memories to motivate us to act badly in our adult lives, before we become able to kill this unfair pain that is keeping our egos and our negative feelings alive inside our conscious minds.

How a Bad Person become a Good Person

I become a bad person when I allow my negative feelings & my ego to control my mind & actions when I intentionally hurt other people, by lying to them or by manipulating them when I treat them as adversaries as I compete with them to obtain my share of the scarce resources in the external world that I hope will supply me with external joy & happiness.

The consequences of my negative hurtful actions generate negative consequences for my future life that are stored in My Soul, which sentences me to experience fair pain & suffering in my future life that is equal to the unfair pain & suffering that I have caused other human beings.

This is the Law of Karma which states that I will experience the fair consequences of my actions.

Now, as I fully reconnect to my internal source of unconditional love, I realize that I have rediscovered an internal source of joy & happiness from my childhood and I realize that I do not need to compete with other people for joy & happiness, because I no longer need external joy & happiness for my life and because my internal source of unconditional love is supplying me with all the joy & happiness that I need, as it supplies me with powerful motivation to accomplish my goals each day.

My internal unconditional love is motivating me to become a good person who is becoming highly motivated to generate only positive actions, which nurture & protect all the life around me and which generates only positive consequences in my life, as my internal source of love fills me with the increasing love, peace, joy & compassion that I share with all life each day, especially with my friends & family.

How do I become a more loving human being who is able to generate increased love, peace, joy & compassion in my life that I can share with my friends & family? Q-134

My experience of reduced unfair pain in my daily life is proving that I am becoming a more loving human being, as I become a better person, who is a good person, as I learn to kill the unfair pain in my memories and as I experience the results of applying The Wisdom of Children to my life as I begin to share my increased love, peace, joy & compassion with all life on Our Precious Mother Earth.

Killing the Worry & Stress in My Life

The process of Practicing The Wisdom of Children to reduce the amount of unfair pain in my life, which has been diminishing the quality of my life, starts with reducing the amount of worry & stress in my life.

Please stop reading Our Book for a few minutes and think about how much better your life would be if you could get rid of all the worry & stress that you may put yourself through each day, especially the worry & stress over the concerns in your life that you cannot stop thinking about, including the possible future negative consequences for you, your family or your friends.

Creating Worry in Our Lives

Examples of worry:

As children we may worry about sharing fun & adventures
As children we may worry about competing with other children

As children we may worry about our social relationships
As adults we may worry about getting the next promotion
As adults we may worry about our families
As married couples we may worry about our jobs, how to pay the
bills on time, how to find time to relax, and how to be better parents,
as we become compulsive thinkers, worrying more & more each
day.

Creating Stress in Our Lives

Examples of stress:

Stress on a young child when he keeps asking his Mom to get him a
dog. He knows that dogs are loyal, loving and trustworthy and that
his own dog would become his playmate & best friend. His mother
understands but she knows that he is too young to take care of a dog
on his own, such as teaching the dog discipline, bathing him, feeding
him, grooming him, and taking him for walks.

When his mother says, "no" to him and explains why, that she does
not have the extra time & energy, that would be necessary to take
care of his dog for him, then the child is disappointed but he
understands that his mother is right because he is not old enough to
take care of a dog on his own, and it is not fair to his Mom to ask her
to take care of his dog for him. His Internal Source of Unconditional
Love helps him to understand the need for fairness in his life and in
his mom's life. His unconditional love helps him to kill the pain of
disappointment so he does not store any unfair painful memories of
his Mom telling him that he cannot have a dog, until he is older and
can take care of the dog. He understands that his Mom is being fair
because he knows that she loves him and wants him to be happy. He
does not feel that life all around him is being unfair to him.

Do I know any parents who find it both stressful & even painful to
say, "No" to their young children who they do not want to
disappoint? Why do parents feel this way? Q-135

Stress on a teenage son when he asks his Dad to help him buy a car,
when he knows he does not deserve help to buy his car because he

no longer confides in his Dad and he is not doing well in school. He wants the car to help him to escape from his life at home, by giving him the ability to easily visit his friends and take his girlfriend on dates.

Unfortunately, the pain of angst from the unresolved unfair pain in his relationship with his Dad, results in an argument which puts even more stress on their tenuous relationship. They still both love each other but he and his Dad end up with more unresolved unfair pain in their memories, as neither of their expectations is being met and his Dad is reluctant to help him buy a car.

If the teenager had grown up still fully connected to his internal source of unconditional love, then he would still be confiding in his Dad and he would still have the motivation from his internal source of unconditional love to help him to do well in school, instead of rebelling against authority and becoming annoyed with his teachers & his parents, who keep giving him advice all the time that he does not want to hear anymore.

The unresolved unfair pain from his childhood memories is flooding the teenager's mind each day, so that all he wants to do is escape, to obtain his freedom that this car represents and this is why he wants it so much. His angst is robbing him of his motivation to do well in school and he is blaming the world & his parents because he is too afraid to look inside himself at the unresolved unfair pain in his memories. He does not have the knowledge to kill the pain that is robbing him of his motivation to well in school and to confide in his Dad because his remembered unfair pain is feeding his angst & his rebellion, against the authority of his parents & teachers.

A teenager may feel that life all around him is unfair to him, except when he is with his friends. Why? Q-136

Please visualize this teenager fully reconnected to the unconditional love that he was born with and then visualize yourself as this teenager as you answer these questions,

How would my teenage life change if I was fully reconnected to my internal source of unconditional love?

How would I change my relationships with my Dad & my teachers?

Would my renewed feelings of love & compassion motivate me to ask my parents & teachers for forgiveness, as I try to forgive myself for all the mistakes that I have made, because I did not know how to kill the unfair pain in my memories that was creating the angst & rebellion in my relationships with my parents & teachers?

Now, please ask yourself this question about your current adult life.

How does worry & stress produce unresolved unfair pain in my adult life, especially when I may worry about things that I feel I have no control over? Why? Q-137

"It is reported that over 90% of what we worry about never happens. That means our negative worries have about a 10% chance of being correct." - Dr. Susan Jeffers [36]

Losing My Connection to Unconditional Love

Unfortunately, we start to lose the internal connection to unconditional love that lives inside our minds & bodies when we start to believe that joy & happiness comes from outside of us and when we start to believe that our mind & body are separate from all life, except our own.

We start to lose our love, peace, joy & compassion when our internal connection becomes clouded over by our memories of the painful feelings, thoughts & images that were caused by the unfair suffering that we experienced as we grew up. These painful memories motivated us to falsely believe that the external world may contain a source of joy & happiness that will help us to compensate for our internal suffering that it is separating us from all the life that lives outside our mind & body.

These painful memories of the unfairness in our lives may have gradually increased during the years of our childhood, as we continued to experience unfairness in our lives. By the time we became teenagers we may have accumulated hundreds of painful memories that were stored in our subconscious minds, as Angst, that we felt each day when our parents or teachers asked us to do something or tried to give us advice.

Childhood disappointments build up over time because the child does not know how to kill the pain of his disappointments caused by the unfairness in his life.

By the time many children become teenagers, a huge amount of angst has been built up between them and their parents, and unfortunately, many parents do not know how to teach their children to kill the pain in their memories and many parents do not know how to teach their children to forgive them, when life at home is not always fair & loving.

"Angst is the unresolved pain of anxiety & anguish that is stored in a child's memories of the negative unfair experiences in his life that he believes were created by someone that he loves, such as his Mom or Dad.

Angst is generated in a child's conscious mind, whenever he allows his Ego to convince him to treat another human being who he loves, as an adversary, when he blames the person he loves for the unfair pain & suffering in his life." (Paraphrase of a quote from the Father Angst section of Our Book Three)

Some of the results of unresolved family pain & angst are:

Teenagers do not want to listen to anyone who tries to give them advice including their teachers & parents

Parents cannot stop giving advice because they are continually worried about how their children are behaving

Mothers become estranged from their daughters

Sons no longer confide in their fathers

The painful memories of rejection or failed attempts at romance that create unresolved pain & suffering in a teenager's life, the loss of friendships with family members, the perceived lack of parental understanding and the angst from always being told what to do, by parents & teachers, may start to re-surface each day in a teenager's life.

They may sprout into the teenager's mind and the teenager's refusal to look inside his mind at his memories of this unfair pain & suffering may start to cut off the teenager from his internal connection to the source of love, peace, joy & compassion of his childhood, that he was born possessing and that he experienced as unconditional love for all life when he was a child.

A teenager can only maintain his internal connection to the source of unconditional love when he continually looks inside his mind & body to consciously maintain his connection to his internal source, which he cannot do if he runs away from the unresolved pain in his teenage life because he does not know to kill this suffering.

To be able to fully reconnect to his internal source of unconditional love, when the unfair pain from his memories is blocking his internal connection, a teenager needs to learn how to kill the major unfair pain in his memories of his relationships with his parents, teachers, siblings & friends.

I am assuming that you may have a few memories from your teenage years that contain unresolved pain & suffering that need to be cleansed with forgiveness.

So, let us practice using The Steps to Emotional Freedom that will enable us to kill the unfair pain that is living in one of these memories.

Then, we can start using The Steps to Emotional Freedom to kill all the major unfair pain in our memories that we are reliving each day of our adult lives. And when this killing is done we will be able to fully reconnect with our Internal Source of Unconditional Love that will start to feed continuous love, peace, joy & compassion into each new day of our future adult lives.

Visualizing Myself as a Teenager

Please visualize yourself when you were a teenager and choose a memory of unfair pain & suffering when a friend, who you trusted, betrayed you. This should be a memory of someone you have not forgiven for creating unfair pain in your teenage life.

And please use this painful memory to learn how to practice killing all the unfair pain in the memories that you may be reliving each day of your adult life.

Start by reviewing the first five steps of The Nine Steps to Emotional Freedom section of Our Book One, until you intellectually understand how these steps work and why they should work for you. They are:

Practicing Detachment
Practicing Friendship
Controlling My Mind
Practicing Fairness
Practicing Forgiveness

Now, please trigger the unfair memory from your teenage life, so you can practice these steps and prove to yourself that this wisdom will work to kill the pain that is buried inside this unfair memory.

First, say the name of the teenager who treated you unfairly. This should trigger the unfair teenage memory to start generating new pain from this unfair experience into your conscious adult mind.

Now, start practicing detachment to enable you to look at the new pain from outside of it, instead of getting lost inside the pain.

Then, start practicing controlling your mind so you can use meditation & mindfulness to calm your mind and help prevent you from mentally running away from this new pain. Just watch the pain and feel all of it. Do not try to control the pain. Just wait & watch until the pain runs out of energy and starts to disappear from your mind.

Now, when the intensity of pain has decreased, start practicing friendship by making the pain your new friend, so it can help you understand why your teenage friend treated you unfairly. And ask yourself questions, such as,

Did I contribute to my friend treating me unfairly by saying something or doing something that my friend did not like?

Now, start practicing fairness by **not** telling yourself that life is being unfair as you relive this memory, as you begin to suffer the old pain from this memory.

If you tell your memory that life is being unfair to you as you relive this teenage memory, your old memory will use the new unfair thinking energy that you have just created in your mind, to generate more pain inside your conscious mind.

Then, start practicing forgiveness by visualizing an image of your teenage friend inside your conscious mind, as you imagine forgiving your friend.

Now, imagine telling your unfair memory that you are willing to live with this unfairness and that you have forgiven your teenage friend for treating you unfairly, so there is no longer any need for the memory to generate any new pain inside your conscious mind in the future, to warn you that your teenage friend may create new unfairness in your life, whenever you relive this unfair memory again in the future because your teenage friend will not treat you unfairly again in the future.

Old unfair memories will not change their self-programmed reaction when I trigger them to generate new pain into my life, until I reprogram them with forgiveness by telling them that I can live with the unfairness because the person who hurt me unfairly in the past will not hurt me again in the future **or** by reprogramming them with the truth, such as by convincing a memory that it does not need to generate new pain into my mind to warn me that I am in danger of being hurt because life is now being fair to me and the potential unfairness that the memory is warning me about will not re-occur in the future, ever again.

If you cannot convince your memory to stop generating pain into your life, then think of this teenager's name, at least once a day for the next few days, to allow the memory to create new pain in your life each day, until it completely depletes its energy supplies that it has stored inside The Room of Feeling Energy inside your subconscious mind, until it has no energy left to generate any new pain into your life.

And make sure you do not think your life has suddenly become unfair to you whenever you relive this now painless memory again in the future because you will give this old unfair memory new thinking energy to start generating new unfair pain into your life, once again.

When you have completed the steps to kill the pain in this memory, please answer these questions.

Have I proven that the five steps to emotional freedom have worked to kill the unfair pain in this memory?

If the steps worked, why did they work?

If the steps did not work, why did they not work?

The benefits of practicing these five steps to emotional freedom are:

You will learn to forgive your friends & family members who have hurt you unfairly in the past, by first killing the unfair pain that they have created in your memories, so you will be able to generate compassion for each one of them, especially when they do not deserve your forgiveness, when you realize that you are **not** doing this to benefit them. You are doing this to stop your memories from creating new pain in your conscious mind in the future whenever you think of the names of the friends or family members who hurt you.

And you will learn to generate the courage that you require to become able to look at all the unfair painful memories that are living inside your mind and then you will realize that as you continue practicing The Wisdom to Kill the Unfairness in Your Memories, you will eventually make all the major painful memories that you may be reliving in your life each day, pain free.

Being pain free allows your internal source of love to generate increasing love, joy, peace & compassion into your life each day until it becomes continuous.

However, please be patience with your progress as you continue practicing the steps to emotional freedom during the next few months, as you kill the unresolved pain & suffering in other memories that require you to forgive yourself for the unfairness you created in someone's life or that require you to forgive someone who created unfairness in your life, as you learn to kill all the major unfair pain in your memories that may be blocking your internal connection to the unconditional love in your heart that will enable you to generate additional love, peace, joy & compassion in your adult life each day, as this connection becomes a clear & fully open pathway to your internal source of unconditional love.

Why do I lose my internal connection to unconditional love when I run away from the pain & suffering that my memories generate inside my mind? Why do I allow this to occur and how can I prevent it in the future? Q-138

Please realize that when you refuse to look inside your mind at your internal suffering, you become cut off from your connection to your internal source of unconditional love. This reduces your ability to feel increasing love, peace, joy & compassion in your adult life.

Fully Reconnecting to Unconditional Love

How do I reconnect to the motivational power that is being continuously generated by My Internal Source of Unconditional Love, to help me to visualize jumping out of bed each morning with a song in my heart, ready & eager to face the opportunities & challenges that this new day is offering me? Q-139

With your new understanding of how The Wisdom of Children works to generate unconditional love & nurture true friendship, please visualize waking up in the morning with a song in your heart, as you imagine being fully connected to your internal source of unconditional love that is filling your mind with powerful motivation to accept new opportunities & adventures in your adult life today and then compare this positive visualization to a negative memory from your past life, when you woke up in the morning filled with worry & stress that was killing your motivation to get out of bed & start a new challenge that day.

Please realize that as you practice Meditation, Mindfulness & The Wisdom to Kill the Unfairness in Your Memories, the intensity level of any worry & stress that may enter your mind during the day will become dramatically reduced.

Then, as you master the steps to emotional freedom that we are teaching you, you will start waking up each day with a feeling of anticipation that this new day will become worry & stress free because you have become able to kill any new worry & stress that may try to enter your life during the day.

To help you to accomplish this, please answer this question,

How do I maintain a continuous connection to my internal source of unconditional love during the day so it can provide me with the powerful motivation that I need to kill any new worry & stress that may enter into my life today? Q-140

When you decide to get rid of all the worry & stress in your life, please go back to your visualization of savoring the positive feelings of love, peace, joy & compassion that you generate, by visualizing yourself going through a day continuously connected to your internal source of unconditional love, as it continuously generates powerful motivation to help you accomplish your goals for the day.

Please use this positive visualization to motivate yourself to make a commitment, to make positive changes in your life, as you allow your visualization to imagine yourself bringing increased love, peace, joy & compassion into your daily life, to help you to increase your motivation & energy level during the day, to help you to complete your goals for the day, as you begin to realize that the intensity level of the worry & stress in your life is diminishing, as you learn to kill the unfair pain in your memories, such as your fear of future loss that something negative is going to happen to you or a loved one, a fear of loss that is living inside a memory that you cannot stop worrying about and stressing over today, until you become able to kill the fear that is living inside the memory.

Please keep visualizing your desire to kill all your worry & stress that is living inside your conscious mind, until you have generated enough courage to fully commit yourself to looking at all the unresolved unfair pain in your memories that is generating new worry & stress into your life each day, as you decide to kill all this worry & stress to become able to stop your daily suffering, even if it may take months to accomplish, as you fully reconnect to your internal source of unconditional love and become able to generate a continuous stream of love, peace, joy & compassion that you will feel during each moment of every day of your future life.

To help you to accomplish these challenges, please answer this question,

How do I use my ability to visualize powerful motivation in my future life, when I wake up each morning, to convince me that I am ready to look inside my mind at my painful memories, and how do I become convinced that I am ready to learn how to kill all the major unfair pain in my negative memories, to become able to stop the

worry & stress in my life by Practicing The Wisdom of Children?
Q-141

(Please refer to the Relieving Worry & Stress section in Chapter 13
of Our Book One)

Deciding to Look at My Painful Memories or Not

However, if you are not ready to look inside your mind at your
painful memories, so you can begin to kill your daily worry & stress,
then please stop reading Our Book.

Hopefully, you will reconsider your choice someday and then you
will pick up Our Book once again, so we can continue our journey of
self-discovery, together, as you study the wisdom in Our Book, once
more.

When I am Being Treated Unfairly

When I am being treated unfairly, it is important for me to not worry
& stress about the unfairness of the experience. When I start to
compulsively think about the unfairness of the experience, I give my
memory of the experience, extra thinking energy, to store in The
Storage Room of Feeling Energy in my subconscious mind. Then,
when I relive this painful memory, sometime in the future, the extra
thinking energy that is stored in The Storage Room of Feeling
Energy will sprout into my conscious mind and generate extra unfair
pain in my mind that is more powerful than it should be, because of
the extra worry & stress that my compulsive thinking has added to
the memory.

False Life Diminishing Thoughts

When I am being treated unfairly in my life and I store extra unfair
thinking energy in The Storage Room of Feeling Energy, I may be
thinking about a False Life Diminishing Thought that is not true. A
few of the hundreds of False Life Diminishing Thoughts that may be
buried inside my painful feelings that are supporting my feelings that
life is being unfair to me are:

My friends & family are always treating me unfairly, so they do not deserve my respect or support.

I am not worthy of living because there is something wrong inside me that will keep me from succeeding, so I am not going to try to succeed.

Life will always be unfair to me, so any future joy & happiness will be taken away from me.

It is painful to try to succeed because I am afraid that I will fail in the future, so I am going to procrastinate and I am not going to work on my goals for today.

It is important for me to look for the False Life Diminishing Thoughts that are living inside my unfair memories that are generating my painful unfair feelings that sprout into my conscious mind when I relive one of these memories.

A False Life Diminishing Thought is an untrue thought, feeling or image that I create in my mind and store in a memory that creates pain & suffering in my life when I relive this negative life diminishing memory in the future, which makes me feel that I am unworthy of living.[55]

What are some of the False Life Enhancing Thoughts that I have stored inside my memories that tell me I am unworthy of living? Q-142

When I identify a False Life Diminishing Thought that is buried inside a memory that is generating an unfair negative feeling inside my conscious mind, I can stop my memory from hurting me again in the future, by making it pain free, by reprogramming the negative unfair memory with A True Life Enhancing Thought that tells me I am worthy of living and capable of creating happiness in my daily life because I was born to be an unconditionally loving human being with the intelligence and the Free Will to choose to succeed at whatever I choose to do in my life, as I accomplish the goals for my life, especially my goal of killing all the major unfair pain in my memories and then using my life enhancing wisdom to help my friends & family to kill the unfair pain in their lives, as we start to replace our unfair pain that is living inside our memories with continuous love, peace, joy & compassion, by fully reconnecting to our internal source of unconditional love that has always lived inside each of us, since birth.

True Life Enhancing Thoughts

A True Life-Enhancing Thought is a true thought, feeling or image that I create in my mind and store in a memory that enhances my future love, peace, joy & compassion when I relive a positive life enhancing memory in the future that tells me that I am an unconditionally loving human being, who is capable of creating continuous love, peace, joy & compassion in my daily life which makes me worthy of living.[56]

Examples of True Life-Enhancing Thoughts are:

I was born with a continuous stream of unconditional love flowing into my mind & body from all the life in the universe that I can share with everyone in my life

I was born with the ability to reason to be able to choose the feelings that I want to experience each day, such as choosing to feel the powerful motivation that My Internal Source of Unconditional Love is offering me, to enable me to accomplish The Goals for My Life each day

I was born with a powerful desire to share unconditional love & true friendship with other human beings who I can convince to work with me in mutual self-interest, to create a fun filled life full of adventures to help nourish, support & protect our lives and the lives of those we love.

What are some of the True Life Enhancing Thoughts that I have stored inside my memories that tell me I am worthy of living? Q-143

The Key to Choosing All My Feelings, Thoughts & Images

The key to becoming able to choose the feelings, thoughts & images inside my conscious mind that I want to experience, is to practice continuous detachment from all the feelings, thoughts & images that are living inside my mind, so I can determine which ones are beneficial or harmful to me or to my friends & family, before I choose to enhance or prolong the life of a beneficial feeling, thought or image with new fair thinking energy.

And I am not thinking about any potential future unfairness in my life, so I do not give a harmful feeling, thought or image any new unfair thinking energy to prolong its life inside my conscious mind.

To help me to understand this process I am repeating the phrase, "I become what I think about" as I decide whether or not to add thinking energy to new feeling, thought or image that enters my mind.

So, I have decided to add new thinking energy to my life enhancing feelings of love, peace, joy & compassion to prolong their lives inside me and I have decided **not** to add new thinking energy to my life diminishing feelings of fear, anger, worry & stress to shorten their lives inside me.

Chapter 24

My Room of Memories

To help you to understand how to choose your feelings, please visualize how your mind creates, stores, and relives the feelings in your memories, as you read this.

My Awareness of My Connection to All Life is feeding my mind 60,000+ feelings, thoughts & images each day. I am watching these feelings, thoughts & images, as they enter my mind to complete the task they were sent to do, and then disappear from my conscious mind.

My Room of Memories

My Room of Memories that is located inside my subconscious mind stores the memories of the feelings, thoughts & images that I experience each day of my life.[66]

Triggering a Stored Memory

When I trigger a memory to sprout into my conscious mind, the sprouted memory may not contain a feeling, such as when I am remembering a fact that I read in a book a long time ago. This is called a neutral memory.

Usually, memories have feeling energy stored in The Room of Feeling Energy located inside My Room of Memories in my subconscious mind that enables the memory to generate a pleasurable or painful feeling, whenever it spouts into my conscious mind.

For example, a memory that is triggered into action, by what I think about, or by what I perceive through my five senses, takes the feeling energy stored in The Storage Room of Feeling Energy and uses this feeling energy to generate pain or pleasure inside my conscious mind, that I begin to experience in weak or strong amounts, that is determined by how much energy the memory has brought with it from my subconscious mind. The amount of energy also determines how long the memory & the feeling can stay in my conscious mind, as the memory burns up its energy reserves to keep generating pain or pleasure. The memory knows that it needs to get a source of new energy to survive, so it tries to tap into my thinking energy to feed itself. It desires to get me to think about it to feed it more thinking energy to keep it alive, while it is in my conscious mind. It also desires to give me a message to get me to act to satisfy its desires.

When a Memory is Painful

When a memory is painful, it is generating pain to get my attention because it thinks that the life that is living all around me is treating me unfairly & I am in danger of being hurt.

The painful memory has a minimal ability to think because it can partially control my thinking energy to get my attention when it is in my conscious mind, to get me to feel pain and to deliver me its message that life may be unfair to me in the future.

It is my objective to convince the painful memory that I have heard its message and that it no longer needs to cause me pain to get my attention. I tell the memory that I agree with its message that life may be unfair to me & I am in danger of being hurt, or I tell the memory that it is wrong because life is being fair to me & I am not in danger of being hurt. When the painful memory realizes that I have heard its message and agrees with my assessment of its message, then it will decide to stop causing me pain and it will disappear from my conscious mind, as long as I stop feeding it new thinking energy about how unfair my life may become, whenever I start to relive this painful memory, again in the future.

When a Memory is Joyful

When a memory is joyful, it is generating joy to get my attention because it thinks that the life living all around me is being fair to me and that I should indulge in the joy that life is generating, as it tries to convince me that I should continue thinking about how fair life is being to me. It wants my thinking energy to continue feeding it, to keep it alive and active in my conscious mind.

Fortunately, I was born with Free Will which gives me the ability to make a choice, either to increase the power and the life expectancy of a joyful memory by feeding it thinking energy that life is being fair to me, or to decide not to indulge in a joyful memory because this indulgence would distract me from working on My Goals for Today.

When I realize a joyful memory is distracting me from working on my goals, then I use my Free Will to decide not to feed it new thinking energy that life is being fair to me, to stop keeping it alive.

When my joyful memory realizes that I have cut off its energy supply, it will return to My Room of Memories in my subconscious mind and then it will wait until it is triggered again in the future by a new thought, feeling or image from my conscious mind, a dream, or an external event in my life.

When a joyful memory decides to leave my conscious mind, it takes the thinking energy with it, that it has remaining in its energy reserve, back to My Room of Memories to store in the energy reserve inside The Storage Room of Feeling Energy, so it can use the energy to feed itself when it is triggered again sometime in the future.

Realizing I am Not My Feelings

As I learn to watch how my feelings are generated in my mind by my memories, I am beginning to realize that I am not my feelings. I am The Compassionate Watcher who is watching them, as they are born, as they enter my mind, as they live for a while in my conscious mind, and then as they disappear from my conscious mind. Where they come from I do not always know and where they go to I do not always know.

What I do know with certainty is my realization that I am the Compassionate Watcher of the feelings, thoughts & images in my mind that are not me because I have the Free Will to choose to kill the feelings that I do not want to experience, by deciding to not feed new thinking energy to the negative feelings, thoughts & images, so they start to die, as they run out of energy and then disappear from my conscious mind,

And I have the Free Will to choose to extend the life of the feelings that I want to experience, by deciding to feed new thinking energy to the pleasurable feelings, thoughts & images to keep them alive & active in my conscious mind.

Chapter 25

Becoming a Master of The Wisdom of Children

In the introduction to the My True Self section of Our Book One, we explored the wisdom of Taking The Nine Steps to Emotional Freedom. Now, we will increase our understanding of how to kill the unresolved pain & suffering in our memories.

When you were given the opportunity to practice the wisdom in Our Book, you were also given the opportunity to make friends with hundreds of memories that may be generating unresolved pain & suffering in your life whenever you relive one of these memories. Please practice killing the pain in these memories to help you become a Master of The Wisdom of Children, a skill you will be able to use in the future when you experience a new painful event in your life, whenever someone hurts you unfairly.

Controlling The Power of Detachment

The Power of Detachment helps me to control the fairness in my conscious mind by detaching from any new unfair pain that may enter my conscious mind. Then, I am using my reasoning ability to convince the memory that is generating the unfair pain in my mind that there is no need to generate any new pain inside my conscious in the future.[67]

My Detachment enables me to get outside of my experience of the unfairness and enables me to start generating a state of Mindfulness, as I become aware of the other mental activities that are happening in my mind in the present moment, while they are happening, no matter what they are.

Only when I am fully detached from the unfairness am I able to look back at the unfair memory that is generating the unfair pain, worry & stress in my mind instead of remaining lost inside the unfairness and feeling helpless because I do not know how to stop the unfairness from hurting me.

Only then, am I able to observe the unfairness with detachment, as it is being powered in my conscious mind by a memory's energy reserves stored inside The Storage Room of Feeling Energy in my subconscious mind.

Only then, am I able to detect the reasons why the unfair memory is generating unfair pain in my conscious mind to get my attention, so it can tell me that life may be unfair to me again in the future and I am in danger of being hurt.

Only then, am I able to fully understand the reasons that the unfair memory is using to justify generating the unfair pain, worry & stress in my conscious mind.

Then, I am looking at my understanding of the reasons to determine if the reasons are true or false.

When a reason for the unfair pain is false, such as A False Life Diminishing Thought that diminishes my love, peace, joy & compassion, I am reprogramming the painful memory with the truth of A True Life Enhancing Thought that tells me that I am an unconditionally loving human being who is capable of creating feelings of immense love, peace, joy & compassion in my daily life.

Then, when I reprogram the painful memory with the truth, it stops generating unfair pain, worry & stress and stops sending these unfair feelings into my conscious mind.

When the reason for the unfairness is based on a true event, I am using the power of my compassion to forgive those who caused my painful experience or to forgive me for causing the unfairness, to become able to stop feeding new unfair thinking energy to the unfair memory that is creating the unfairness in my mind, to stop keeping this new unfair pain, worry & stress alive inside my conscious mind.

I am telling the unfair memory that I am able to live with the unfair event in my past life without the need for my memory to tell me that life has been unfair. This is how I convince the unfair memory that there is no longer any need to generate new unfair pain, worry & stress in the future to get my attention, by telling the unfair memory that I understand why the painful past event was unfair.

Now, the unfair memory will realize that there is no longer any need to cause me new unfair pain in the future, to get my attention to tell me that life has been unfair to me in the past and to tell me that I should obtain justice or seek revenge from those who have hurt me unfairly, or to tell me that I should obtain forgiveness from those I have hurt unfairly because I have decided to stop thinking about the unfairness of the painful event from my past life.

How does The Power of Detachment control the fairness in my mind? Q-144

Controlling The Power of My Mind

The Power of My Mind helps me to control My Thinking Energy to enable me to control the fairness in my mind by stopping my thinking energy from feeding an unfair memory the energy that it needs to be able to generate new pain inside my conscious mind. Without this thinking energy the unfair memory cannot generate new unfair pain into my conscious mind, unless it has energy already stored inside The Storage Room of Feeling Energy in my subconscious mind. So, with this understanding of how my mind works I am using my thinking energy to feed fair memories only, so only fair feelings will be fed thinking energy inside my conscious mind.[68]

As I experience unfair painful thoughts, feelings or images in my daily life, it is important for my future well-being to not become stressed out and to not start worrying about the negative impact of this current unfair pain on my life, or how unfair the experience is, that is causing the current unfair pain that I am now experiencing. Because doing so, increases the amount of unfair thinking energy that I will store inside The Storage Room of Feeling Energy for the new feeling's memory to use in the future.

Then, the extra thinking energy that I gave my memory by compulsively thinking about the unfairness in my life will be liberated from storage inside The Storage Room of Feeling Energy and be used by the pain generating mechanism of my memory, to enhance my future unfair pain, to make it more intense, and to enable my feelings of unfair pain to stay longer in my conscious mind, when at some future date I start to relive a memory of how unfair life has been to me.

Controlling The Power of Friendship

The Power of Friendship helps me to make an unfair memory my new friend so I can ask the unfair memory to help me understand why it is generating unfair mind into my conscious mind.

This does not mean that I should suppress the unfair pain, when it sprouts into my conscious mind and starts to demand my attention. Instead of suppressing the unfair pain, I am asking the unfair painful feeling & its memory that is in my conscious mind to become My New Friend, to help me to understand the unfair experience in my past life, so I can learn how to convince the memory to stop generating new unfair pain into my conscious mind.

And I am trying not to think about the unfairness of the experience, so that I do not give the painful memory any new unfair thinking energy, so the memory will not be able to re-energize itself & become able to generate extra unfair pain in my conscious mind which will cause the unfair pain to become more intense. This will not happen when I stop feeding the memory new unfair thinking energy, to stop powering it, to stop keeping the pain alive & active in my conscious mind, when I stop thinking about the unfairness of this experience from my past life.

My strategy is to leave the painful feeling & its memory alone, by not trying to control them and by not trying to change them, as I observe them with My Compassionate Watcher when I an reliving an unfair memory inside my conscious mind, as it continues to hurt me because I know that it will use up its energy reserves and then disappear from my conscious mind.

Then, the next time at some future date, when the painful memory sprouts again into my conscious mind, the remembered pain of the unfair experience will not be so intense because the painful memory has used up a lot of the energy that was stored in The Storage Room of Feeling Energy, the last time it visited me, and so it has less stored energy to cause me unfair pain this time around.

Eventually, after I relive the memory many times, the memory will no longer have any energy left in storage in The Storage Room of Feeling Energy in my subconscious mind to cause me unfair pain in the future. I will still remember the experience that caused the unfair pain, but the memory will no longer have any energy left to be able to hurt me. Of course, I must not think about how unfair the experience was that created the memory or I will give the memory new thinking energy to start hurting me again, when I relive the memory again in the future.

Then, in the future when I start to experience a new unfair memory that I know is painful, I am telling myself not to run away from feeling the unfair pain because I now know that I have to experience the unfair pain and feel its full intensity, to be able to deplete the memory's energy reserves that are feeding energy to the unfair pain in my conscious mind, in order to kill the energy source of the unfair pain that is stored in The Storage Room of Feeling Energy, so the negative memory will have no energy left to create new unfair pain in the future, so it will not be able to hurt me again in future.

Now I am welcoming a new painful feeling & its memory as My New Friends, as I fully embrace the new unfair pain, as I welcome feeling all the new unfair pain being generated by a painful memory because I realize that this is the method that I must use to allow the memory to consume all of its energy supplies, until it runs out of energy, so it cannot generate any new unfair pain, to create new suffering in my life in the future.

During the process of helping an unfair painful memory to use up its energy supplies, until it is exhausted, when the unfair pain is at a low intensity level in my conscious mind, I am asking the painful memory who has become My New Friend to tell me its story of how unfair life has been to me, as I compassionately feel its sorrow & suffering. I have to be careful when I ask this question to not agree with My New Friend that life is still being unfair to me because this will trigger the painful memory to start increasing the intensity level of the unfair pain that is currently in my conscious mind.

And I do not make judgments about what My New Friend is telling me. I do not agree and I do not disagree with My New Friend, when it is telling me its story about its understanding of the unfairness in my past life. I let My New Friend do the talking and I make sure that I shut up and just listen to what it is telling me, without making judgments.

My New Friend's story may be a true description of the events in my past life or its story may be untrue. After I have listened to My New Friend's complete story and I fully understand what My New Friend is telling me, I explain to My New Friend that I want to examine the other memories that I have about the unfair experience for truth, so they can help me to understand why the painful experience occurred. Then, when the pain that is being generated by this memory runs out of energy and disappears from my conscious mind, I will ask,

Is My New Friend's story true?

And I will ask,

Does the memory's story agree with the events that my other memories tell me are true?

I will ask My New Friend to help me to answer these questions, without triggering the unfair painful memory to start generating new unfair pain into my conscious mind.

When a Memory is Untrue

When My New Friend & I look at the available evidence for truth about the unfair painful experience and when we determine that the story is not true, we can work together to reprogram the untrue memory with the truth, to enable this re-programming to prevent the memory from producing new unfair pain in my future life. My New Friend now realizes that life has not been unfair to me in the real world and that the untrue memory does not need to generate new unfair pain to get my attention to tell me that life may be unfair to me in the future because life has not been unfair to me in the past.

Now, I no longer relive the unfair pain of this untrue memory in the future because I have reprogramed the memory with the truth to make the memory agree with reality that life has not been unfair to me.

When a Memory is True

To be able to the kill the unfair pain remaining in a true memory that is left over by a true story about the unfairness in my life, I am using my connection to My Internal Source of Unconditional Love to give me the energy of compassion, to be able to forgive those who caused the unfair true experience that is stored in my true memory.

With some of my true memories, I will have to forgive me or I will ask others to forgive me, to become able to kill unfair pain, when I realize that I am responsible for the unfair painful experience stored in my true memory, when I realize that I have hurt another human being by my act of unfairness.

How does The Power of My Mind control the fairness in my mind? Q-145

Controlling The Power of Fairness

Controlling the Power of Fairness helps me to convince an unfair memory to become fair to me, when it is being unfair by generating new unfair pain inside my conscious mind. To do this I detach from any unfair pain that is created inside my conscious mind by an unfair memory that starts to live inside my conscious mind. My detachment allows me to get outside of this new pain instead of staying trapped inside of it. Then I am asking the pain & the memory to become My New Friend to help me find the reason why the unfair memory has entered my conscious mind and why it is creating new pain in my mind. When I learn what is causing the memory to remain in my conscious mind, I can convince the memory to become fair to me by not generating any new pain inside my conscious mind and then I can convince the memory to leave my conscious mind.

And I am convincing this unfair memory that there is no longer any need to generate new unfair pain in my future life, to get my attention when I relive this unfair memory, because it no longer needs to tell me that life has been unfair to me in the past and may be unfair to me again in the future.

To accomplish this, I am forgiving those who caused the unfairness in my past life, so my forgiveness will allow my life to be become fair once again, by restoring the balance between the joy & pain that is being maintained by The Law of Karma. This balance prevents my memory from creating new unfair pain again in my future life.

Now, my unfair memory has been transformed into a painless memory.

How does The Power of Fairness control the fairness in my mind? Q-146

Controlling The Power of Forgiveness

The Power of Forgiveness helps me to control the fairness in my subconscious mind with forgiveness, which kills the unfairness that is buried in the memories that are stored inside my subconscious mind inside My Room of Memories, so now I am using the power of my forgiveness to only allow fairness to live inside my subconscious mind.[70]

I am starting the process of forgiveness to kill the unfair pain in my true memories in my subconscious mind. I am killing each memory's source of energy by not feeding it new unfair thinking energy whenever I start to relive this memory.

Whenever new unfair pain from a memory sprouts into my conscious mind, I recognize it as My New Friend, as I try to convince it to stop causing me pain, as I start the process of forgiveness by not giving it new unfair thinking energy, by not thinking about how unfair my life has been.

1) My act of forgiveness is the conscious decision that I make to be able to excuse or pardon someone for a mistake or an offense against me. This is not always easy to do. It takes time to allow my feelings of pain, my desire for revenge, and my need for justice to lose their energy, so they no longer try to manipulate me into providing them with new thinking energy that is generated, when I worry & stress about how unfair my life has been.

2) My act of forgiveness depletes the energy reserves of the memory that is stored inside my subconscious mind that is generating the unfair pain, each time I relive the memory. I do not add new unfair thinking energy to the memory's energy reserves by not thinking about how unfair my life has been. Eventually, after I relive the memory many times, the memory will deplete its energy reserves until it has no energy left to hurt me again in the future. Then my memory will no longer be painful when it enters my conscious mind, as the now painless memory returns to tell me to obtain justice or seek revenge.

388 Coulson/Practicing The Wisdom Of Children Our Book One

3) My act of forgiveness cuts off the memory's need to cause me pain in the future, as I make the decision to tell the memory that there is no longer any need to cause me unfair pain. The memory now realizes that it no longer needs to generate pain in my conscious mind to get my attention, so it can tell me that life has been unfair to me and that I should obtain justice or seek revenge. The memory now realizes that I have forgiven those who have caused me unfair pain & suffering.

4) To forgive is to cease to feel my anger for, or to feel my resentment against, someone who has treated me unfairly. It takes time, sometimes days or weeks, to allow the unfair pain to lessen in intensity until I realize that I am able to forgive.

5) I forgive whoever caused the unfair pain, to be able to get the unfair pain to stop, even though whoever caused the pain may not deserve forgiveness. I have a choice. I can continue to feel the unfair pain again in the future, as I continue to worry & stress about how my life has been unfair, I can continue to demand that justice should prevail, and I can continue to demand that whoever caused the unfair pain should be punished because I desire revenge, or I can stop the unfair pain with my conscious decision to use my unconditional love, compassion & forgiveness, to kill the source of the continuing unfair pain that is buried inside my painful memory. I am not doing this to benefit the person who treated me unfairly. I am doing this to stop my memory from creating new pain in my conscious mind in the future.

6) Forgiveness is my decision to stop feeding new unfair thinking energy to the unfair memory's energy reserves that are stored in The Storage Room of Feeling Energy, as I use my Free Will to decide that whatever unfairness has occurred, I can still live with unfairness without thinking about the need to obtain justice or seek revenge.

7) The act of forgiveness is my acceptance that life is sometimes unfair and I can endure the unfair pain caused by other people, without making the mistake of adding to my unfair pain by continually worrying & stressing about how unfair life has become.

8) In the future, whenever life is unfair to me, I have the choice to forgive the unfairness in life, even when this unfairness does not deserve forgiveness, or I can start to feed new thinking energy to this memory of unfairness which will begin to generate new pain into my conscious mind, as I try to obtain justice or seek revenge for being hurt.

Obtaining justice or seeking revenge is important when loved ones are hurt. If I had lost a family member in the World Trade Center terrorist attack on September 11, 2001, I would continue to try to obtain justice, until the terrorists were caught and punished.

Personally, I would never forgive the terrorists who are beyond redemption. I would want them to burn in hell forever, if there is such a place. Even so, I would still try to kill the unfair pain in my memories, by realizing that even though life has been terribly unfair to us, I do not want the terrorists to succeed in their goal of instilling continuous pain & fear into the hearts of the American people.

I would learn to live with my loss by living my life as our lost loved ones would want us to live it, by remembering the joy & happiness that our lost loved ones brought into our lives and by cherishing their memories. In this way, I would honor them and I would continue to miss them, but I would also continue to try to kill the pain of the unfairness of their loss, so that as I remember them, my memories will be joyful without the need of feeling the unresolved pain of the unfairness of their loss, as I keep my loved ones alive in my heart, not just my family member, but all those who lost their lives in the World Trade Center terrorist attack.

I learned the importance of forgiveness, when I suffered great pain & loss, when my mother died when I was a teenager. I was angry & resentful at the unfairness in my life, when my mother was taken away from me. I was not able to understand why my mother died or how to kill the immense unfair pain in my heart that continued to grow, as I kept thinking about how unfair life had been to take my mother away from me. It took me many years to acquire the wisdom of forgiveness by forgiving life, even when life does not ask for

390   Coulson/Practicing The Wisdom Of Children Our Book One

forgiveness, so I could learn how to kill the unfair pain in my memories of my mother's death, before I could live with the memories of my love for My Mom, without also feeling the unresolved pain of the unfairness of her death.

These unfair events are tragic for us, but fortunately, we are able to kill the unfair pain in our memories by forgiving ourselves, by forgiving other people, or by forgiving life for being unfair to us, so we can stop experiencing future unfair pain that we generate whenever we feed new thinking energy to our memories about how unfair life has been.

As we continue to apply the wisdom in Our Book to our lives, we have the opportunity to use the powerful compassion that we are starting to receive from our reconnection to our internal source of unconditional love, to practice killing the feelings of unfairness that are buried inside our memories, so we can generate a powerful desire to forgive, when those we are forgiving do not deserve our forgiveness, or when events do not deserve forgiveness, especially in situations where obtaining justice or seeking revenge is no longer possible or feasible.

Please ask yourself these questions when you experience unfairness in your mind.

Why am I feeling the pain of unfairness, when those who caused the pain are not feeling my pain and they may not even care that I am experiencing pain?

Why am I continuing to experience the pain of unfairness, when I can make the decision to stop the unfair pain from occurring in the future by practicing forgiveness?"

Some pain in my life is fair & healthy, when it makes me realize that I should not treat other people unfairly, or I should not do things that cause others unnecessary pain.

Keeping the pain of unfairness in my memories alive and allowing this unfair pain to continue to hurt me is not healthy for my future well-being.

Please make a decision to use The Wisdom of Children to kill the Unfairness in Your Mind by searching for the suppressed memories of the major unfair events in your life, so you can learn to kill the pain of unfairness whenever you relive these unfair memories. The benefits of this wisdom will become known to you, as you begin to experience more love, peace, joy & compassion and less remembered unfair pain, each day of your future life.

As I start to forgive each member of my friends & family for causing many of my painful memories, I realize that I am starting to feel unconditional love for them, when I see them, talk to them, or think about them.

For example, when a friend betrays me, as we described in the How I Nurture True Friendship section in Chapter 22 of Our Book One, I feel the hurt & unfairness of the betrayal which blocks my ability to feel unconditional love for my friend. As I start to forgive my friend by using The Power of My Forgiveness, to stop the unfair pain of betrayal from hurting me in the future, my unconditional love for my friend automatically starts to enter my mind & body from my internal source of unconditional love for all life, when I think about my friend or spend time with him in the future.

In the future when I forgive my spouse for not living up to my expectations or for causing unfair pain & suffering in our marriage, I start to automatically feel unconditional love for my spouse, whenever I think about my spouse or spend time with her in the future.

When I forgive a parent, a brother, or a sister, I start to feel unconditional love for them, whenever I think about them or spend time with them in the future.

It may take me days or months, to fully forgive a member of my friends & family, depending on how much unfair pain & suffering they have created in my life, by being unfair to me.

How does The Power of Forgiveness control the fairness in my mind? Q-147

Helping Loved Ones to Control the Fairness in Their Lives

I am praying for each member of my friends & family to obtain the courage to look inside their minds, to begin to use The Wisdom of Children to Control the Fairness in Their Minds and to tear down the wall of painful memories that is preventing them from fully reconnecting to their internal source of unconditional love, so they can begin to generate enough compassion to help them to realize that they need to ask for my forgiveness, as they show me that they are now able to treat me fairly and that they are now determined to start loving me unconditionally.

I realize that this may be difficult for many members of my friends & family to do, so I am committed to helping each one to become fully reconnected to their internal source of unconditional love, so they can begin to obtain the power & the motivation they need, to enable them to love other human beings unconditionally, so they can begin to learn how to treat other human beings fairly with honesty & respect, so they will not need to seek forgiveness again in the future, and so they will not start to treat someone unfairly, as they have unfairly treated me in the past.

I realize that each member of my friends & family has the Free Will to choose to learn how to generate Compassion to become able to kill the unfair pain in their memories and to practice forgiveness. I realize that many members of my friends & family are not willing to make the decision to try to learn this wisdom because they are afraid of the painful memories that they may experience inside their minds, when they try to search for their internal source of unconditional love that is capable of supplying them with the immense power of compassion, to enable them to kill all the unfair pain in their memories, to stop their memories of unfairness from hurting them again, when they relive these memories in the future.

I am being patient, as I wait for a member of my friends & family to find the courage to look inside himself, to fully reconnect to the immense power of his internal source of unconditional love for all life. I realize that members of my friends & family may find it very difficult to obtain the courage to do this. So, I am helping them, whenever they are willing to listen to the wisdom of unconditional love, as I continue to love them unconditionally. And I am continuing to feel personal compassion for their unfair pain & suffering, as they try to love me, whenever their unconditional love is not hiding behind the wall of fear & suffering that is generated inside their conscious minds, whenever they relive one of their painful memories of the unfairness that they have experienced in their lives.

My Personal Compassion

My Personal Compassion is my personal desire to share unconditional love & nurture true friendship to enhance the well-being of my friends & family.[71]

Now, when a member of my family, friends, neighbors, or a stranger hurts me unfairly, I realize that I am able to kill this new unfair pain and I am able to generate powerful personal compassion for the person who hurt me, even when it is important to punish the person who has hurt me unfairly or when it is important to seek compensation for my unfair pain & suffering.

The process of continually killing the unfair pain in my present & future life is helping me to maintain & enhance my continuous connection to My Internal Source of Unconditional Love to generate powerful personal compassion for my friends & family.

Now, I realize as I practice The Power of My Forgiveness that I am acquiring The Power of My Thankfulness, as I realize that my painful memories of unfairness have blocked my ability to say,

"Thank You" to each member of my friends & family for all the love & support they have given me over the years.

I am beginning to realize that the painful memories of unfairness that I have carried with me for many years have prevented me from realizing that I have the ability to love my friends & family unconditionally, when these painful memories block my connection to my internal source of unconditional love for my friends & family.

So, I am beginning to increase my desire to kill the major unfair pain & suffering that my friends & family have created in my life because it has hidden my ability to feel the love that they have shown me in the past, as they try to fully reconnect to their ability to love me unconditionally in the present, as they struggle with the unfair pain & suffering in their lives that may motivate them to treat me unfairly, again.

There may be a family member or a friend who does not deserve forgiveness and who does not have any love to offer me because he is experiencing unfair pain & suffering in his current life, and his ability to love me is not working.

I realize that I can help him to learn how to use The Wisdom of Children to Kill the Unfairness in His Memories, to help him to reconnect to his internal source of unconditional love, to help him to restart using his ability to love unconditionally, when he is willing to accept me as his role model because of my proven ability to offer him continuous unconditional love, so he can end his unfair pain & suffering and so he can start to experience the continuous unconditional love & compassion that he felt as a child and that he now sees in me.

My Global Compassion

My Global Compassion is my global desire for universal unconditional love to enhance the well-being of all human beings on Earth who are members of my family of unconditional loving human beings.[72]

Now, that I have started the process of forgiving my friends & family, I realize that I am able to use my growing global compassion for all human beings on Earth, to help them to start killing the pain in their memories of the unfairness of their neighbors and the unfairness of all human beings in the world, who have hurt them, as I feel global compassion for the victims of this senseless unfair suffering, who I have witnessed personally or watched on TV or read about. This is helping me to become more optimistic, that someday, all human beings in the world will learn The Wisdom of Children and will learn how to use this wisdom to kill the unfairness in their memories, to enable them to increase their unconditional love & compassion, as they learn to treat other human beings fairly, with honesty & respect.

Using My Personal Power

Now, as I practice using My Personal Power,

I am beginning to realize that I am cultivating an increasing desire to say, "Thank You" to each of my friends & family for their love & support.

I am beginning to experience a strong desire to tell them of the love that they have shown me that was blocked by my feelings of the pain of unfairness that they created in my life.

I am starting to feel increasing unconditional love & compassion for them, as I continue to kill the major unfair pain in my memories that is helping me to fully reconnect to My Internal Source of Unconditional Love for them.

I am making a list of the qualities of unconditional love & compassion that each of my friends & family has offered me in the past.

I am thanking each one of them for these qualities. I do not speak to them about the unfair pain that they created in my past life because I have forgiven them, and I do not want to give my negative memories any new unfair thinking energy to start causing me new unfair pain in the future.

Each of my friends & family has different abilities to love me with fairness, honesty & respect, as they learn to become unconditionally loving human beings, once again, as they once were when they were young children.

I am telling them how their childhood abilities make them special and how their childhood abilities enable them to live life passionately, which enables them to become unconditional loving human beings, as they try to fulfill the purpose of their lives, whether or not, they have identified what they want to accomplish in their lives.

I am saying to each of them,

"The purpose & meaning of your life may be different than mine. It is as if each of us is born as a unique human being with a particular skill set of abilities, that no one who has ever lived has had and that no one in future will have. It is as if each of us is an experiment for living life successfully that will never be created in the same way again. Your unique set of skills is inspiring you, to fulfill the unique purpose and to experience the special meaning, of your life. You are unique, special & blessed to be given the opportunity to experience life as an unconditional loving human being on our precious Mother Earth." (Quote from A Spiritual Journey with My Son Wil section in Chapter 6 of Our Book One)

Such is The Power of My Thankfulness that enables me to persuade my friends & family that they have the ability to love me unconditionally and they have the ability to accept & appreciate my unconditional love for them.

When I say, "Thank You" to an unconditional loving human being, he becomes obligated by his childhood abilities to accept my "Thank You" and to love me for my ability to appreciate him as a human being because I am a member of the family of all human beings on Earth, to which he belongs. He is required by his childhood nature as an unconditionally loving human being to begin to accept me as his spiritual brother, as he begins to realize that I love him unconditionally, as he begins to realize that he is genetically & spiritually connected to me and to all human beings on Earth, by his innate childhood ability to share unconditional love & nurture true friendship with all human beings in his life, especially me.

It is The Wisdom of Children that enables me to understand & manage The Power of Detachment, The Power of Controlling My Mind, The Power of Fairness, The Power of My Forgiveness, and The Power of My Thankfulness, to help me to increase the amount of unconditional love that is being shared by all human beings on Earth.

As I practice The Wisdom of Children each day of my life, I am continuously confirming that I am the Unconditional Loving Human Being who I was born to be. My life is not about doing, it is about being who I was born to be.

And I am asking for forgiveness for my unfairness and I am forgiving others for their unfairness to me.

The Unfairness in My Mind

All Human beings are born fully connected to their Internal Source of Unconditional Love which gives us the ability to share unconditional love & nurture true friendship with everyone in our lives.

Unfortunately my connection to this source of love became blocked by the unfair pain in my memories that I started to accumulate, as I experienced unfair pain & suffering in my life, as I grew from childhood into adulthood.

To remove this pain blockage, I am learning to kill the unfair pain in my memories by learning to choose my feelings and by practicing Meditation & Mindfulness to become able to monitor how my memories are created, stored and relived in my mind, each day of my life.

It is critical for my future joy & happiness to become able to choose my feelings especially when they become negative habit energies, such as my fear of the darkness at night when I was a child, when I was afraid that someone or something was going to come into my bedroom during the hours of darkness when I was sleeping and steal my joy & happiness by hurting me or stealing something from me.

This is the unfair pain of the fear of the unknown. This fear is the negative habit energy of The Primordial Fear of Future Loss & Potential Failure that many adults feel when the worry & stress in their lives becomes intense, which we will explore in Our Book Three.

Another negative habit energy many adults feel is doubting their ability to achieve success in life because they believe that there is something wrong inside them, which is generating a feeling that they are not worthy of living, which they believe is true, each time they make a mistake, such as causing unfair pain in the life of another human being, which adds power to their negative habit energy of Self Hatred, which we will explore in Our Book Three when we learn how to kill the unfair pain in these negative habit energies so they can no longer hurt us in the future.

When my memories of unfair pain sprout into my conscious mind, they use the energy they brought with them from The Room of Feeling Energy in my subconscious mind, to generate new unresolved pain & suffering into my conscious mind and then they begin to die, when they run out of the energy that they brought with them because I have decided to kill their ability to hurt me, by not giving them any new unfair thinking energy to stop keeping their unfair pain alive in my conscious mind.

By the time I became an adult, I had acquired thousands of memories of unfair pain & suffering that I am learning to kill, one at a time, as they sprout into my conscious mind.

Only when I have killed the energy reserves of an unfair painful memory, am I able to forgive the person who created the unfair experience in my life that caused this unfair pain. This person I want to forgive could be me.

I am learning to forgive me first, before I forgive another human being.

I am forgiving me first, for keeping all my memories of unfair pain alive by continually feeding my memories new unfair thinking energy to allow them to continue hurting me each day of my future life. I did this because of my ignorance of not knowing how to kill the unfair pain in my memories and by not knowing how to stop feeding my memories new unfair thinking energy.

Now that I know how my mind works, I am able to kill all the unfairness in my mind.

The Three Steps to Freedom from Unfairness

1) I am using My Free Will to stop generating new thoughts inside my conscious mind that life is being unfair to me, whenever I start reliving an old unfair memory, so I will not give new thinking energy to this unfair memory that it will use to generate new unresolved pain & suffering into my conscious mind, now or in the future.

2) I am detaching from any unresolved pain & suffering that may already be living inside my conscious mine by not thinking about how unfair my life became when I started to feel this new pain & suffering. Then, I am using meditation to observe this new pain & suffering until it runs out of energy and disappears from my conscious mind because I am not feeding it any new unfair thinking energy to keep it alive inside my mind.

3) After this new pain & suffering has disappeared from my conscious mind, I am forgiving myself & anyone else who created the experience of this unfairness in my past life that is buried inside my old unfair memory, so I can kill this unfairness which will stop the memory from generating any new unresolved pain & suffering into my life in the future.

These three methods kill the unfairness in my mind, to ensure that only fairness remains inside the memories that are living inside my subconscious mind.

When my task of killing the unfairness in my mind is complete, I will have killed My Pain Body, which we will explore in Our Book Three and I will have removed the pain blockage from my connection to my internal source of unconditional love. Then, I will be fully reconnected to my internal source of unconditional love which will maximize the amount of love, peace, joy & compassion that I experience each day of life, as I learn to choose all my feelings and as I learn to kill any pain & suffering that I may experience in my future life.

It was necessary for me to learn how to kill the unfairness in my mind that was blocking my connection to my internal source of unconditional love before I could bring increasing love, peace, joy & compassion into my daily life.

Now, that I have learned to kill any new unfair pain & suffering that may enter my future life, I am looking forward to accepting new challenges in the real external world that were not possible for me to enjoy in the past, when I spent most of my free time hiding away in a make believe world inside My Bubble of Protection when I tried to hide from the external world of new challenges & responsibilities, as I tried to feed my mind pleasure & avoid pain, such as when I read an enjoyable novel because I was afraid of being hurt if I accepted a new adventure in the external world that would require me to leave my bubble of protection that I had erected around myself to protect me from possible future failure or rejection in the real external world of people & events, outside of my home.

Now, for the first time in many years, I have the motivation and the eagerness to accept exciting new challenges in the real external world outside my bubble of protection.

And I realize that all I have to do, to bring additional fun & joy into my life, as I accept new challenges in the external world, is to

Practice Choosing My Feelings, as described in Step 6 of the Nine Steps to Emotion Freedom section in Chapter 13 of Our Book One, so I can stay connected to The Present Moment and not get lost in thinking about my past life or my possible future life, as I venture out into the real external world with the understanding that I am an unconditionally loving human being who was born to be successful when I face new challenges in the real external world, as I feel the unconditional love surrounding me from all the life that lives in the external world, a powerful love that will protect me from fear as I look forward to sharing new fun & adventures with my friends & family. (We will explore the concept of My Bubble of Protection in more detail in the Killing My Bubble of Protection section in Chapter 1 of Our Book Two)

What choices am I asking My Free Will to make each new day of my life to help me kill the unresolved pain & suffering & unfairness that is living inside my unfair memories? Q-148

My Need for Mindful Breathing Meditation

Mindful Breathing Meditation enables me to manage my state of Mindfulness to enable me to choose my feelings.

I am starting Mindful Breathing Meditation by practicing Control Meditation to enable me to maintain an awareness of my breathing, at all times, to keep my body anchored in the now to the Present Moment. Then I am starting Release Meditation to become able to expand my awareness outwards from my breathing to all the revealed activities of my mind to achieve Mindfulness, to enable me to spot new distractions when they enter my mind, and then I am stopping the causes of these new distractions to prevent them from gaining partial control of my mind and to prevent them from becoming able to stop me working on my goals.

Meditation is practicing detachment from all the feelings, thoughts & images in my mind that are preventing me from achieving a state of Mindfulness. Whenever I achieve a state of Mindfulness, I become able to perceive all the feelings, thoughts & images in my mind clearly & correctly without distraction or falsehood, I become able to choose to live in the present moment without accepting distractions from the past or the future, and I become able to choose to feel the continuous love, peace, joy & compassion emanating from all the life in the universe as I fully reconnect to my internal source of love that lives inside me.

I am not my feelings, thoughts, or images. I become A Compassionate Watcher as I observe them, learn to understand them, and then choose what I want to experience.

Choosing The Feelings I Want to Experience

My Life has become a contest between Me Trying to Choose My Feelings and My Feelings Trying to Control Me. The winner gains control of my mind & actions and the direction of my present life & my future destiny.

I am learning to choose my feelings instead of following my feelings, as I gain more control of my mind & actions, as I apply the understanding of how my mind works to my life, to become able to increase the amount of love, peace, joy & compassion that I feel today.

I am no longer following my feelings by allowing my feelings to tell me how to think & act to satisfy the desires that my feelings are telling me are beneficial for my future well-being.

Instead, I am choosing my feelings by not allowing my feelings to distract me from working on My Goals for Today. I am listening to what my feelings are telling me and then I am saying, "No" to following a feeling's desire for me to act in a certain way, unless I become convinced that the feeling is trying to help me to accomplish My Goals for Today.

My Major Goal for Today is to increase the number of times I say, "No" to following my feelings as I learn to Choose My Feelings instead of following my feelings and allowing them to control me. I am learning to choose my feelings by asking,

What Feelings Am I Following Today? Q-149

How do I say, "no" to following a feeling so I can observe it and not follow the feeling's desire for me to grasp or reject the action the feeling wants me to take, such as grasping onto the pleasure of listening to music or rejecting the desire to start working on a goal that may require hard work? Q-150

How do I listen to the message that a feeling is trying to tell me, so I can understand its message without following its desire for me to act, to satisfy its desire to improve the quality of my life, such as when a feeling tries to bring more pleasure into my life or when a feeling tries to reduce my pain & suffering by telling me to avoid being hurt, when it decides that I am in danger of suffering potential future loss or future failure? Q-151

For example, How do I motivate myself enough to become able to say, "No" to a feeling's desire for me to start procrastinating when it tries to convince me to stop working on My Goals for Today?

I know that my feeling of procrastination wants me to experience pleasure at all times and my procrastination does not want me to feel any pain. My procrastination is always rejecting the prospect of worry, stress & fear of future failure by seeking pleasure in doing things, such as watching TV that may not be on My List of Goals for Today.

To be able to kill my feelings of procrastination, I have decided to choose to feel any worry, stress or fear of future failure that I must feel, to be able to accomplish My Goals for Today that I have listed in my mental goals notebook this morning.

I am learning to understand how my mind should work, to enable me to choose all my feelings, especially enabling me to say, "No" to following my desires to procrastinate.

What is My Wisdom for Choosing My Feelings?

I asked My Son to answer this question, to give you an example of an answer that I am challenging you to write in your own words, to help you to practice choosing your feelings.

Chapter 26

My Son Wil's Wisdom for Choosing His Feelings

The Compassionate and Loving Nature of Children

Children are innately compassionate and loving. This is a result of their strong connection to their internal sources of unconditional love. This connection is strong due to the proximity of their age to their birth. Young children have not as yet had enough discouraging interactions with disconnected people and insane situations to erode their faith in their wisdom. Children will eventually grow into jaded adults but as long as they remain children they continue to live joyfully.

Examples of the compassion of children are provided by Maria Montessori and Theodore Rubin. They express how the compassion that exists amongst children is remarkable. It is remarkable because it does not generally exist to the same degree among adults. In this way, children offer the example of how we all should live, regardless of age. Remembering how I was as a child is the key to reconnecting with my internal source of unconditional love. This is because that connection is still there; I've simply forgotten how to use it. Remembering how I was as a child and acting as I did then is my means of reconnection.

I cannot prove to anyone that unconditional love is the inherent state of spiritual existence for all human beings. Each individual must prove that for himself or herself. Practicing The Wisdom of Children exists to help people through that process with the goal of improving the quality of their lives and spiritual existence. This work is important because it's true. It works for me. Reconnecting with the unconditional love I felt as a child makes me happier, more motivated and more able to accomplish my goals.

I am inherently an unconditionally loving person. However I find it difficult to be my true self due to my acceptance of the false expectations the world has thrust upon me.

Reconnecting with the unconditional love I felt as a child is a simple process because it doesn't require any additional evidence beyond my early life experiences. The evidence is there and it is irrefutable. Once I accept the truth of my childhood, I can begin practicing unconditional love immediately.

Improving the Quality of My Life

I am an unconditionally loving human being. I can choose to use my knowledge to improve the quality of my life. I do so by unconditionally loving myself and those around me.

I have an alternative choice. This choice is to go on living as I am. To do so I must ignore my ability to love unconditionally and fail to acknowledge my natural state of connectedness. I must reject the evidence that is provided by my childhood memories and refuse the benefits of an unconditionally loving life.

This, as I see it, is no choice at all.

The only challenge I must meet is to truly and continuously believe in the power of unconditional love. For this to work, I must change my mind and master my ego. I must undo the damage done to me by my interaction with spiritually disconnected people and therefore the insane world I live in. In fixing myself and helping others to fix themselves, I can contribute to repairing and changing the world as I help the world to reconnect to unconditional love and to me.

The Duality of My Spiritual Existence

"My existence is broken into two parts: my spiritual existence and my material existence. I experience my spiritual existence when my mind is free of thoughts. This state involves experiencing life entirely as My Soul and is known as being my watcher. My spiritual existence is my true existence because My Soul is who I truly am. I experience my material existence when my mind is full of thoughts. This state involves obsessing over the material world and is known as being my ego. My material existence is my false existence because the material world, including my body, is arbitrary.

The Fundamentality of My Soul

Existence is experience. How I experience life at any given moment is how I exist at that moment. Experiencing life as my watcher is true while experiencing life as my ego is false. This dichotomy exists because My Soul is unchanging while the material world is arbitrary. My Soul is the origin of my sentience. I know this because it is the only part of my experience that is fundamental. I can choose not to think but I must be My Soul. In fact, being my watcher is the only thing I can do consciously to the exclusion of all other conscious activities. Thus, My Soul is who I truly am.

The Arbitrary and Irrelevant Nature of the Material World

The material world is arbitrary because it is ultimately irrelevant to My Soul. Everything that exists in the material sense is the result of infinite physical and evolutionary interactions. The physical conditions of my body and the world are largely out of my control. History has progressed in my absence and will continue to progress in my absence. Thus, the world is as it is, not because of me, but because of the works of infinite others.

My Soul can direct my actions but my actions have no impact on My Soul. This is because My Soul exists prior to all other things. My Soul is unchanging, immune and benevolent. Thus, the material world is irrelevant to my true existence and experiencing life as my ego is false because it involves material obsession." (Quote from My Soul, My Ego and My Father Angst by Wil Coulson section of Our Book Three)

The Choice between Compassion and Entitlement

In the battle between competing philosophies of the mind, and by extension, the spiritual existence of the soul and the mental existence of human thought, there is the choice to believe in either compassion or entitlement.

The stance of compassion, a component of unconditional love, is represented by the phrase, "I am, therefore I think." This statement represents the primacy of soulful existence over mental existence. In other words, the soul exists before the mind within this school of thought. The stance of compassion explains the natural inclination of human beings to exist in partnerships of mutual self-interest.

The stance of entitlement is represented by the phrase, "I think, therefore I am." This statement represents the primacy of the mental existence over soulful existence. In other words, the mind exists before the soul within this school of thought.

The stance of entitlement argues for the natural entitlement of the mind and those with superior mental faculties. This belief leads to human beings existing in a state of constant competition and conflict.

Since the soul exists before the mind the stance of compassion is true while the stance of entitlement is false. Thus, the state of nature that exists between human beings who love unconditionally is one characterized by cooperation. The state of nature characterized by every man for himself, as envisioned by Hobbes, only exists as a result of the false premise of entitlement that results from being spiritually disconnected from other people.

Human beings are meant to cooperate, not compete. Cooperation only arises from a spiritual connection to other human beings. Thus, when I make the choice to love unconditionally, to share my love and wisdom with those around me, I also make the decision to cooperate with the world in a beneficial manner rather than to carve my own exclusive slice of it out for myself, to which I deny access to others. I choose to love and share because that is my true nature as evidenced by my childhood memories.

I have not, in the past, decided to be cooperative. This is a result of my spiritual connection with others. There are those that will continue to be competitive and disconnected spiritually. I must help myself and those around me who are willing to be helped and not concern myself too much with the refusals of others because they must discover the truth of unconditional love for themselves. I cannot prove it to them; they must prove it to themselves with evidence from their own childhoods.

Proving that I am an Unconditional Loving Human Being

The main theme of Practicing The Wisdom of Children is proving the truth of our inherent unconditionally loving nature to ourselves using the evidence provided by our childhood memories. Doing so requires removing all the blockages caused by patterns of egoic thinking accumulated since childhood through the interaction with spiritually disconnected individuals and situations.

This process requires that I master the wisdom of killing the unfairness in my memories so that I can reconnect with my internal source of unconditional love. Killing the unfairness in my memories is important because the unfair pain I've accumulated throughout my life has created a wall that blocks my internal connection to the unconditional love inside me by confusing, distracting and disconnecting me from my true nature.

Killing the Unfairness in My Memories

I accumulate unfair pain in my memories whenever I'm treated unfairly and I compulsively think about the unfairness of my experience. The more I compulsively think about the unfairness of my experience, the more I give the feeling of unfairness energy. Although it may be fiction, it becomes a belief that I start treating as a fact. Although it is ultimately irrelevant, I make it out to be the biggest thing in my world. This is dangerous behavior because the unfair pain in my memories exponentially grows in power and diversity. In the future, when I relive my memories of unfairness, they sprout from my subconscious into my conscious mind, forcing me to experience extra unfair pain in addition to any unfair pain I may be feeling as a direct result of events in the present. The progressively intensifying power of unfair pain that I experience as a result of this pattern of compulsive thinking and memory retention contributes to my disconnection from my internal source of unconditional love by convincing me that life, living all around me, is not only unfair but also unfair in increasingly escalating degrees. The belief that life, living all around me, is unfair is ultimately irrelevant and only serves to hurt me in the present moment and in the long run. I must learn to choose my feelings and my memories in order to diminish their power over my thinking and perception. This will allow me to become who I truly am, an unconditionally loving person.

My wisdom for killing the unfair pain in my memories is relatively easy. False life diminishing thoughts are thoughts that are ultimately untrue, irrelevant and hurtful to the quality of my existence. They serve no other purpose than to present me with a challenge on my quest to fulfill my true purpose in life. Dealing with them is simple. I catch and identify them in their moment of arising: the moment in which they sprout into my conscious mind. I then choose not to compulsively think about them. Thus, I refuse to feed them power. I acknowledge their existence and seek to understand them while realizing they are not who I am, how I have to be or how I have to feel. They present me with an option to feel negatively that I refuse. I remind myself that I am worthy of living and capable of success. I know that I can reprogram my memories in order to remove their mastery of me. I allow my false life diminishing thoughts to arise and then subside back into my subconscious without compulsively thinking of them. Starved of attention, my false life diminishing thoughts, and the unfair pain associated with them, lose their power in the present moment and in the long term. Over time, the unfair pain in my memories diminishes. The wall blocking my connection to my internal source of unconditional love is eroded. As a result, I become more and more the person I am meant to be.

In this way, I master the mechanic of my memory. Memories are packets of emotion, both negative and positive, that are associated with my past life experiences. Memories are the vehicles through which my unfair pain is stored and the mechanism through which past emotions sprout into my mind.

When my memories contain positive emotions I can be tempted to compulsively think about the acquisition of pleasurable experiences. This compulsive thinking distracts me from my true purpose in life and leads me to indulge in pleasurable experiences for the sake of pleasure, no matter how detrimental they may be to me in the present moment and in the long run. This is the source of my addictions. I obsessively indulge in activities I enjoy to the exclusion of accomplishing my goals because those goals require work to attain. When the positive emotions released by my memories convince me to compulsively think about the pleasurable experiences I'm having and cause me to work towards perpetuating them, I must remember that this pleasure is in large part a false alternative to my true existence.

Pleasure in itself is a worthy reward and a worthwhile experience. However, false pleasure in excess of that to be found in the present moment is to be avoided because it serves as a mental distraction from my true existence. Ultimately, pleasure derived from material experience pales in comparison to the pleasure that I feel as a result of my internal connection to unconditional love. Thus, I must control how much I indulge in material pleasure, ensuring that I'm not led to compulsive thinking by the emotions stored within my memories, and making sure that my enjoyment of material pleasure never blocks my connection to my internal source of unconditional love. I must truly enjoy, not falsely indulge.

When my memories contain negative emotions I can feel as if the world is being disproportionately unfair to me and this feeling can cause me to lose my motivation. When a negative memory sprouts into my conscious mind, I have the choice of whether to feed it energy or not. By choosing not to feed it energy, choosing not to compulsively think about the negative thoughts and emotions that it contains, I diminish its power over me. I realize that negative emotions and thoughts contained within my memories are irrelevant. My memory of being treated unfairly in the past is irrelevant to the present moment. While I may be in the process of being treated unfairly in the present moment, I remember that in the grand scheme of things, life is fair and this too shall pass. I'm never in danger of being hurt, not truly. The magnificence of My Soul and its connection to unconditional love is untouchable and always available to me if I choose to connect with it. That's all I ever need in life to be happy, joyous and secure. The only things that can hurt me are my worries.

It is important for me to remember that I am not my feelings. I am not my mind either. I am the compassionate watcher that exists before thought. I am who I truly am when I'm not thinking. This primacy means that I have control over what I think about and how I feel. Life is entirely experiential. It flows through the filter of perception. Nothing exists for me divorced from how I perceive it. Thus, I can control my existence, make it pure, by controlling how I think so I can choose how I feel. This is free will.

Using My Free Will to Choose My Feelings

Free will allows me to decide between being either inside or outside my unfair pain. I can be lost inside my unfair pain. I can compulsively think about it and let it consume me. Or I can exist outside my unfair pain and realize that it needn't define who I am, that it needn't consume me. I can look back at the unfair experience that is the source of my unfair pain and realize that it is over and ultimately irrelevant to the present moment. I can use my free will to free myself from the burden of the hurt of my past. I stop feeding my unfair memories and they lose their power. I stop them from hurting me now and in the future.

Stress and worry are caused by disproportional, inappropriate and inaccurate thoughts and emotions. The past is impossible to change and the future has yet to happen. All that exists is the present moment. Thus, thoughts and emotions should be tailored in size and shape to appropriately suit the demands of the present moment. How much energy does this task need to get done? How should I feel about this task truly?

In my process of self-discovery, I must realize that the challenges presented by my mind are my friends. The unfair pain in my memories provides me with learning opportunities and the opportunity to grow and excel spiritually. Perfection is boring because upon its attainment, there's nothing left to do. Every story needs a hero and every hero needs a flaw. Flaws exist to be improved upon and improvements provide the arc of the story. If there is no deficiency, there can be no goal. So I welcome the unfair pain in my memories, my false life diminishing thoughts and my memories as companions and friends on my journey of spiritual discovery.

Exercising understanding, self-discipline and mindfulness allows me to attain my goal of living a meditative life characterized by my connection to my internal source of unconditional love. The energy supplies that are present in The Storage Room of Feeling Energy for my unfair memories, false life diminishing thoughts and memories will eventually be exhausted. I am gaining a better understanding of my mind, how it works, the dangers it presents and most importantly the potential that it offers.

Throughout my journey it's important not to judge myself, my thoughts or my emotions. They are ultimately all neutral in nature. They are only positive or negative when I project those qualities upon them. Judgment leads to more thinking, often negative, that I must avoid. I must only concern myself with the demands of the present moment, for that is all that truly exists, and then focus on being the best I can be in the now.

I can find the truth behind my memories by reflecting upon them. My unfair pain, false life diminishing thoughts and memories often spout into my conscious mind incomplete and inaccurate. The unfair pain in my memory exists to intensify my pain now and in the future. It seeks to grow its strength, perpetuating itself and increasing its power over me. This process, as it is in any competition, is more about winning than it is about fair and balanced play. My unfair pain is by definition unfair. It fights dirty and is unconcerned about its legitimacy. Knowing this, I can reflect on the unfair experience that originally caused my unfair pain and realize that it wasn't nearly as unfair as my memory makes it out to be. I also remember that anything that happened in the past is ultimately irrelevant in any case. Seeking accuracy in my remembrance leads me to replace my disproportionately unfair memories with true memories to which I can feel a vastly diminished feeling of unfairness.

Practicing Forgiveness

Mastering the unfair pain in my memories ends with me practicing forgiveness. I forgive when I consciously decide to excuse or pardon someone for treating me unfairly. By forgiving someone, I dismiss any desire for revenge or demands for justice. I relieve myself of the burden of pain, guilt and obligation associated with being taken advantage of and putting myself in a position to be victimized. I remove my need to exact retribution.

Forgiveness is ultimately superior to vengeance because of the primacy of the present moment, the irrelevancy of the past and the necessity of maintaining my connection to my internal source of unconditional love. Exercising forgiveness allows me to diminish the power of my unfair pain, false life diminishing thoughts and memories because it prevents me from compulsively thinking about the injustice that was done to me.

To forgive others I must first forgive myself. I must forgive myself for feeling the way I do when I'm treated unfairly. I must forgive myself for the way I may act in the heat of the moment, the shame I may feel at being victimized and the desire for brutal vengeance that I feel. I must understand that what happened to me was not my fault and that, ultimately, everything will be ok. Letting go of my feelings of unfairness and not judging my thoughts and emotions while understanding what they are and why they occur, enables me to free my mind of this unfairness.

Once I'm free of my personal obligations to the unfairness I endured, I can then free others of their personal obligations to me. In most cases, revenge and the process needed to obtain it are not worth the cost of losing my connection to my internal source of unconditional love. There may be times when revenge must be obtained but it's unlikely that I will encounter such a case in my lifetime. Also, forgiving does not necessarily mean dismissing unfair actions and their perpetrators completely. Instead, forgiving myself and the others associated with the unfairness perpetrated against me is meant to prevent disproportionate reactions. Ideally, I will act appropriately and proportionately to address the demands of the present moment, divorced from its connection to the past and free of any emotional reaction. This will make me more prudent and most importantly happier. I will be free to spend more time maintaining my connection with my internal source of unconditional love.

Practicing Thankfulness

Diminishing the unfair pain in my memories will allow me to practice thankfulness. As I connect with my internal source of unconditional love, I begin to be filled once more with joy. I begin to feel unconditional love for myself and all living things around me. I become empowered and astonished at the wonders in life. Becoming unconditionally loving works in a similar way to becoming obsessed with unfairness but with opposite results. Unconditional love begets more unconditional love and loving unconditionally empowers me to become more unconditionally loving now and in the future.

Unconditional love leads to thankfulness. I feel thankful for life because it's miraculous. I feel thankful for all living things because they are also miraculous because they have the ability to share their love for living life with me.

My unconditional love and thankfulness improves my existence and the existences of others. This is because unconditional love and thankfulness are infectious. Sharing my joy and the methods through which I attain it allow me to spread unconditional love to those around me. This is how I nurture true friendship. True connections between me and another person occur when our souls interact. This connection exists free of the thought and pretense that is the basis for thought based human interaction. The most meaningful communication between people occurs when they're not saying anything and instead completely present in the now with each other as their spiritually based unconditional love bonds them together.

Pay-It-Forward

Unconditional love thus spreads exponentially within me through reinforcement and throughout others through a pay-it-forward method. As I learn to connect to my internal source of unconditional love I can teach others to connect to their internal sources of unconditional love and they, in turn, can teach others similarly. Thus, in helping myself, I help others. They in turn help yet more people and this is how the world is changed.

Unconditional love leads to personal compassion. Personal compassion is my personal desire to share my unconditional love with others. Personal compassion stems from the natural sense of giving that comes with unconditional love. This feeling comes from the interconnectedness of unconditional love. We each have a personal connection to our internal sources of unconditional love. However, this personal connection leads to a larger universal internet of love.

If all living things are unconditionally loving then that unconditional love encompasses and unites all those who are simultaneously connected. As I log onto the social network of unconditional love, I join the chat room of like connected people. In this chat room we can communicate in the language that exists before thought. This language comes from knowing the truth of our unconditionally loving natures.

The interconnectedness of unconditional love extends personal compassion to global compassion. Global compassion is the extension of personal compassion to the global level encompassing all human beings on earth. On the largest scale, many of my hopes and dreams are limited by the society I live in, on the local, municipal, national and global levels. My grandest aspirations are entwined with those of the human race as a whole. My ultimate goal is to make a meaningful difference in the world on the macro scale. I want to change the world.

Fostering my global compassion enhances my sense of purpose because material concerns become less trivial as they grow beyond my own personal concerns to a level where they consider grand change in a giving manner. Becoming more optimistic about the state and future of the human race helps me feel more optimistic about my place in the world and the positive changes I'm enacting in the present moment.

Spreading unconditional love and thankfulness to others begins with projecting my positive and loving attitude to those around me through my aura and actions. Projecting a positive attitude makes me magnetic.

Spiritual Resonance

Spiritual resonance exists between souls. Souls project frequencies dependent upon how connected their owners are with their internal sources of unconditional love. The more connected I am, the more unconditional love I feel and, thus, the more unconditional love I project outwards to those around me.

This unconditional love is interpreted by the senses as happiness, positivity and love. In the minds of others, I am perceived as a loving and positive guy. In the souls of others I am perceived as an unconditionally loving spiritual entity. This spiritual perception fills anyone who interacts with me with a sense of connection. If the person is connected to their own personal source of unconditional love, they will recognize what I am and what I am projecting. If the person is not connected to their personal source of unconditional love they will sense a special feeling from me they will not necessarily be able to identify but will like and wonder about.

My outward projection of unconditional love and its reception by others on a spiritual level is my spiritual resonance and aura. My spiritual resonance and aura are magical because they have the power to attenuate other souls to my positive frequency through passive interaction. Thus, my projections of unconditional love cannot help but fill others with unconditional love. Filling others with unconditional love from my internal source will help them to reconnect with their own personal sources.

My Spiritual Purpose in Life

My spiritual purpose in life and my material purpose in life are different but united. My spiritual purpose is to live in accordance with my spiritual meaning. My spiritual meaning is to exist in the present moment by practicing mindfulness through meditation. My spiritual purpose is to exist as much as possible in the present moment. My material purpose is to use my unique set of material abilities in accordance with, and under the direction of, my spiritual purpose.

I was born with an exceptional intellect and charismatic personality. I was given compassionate parents and born Canadian. My father is uniquely enlightened and interested in spirituality. These advantages comprise my unique set of material abilities. What am I supposed to do with them?

Living spiritually requires that presence permeate all of my actions whether they are spiritual, mental or physical. As I exist in the present moment, My Soul focuses and directs my mind and body. This focus and direction is presence. Thus, presence is the force exuded by My Soul. Presence is soul power.

My Material Purpose in Life

Fulfilling my material purpose requires that I allow My Soul, not my mind, to direct my material actions. When I am present, my next action is clear because my next action is directed by My Soul. Therefore, living spiritually is a process of moving from this action to the next under the direction of My Soul. My Soul guides me from moment to moment while I exist in the present moment. Moving from one action to the next allows me to complete the sequence that fulfills my material existence. In this way, I don't worry about step 2 when I'm on step 3. When I'm on step 3 I don't worry about step 5. I just complete Step 3 in the present moment to the best of my ability and then move to step 4. Only once I complete step 3 will I know what step 4 entails. I move from step to step in the present moment. I trust in My Soul's direction and know that what I'm doing is in tune with My Soul.

Living Spiritually Contrasted with Living Materially

Living spiritually contrasts with living materially. Living materially is what I do most of the time at present. I allow my mind, not My Soul, to direct my actions. When I do this I'm focusing on everything but what I'm presently doing. When I'm on step 3 I'm worrying about how much I failed at completing step 2. I'm also worrying about how hard step 5 will be. Else wise, I'm regretting how hard step 3 is in comparison with step 1. I'm worried about whether the last step will allow me to achieve anything of meaning. Meanwhile, I'm wondering how I can avoid doing step 3 right now and am searching for something more fun to do instead. These are the trappings of living materially. Living materially involves living without direction and for all the wrong reasons while avoiding living truly at all. This is because living truly only happens in the present moment and living materially involves avoiding the present moment at all costs because it usually requires self-discipline and hard work.

Living spiritually provides me with the ability to live truly and to live with certainty in life. I know that My Soul is who I truly am. When I allow my existence to flow from My Soul I know that this is the true way for my existence to be. I take comfort in the fact that I am who I am truly meant to be and that my actions are flowing in the right direction. This requires me to have faith in My Soul and connect with my internal source of unconditional love, as this love motivates me to work in a self-disciplined manner with a willingness to accept doing the work required to complete my spiritually motivated goals.

Everyone's material purpose is unique because each of us possesses a unique set of material abilities. Essentially, all of our souls are the same. It is only our unique material abilities that make us different. We must all connect with our internal sources of unconditional love and allow our souls to direct us. When we do this, we interact materially as unique expressions of the same soul. Thus, we are colored by different materials and directed down different material paths by the same spiritual hand.

I have the capacity to treat others unfairly. This is because I am still imperfect. I often live materially. My existence is often dominated by my mind. When my mind controls my actions, I am capable of insanity. Thus, treating another person unfairly is an insane action that I am capable of. When I do treat someone unfairly it is important that I forgive myself for my actions. I am allowed to make mistakes. I must try not to repeat my mistakes in future. The best way to do so is to return to living spiritually. In order to do so I must avoid compulsively thinking about the negativity surrounding my actions. Thus, self-forgiveness is essential because it allows My Soul to continue to direct my mind.

Avoiding Self Hatred

It is very important that I avoid self-hatred. I am my own biggest obstacle in life. Worrying has the potential to paralyze me mentally and physically. If I believe there is something wrong inside me that will prevent me from achieving my dreams then I will automatically fail to achieve them. This is a self-fulfilling prophecy. My worries needn't be based in truth. In fact, they almost never are. Instead, they become true because I manifest them on my own. I make them a reality. I need to avoid this from happening by refusing to worry. I acknowledge my fears but do not feed them energy. Thus, I allow them to subside back into my subconscious and refocus my attention on the present moment. By controlling my primordial fear of future loss, I kill the unfair pain in my memories. By killing my unfair pain, I release myself from my mental burdens. Thus, I allow myself the freedom to make my dreams come true instead of my fears.

Manifesting My Dreams

I have the ability to manifest my positive life enhancing dreams, to make them happen. I do this is the same way I might manifest my fears. If I believe that there is something right inside me that will allow me to achieve my dreams then I will automatically succeed. This is also a self-fulfilling prophecy. My dreams needn't be based in truth. Instead, I make them true by first believing that they are true. My self-belief will then give me the necessary motivation to make my dreams reality.

Mindfulness allows me to remain outside my thoughts and emotions. I am My Compassionate Watcher who lives inside My Soul. I am that which exists prior to thought. Thus, my fundamental perception exists outside of my thoughts and emotions.

However, I can perceive myself to exist inside my thoughts and emotions. This happens when I think compulsively. When I allow my mind to take control of my perceptual existence, I become my thoughts. I identify with the pleasure or pain that I'm feeling. I become the mental persona I've created for myself. I am my position in life. I am what I have, what I need, what I feel and what I want. When I am inside my thoughts and emotions I believe that they are real and tangible. Thoughts and emotions are truly intangible. Thus, they are transient and ultimately irrelevant. But I think they are entirely relevant when I think compulsively. Thinking compulsively makes it easy for me to forget that I am not my thoughts and emotions.

Curing My Compulsive Thinking

The cure to compulsive thinking is simple. I need only remind myself that I am My Compassionate Watcher living inside My Soul as I observe everything that is happening in the present moment, while it is happening, no matter what it is. Doing so instantly brings me back to the present moment. Remembering that I am My Compassionate Watcher is like a switch that I flip to reconnect with My Soul and with all spiritual life in the universe. I do this to gain control of my existence.

The Key to Choosing My Feelings

In conclusion, the key to happiness & success in life is managing my thoughts and emotions through continuous meditation.

Meditation is practicing Mindfulness to maintain my connection to the continuous present moment, which enables me to feel continuous love, peace, joy & compassion from all the life in the universe.

I am meditating continually with the goal of maintaining perpetual mindfulness.

Doing so allows me to exist as I truly am. Everything else, all the techniques that I will learn, all the understanding I will gain, all relates back to this central goal. I'm removing the obstacles, such as killing the unfair pain in my memories, that are preventing me from regaining mindfulness and I am learning to use the tools necessary to maintain mindfulness.

Living Spiritually and Mindfully

Living spiritually means living mindfully to enable me to fully connect to my internal source of unconditional love, to enable my unconditional love to supply me with continuous peace and joy, plus powerful motivation, to help me fulfill my purpose in life.

Living Mindfully is knowing what is happening inside my conscious mind in the present moment, while it is happening, no matter what it is, to become able to spot any new distractions that may enter my mind, to enable me to manage my distractions by preventing them from gaining control of my mind and actions.

All I need to do is regain mindfulness whenever I lose it and then practice maintaining continuous mindfulness, to enable me to manage all my feelings and to prevent me from being distracted, as I work on my goals to fulfill my life's purpose." (End of Quote from My Son Wil)

I helped My Son to learn to understand and then eliminate the unfair pain in his mind & memories as he learned to live in the continuous present moment, to become able to reconnect to his internal source of unconditional love whenever he lost this connection. When he is fully connected to his internal source, it supplies him with continuous feelings of love, peace, joy & compassion and with immense motivation to fulfill the purpose of his life, as he shares his hopes & dreams for a wonderful life with his friends & family.

To accomplish this My Son learned to embrace the nature of his True Self, a process described in The Seven Spiritual Laws of Success by Deepak Chopra.

Chapter 27

Living as My True Self in the Never Ending Present Moment

I become My True Self when I start to live as My Compassionate Watcher who is the embodiment of the unconditional love that lives inside me.

My Compassionate Watcher gives me "the ability to create unlimited wealth with effortless ease and to experience success in every endeavor." (Modified Wisdom from The Seven Spiritual Laws of Success by Deepak Chopra)

And My Compassionate Watcher gives me the awareness that I was born as an unconditional loving human being with an immense passion for living and a compelling desire to share unconditional love & nurture true friendship with my friends.

My Compassionate Watcher also gives me power to use my unconditional love to attract human beings into my life who will help me to create wealth & success in my life. "This power draws people to me and it draws things that I want, to me. It magnetizes people, situations and circumstances to support my desires, as this power creates a bond with people, a bond that comes from true love. I enjoy a bond with people and people enjoy a bond with me." (Modified Wisdom from Deepak Chopra)

When I talk, people want to listen to me and want to believe what I am saying. It is not what I say, it is how I say it that attracts people to my ideas. It is the unconditional love emanating from My Compassionate Watcher that gives me this power to convince other people of my ideas.

The Spiritual Energy Field of Unconditional Love

The Field of Pure Potential that Deepak Chopra describes is the same universal spiritual energy field that I describe as The Spiritual Energy Field of Unconditional Love that is living inside me. I am automatically reconnected to this field of unconditional love when I am not being temporarily disconnected by unfair events in my life, my ego or my memories when they are creating fear, anger, worry or stress in my life, especially when my ego is lying to me, when it tells me that I am spiritually separate from all human beings who are my adversaries, who I must compete with to obtain the scarce resources in the world that I need to obtain external joy & happiness.

Reducing the worry & stress in my life is much easier to accomplish than killing the fear & anger that my ego tries to generate in my life each day. (Please refer to the Killing the Worry & Stress in My Life section in Chapter 23 of Our Book One)

Killing My Ego's Ability to Hurt Me

To stop my ego from hurting me, I am using meditation to detach from the feelings of fear & anger that my ego generates inside my conscious mind, when it uses the unfair energy stored inside my memories of the unfair painful experiences from my past life, or when my ego uses the unfair energy from new painful unfair experiences in my future life, to generate new suffering in my life.

I am also detaching from any false judgmental thinking about how unfair my life becomes, whenever my ego starts creating new suffering in my life.

Stopping this suffering starts with my determination to kill it, when I ask My Compassionate Watcher to just observe it and not try to control it, as I feel the pain and I decide not to run away from the suffering.

To help stop this suffering, I remember that my ego needs me to feed it new unfair thinking energy, so it can use this energy to create new suffering in my current life.

So, when I decide to stop feeding my ego any new thinking energy about the unfairness of the suffering that my ego is currently creating in my life, I begin to cut off this new potential energy supply from being used by my ego, as I stop thinking about the unfairness that my ego needs me to think about, so it can continue using the unfair thinking energy that I am creating, to continue generating new suffering inside my mind.

Then, when my ego's energy supply becomes depleted, when it runs out of the energy that my unfair painful memories have given my ego and I stop giving my ego new unfair thinking energy, the suffering that I am feeling, starts to disappear from my mind.

Fortunately, when the fear & anger are gone from my conscious mind, My Compassionate Watcher automatically starts to reconnect me to the unconditional love from all the life around me, love that my fear & anger was hiding from me behind the suffering I was feeling.

I was born with the ability to harness the love from all the life around me, to help me generate abundant internal love, peace, joy & compassion in my life, as long as new suffering in my life does not start to hide it from me, once again.

The practice of detachment and the practice of not thinking about potential new unfairness in my life, takes away my ego's ability to hurt me again in the future, as I start to feel increasing love, peace, joy & compassion in my daily life, as my ego's power over me starts to decline during each new day of my life.

This increasing love, peace, joy & compassion motivates me to accomplish more of the goals for my life each day, and then when my ego's ability to hurt me in the future is minimized, I start to experience happiness in my life.

My "Happiness is contentment, exhilaration, delight, satisfaction, & well-being. My happiness is my supreme state of contentment with the possession or attainment of my well-being in my relationship with the life, living all around me, especially with my friends & family. It is a blissful state where I am resting in continuous love, peace, joy & compassion without desires, even though my every wish may not have been fulfilled.

My continuous personal feeling of satisfaction with my state of well-being in the world may be interrupted by short term pain, but my happiness returns when the pain disappears, because of my internal personal conviction that the future events in my life will continue to enhance my well-being, especially with my friends & family because The Law of Karma is working to ensure that my life is blessed with fairness in the long term that will ensure my future happiness, even though I may experience unfairness in my life in the short term." (Quote from The Elements of Unconditional Love section in Chapter 23 of Our Book One)

As I wake up each morning, the power of the love emanating from all the life in the universe fills my heart with powerful motivation to face the opportunities & challenges that this new day is offering me.

"I am able to experience this love from all life when I use my state of mindfulness to maintain a connection to the present moment, as I become one with this love, as I merge into it, as I start to experience a fire, a glow, and a sparkle of ecstasy throbbing in every living being. I begin to experience this exultation of spirit in everything that is alive, as I become intimate with the love that I am receiving from all life, as I confirm that my life is worth living." (Modified Wisdom from Deepak Chopra)

DISCLAIMER – This modified wisdom from The Seven Spiritual Laws of Success by Deepak Chopra does not necessarily reflect the views of Deepak Chopra

Now, I am winning my battles with my ego as I practice Choosing My Feelings each day, as I kill any new fear & anger that may be generated by my ego, by stopping my thinking about the unfairness in my life, as I become able to maintain a continuous connection to The Field of Unconditional Love that is living inside me, as I ask My Compassionate Watcher to bring increasing love into my life, as I share this love with my friends & family, who are helping me to become more successful each day of my future life, as I help them to reach their full potential to lead happy & successful lives, as they fulfill the unique purpose & experience the special meaning of their lives. (Please refer to the Practicing The Wisdom of Children is Hazardous to My Ego! Section in Chapter 18 of Our Book One)

Reaching My Full Potential

As I continue to control my ego's ability to hurt me in the future, I am beginning to realize that our lives as human beings on Our Precious Mother Earth reach their full potential when we share our unconditional love & we nurture true friendship with all human beings, as we savor sharing their love for all life, especially their love for us, as we become their spiritual brothers & sisters.

I feel grateful for my gift of being born with the ability to share unconditional love & nurture true friendship, as I say, "Thank You" to my friends & family for sharing their love with me, as I share my love with them, as I experience becoming who I was born to be, as I choose to be an unconditionally loving human being, each moment of every day of my future adult life.

Our ancient sages have tried to convince us to practice the wisdom for sharing unconditional love. This ancient wisdom is contained in the memories of the unconditional love of our childhood, when we felt our love **for** all life and when we felt the love **from** all life, growing inside us. This ancient wisdom benefits us, as adults, when we remember experiencing the unconditional love & the desire for true friendship during our childhood.

To help you to relive these childhood memories, it is important to learn the wisdom in Our Book that will give you the tools to understand how your mind works, to make it easier to relive the unconditional love of your childhood. These memories are important for you to experience, so you can prove that you were born as an unconditionally loving human being. Then, upon this proof of your childhood wisdom that helped you to unconditional love all life when you were a child, you can start to add the adult wisdom in Our Book to your adult life, to increase the love, peace, joy & compassion that you now share with your friends & family, as you begin to realize that you have not lost your childhood ability to feel an immense passion for living and a compelling desire to share new fun & adventures with your friends & family, as you learn to live as a child again, as you start to re-experience the intense unconditional love that you felt as a child, as you remember, "This unconditional love continuously supplied me with abundant passion for enjoying my life and with powerful motivation to fill each day of my childhood with fun & adventures." (Quote from the Learning to Understand My True Self section in Chapter 6 of Our Book One)

One of the major tools available for you to use to facilitate this process of increasing the passion in your adult life is "Rewriting The Wisdom of Children In Your Own Words" about how the wisdom is able to bring increasing love, peace, joy & compassion into your adult life, as you practice The Wisdom of Children each day. Writing about your experiences in your own words will make it easier for you to explain this wisdom to your friends & family, when they ask you why you are a happier human being who has a renewed passion for sharing fun & adventures with them.

May your love, peace, joy & compassion continue to increase each day of your future life. This will come true when you are willing to work hard to achieve it, as My Son & I have been able to do. Then, as you continue to practice The Wisdom of Children, you will eventually achieve the objective stated at the beginning of the Sharing Love & Adventures with Friends & Family section in Chapter 2 of Our Book One, that says,

"Our Book is a Self Help Guide for all adult human beings who desire to live in a state of continuous love, peace, joy & compassion, as they share unconditional love & nurture true friendship with their friends & family."

And if you have already achieved the state of experiencing continuous love, peace, joy & compassion each day of your adult life, then I congratulate you, for you are indeed a rare & precious human being.

Unfortunately for many of us, it is a long & difficult path to navigate, to become able to choose our feelings, so we can kill all the major unfair pain in our memories, so that we can become able to achieve the state of **continuous** love, peace, joy & compassion. And if you are a slow learner of this wisdom, like me, "Do Not Ever Give Up" trying to use the power of this wisdom, as you work hard to implement this wisdom into your daily life, because it is worth all the hard work that it may take, to prove to yourself that you are a rare & precious unconditionally loving human being who is reaching your full potential, as you begin living in a state of continuous love, peace, joy & compassion, and as you share unconditional love & nurture true friendship with all human beings, especially your friends & family.

Chapter 28

Thank You for Embracing the Love in Your Heart

Thank you for embracing the unconditional love in your heart to become able to increase the joy & happiness that you share with your friends, your family & the world, which includes me who is a member of your spiritual family.

I hope & pray The Wisdom of Children described in Our Book One will continue to help you, as it is still helping My Son & me, to fully reconnect to our childhood ability to share continuous unconditional love & nurture continuous true friendship with our friends, family & all the life that surrounds us, which includes you.

Please learn to become a Master of Meditation, Mindfulness & How to Control the Fairness in Your Mind, so you will become able to forgive those members of your friends & family who have hurt you unfairly over the years, so you will become able to start loving them unconditionally once again, as you were able to do as a young child, with every human being that you met in your childhood, as you offered each one an opportunity to share unconditional love & nurture true friendship with you.

Your challenge as an adult is to fully re-learn The Wisdom of Children that you intuitively understood and experienced as a young child, so you can forgive those who have hurt you unfairly, especially those who do not deserve your love because of their bad behavior.

This may not be an easy challenge for you, when you decide to accept this challenge. If you do not accept this challenge you will continue to carry around unresolved unfair pain & suffering that you will continue to feel whenever you relive one of your unfair memories. After you forgive the person who created this unfairness in your memory, the unresolved pain & suffering will disappear forever. The choice to forgive is completely yours to make, but it may not be easy for you to forgive. Forgiveness sometimes takes a long time to accomplish. Please remember that you are not doing this to benefit those who hurt you unfairly in the past. You are doing this to stop your memories from creating new unresolved pain & suffering in your life in the future.

This is why it may take you months or years to forgive not just one person, but all those who have hurt you unfairly over the years. How long it takes will depend on how much unresolved pain & suffering you have stored in your memories of the unfair experiences in your life, as you grew from a young child into the adult you are today, experiences that have created unfair memories that continue to generate unresolved pain & suffering in your life whenever you relive one of these unfair memories. You need to learn how to kill each memory's ability to generate new pain & suffering into your life, pain & suffering that may be blocking your access to your internal source of unconditional love, before you can fully reconnect to your childhood ability to share continuous unconditional love & nurture continuous true friendship with those you love, today.

When you start this challenge you will begin to experience reduced unfair pain & suffering and increasing love, peace, joy & compassion in your daily life within the first month of practicing this wisdom. This positive result of embracing The Wisdom of Children will help motivate you to continue learning more of the wisdom in Our Books, to enable you to increase the amount of unconditional love that you experience each day and then share with your friends & family, as a result of applying The Wisdom of Children to your life.

I know this is true because My Son & I experience increasing unconditional love, peace, joy & compassion in our daily lives as we continue to practice The Wisdom of Children.

Please generate the courage that you need inside you, to become able to look at your painful memories, so you can start killing the unresolved pain & suffering that is buried inside them, so they will lose their ability to hurt you in the future, to enable you to start increasing the amount of unconditional love, peace, joy &

compassion that you are able to experience each day of your future life.

My Son and I will continue to help you to practice this wisdom, as you become a Master of Meditation, Mindfulness & How to Control the Fairness in Your Mind, to enable you to learn to choose more of your life enhancing feelings, instead of allowing the unresolved pain & suffering to continue living inside your conscious mind, by providing you with additional wisdom that will help you to improve your ability to share unconditional love & nurture true friendship with your friends & family.

For example, when you were a child, did you have loving parents or guardians who were able to help you to feel the love **from** all the life living around you and who helped you to feel love **for** all the life surrounding you?

If you felt loved by your friends & family when you were a child, then it should be easier for you to remember this love living inside your heart when you were a young child, as this love helped you to experience that your life as a child was worth living, as you felt an immense passion for living when you woke up each morning, as you started to imagine your new day becoming filled with new fun & adventures.

And if you did not have loving parents or guardians when you were a child, then we will help you to understand how children learn to cope with feeling unloved and how a child learns to fully reconnect to his internal source of unconditional love, as he starts to feel loved by all life once again, when he is able to share love with a new unconditional loving human being, who he meets for the first time, even if it is only for a few minutes, as he continues to struggle, as he never gives up trying to fully reconnect to his innate ability to unconditionally love all life, an ability that he were born possessing.

As Psychiatrist Theodore Rubin says in his book, Compassion & Self Hate, "children will not easily give up their desire to lead a compassionate life". A young child may struggle during his childhood when he feels unloved, but he will not easily give up his desire to share unconditional love with another unconditionally loving human being. We will explore this innate capacity of a young child to continue offering other human beings unconditional love, even when he is being treated unfairly by members of his family or friends, when we explore the wisdom in Our Book Four.

Please make a commitment to continue studying the wisdom in Our Book One and please be patience with you progress as you implement this wisdom into your daily life, as this wisdom helps you to share increasing love, peace, joy & compassion with your friends & family.

There may be many questions waiting for you to answer in your own words, about the wisdom contained in Our Book One.

And please try to answer all the questions in the Questions to Answer section of Our Book One, especially Question 64, which asks you to remember when you felt unconditional love for everyone in your life, when you were a young child, i.e.

"What is my written description of two memories of my childhood, when I played with friends and I felt our mutual love for the fun & adventures that we shared? Q-64"

Now, My Son & I offer you with one additional challenge that I hope will help you to embrace the unconditional love in each moment of every day of your future life, starting with today.

Please allow this challenge, which we will describe for you, to generate a feeling inside your conscious mind that you are worthy of living because you have the ability to share continuous love, peace, joy & compassion with your friends & family, which will motivate them & you to cherish & protect all life on our precious Mother Earth. And please allow these life enhancing feelings to become your constant friend & companion, as they continuously motivate you to live your future life, courageously each day.

When you rewrite this challenge in your own words, please say these rewritten words of wisdom to yourself repeatedly, especially when you look at yourself in the bathroom mirror each morning at the start of a new day of your life. It will only take a few moments for you to say these words to yourself, as you allow these words to motivate your mind to remain fully connected to your universal source of unconditional love, whose energy you will use each day to help nourish yourself and those you love. This will become your daily challenge as you become the physical embodiment of these words during each moment of every day of you future life.

Please rewrite "The Wisdom of My Perfection Makes Me Worthy of Living" in the next section of Our Book and repeat it to yourself each morning to help energize your motivation to live your life courageously with a high level of determination & perseverance to help you achieve your goals for the day.

Chapter 29

The Wisdom of My Perfection Makes Me Worthy of Living

I am perfect because I was born this way, with the perfect ability to love all the life that is surrounding me and to feel the reciprocal love from all this life, as it nourishes me, as I wonder how it was created, as I enjoy its beauty, and as its desire to live & thrive, fills me with its powerful passion for living and encourages me to seek out new life giving fun & adventures with my friends & family, as this passion makes me feel worthy of living, as it flows through me into my life experiences.[72]

I am choosing to embrace these life enhancing feelings and I allow them to blossom in my heart, as I learn to detach from any unresolved pain & suffering that may enter my conscious mind, as I share the unconditional love, beauty & passion for living that I am continuing to receive from all the life surrounding me.

This ability to share love enables me to love my friends & family and to forgive them when they hurt me unfairly and it makes me worthy of living my unique & blessed life as an unconditional loving human being on Our Precious Mother Earth.

This loving energy from all the life in the universe flows through all living things and that is why I am blessed as this love energy flows through me and encourages me to work on My Goals for Today. This happens automatically, as long as I am able to stop any fear, anger, worry or stress that enters my conscious mind and tries to block my pathway to this energy of life, which is the love energy that is continuously flowing into my conscious mind from My Internal Source of Unconditional Love.

To be able to do this, I have decided to practice The Wisdom of Children to pay the price required to replace the fear, anger, worry or stress that may enter my mind in the future, with continuous love, peace, joy & compassion by using this wisdom to keep the pathway to My Internal Source of Unconditional Love fully open & clear of obstacles that will start to close down this pathway, when I allow negative unfair feelings to take control of my conscious mind.

A clear pathway to this love energy enables me to accomplish my primary goal for today which is to share continuous unconditional love & to nurture true friendship, a goal which may be delayed, whenever I start to relive the fear, anger, worry or stress that starts to creates despair in my life, whenever my unfair memories or my ego begin to generate painful feelings inside me, as they start to block the pathway to my internal source of love, as they begin to diminish my motivation to continue working on my goals, unless I practice killing these unfair painful feelings quickly to clear my pathway to the full power of the love energy in my internal source of unconditional love.

As this new day of my future life begins, the universal love that I am receiving from all the life around me is encouraging me to share unconditional love & true friendship with friends & family and others who I will meet today, even if the opportunity to share our passion for living will last for only for a few moments, as I continue to ask myself these questions during this new day of my life.

How will I nurture friendship with each person that I meet today? Q-152

How will I practice the Nine Steps to Emotional Freedom to enable me to kill any new feelings of pain & suffering that may enter my life today? Q-153

How will I practice controlling my thinking energy so I can stay fully connected to my internal source of love today, to enable me to greet those I meet today with abundant feelings of love that they will feel when they look into my eyes? Q-154

Chapter 30

Using My Perfection to Help Others become Perfect

Please write answers to all the questions in Our Book One. Answering the questions in your own words will make it easier for you to practice The Wisdom of Children and easier for you to explain this life enhancing wisdom to your friends & family. Their questions & feedback about this wisdom will help you to become a master of this wisdom.

"The Wisdom of Children is composed of a mental & physical practice. The mental practice is the nurturing & protecting of the love, peace, joy & compassion that lives inside me and the physical practice of sharing this unconditional love when I offer true friendship to another human being." (Quote from The Essence of The Wisdom of Children section in Chapter 8 of Our Book One)

Once this wisdom starts to benefit you, you will begin to help your friends & family to bring more joy into their lives, just by becoming a more loving & compassionate human being who exhibits an increasing desire to share unconditional love & nurture true friendship.

And please forgive us for the repetitive nature of the questions. We have asked you similar questions, in slightly different ways throughout Our Book One, to help you to obtain a clearer & more precise understanding of this wisdom, as your daily practice of this wisdom increases, as your mind makes this wisdom into a belief structure that your mind automatically uses to understand why other human beings treat you fairly or unfairly in your future life, when they try to share joy or pain with you and when they accept or reject your offers of love & understanding.

Unfortunately, why another human being treats me fairly or unfairly will often remain a mystery to me when he does not reveal his thoughts or feelings to me because he is afraid of my rejection of him, a fear of rejection that may have started to develop during his childhood and which now stops him from sharing his fear, anger, worry or stress with me & others.

As his friend, I will ask him to allow me to help him to understand that under all the fear, anger, worry or stress in his mind is the realization that he was born as a perfect human being, a realization that Buddha taught us to accept & understand. Once he begins to realize this, then he will become able to forgive himself for carrying the burden of fear, anger, worry or stress around with him during his life, a burden that is not part of his perfection.

Fortunately, this new understanding of his perfection will help motivate him to start killing all the unfair fear, anger, worry or stress that he now feels in his life so he can replace it with love, peace, joy & compassion, which will become a powerful stream of life enhancing energy that he will feel continuously when he is able to fully reconnect to The Internal Source of Unconditional Love that he was born possessing and that still lives inside him of him, waiting for him to fully reconnect to.

This process will enable him to begin sharing his fear, anger, worry or stress with me & others and will help him to begin to kill his old fear of rejection that will allow him to start creating new hopes & dreams for a better life with his friends & family, as a more loving & emotionally open person, because he will start believing that his future life will become fair to him and that he will no longer be afraid of a starting a new relationship in the future because he is no longer afraid that it will fail just because someone may reject him.

Then hopefully, as we start to share increasing unconditional love with each other, he will acquire the belief, that I will not reject him even if he acts badly in the future because I will forgive him when he unintentionally hurts me, that I will not betray his trust in my integrity & honesty, that I will not tell anyone about the experiences in his life that he has told me about without his permission, that I will continue to respect him as a unique & unconditionally loving human being even when his life experiences may make him appear to be less than worthy of my respect, and that I will ask him for his forgiveness when I say or do something that hurts our relationship.

In this way, the sharing of our mutual unconditional love and the mutual respect for one another's ability to nurture love, honesty, understanding, caring, support, sacrifice, forgiveness & eventual happiness in our relationship, will continue to increase as we spend time together, even though other priorities may get in the way of our spending additional time together in the future.

As I move through life, old friendships are put on hold and new ones take their place, as the priorities for how I spend my time change. Then, I am left with my memories of the old relationships, many of which I cherish inside my heart when I start to relive some of my memories of sharing love & friendship, especially the wonderful memories of growing up with my parents & my childhood friends.

This is an example of how we use The Wisdom of Children to increase the quality of life that we share with another human being who is hurting, and who may be like many of us are today because we may also be recovering from painful experiences with the help of our friends & family, as we try to share love & forgiveness with those who hurt us, with the hope that they will eventually become our true & loving friends, even though this process may take months or years to accomplish and then sometime in the future our sharing of mutual love & respect may end, at least for a while, as our life moves on to new relationships and we say goodbye to old friends.

This process of increasing the passion for living that I share with other human beings is made possible by my daily practice of The Wisdom of Children as it helps me to understand the new feelings that I experience each day and also helps me to understand & respect the privacy of the feelings of my friends & family, as I wait for them to share their thoughts & feelings with me, as I allow them to live their lives with me or without me, but also without my advice, if possible, unless they ask for help & advice when they share their thoughts & feelings with me as I endeavor to love & respect them unconditionally, continuously & forever.

Knowing that my friends & family are trying to live their lives as unconditional loving human beings and are also trying to share true friendship with those they love, is what is important to me, even if I may be unable to share my life with them, at this time. But then again, who knows what may happen in the future as our mutual love motivates us to be together, as one big family who shares hopes & dreams and then works together to make some of those dreams become a reality.

And hopefully in the future, I will become able to share more of my life with those I love, as my desire for a fun filled future life continues to inspire me and as I realize that our ultimate human destiny is to be together, loving one another in this life & the next, as I cherish my future vision of all human beings on Our Precious Mother Earth coming together in mutual self-interest as we; help one another, love each other, support one another, and of course forgive each other, especially when those who hurt us do not deserve our forgiveness or when we hurt ourselves & others when our plans for a better life go awry.

Then, as we try to live peacefully together once again, as our mutual love for all life starts to heal the wounds of our failures & disappointments, as best it can, hopefully we will realize that sharing unconditional love & nurturing true friendship is what all human beings are born to do.

I can prove this is true in my own life, by looking back at the memories of my childhood when I felt love for everyone & when I felt loved by all the life in the universe, and by looking at my friends & family as my desire to share love & friendship with them continues to grow.

Please Forgive Us

The wisdom in Our Book One is very repetitive. We have written it this way on purpose to help you loosen the grip that your ego may have on you. Please forgive me & my son for this repetition.

"Aristotle once commented on the importance of repetition in education by noting, "It is frequent repetition that produces a natural tendency." Many teachers strive to help their students acquire new skills and repetition can be a highly effective way to do so, for as Aristotle mentions, it is how tasks and knowledge can become second nature for students.

Repetition is a key learning aid because it helps transition a skill from the conscious to the subconscious. Through repetition, a skill is practiced and rehearsed over time and gradually becomes easier. As the student improves, he does not need to think consciously about the skill.

This is how repetition makes the skill of Practicing The Wisdom of Children easier to learn & perfect." (Modified quote from Focus & Repetition in Learning)

The next chapter will reduce all this repetition into concise questions, whose answers will enable you to more easily understand and then practice The Wisdom of Children in your life.

Chapter 31

Questions to Answer in My Own Words

We have provided you with a list of questions from Our Book One that will help you to master The Wisdom of Children. Hopefully, you have already answered some of the questions in your own words as you read through Our Book One. Please write down your answers to the questions you have not answered and then store all your answers in a secure location that you can access in the future, as you use these answers to help you to become a master of The Wisdom of Children. And I hope you will become motivated to write a book or produce a video about your wisdom, when you decide to start sharing your wisdom of unconditional love with all human beings in the world, not just with your friends & family.

As you describe the wisdom of your life experiences, hopefully, you will use your own words to describe your desire to share love with everyone on Our Precious Mother Earth and you will also describe the child who you were many years ago, who stills lives inside you, and who confirms that you were born to love everyone in your life, as you tell your life story about how you continue to love & forgive friends & family members, especially those who do not deserve your love & forgiveness.

This is what My Son & I are trying to do, to allow the readers of Our Book to look inside our hearts and feel the unconditional love that we are offering to share with them & you and to enable our readers to look deeply inside their own hearts & minds to help them to learn how to share more love & friendship with the loved ones in their lives.

Before you attempt to answer a question, please read the section of Our Book in which the question appears so you can understand why the question was asked. And if you have answered a similar question, then, please try to capture the context of the wisdom in this new section of Our Book when you answer this new similar question for the first time.

And when you have answered this new question to the best of your ability at this time, please write an introduction to the question that explains the context of the wisdom that the question is derived from, to enable a friend of family member, to read what you have written and to understand why the question was asked and why you answered it this way.

Please realize that you may not be able to answer some of the questions, until you have practiced The Wisdom of Children enough to realize the benefits that the answer to this question has for your life.

So, please answer the questions you can at this time and then, come back and answer additional questions when The Wisdom of Children enables you to see more of the answers to these questions in your life experiences.

Sharing Love & Adventures with Friends & Family

Can I remember when I felt immense love for all the life around me, when I was a young child, as I shared new fun & adventures with my family & friends?   Q-1

Will I endure the pain & suffering that my childhood memories may reveal to me, as I search my memories for the source of my childhood ability to love life passionately? Q-2

Will I forgive those who hurt me unfairly during my childhood, to enable me to kill the unresolved pain & suffering that is hiding my childhood memories of the unconditional love that I felt for other human beings, before they hurt me? Q-3

Will I use the unconditional love for the fun & adventures of my childhood, that I find living inside my childhood memories, to help motivate me to try a new adventure in my adult life? And what is my description of the fun & joy that I want to share with others on this new adventure? Q-4

Will I pay any price that is required to fully reconnect to the passion of my childhood, to enable me to feel continuous love, peace, joy & compassion in my adult life? Why? Q-5

How do I begin to share this powerful childhood life enhancing energy of love? Q-6

Such as:

Hug & Kiss someone more often? Q-7

Forgive someone who doesn't deserve it? Q-8

Tell someone "I love you", maybe a friend I haven't told before? Q-9

Share a new exciting adventure with someone I love? Q-10

Overview of the Wisdom in Our Books One through Four

Is it possible to believe that this wisdom may work to increase the joy & happiness in my adult life? Why? Q-11

How does The Wisdom of Children become a belief structure that anchors itself to my real childhood ability to unconditionally love all the life around me and to my adult ability to love my friends & family? Q-12

Introduction to My True Self

Can I remember a childhood experience when I felt connected to a source of unconditional love that lived inside me and powered my motivation to learn to walk, talk & play and nourished my sense of wonder & delight when I shared fun & adventures with my friends & family? Q-13

As I look back through my childhood memories, can I remember when I was able to embrace my childhood wisdom for sharing unconditional love & nurturing true friendship, by opening my heart and offering my unconditional love to potential friends, with my innocent expectation that we could share fun & adventures and become true & loving friends? Q-14

Why did I diminish or lose the passion of my childhood by the time I became an adult? Q-15

What can I do as an adult to increase my passion for living and increase my eagerness to share new fun & adventures, so I can fully enjoy my life again, as I once did when I was a young child? Q-16

How do I fully reconnect to the internal source of love, peace, joy & compassion of my childhood, so I can start to feel & then share this powerful unconditional love with all the life that is surrounding me, especially with my friends & family? Q-17

How do I kill the unfair fear, anger, worry & stress in my mind that is being generated by my unfair painful memories and that is blocking my connection to the source of unconditional love of my childhood and diminishing my ability to increase the love, peace, joy & compassion in my adult life? Q-18

My Childhood

Why I was born? Q-19

A Spiritual Journey with My Son Wil

Who am I? Q-20
Where did I come from? Q-21
Why am I here on Earth? Q-22
What is my life's purpose? Q-23

Practicing Meditation & Mindfulness When I Wake Up Each Morning

Was I born with an internal source of unconditional love that nourished me with continuous love when I was young child and can I use this internal source of love, now that I am an adult, to enable me to share increasing love, peace, joy & compassion with all human beings, especially with my friends & family, until it becomes continuous? Q-24

If my answer to this question is Yes, Why is it Yes? Q-25

If my answer to this question is No, Why is it No? Q-26

Continuous Love Requires Freedom from Unfair Pain & Suffering

How do I use The Wisdom of Children to achieve Emotional Freedom from unfair painful feelings that enter my mind and try to control me, as they start to destroy the love, peace, joy & compassion that I am feeling at the present moment? Q-27

How do I start to experience continuous feelings of love, peace, joy & compassion in my adult life? Q-28

How do I prove that this wisdom works? Q-29

The Balance Between Joy & Fear Inside My Mind

What is the balance between joy & fear inside my mind and what causes this balance to change inside my mind? Q-30

Did I fight or run away from the cause of the unfairness in my childhood whenever someone treated me unfairly? Why? Q-31

The Nine Steps to Emotional Freedom

Step 1) Practicing Detachment

What is detachment? Q-32

How do I detach from unfair pain & suffering? Q-33

Parents & Teenagers

Why do many parents continue to give their children advice, when their children tell them that they do not need or want their advice? Q-34

An Unbreakable Bond of Love

How does an unbreakable bond of love develop between children & their parents? Q-35

Step 2) Practicing Friendship

Killing Unfair Pain & Suffering

When I experience unfair pain & suffering, am I spiritually alone in the universe and does my consciousness live solely inside my head, or am I spiritually connected to a universal consciousness that lives outside my body, a universal consciousness that I can use to help me to kill future pain & suffering, so I can start to live my life more fairly & successfully? Q-37

Where do my thoughts & feelings come from? Q-38

Step 3) Controlling My Mind

How does meditation & mindfulness help me to keep control of my mind? Q-36

My Pain Needs to be Embraced before I Can Make Pain My Friend

When I am able to make the pain my friend, then I try to convince the unfair memory that is generating the pain to become my friend also, when I ask a memory,

What are you trying to tell me, each time I relive your pain? Q-39

Please ask yourself this question. Your answer to this question will be different from mine, however, the answer will probably include one of these phrases, "life is being unfair to me, life has been unfair to me, or life is going to be unfair to me."

If so, then your next question should be similar to this one,

How do I use friendship to understand an unfair memory, so I can find the source of this unfairness and then learn how to kill the unfairness, so my memory will not hurt me again in the future, when I relive it?
Q-40

How do I convince an unfair painful memory that life will be fair to me in the future, so it will Stop generating new pain in my life, the next time I relive this memory, because it now realizes that it No longer needs to use pain to warn me that l am in danger of being hurt? Q-41

Step 4) Practicing Fairness

Questions to Ask Myself when I am Practicing Fairness in My Life

Why did I start running away from my memories of pain & suffering when I was a child? Q-42

Does a memory use up its store of available energy when it creates new pain & suffering in my mind Q-43

How does a memory obtain new unfair energy to become able to create new pain & suffering in my mind in the future? Q-44

Why does a memory create new pain in the future whenever I feed it new energy of unfairness? Q-45

Can I learn why a memory thinks my future life will become unfair to me, once again? Q-46

When I learn why the past was unfair, can I convince a memory to Stop generating new unfair pain in the future, with the unfairness energy it has stored in its energy reserve? Q-47

What happens when I cannot convince a memory that life will become fair to me in the future? Q-48

What is fairness and how may I create more fairness in my life, today? Q-49

Step 5) Practicing Forgiveness

Is there anyone in my life who will benefit from my forgiveness, today? Q-50

How will my forgiveness reduce the pain that I feel, whenever I relive the unfair experience that this person created in my life? Q-51

What is forgiveness and how does it stop unfair pain from reoccurring when I relive a painful memory? Q-52

Step 6) Choosing My Feelings

What do I ask my mind to do to help me choose my feelings of Childhood Love, Peace, Joy & Compassion? Q-53

The Qualities of a Hero

What are the qualities of a hero that are living inside me, waiting to re-born? Q-54

Step 7) Practicing Self-Discipline

How does self-discipline help me to continuously share unconditional love & nurture true friendship with everyone in my life? Q-55

Step 8) Practicing Thankfulness

How does thankfulness help me to cherish my friends & family as they keep loving me & keep forgiving me, especially when I do not deserve their continuing love & forgiveness? Q-56

Step 9) Sharing All The Love in The Universe

How do I maintain a continuous connection to all the love in the universe during each moment of every day of my future adult life? Q-57

What am I Asking My Mind to Do, when I Practice The Nine Steps? Q-58

This is the most important question in Our Book One. The answer to this question gives my mind the mental tools that it needs to maintain my connection to continuous love, peace, joy & compassion during every present moment of my life, especially when I am with my friends & family, so I can share these wonderful feelings with those I love.

A Last Word at The Beginning

Why is my ability to unconditionally love all the life that surrounds me, so perfect? Q-59

Why was I born with the perfect ability to unconditionally love all life? Q-60

Do I want to increase the passion in my adult life by fully reconnecting to my intense childhood desire to seek new fun & adventures, by fully reconnecting to the internal source of unconditional love & motivation of my childhood? Q-61

When I decide to increase the passion in my adult life, how do I start to fully reconnect to my childhood source of unconditional love & motivation? Q-62

My Childhood Ability to Share Unconditional Love with All Life

Are these statements about my childhood also a true description of your past life? Q-63

What is my written description of two memories of my childhood, when I played with friends and I felt our mutual love for the fun & adventures that we shared? Q-64

Will these memories help me to rediscover & embrace my childhood ability to love all life passionately, to help me to bring more love, peace, joy & compassion into my adult life? Q-65

What is the next step that I must take, to be able to continue on my adult journey to fully rediscover my childhood ability to feel increasing love from all the life that is surrounding me and to feel increasing love for all this life? Q-66

Practicing The Wisdom of Children is Hazardous to My Ego!

Do I have an Ego and if so, how do I learn to control my ego so it will no longer be able to control me, when I feel that the life all around me is being unfair to me and when I start to feel afraid of the future events in my life? Q-67

Does every human being in the world have an Ego, such as the one that is trying to control my mind & actions as it motivates me to feel separate from other human beings, so it can convince me to start competing with other human beings by lying, cheating & stealing from them, to become able to obtain my share of the scarce resources in the world that I mistakenly believe will bring me continuous external joy & happiness? Q-68

What is my ego trying to convince me to do and what impact will this action have on my life, today? Q-69

My Ego's Belief in Separation

How does my ego try to make me feel spiritually separate from my friends & family, at times, when I become upset with the unfairness in my life and I start to treat those I love as my adversaries when I start to crave fairness, justice or revenge because of the unfairness they are generating in my life? Q-70

How do I learn to Choose My Feelings so I can choose to forgive those who treat me unfairly and then, so I can start to offer them unconditional love, once again, when I am able to kill my ego's desire to treat my love ones as my adversaries? Q-71

Who Loves Me Enough

Who loves me enough to save me, when I am danger of being hurt? Q-72

The Desire for Unconditional Love & True Friendship

Who do I want to share unconditional love with today? Why? Q-73

Who do I want to nurture true friendship with today? Why? Q-74

The Energy Strings of The Universe

Inside the atoms in our human bodies, the electrons have been spinning around the core of each atom for billions of years and have not slowed down, which begs obvious questions in our minds,

Were electrons designed by a creator or by random chance, to keep spinning forever? Q-75

Where does an electron's continuous self-sustaining energy come from? Q-76

Questions about The Meaning of My Life

Was my birth as a human baby the result of random chance? Q-77

Or divine creation? Q-78

Is there a divine intelligence that helped create the universe & all human beings? Q-79

The Choice to Acquire Faith

When I physically die, does my spiritual essence that is contained in My Soul, live on, because there is a Creator or a God that gives human beings eternal spiritual life or is my life at an end with No possibility of a future life for me? Q-80

We will no longer explore where our ability to offer unconditional love to other human beings may have come from, other than to ponder this question,

Does my ability to love come from a creator or from the random chance of evolution? Q-81

What we will do instead is try to except that our ability exists because we were born with the perfect ability to love all life, without knowing why we were blessed with this ability.

Understanding The Awareness of My Connection to All Life

To understand the concept of My Awareness of My Connection to All Life as an adult, I began to realize that this experience is real when I am feeling continuous love, peace, joy & compassion and when I am feeling the unconditional love emanating from all life in the universe.

To be able to understand the truth of this statement, please look inside your mind at your earliest memories of when you were a baby and ask yourself these questions,

What is my earliest memory as a baby, when I was aware of the unconditional love living inside a family member or a guardian? Q-82

How did I express my unconditional love for all life when I was a child by expressing my love & joy when I played games or went on adventures with my family, by laughing, singing or shouting my excitement & delight to everyone, so they could share in my joy of being alive to experience these wonderful feelings of new fun & adventures? Q-83

What is My Awareness of My Connection to All Life in the universe? Q-84

My Nature as an Unconditionally Loving Human Being

What is Pure Eternal Spiritual Energy? Q-85

Is the primordial spiritual energy of the universe powering the energy of My Mind & Body? Q-86

Will I be united with a new body when my spiritual essence goes to Heaven? Q-87

Will I be reincarnated into a new body and start a new life on Earth? Q-88

Or, Will I cease to exist because My Spirit dies when My Body dies? Q-89

What is The Mirror in My Mind? Q-90

What is The Energy of My Mind? Q-91

What is The Light of My Mind? Q-92

What is The Clarity & Truth of My Mind? Q-93

What is The Creativity of My Mind? Q-94

How does The Mirror in My Mind work to reflect the truth of the contents of my mind? Q-95

Why am I not my feelings, thoughts or images? Q-96

What is The Primordial Awareness of My Mind? Q-97

What are the different types of Primordial Awareness of My Mind? Q-98

What are My Definitions of the feelings, thoughts & images in my mind? Q-99

Am I a Mind without a spirit & a soul and am I destroyed when My Body dies? Q-100

And

Are love, peace, joy & compassion only found outside of My Body and not inside me? Q-101

Or

Am I pure primordial spiritual energy called My Spiritual Being who is absolutely connected to all living things in the universe and do I exist forever? Q-102

And

Are love, peace, joy & compassion found inside of My Body and will this internal unconditional love continue to stay connected to My Spiritual Being after My Body dies? Q-103

How I Stopped Being Connected to Unconditional Love

Why do I sometimes allow my feelings of being spiritually separate from other human beings to convince me to believe my ego? Q-104

How I Started to Fully Reconnect to Unconditional Love

My childhood memories are my proof that I was born with the ability to feel love for all life and to feel loved by all life, continuously, every moment of every day of my adult life.

How do I get confused, when I start to falsely believe that the love I need to motivate me to live my life with passion exists in the external world? Q-105

How I Nurture True Friendship

How do I choose feelings that increase my love, peace, joy & compassion and nurture true friendship instead of indulging in feelings that are motivating me to seek justice or revenge for a betrayal of our friendship when I am trying to forgive a friend who hurt me? Q-106

The Nature of True Friendship

What is the nature of True Friendship and how can it improve the well-being of my life? Q-107

Is my life blessed with a True Friend? Who? Why? Q-108

Questions for Parents

Is it not a mother's right to give her children unsolicited advice, as often as a mother feels it is appropriate to do so? Q-109

Do fathers feel the same need to give unsolicited advice to their children? Q-110

When I give my children unsolicited advice, am I being a True Friend? Q-111

Is unsolicited advice harming our relationship with our child? Q-112

Questions for Adults

Should I stop giving advice to my friends when it is not asked for?
Q-113

Do I find unsolicited advice from my friends, helpful? If so, When?
Q-114

Is unsolicited advice hurting my friendships? Q-115

How I Benefit from Studying The Wisdom of Children

Can I say that the person I love, who I want to share my life with,
who I may be engaged to, married to, or in a complicated romantic
relationship with, is a True Friend? Q-116

Can I bring True Friendship to my family relationships? Q-117

Will I make a journey of self-discovery with Bill & Wil, as I read
Our Book One to discover The Wisdom of Children and apply this
wisdom to my life to increase the Unconditional Love & the True
Friendship in my life? Q-118

Unlocking The Meaning of My Life

What is The Meaning of My Life? Q-119

**Making a Commitment to study The Wisdom of The Meaning of
My Life**

Am I willing to make a commitment to perform the hard work
required to find all the keys for unlocking The Wisdom of The
Meaning of My Life, to be able to maximize the love, peace, joy &
compassion in my daily life? Why? Q-120

The First Key for Increasing the Love, peace, joy & compassion in
My Life

"I am learning to share my unconditional love & forgiveness to
become able to nurture true friendship with those I love"

Unfortunately, I may quit my journey of self-discovery to increase the unconditional love in my life soon after I start. Why? Q-121

The Second Key for Increasing the Love, peace, joy & compassion in My Life

"I am learning to become courageous by looking inside my mind at my painful memories to transform my memories by melting away their power to inflict unfair pain & suffering, so they cannot hurt me anymore."

Am I afraid to look inside my mind at my painful memories? Why? Q-122

How do I acquire painful memories? Q-123

How many painful memories do I have? Q-124

My Childhood Memories of My Connection to Love & Friendship

What is my earliest childhood memory of my unconditional love for a family member or a guardian? Q-125

The Elements of Unconditional Love

My unconditional love is the love, peace, joy & compassion of my childhood that I become able to share with all human beings in my adult life, when I become a child of love, once again.

What is my definition with an example from my personal experience of each subcomponent of unconditional love? Q-126

Fear & Anger that Creates Despair in My Life

What will maintain the fairness in my future life, so I can use this fairness to kill any future fear & anger that may try to enter my mind? Q-127

A Formal Definition of The Law of Karma

Why is it important for me to learn that there is no permanent self and that my body, my mind, my name & my human life are impermanent? Q-128

Unconditional Love is like a Precious Coin that I Spend when Sharing Love

How often do I spend My Coin of Unconditional Love? Why? Q-129

Accepting My Unconditionally Loving Nature

What is my written description of two memories from my childhood of the fun & adventures I experienced as a young child, when I felt love for all life & I felt the love from all this life, as I enjoyed playing games with my friends & family?
Q-130

Distilling The Main Theme of Our Book

Have I diminished or lost my internal connection to unconditional love? Q-131

If so, Why? Q-132

How do I fully reconnect to my source of continuous love? Q-133

How a Bad Person become a Good Person

How do I become a more loving human being who is able to generate increased love, peace, joy & compassion in my life that I can share with my friends & family? Q-134

Reducing Worry & Stress in My Life

Do I know any parents who find it both stressful & even painful to say, "No" to their young children who they do not want to disappoint? Why do parents feel this way? Q-135

A teenager may feel that life all around him is unfair to him, except when he is with his friends. Why? Q-136

How does worry & stress produce unresolved unfair pain in my adult life, especially when I may worry about things that I feel I have no control over? Why? Q-137

Losing My Connection to Unconditional Love

Why do I lose my internal connection to unconditional love when I run away from the pain & suffering that my memories generate inside my mind? Why do I allow this to occur and how can I prevent it in the future? Q-138

Fully Reconnecting to Unconditional Love

How do I reconnect to the motivational power that is being continuously generated by My Internal Source of Unconditional Love, to help me to visualize jumping out of bed each morning with a song in my heart, ready & eager to face the opportunities & challenges that this new day is offering me? Q-139

How do I maintain a continuous connection to my internal source of unconditional love during the day so it can provide me with the powerful motivation that I need to kill any new worry & stress that may enter into my life today? Q-140

How do I use my ability to visualize powerful motivation in my future life, when I wake up each morning, to convince me that I am ready to look inside my mind at my painful memories, and how do I become convinced that I am ready to learn how to kill all the major unfair pain in my negative memories, to become able to stop the worry & stress in my life by Practicing The Wisdom of Children? Q-141

False Life Diminishing Thoughts

What are some of the False Life Enhancing Thoughts that I have stored inside my memories that tell me I am unworthy of living? Q-142

True Life Enhancing Thoughts

What are some of the True Life Enhancing Thoughts that I have stored inside my memories that tell me I am worthy of living? Q-143

Becoming a Master of The Wisdom of Children

How does The Power of Detachment control the fairness in my mind? Q-144

How does The Power of My Mind control the fairness in my mind? Q-145

How does The Power of Fairness control the fairness in my mind? Q-146

How does The Power of Forgiveness control the fairness in my mind? Q-147

The Unfairness in My Mind

What choices am I asking My Free Will to make each new day of my life to help me kill the unresolved pain & suffering & unfairness that is living inside my unfair memories? Q-148

Choosing The Feelings I Want to Experience

My Major Goal for Today is to increase the number of times I say, "No" to following my feelings as I learn to Choose My Feelings instead of following my feelings and allowing them to control me. I am learning to choose my feelings by asking,

What Feelings Am I Following Today? Q-149

How do I say, "no" to following a feeling so I can observe it and not follow the feeling's desire for me to grasp or reject the action the feeling wants me to follow, such as grasping onto the pleasure of listening to music or rejecting the desire to start working on a goal that may require hard work? Q-150

How do I listen to the message that a feeling is trying to tell me, so I can understand its message without following its desire for me to act, to satisfy its desire to improve the quality of my life, such as when a feeling tries to bring more pleasure into my life or when a feeling tries to reduce my pain & suffering by telling me to avoid being hurt, when it decides that I am in danger of suffering potential future loss or future failure? Q-151

The Wisdom of My Perfection Makes Me Worthy of Living

How will I nurture true friendship with each person that I meet today? Q-152

How will I practice the Nine Steps to Emotional Freedom to enable me to kill any new feelings of pain & suffering that may enter my life today? Q-153

How will I practice controlling my thinking energy so I can stay fully connected to my internal source of love today, to enable me to greet those I meet today with abundant feelings of love that they will feel when they look into my eyes? Q-154

Chapter 32

Recommended Books & Videos

The Nature of Unconditional Love

Loving What Is by Byron Katie – Highly Recommended!
The Absorbent Mind by Maria Montessori
The Montessori Method by Maria Montessori
The Secret Millionaire TV Series
Stick Up for Yourself! Every Kid's Guide to Personal Power &
Positive Self-Esteem by Gershen Kaufman
The Natural History of Love by Morton Hunt
Open Marriage by Nena & George O'Neill
The Five Love Languages by Gary Chapman

Unconditional Love for All Life in the Universe

Earth The Power of the Planet presented by Iain Stewart - BBC
miniseries - Highly Recommended!
Evolution DVD by Nova - PBS Mini Series - Narrated by Liam
Neeson
Unlocking the Mystery of Life DVD by Illustra Media
The Elegant Universe DVD by Nova - PBS Mini Series
The Elegant Universe book by Brian Greene
Cosmic Voyage DVD by Imax

Learning to Love Other Human Beings

Zen Heart by Ezra Bayda - Highly Recommended!
Toward a Psychology of Being, 3rd Edition by Abraham H. Maslow
The Seven Habits of Highly Effective People by Stephen Covey
The Eighth Habit by Stephen Covey
The Fountainhead novel by Ayn Rand

Love for God

How to Know God - Book & DVD by Deepak Chopra - Highly Recommended!
The Third Jesus by Deepak Chopra
Living Buddha Living Christ by Thich Nhat Hanh
Going Home, Jesus and Buddha as Brothers by Thich Nhat Hanh
How to Hear From God by Joyce Meyer
The Good Heart, A Buddhist Perspective on the Teachings of Jesus by the 14th Dalai Lama

Meditation & Mindfulness

Diamond Mind by Rob Nairn - Highly Recommended!
What is Meditation by Rob Nairn

Living Spiritually

Many Lives, Many Masters" by psychotherapist Dr. Brian Weiss - Highly Recommended!

Habit Energies

Feel the Fear and Do It Anyway by Susan Jeffers - Highly Recommended!
Understanding Our Mind by Thich Nhat Hanh
Buddha Mind, Buddha Body by Thich Nhat Hanh

The Ego

Your Sacred Self by Wayne Dyer - Highly Recommended!
Understanding The Power of Now by Eckhart Tolle
The Power of Now by Eckhart Tolle
Stillness Speaks by Eckhart Tolle
A New Earth by Eckhart Tolle

Procrastination

Procrastination, Why You Do It, What To Do About It by Jane Burka & Lenora Yuen - Highly Recommended!

Forgiveness of False Pride & Self Hate

Compassion and Self Hate by Theodore Isaac Rubin - Highly
Recommended!
Neurosis And Human Growth by Karen Horney

Creating Personal Wealth & Personal Power

The Seven Spiritual Laws of Success by Deepak Chopra - Book &
DVD - Highly Recommended!
Wishes Fulfilled by Wayne Dyer

Chapter 33

Bibliography

The bibliography contains references to the literary & video material of the authors who have inspired us. My Son & I are indebted to these authors to whom we offer our thanks and our respect & admiration.

We apologize to any authors whose wisdom we may have used without referencing their literary material in Our Book One. Please advise us so we can include the proper references in future revisions of Our Book One

The References also contain specialized definitions that we have created to help the reader to understand the wisdom in Our Book One.

1-Specialized Definition by Bill Coulson

The Wisdom of Children is the wisdom of using my childhood ability to share unconditional love & nurture true friendship. It is also the wisdom of accepting the love from all the life around me, especially the love from other human beings and the wisdom of embracing my love for all this life. This unconditional love of my childhood is a deep affection for the well-being of all the life on Our Precious Mother Earth. It is a love that lives continuously in my heart as it encourages me to take actions to help create, nurture, serve & protect the life that I observe & interact with each new day of my adult life, as I share this love with friends & family and they share their love with me. It is a powerful love that I was born possessing, a love that has been living inside me all my life, as it fuels my motivation to live my life with great passion. (Please refer to the Sharing Love & Adventures with Friends & Family section in Chapter 2 of Our Book One)

2-Specialized Definition by Bill Coulson

Wisdom is a wise act or saying that improves the future well-being of our lives. (Please refer to The Essence of The Wisdom of Children section in Chapter 8 of Our Book One)

3-Specialized Definition by Bill Coulson

Practicing The Wisdom of Children is acting wisely when I use my childhood ability to fully reconnect to my internal source of unconditional love for all life, to become able to generate a powerful passion for living and a compelling motivation to share unconditional love & nurture true friendship with all human beings, especially my friends & family. The Wisdom of Children is also the wisdom of accepting the love from all the life around me & feeling love for all this life. (Please refer to The Essence of The Wisdom of Children section in Chapter 8 of Our Book One)

4-Specialized Definition by Bill Coulson

The Wisdom of Children is composed of a mental & physical practice. The mental practice is the nurturing & protecting of the love, peace, joy & compassion that lives inside me and the physical practice of sharing this unconditional love when I offer true friendship to another human being. (Please refer to The Essence of The Wisdom of Children section in Chapter 8 of Our Book One)

5-Specialized Definition by Bill Coulson

True friendship is nurtured between us when we share love, peace, joy & compassion with each other and we practice forgiving each other for the mistakes we make in our relationship. (Please refer to The Essence of The Wisdom of Children section in Chapter 8 of Our Book One)

6-Specialized Definition by Bill Coulson

As I start applying The Wisdom of Children to my adult life each morning, I begin to practice Meditation & Mindfulness as I as soon

as I wake up from sleep to the start of a new day of fun &
adventures.

Meditation is practicing detachment from all the thoughts feelings &
images in my mind that are preventing me from achieving a state of
Mindfulness. When I achieve a state of Mindfulness, I become able
to perceive all the thoughts, feelings & images in my mind, clearly &
correctly, without distortion or falsehood, as I become able to choose
to live in the present moment without accepting distractions from the
past or the future.

And then, I become able to choose to feel the continuous love,
peace, joy & compassion emanating from all the life in the universe,
as I fully reconnect to my internal source of love that lives inside me.

Mindfulness is knowing what is happening inside my conscious
mind in the present moment, while it is happening, no matter what it
is. (Modified quote from What is Meditation by Rob Nairn)

Achieving The State of Mindfulness is made possible by following
The Middle Path (or The Middle Way) of Meditation that Buddhists
practice when they meditate. As Buddhists practice meditation, they
simply observe, without additional mental effort and without striving
for meditation results, as they observe all the mental activities inside
their conscious minds without trying to control them and without
trying to change them, as they concentrate on their breathing that
helps to calm the mind by reducing the energy & speed of the mind's
mental activities, similar to taking one's foot off the gas pedal when
driving a car.

In this way, the meditator stops giving thinking energy (similar to
cutting off the gas supply to the car's engine) to the feelings,
thoughts & images in the mind by not thinking about them so the
they run out of the thinking energy that they need to continue living
inside the meditator's conscious mind. When they run out of this
energy for living, they have no choice but to leave the conscious
mind which results in the mind's activities slowing down, as the
mind starts to calm, as the number of feelings, thoughts & images in
the mind is reduced.

When I follow The Middle Path of Meditation, I realize that I am not my feelings, thoughts & images because I can kill them by not feeding them the thinking energy that they need to stay alive inside my conscious mind, as I become a watcher of the activities in my mind and as I become mindful of them, as I begin to know what is happening inside my conscious mind in the present moment, while it is happening, no matter what it is.

Unfortunately, I sometimes find meditating extremely difficult to practice, when the pain inside my mind becomes intense, whenever I start to relive a powerful unfair memory that starts to generate new pain inside my mind, as my desire to run away and hide from this intense pain becomes overwhelming, as this pain tries to take control of my mind away from me.

Fortunately, I was born with an equally powerful stubborn streak which makes it difficult for me to give up and run away from pain, when I decide to continue meditating until the pain runs out of energy and disappears from my conscious mind. So, I just wait and feel the full intensity of the pain as I continue to observe it, as I strengthen my resolve to continue waiting for the pain to go away, by telling myself that the pain will eventually end. This painful waiting practice is part of the price that I am willing to pay to become able to gain the benefits that Practicing The Wisdom of Children will bring into my future adult life. These benefits far outweigh any pain that I am required to endure. They are my reward for continuing the meditation practice, as they enable me to increase the love & friendship that I share with everyone in the world.

In this way, I become My Compassionate Watcher as I observe my mental activities, as I learn to understand them and then as I sympathize with their desire to take control of my mind, as I remain in control of my mind, by taking control of the thinking energy in my mind to become able to choose the feelings, thoughts & images that I want to experience at this present time.

Once my mind calms and enters a state of mindfulness & bliss, I start to give new thinking energy to the feelings, thoughts & images that I want to experience, as I watch the other feelings, thoughts & images disappear from my mind because I am no longer giving them the thinking energy that they need to feed on, to be able to stay alive inside my conscious mind. As these unwanted feelings, thoughts & images run out of this energy for living, they start to disappear from my conscious mind, as my mind becomes calm and becomes focused on the mental activities that I want to experience inside my conscious mind. (Please refer to the Practicing Meditation & Mindfulness section in Chapter 9 of Our Book One)

7-Specialized Definition by Bill Coulson

FEAR, ANGER, WORRY & STRESS is UNFAIR when the love, peace, joy & compassion in my life is diminished by the unfairness that enters my conscious mind when I keep reliving the same unfair memory each day, and I do not know how to stop the unresolved pain & suffering that is being generated by a memory from hurting me, each time I relive an unfair memory. I am being punished needlessly by an unfair memory of a real or imaginary experience from my past that may have no relevance to my present or future life. It is like being sentenced to life long punishment with no possibility of parole for good behavior, unless I can learn & then practice the wisdom to kill all the major fear, anger, worry & stress that is being generated by the unfair memories that I am reliving each day of my adult life. (Please refer to the Unfairness in Our Adult Lives section in Chapter 11 of Our Book One)

8-Specialized Definition by Bill Coulson

Fairness is the state, condition, or quality of being free from bias or injustice in my relationship with my feelings, thoughts & images or with another human being. . (Please refer to the Unfairness in Our Adult Lives section in Chapter 11 of Our Book One)

9-Specialized Definitions by Bill Coulson

The Balance between Joy & Pain inside My Mind

When my fear of future unfairness starts to increase, such as when pain is generated by my thoughts, images or my dreams of someone or something treating me unfairly in the future, the flow of energy from my internal source of love to my mind starts to become blocked by this new pain and the amount of joy inside my mind starts to decrease as my joy runs out of the energy it needs to stay alive inside my mind.

Fortunately, when I stop thinking about the potential future unfairness in my life, I stop feeding new thinking energy to the pain in my mind so it no longer receives the energy that it needs to stay alive. This pain could also be receiving energy from an old memory which I started reliving when I started thinking about the unfairness in my life. Even so, my old unfair memory will also run out of the available energy that it has stored inside The Storage Room of Feeling Energy that it needs to continue feeding energy to the pain in my mind

Then, when the pain in my mind runs out of energy, it starts to disappear from my mind and when this happens, my internal energy of love automatically starts to flow faster as it travels from my internal source of unconditional love to my mind because pain is no longer blocking my mind's pathway to my internal source of love.

Then, the balance between joy & pain inside my mind shifts over to joy as I fully reconnect to my internal source of unconditional love, when the pain inside my mind has dissipated and new joy fills the empty space in my mind that was created when the pain disappeared.

Now, joy becomes the predominant feeling in my mind for as long as the pathway to my internal source of love remains fully open to allow the energy of joy to continuously fill my mind, until I start to think about a new or imaginary unfair event in my life that triggers another old memory or triggers my fight or flee warning system, to create new pain inside my mind, once again.

Then, the pathway to my source of unconditional love becomes blocked once again by this new pain, as pain becomes the predominant feeling in my mind, once more, when the joy inside my mind starts to disappear from my mind, once again. This is how the balance between joy & pain inside my mind shifts from pain to joy and back again. (Please refer to The Balance Between Joy & Pain inside My Conscious Mind section in Chapter 11 of Our Book One)

10-Specialized Definitions by Bill Coulson

My Feeling of Self-Worth is the emotional assessment of the value of the joy & fairness or pain & unfairness in my life at the present time. This feeling of self-worth may be, or may not be, an accurate emotional assessment of how much joy & fairness or pain & unfairness I will receive in my future life. (Please refer to The Balance Between Joy & Pain inside My Conscious Mind section in Chapter 11 of Our Book One)

11-Specialized Definition by Bill Coulson

A Mind Controlling Feeling is any feeling that becomes so intense that it starts to control my mind's ability to think & act, as I indulge in this feeling and allow it to take control of me as I begin to live inside this feeling and as I begin to fully indulge in the pain or the joy that this feeling brings into my life in the present moment. (Please refer to the Mind Controlling Feelings section in Chapter 12 of Our Book One)

12-Specialized Definition by Bill Coulson

Detachment occurs when I disengage, separate or remove something from something else that it is connected to (Cambridge English Dictionary)

Practicing Detachment is to disengage, separate & remove my mental awareness of being inside a distracting feeling, thought or image to become aware of moving outside of it, and then to become aware of looking back at it from outside of it. Practicing Detachment is also asking my mind to stop me from becoming lost inside a distracting feeling, thought or image when it tries to take control on my mind. (Please refer to Step 1 of The Nine Steps to Emotional Freedom section in Chapter 13 of Our Book One)

13-Specialized Definition by Bill Coulson

Friendship is a relationship between people & feelings that is based on mutual trust, attachment and common interests.

Practicing Friendship is asking my mind to make friends with the painful feelings, thoughts & images that are generated inside my mind when life is being unfair to me.

And Practicing Friendship is asking my mind to make friends with the joyful feelings, thoughts & images that are generated inside my mind by the unconditional love from all the life surrounding me, as this joy flows into my heart, when life is being fair to me. (Please refer to Step 3 of The Nine Steps to Emotional Freedom section in Chapter 13 of Our Book One)

14-Specialized Definition by Bill Coulson

The Power of Fairness is the ability that I was born possessing which enables my adult life to be fair to me in the future, as long as I practice The Nine Steps to Emotional Freedom.

I am asking my mind to help me practice fairness by treating all human beings equally with the same love & forgiveness that I offer my friends & family.

And I am asking My Mind to help me kill any unfairness that is living inside me to restore the long term fairness in my life.

15-Specialized Definition by Bill Coulson

Forgiveness occurs when I stop feeling anger or resentment toward someone, for an offense, a flaw, or a mistake made against me and forgiveness occurs when I no longer desire to punish or expect compensation from this person because I have killed my desire for justice & revenge and replaced this desire with renewed unconditional love & forgiveness for this person. (Modified quote from the Cambridge English Dictionary)

And Practicing Forgiveness is asking my mind to help me to convince a painful memory that I am forgiving those who created this painful experience in my past life and as a result of this forgiveness, that my future life will become fair to me. (Please refer to Step 5 of The Nine Steps to Emotional Freedom section in Chapter 13 of Our Book One)

16-Specialized Definition by Bill Coulson

The mental process of Choosing My Feelings during the day occurs when I ask my mind to help me choose the feelings that I want to experience. I am also asking my mind to help me to stop telling my unfair memories or my ego that life is being unfair to me, so I can stop feeding my memories the unfair thinking energy they need to start generating new painful feelings into my life in the future because I now realize that I am not my feelings (Please refer to Step 6 of The Nine Steps to Emotional Freedom section in Chapter 13 of Our Book One)

17-Specialized Definition by Bill Coulson

Self-discipline is the ability to make myself do things that I know I should do even when I do **not** want to do them. (Cambridge English Dictionary)

I am practicing Self-Discipline to enable me to continuously think that my life will be fair to me in the future, to enable My Internal Source of Unconditional Love to motivate me to continuously share unconditional love & forgiveness with everyone in my life.

And practicing Self-Discipline enables me to detach from all the feelings, thoughts & images that are trying to control my mind, so I can use My Free Will to choose my feelings that I want to experience.

18-Specialized Definition by Bill Coulson

Practicing Thankfulness is asking my mind to help me to thank the members of my friends & family who have been supporting me with encouragement, hope, sympathy, forgiveness & unconditional love, as I start to fully appreciate how much I love them and how much I owe them for their support, as I use my re-acquired childhood ability to share increasing love, peace, joy & compassion with friends & family, feelings that are being continuously generated inside my conscious mind by the internal source of unconditional love that is living inside me, when painful unfair feelings are no longer blocking my mind's access to this love, whenever I am able to convince my memories & my ego to stop generating new fear, anger, worry & stress into my adult life, both now and in the future. (Please refer to Step 8 of The Nine Steps to Emotional Freedom section in Chapter 13 of Our Book One)

19-Specialized Definition by Bill Coulson

I am maintaining a continuous connection to all the love in the universe that is flowing through me during every moment of every day of my adult life, as I feel this powerful love automatically recharging My Internal Source of Love that lives inside me, as I share this newly acquired love with all the life that is surrounding me on Our Precious Earth, especially with my friends & family. (Please refer to Step 9 of The Nine Steps to Emotional Freedom section in Chapter 13 of Our Book One)

20-Specialized Definition by Bill Coulson

The Parents' Credo is a parental doctrine, tenet or philosophy for relating to a child:

I will only give my child advice or offer my suggestions, when my child asks for help! And when I offer advice, I will offer it only once. Then later, I will not ask if my advice has been useful.

I will not be a bossy & controlling parent and I will not nag my child to do better, when my child does not live up to my expectations or my desires. (Please refer to The Parents' Credo for Teenage Children section in Chapter 13 of Our Book One)

21-Specialized Definition by Bill Coulson

My Ego is the name I give to my feelings of fear & anger that live inside me when I allow them to take control of my mind & actions as I start to become lost inside these painful feelings, when I cannot stop them from controlling me. I started to experience these painful feelings of fear & anger during my childhood and I started to store these painful feelings inside my memories, whenever someone rejected my offers of love & friendship when I was a young child. (Please refer to Practicing The Wisdom of Children is Hazardous to My Ego! section in Chapter 18 of Our Book One)

22-Dictionary definition

23-Nova PBS Miniseries called The Elegant Universe - Narrated by Brian Greene who also wrote the book The Elegant Universe

24-Your Sacred Self by Dr. Wayne Dyer - Page 99

25-Specialized Definition by Bill Coulson

God is the source of all unconditional love in the universe including mine. (Please refer to Killing My Fear Of Death Is Worth The Price Of My Faith section in Chapter 22 of Our Book One)

26-Proof of Heaven by Eben Alexander- Page 171

27-Renascence and Other Poems by Edna St. Vincent Millay- New York, Harper, 1917

28-Specialized Definition by Bill Coulson

I am Spiritual Energy who lives inside My Mind & Body, who has the ability to observe the revealed feelings, thoughts & images in My Mind and who has the Free Will to manage My Mind & Body to use my ability to reason to choose to act as a human being, to enhance or diminish the well-being of my human life. (Please refer to Becoming an Unconditionally Loving Human Being section in Chapter 22 of Our Book One)

29-Specialized Definition by Bill Coulson

The Mirror in My Mind reflects the way my mind works as it processes the perceptions of my life experiences each day that come, from the external world, from my memories, from my ego & from my imagination. To help me to understand this process, I am visualizing my mind & body being powered by the Pure Eternal Spiritual Energy of the universe, which I call by several names including My Compassionate Watcher, who is sitting inside The Mirror in My Mind watching all my revealed feelings, thoughts & images being reflected as they go by the surface of The Mirror in My Mind as these reflections are processed by my mind each & every moment of my life as a human being. (Please refer to The Mirror in My Mind section in Chapter 22 of Our Book One)

30-Specialized Definition by Bill Coulson

The Energy of My Mind is generated by the Pure Eternal Spiritual Energy of the universe to power a search light attached to The Mirror in My Mind to be able to shine a powerful light on the contents in each room of My Mind. (Please refer to The Mirror in My Mind section in Chapter 22 of Our Book One)

31-Specialized Definition by Bill Coulson

I use The Light of My Mind to make the contents of a room of my choosing to appear bright & clear (Please refer to The Mirror in My Mind section in Chapter 22 of Our Book One)

32-Specialized Definition by Bill Coulson

The Clarity & Truth of My Mind are the clear & true reflections of the feelings, thoughts & images in my mind that My Compassionate Watcher uses to create new possible future actions that I may take that will improve my life. (Please refer to The Mirror in My Mind section in Chapter 22 of Our Book One)

33-Specialized Definition by Bill Coulson

The Creativity of My Mind is the mental process that My Compassionate Watcher uses to create potential new actions & outcomes for my future life, to help me to decide which of the possible futures I should try to create in my life, a life that My Compassionate Watcher wants me to fill with joy & happiness that I can share with my friends & family. (Please refer to The Mirror in My Mind section in Chapter 22 of Our Book One)

34-Specialized Definition by Bill Coulson

The Primordial Awareness of My Mind is my mental Awareness of My Existence as an Unconditionally Loving Human Being. (Please refer to The Primordial Awareness of My Mind section in Chapter 22 of Our Book One)

35-Dzogchen, The Self Perfected State by Chogyal Namkhai Norbu Pages 25 –30

36-Feel Fear and Do It Anyway by Dr. Susan Jeffers - Page 62

37-Specialized Definition by Bill Coulson

True Friendship occurs when one human being offers unconditional love to another human being, who accepts the unconditional love and then offers unconditional love in return. (Please refer to The Nature of True Friendship section in Chapter 22 of Our Book One)

38-Spiritual Friendship by Cistercian Publications – Chapter Three – Verse 62

39-Memo to Wil from Dad - January 20, 2007 – Page 1

40-Abraham H. Maslow's Hierarchy of Needs – Wikipedia

41-Specialized Definition by Bill Coulson

The meaning of life for each human being becomes the purpose & significance of that person's life. (Please refer to Unlocking The Meaning of My Life section in Chapter 22 of Our Book One)

42-Wild Awakening – The Heart of Mahamudra and Dzogchen by Dzogchen Ponlop Pages 44-46

43-Bible - Matthew 22:36-40

44-Specialized Definition by Bill Coulson

Practicing The Wisdom of Children is acting wisely when I forgive those who hurt me, when I believe they are able to fully reconnect with their internal source of unconditional love, to become able to ask for my forgiveness, sometime in the future, as they become able to start sharing unconditional love & nurturing true friendship with me, once again. (Please refer to The Essence of The Wisdom of Children section in Chapter 8 of Our Book One)

45-Dictionary definition

46-The Absorbent Mind by Maria Montessori - Owl Book Edition
    Pages 288-289

47-The Absorbent Mind by Maria Montessori - Owl Book Edition
    Page 229

48-Compassion and Self Hate by Theodore Isaac Rubin – Page 135

49-Compassion and Self Hate by Theodore Isaac Rubin – Page 135

50-Toward a Psychology of Being by Abraham Maslow – Three
    Edition Page 123

51-Toward a Psychology of Being by Abraham Maslow – Three
    Edition Page 81

52-Toward a Psychology of Being by Abraham Maslow – Three Edition Pages 216 - 217

53-Toward a Psychology of Being by Abraham Maslow – Three Edition Page 224

54-Compassion and Self Hate by Theodore Isaac Rubin – Page 136

55-Specialized Definition by Bill Coulson

A False Life Diminishing Thought is an untrue thought, feeling or image that I create in my mind and store in a memory that creates pain & suffering in my life when I relive this negative life diminishing memory in the future, which makes me feel that I am unworthy of living. (Please refer to False Life Diminishing Thoughts section in Chapter 23 of Our Book One)

56-Specialized Definition by Bill Coulson

A True Life-Enhancing Thought is a true thought, feeling or image that I create in my mind and store in a memory that enhances my future love, peace, joy & compassion when I relive a positive life enhancing memory in the future that tells me that I am an unconditionally loving human being, who is capable of creating continuous love, peace, joy & compassion in my daily life which makes me worthy of living. (Please refer to True Life Enhancing Thoughts section in Chapter 23 of Our Book One)

57-Specialized Definition by Bill Coulson

My Thoughts are the products of my mental activities that contain the words & symbols that flow through my mind, as I think & reason. My thoughts are being fed by what I perceive through my five senses, my memories, my feelings, my images & my sense of My True Self. (Please refer to Our Book Four to explore Becoming My True Self)

58-Specialized Definition by Bill Coulson

Each of My Feelings contains a pleasant, neutral or painful desire to act in a certain way. My feelings are stored inside My Room of Memories along with the thoughts & images of my life experiences, my dreams & my fantasy worlds that I create in my mind. (Please refer to the Definitions of My Feelings, Thoughts & Images section in Chapter 22 of Our Book One)

59-Specialized Definition by Bill Coulson

Each of My Desires is a pleasant, neutral or painful mental energy that is contained inside a feeling that is telling me to attain or possess something in the real external world or in my imagination that is within reach of my potential future mental & physical actions. . (Please refer to the Definitions of My Feelings, Thoughts & Images section in Chapter 22 of Our Book One)

60-Specialized Definition by Bill Coulson

My images are my mental creations of the physical likeness of the real external world, or the representation of my mental pictures & videos of my real life experiences, my memories, my dreams & my fantasy worlds that I create in my mind. . (Please refer to the Definitions of My Feelings, Thoughts & Images section in Chapter 22 of Our Book One)

61-Specialized Definition by Bill Coulson

My Feelings, thoughts & images enter my mind, stay for a while and then disappear. When they disappear from my mind, a copy of the feelings, thoughts & images is stored in my subconscious mind, as a memory. (Please refer to the Definitions of My Feelings, Thoughts & Images section in Chapter 22 of Our Book One)

62-Specialized Definition by Bill Coulson

A memory is the mental capacity or faculty for retaining and reviving information that is stored in my subconscious mind inside My Room of Memories which stores the feelings, thoughts & images that I experience during the day. . (Please refer to the Definitions of

My Feelings, Thoughts & Images section in Chapter 22 of Our Book One)

63-Specialized Definition by Bill Coulson

I am not the contents of my mind. I am the Compassionate Watcher who is sitting inside The Mirror In My Mind, who is choosing which feelings, thoughts & images to reflect in The Mirror In My Mind, to enable me to clearly observe them, think about them, and understand them. . (Please refer to the Definitions of My Feelings, Thoughts & Images section in Chapter 22 of Our Book One)

64-Specialized Definition by Bill Coulson

My External World consists of all the revealed activities in The Real External World, outside my mind & body that I am reflecting in The Mirror in My Mind at the present time. . (Please refer to the Definitions of My Feelings, Thoughts & Images section in Chapter 22 of Our Book One)

65-Specialized Definition by Bill Coulson

My Internal World consists of all the revealed mental & physical processes inside my mind & body that I am reflecting in The Mirror in My Mind at the present time. . (Please refer to the Definitions of My Feelings, Thoughts & Images section in Chapter 22 of Our Book One)

66-Specialized Definition by Bill Coulson

My Room of Memories located in my subconscious mind stores the memories of the feelings, thoughts & images that I experience each day of my life. (Please refer to My Room of Memories section in Chapter 24 of Our Book One)

67-Specialized Definition by Bill Coulson

The Power of Detachment helps me to control the fairness in my conscious mind by detaching from any new unfair pain that may enter my conscious mind. Then, I am using my reasoning ability to convince the memory that is generating the unfair pain in my mind that there is no need to generate any new pain inside my conscious in the future. (Please refer to Controlling The Power of Detachment section in Chapter 25 of Our Book One)

68-Specialized Definition by Bill Coulson

The Power of My Mind helps me to control My Thinking Energy to enable me to control the fairness in my mind by stopping my thinking energy from feeding an unfair memory the energy that it needs to be able to generate new pain inside my conscious mind. Without this thinking energy the unfair memory cannot generate new unfair pain into my conscious mind, unless it has energy already stored inside The Storage Room of Feeling Energy in my subconscious mind. So, with this understanding of how my mind works, I am using my thinking energy to feed fair memories only, so only fair feelings will be fed thinking energy inside my conscious mind. (Please refer to Controlling The Power of My Mind section in Chapter 25 of Our Book One)

69-Specialized Definition by Bill Coulson

The Power of My Forgiveness helps me to control the fairness in my subconscious mind with forgiveness, which kills the unfairness that is buried in the memories that are stored inside my subconscious mind inside My Room of Memories, so now I am using the power of my forgiveness to only allow fairness to live inside my subconscious mind. (Please refer to The Power of Forgiveness section in Chapter 25 of Our Book One)

70-Specialized Definition by Bill Coulson

My Personal Compassion is my personal desire to use my unconditional love to enhance the well-being of all human beings, especially my friends & family. (Please refer to My Personal Compassion section in Chapter 25 of Our Book One)

71-Specialized Definition by Bill Coulson

My Global Compassion is my global desire for universal unconditional love to enhance the well-being of all human beings on Earth who are members of my family of unconditional loving human beings. (Please refer to My Global Compassion section in Chapter 25 of Our Book One)

72-Specialized Definition by Bill Coulson

I am perfect because I was born this way, with the ability to love all the life that is surrounding me and to feel the reciprocal love from all this life, as it nourishes me, as I wonder how it was created, as I enjoy its beauty, and as its desire to live & thrive, fills me with its powerful passion for living and encourages me to seek out new life giving fun & adventures with my friends & family, as this passion makes me feel worthy of living, as it flows through me into my life experiences. (Please refer to The Wisdom of My Perfection Makes Me Worthy of Living section in Chapter 29 of Our Book One)

About the Author

William (Bill) Coulson experienced the reality of The Wisdom of Children in his everyday life as a young child, whenever he received unconditional love or forgiveness, especially when he did not deserve it, from a childhood friend, a family member or one of his teachers, who continued to offer him wonderful opportunities for fun & adventures during his childhood in a small rural farming community in Nova Scotia, Canada.

A quote from Bill, "When I became an adult, I began to understand how it is possible to relive the powerful unconditional love of my childhood by embracing the love from everyone around me, as I once did when I was a child, when I intuitively understood that the primary purpose of my life is to share unconditional love & nurture true friendship with my friends & family.

The wisdom I learned as I reconnected with my childhood ability to love life passionately enabled me to help other adults to kill the pain & suffering in their lives that was preventing them from feeling the continuous love, peace, joy & compassion of their childhood during each moment of every day of their future adult lives.

This is why I wrote our book called "Practicing The Wisdom of Children" with the help of my son, so I could leave a legacy of wisdom for my friends & family and my future grandchildren, so they will become able to protect their childhood ability to love life passionately and not lose it as I did and then have to find it again. And now this desire to help other human beings has expanded to include you, the reader of our book, who will benefit from practicing this wisdom, as you begin sharing the increasing unconditional love that this wisdom will bring into your future life.

When we are born, each of us is given a compelling desire to seek a unique & special purpose for our life that motivates us to start asking questions about the meaning of our lives on Earth, whose answers will help us to understand why each of us is given this opportunity to live a potentially wonderful human life, as we begin to ask & answer these questions:

> Who am I?
> Where did I come from?
> Why am I here on Earth?
> What is my life's purpose?

Your life's purpose may be different from mine, but I know from my personal experience that fully reconnecting to your childhood ability to live your life with wonder, excitement, intrigue, puzzlement, and the profound satisfaction of loving everyone around you, will add powerful childhood passion to your adult life.

Fortunately, The Wisdom of Children helps us to embrace our childhood ability to love life passionately, as we share ever increasing unconditional love & forgiveness with our friends & family and as we fulfill the unique & special purpose for each of our lives, which makes us worthy of living on Our Precious Mother Earth."

I Am Never Satisfied With My Accomplishments

I try to accomplish the Goals for My Life, as I struggle
To fully embrace my childhood ability to live with great passion,
During each new day of my adult life, as I accept that:

I am never satisfied with my accomplishments
Succeeding is a satisfying pause on my journey through life
Until a new goal entices me with future fun & adventures

And I try to be creative as I accept this new challenge
As I start struggling to succeed, once again,
With self-discipline & fairness and without fear & anger

As I try to nourish & protect all the life around me
On my journey to fulfill my life's purpose
To share unconditional love & nurture true friendship

And to forgive those who do not deserve it
As others forgive me when I hurt someone or I fail
And I pick myself up & try to be the best that I can be, once again

Because love keeps motivating me, to keep on struggling
And to not worry about the outcome of my efforts
By making my journey important, not my destination

As I work on my goals in the present moment, while
Practicing the wisdom of our ancestors and correcting
Any mistakes I make, as I continue to love without end

And in the end, only love remains
As it was in the beginning, so it is now
Forever inside me, motivating me to share love & forgiveness

William (Bill) Coulson

www.ingramcontent.com/pod-product-compliance
Lightning Source LLC
Chambersburg PA
CBHW060448090426
42735CB00011B/1947